PERCEPTION AND LIGHTING
AS FORMGIVERS FOR ARCHITECTURE

PERCEPTION
AS FORMGIVERS

AND LIGHTING
FOR ARCHITECTURE

WILLIAM M. C. LAM

edited by CHRISTOPHER HUGH RIPMAN

McGRAW-HILL BOOK COMPANY

New York   St. Louis   San Francisco
Auckland   Bogotá   Düsseldorf   Johannesburg
London   Madrid   Mexico   Montreal   New Delhi   Panama
Paris   São Paulo   Singapore   Sydney   Tokyo   Toronto

Library of Congress Cataloging in Publication Data
Lam, William M C
    Perception and lighting as formgivers for architecture.

    Bibliography: p.
    Includes index.
    1. Space (Architecture)   2. Visual Perception.
3. Light in architecture.   I. Title.
NA2765.L35   729'.28   76-2554
ISBN 0-07-036094-4

1234567890   HDHD   786543210987

The editors for this book were Jeremy Robinson and Virginia Anne Fechtmann,
the designer was Edward J. Fox, and the production supervisor
was Teresa F. Leaden. It was set in Palatino by The Clarinda Corporation.

It was printed and bound by Halliday Lithograph Corporation.

Of the Mulla Nasrudin stories which appear in this book
"The Use of Light," "More Useful," and "Anachronism" are
from *The Exploits of the Incomparable Mulla Nasrudin* by
Idries Shah and illustrated by Richard Williams (text and
illustrations copyright © 1966 by Mulla Nasrudin Enterprises,
Ltd.). "Salt is not Wool," "Nasrudin and the Wise Men,"
"There is more light here," and "The Child is Father to the Man"
are from *The Pleasantries of the Incredible Mulla Nasrudin*
by Idries Shah and illustrated by Richard Williams and Errol Le Cain
(text and illustrations copyright © 1968 by Mulla Nasrudin
Enterprises, Ltd.). Reprinted by permission of the publishers,
E. P. Dutton & Co. Reprinted in the British Commonwealth by
permission of Idries Shah and Jonathan Cape Ltd.

Inside cover art: Concordia Hall, Place Bonaventure, Montreal (photo by Michael Drummond).

Contents

What do we look at? 35

Attributive classification of visual stimuli: assignment of meaning 40

Expectation as a component of the process of perception 51

The affective component of perception 52

How well do we see? 57

Summary 69

4 The Design of the Luminous Environment 71

The conventional process of lighting design 71

A new process of design 83

Summary: new objectives and design implications 96

CASE STUDIES: Principles Applied in Practice 100

Group A: Buildings dominated by a single major space 103

Acknowledgments

This book is the culmination of a twenty-year team process and I am indebted to all those who have contributed to it by working with me. My biggest debt of gratitude has always been to those architects who have allowed me to work with them in developing new and often unconventional solutions to old problems. In having the courage to experiment, modify, and reformulate ideas, they have made it possible for us to come up with solutions in which I can take real pride. I hope that they will take equal pride in the projects which I have selected as representative of our best efforts.

The enthusiastic support and feedback of my associates during the past fifteen years has been invaluable. Jon Birdsey, Marietta Millet, Peter Coxe, John Powell and Chris Ripman, my editor, have all made their special contributions which go far beyond those which one might expect from professional associates.

Numerous other groups have contributed to the production of this book: The National Endowment for the Arts gave me a substantial grant for the preparation of illustrations; the State University Construction Fund of New York provided me with the opportunity to formalize many of my thoughts in the course of preparing a number of documents on performance criteria for the luminous environment; and the Boston Architectural Center, MIT, and the Harvard Graduate School of Design have all contributed by giving me the opportunity to air my ideas in a classroom context.

Many individuals in the publishing field have also lent their support. I want to thank the editors and staff of all of the architectural magazines which have generously allowed us to reproduce illustrations; special thanks also to the many architectural photographers who have contributed, particularly, George Cserna, Alexandre Georges, J. O. Hedrich, Roger Jowett, Balthazar Korab, Louis Reens, Steve Rosenthal and Ezra Stoller. Harold Lewis of Photo International in Newton, Mass., trekked across the country to photograph a number of projects and has been producing top quality prints for us on short order ever since. Gary Fujiwara gave invaluable professional advice on book format.

I am particularly indebted to Virginia Anne Fechtmann of the McGraw-Hill organization for the many long hours and the particular care which she devoted as Editing Supervisor to improving the quality of this book.

Judy Stein, Rosie Hooper, Christine O'Bryan and Cathy Shupe have all been tested at one time or another in converting my illegible scrawls into legible typescript. Pam Reiser, who joined us at the last minute, embarrassed us all with her encyclopedic knowledge of the rules of grammar. I am also grateful to my sons, John and Tom, for their help throughout.

Finally, I am most indebted to my editor, Chris Ripman. Although he originally joined my forces as a photographer, he soon proved himself to be not only a first-rate photographer, but also a competent editor. His help over the past two years in developing more thorough discussions in the text, sharpening statements, and in many cases adding his own examples to clarify a point has been invaluable. Effectively, he took over the book in all its details and I became the consultant. I am grateful, both for being relieved of the details, and for the knowledge that the end result is that much better for his input.

Preface

hy are you sitting at the crossroads, Mulla?

'One day something will happen here, and a crowd will gather. When that comes about, I may not be able to get close enough—so I'm putting in my time now.'

——*The Pleasantries of the Incredible Mulla Nasrudin*

[1]*For those who may be unfamiliar with the technical terminology of lighting, a glossary has been included at the end of this preface.*

[2]*See, for instance, Parry Moon and Domina Eberle Spencer, Lighting Design, Addison-Wesley, Cambridge, Mass., 1948, p. 358, Table 9.08.*

[3]*By the term luminous environment I mean the visual environment illuminated by natural and artificial light sources.*

[4]*Brightness ratios compare the measured surface brightness or luminance of any two objects in the visual field.*

In the 1940s, as a candidate for a degree in architecture from M.I.T., I took two semesters of a required course in architectural lighting taught by Parry Moon. Compared to the training received by most architects and engineers even today, it was an excellent education in terms of the mathematics and geometries of light, the essentials of task illumination, and the need for comfortable visual environments as revealed by psychophysical research.

Even in those days, Moon cautioned us to be suspicious of the role of the Illuminating Engineering Society as a persistent promoter of ever higher illumination levels by its advocacy of oversimplified minimum footcandle standards.[1]

We learned the applicability of the law of diminishing returns to the relation between illumination levels and task visibility, and the effects of such factors as reflected glare, shadows, and veiling reflections on the quality of human vision. In addition to covering in depth computational techniques for calculating light levels from both daylight and artificial sources, Moon introduced his students to psychological and aesthetic design considerations, and taught us ways to give them more than just lip service by using sophisticated evaluation techniques for the analysis of alternative designs.[2] With his persistent emphasis on the need to design luminous environments[3] which were *comfortable* as well as successful in the conventional sense of providing adequate illumination for formal visual tasks such as reading, Moon urged us to use brightness ratios[4] as a major design criterion, and suggested the luminous ceiling as the answer to the problems of school and office lighting.

But even as a student, I could see that something was wrong with this approach. To me, the luminous ceiling seemed unpleasant and uncomfortable, despite the uncontestable fact that it typically produces almost perfect (i.e., very low) brightness ratios in the spaces which it illuminates. Nor could I accept as desirable and useful design guidelines criteria such as "brightness ratios of 3 to 1, with a maximum of 10 to 1," when I could see for myself that the environments which I and others liked best simply did not conform to these abstract, simplistic, and highly restrictive standards. I felt strongly that both the conventional criteria for lighting design and the conventional hardware applications such as the luminous ceiling failed in some essential way to address the underlying issues in the design of really good luminous environments.

In the intervening years, beginning with the impetus provided by occasional teaching assignments and further stimulated by the demands of designing and consulting on projects and government policy, I searched out and read everything I could find on the experimental measurement of psychophysical phenomena such as glare, in the hope of finding more meaningful criteria for the luminous environment. I came across many formulas which looked promising at first, but I found that my daily experience contradicted their predictions. For example, Hopkinson[5] predicts that looking at large light sources with a surface brightness of 150 footlamberts[6] will cause discomfort. This may be true in a laboratory setting, yet most people derive considerable pleasure from looking at sunny outdoors scenes, which are typically many times brighter than 150 footlamberts. Once again, it became clear to me that something was seriously amiss here, and that apparently results obtained in the abstraction of the laboratory environment could not be converted directly into useful, valid criteria for real-world design.

At that time the majority of lighting criteria were stated in quantitative terms — as they still are today, though there are signs of change. Could it be that quantitative criteria per se were in some essential way deficient? The question of *quality*, which was given little consideration in both codes and research except in quantitative terms, began to fascinate me more and more, and I kept coming back to a basic question which was bothering me: *Could a good luminous environment be defined meaningfully in purely quantitative terms?*

At the same time, I became increasingly aware that the conceptual tools at the disposal of the lighting designer were weak, inconclusive, incomplete, and sometimes even positively misleading. For example, consider the Visual Comfort Probability Index,[7] or VCP, a measure intended to evaluate the probability that people will be able to tolerate glare conditions resulting from a given lighting arrangement. Unfortunately, one can only assign VCP ratings to standard patterns of standard light fixtures. Daylight scenes and brilliantly illuminated crystal chandeliers — in fact every scene that we find positively attractive — cannot be evaluated and classified according to VCP. How, then, could we as design professionals have faith in our tools when all they could tell us was the proportion of users who would probably find the resulting environment *intolerable?* It seemed a little like trying to grow a beautiful garden with only weed killer and hope.

Thus frustrated, I became increasingly aware that the difference between sparkle and glare, like the difference between music and noise, did not lie in measured intensity ratios or absolute intensity levels, the conventional criteria for the luminous environment. More light was, indeed, often less pleasant, less comfortable, and even less safe. Yet lighting handbooks, codes, and the spokesmen of the power and lighting industries all seemed to be saying that more light was a good thing under all circumstances — something to strive for in the design of the luminous environment.

In searching for explanations for these seeming paradoxes, I turned to books about perception, a subject never mentioned during my formal education and hardly referred to even today in the literature of illuminating engineering. As a consultant interested in practical applications rather than a scholar preparing for a thesis, I read widely, without taking notes, absorbing ideas from many sources to be subsequently tested by personal experience and observation. I was after an explanation of *how* and *why* I perceived the world around me, so that I could put that understanding to work in the design of environments which would have predictable and positive effects on those who experienced them. I read a broad range of material,

[5]R. G. Hopkinson and W. M. Collins, "An Experimental Study of the Glare from a Luminous Ceiling," *Building Research Station Note No. E 1275.*

[6]*The luminance of a surface expressed in footlamberts is equal to the product of its reflectance in percent and the incident illumination in footcandles.*

[7]*Described in John E. Kaufman (ed.), IES Handbook, 5th ed., The Illuminating Engineering Society, New York, 1972, pp. 3.24–3.27.*

published and unpublished, in fields such as psychology, anthropology, and sociology, the best of which I have included in the bibliography at the end of this book. Peter Jay, an articulate London electrical engineer with an unusually broad education whose articles about lighting in *The Architects' Journal* helped to stimulate my original interest in perception, opened his library to me and, without realizing it, gave me invaluable help in my search.

As I read, I found my greatest inspiration in the work of the early pioneers in the field of perception such as William James and Ewald Hering: here at last were thoughtful men who addressed the real problems of man in relation to his total environment. In reading reports of more recent experimentation in visual perception, however, I found my initial excitement turning to disappointment time and time again as I realized that many of the phenomena studied under the carefully controlled conditions of the laboratory would retain little or none of their validity in the real world. I could sympathize with the pure theorists who sometimes neglect to qualify the applicability of their results. Qualification may be more properly the field of the applied researcher. But it is less forgivable when applied researchers working to provide the basis for real-world codes and regulations either ignore essential aspects of reality, so that their results are deceptive or incomplete, or publish those results without appropriate *caveats*, so that the limitations of their validity are surreptitiously concealed.[8]

I do not mean to imply that all modern authors in the field of psychophysical research are incompetent—far from it. I found the results of many psychological experiments interesting and encouraging; they confirmed my intuitive belief that there was no simple correlation between the measured strength of sensory stimuli and the importance of the perceptions which they produce in the brain. I found that it was the *information content* of the incoming stimuli, and not their absolute intensity, which appeared to be the key to understanding why we evaluate our environments as good or bad, pleasant or uncomfortable. In the real world, *quality* seemed to dominate quantity as a determinant of perceptual evaluation. My suspicions of simplistic numerical techniques for evaluating the luminous environment deepened as I grew increasingly aware of the extraordinary complexity and adaptibility of human perception.

The work of many modern writers provided me with invaluable insights into the subtle workings of the human mind. Gibson's *The Perception of the Visual World*[9] led me to understand that we perceive a *visual world*—a complete and meaningful gestalt—and not merely a sequence of independent, unique scenes. Gibson made it clear that perception is an active, information-seeking process, not a string of unconscious and mechanistic responses to external stimuli. Other works which proved unusually helpful were Warr and Knapper's *The Perception of People and Events*,[10] Broadbent's *Perception and Communication*,[11] Hurvich and Jameson's *The Perception of Brightness and Darkness*,[12] and Hall's *The Hidden Dimension*[13] and *The Silent Language*.[14]

Of those directly involved in lighting research, I was most impressed by Ralph Hopkinson of London University, formerly of the Building Research Station—the rare psychophysicist who, though highly involved in numbers, remained a balanced human being. In his *Architectural Physics*, which should be required reading for anyone involved with the luminous environment, Hopkinson states that

[8] *An example of this sort of misleading study is the publication of "ideal color combinations," based on experiments which deal with color only in the abstract on meaningless pieces of paper. The appropriateness of color is directly dependent on the nature of the colored object: there is obviously a basic difference between a blue sky and a blue banana, yet the experiments which suggest the "desirability" of a particular shade of blue ignore completely this effect. Our evaluation of visual phenomena is always conditioned by the meaning we give them in the process of perception, and it is misleading and deceptive to pretend otherwise.*

[9] *James J. Gibson*, The Perception of the Visual World, *Houghton Mifflin, Boston, 1950.*

[10] *Peter B. Warr and Christopher Knapper,* The Perception of People and Events, *Wiley, Inc., New York, 1968.*

[11] *D. E. Broadbent*, Perception and Communication, *Pergamon, New York, 1958.*

[12] *Leo M. Hurvich and Dorothea Jameson,* The Perception of Brightness and Darkness, *Allyn and Bacon, Boston, 1966.*

[13] *E. T. Hall*, The Hidden Dimension, *Doubleday, Garden City, N.Y., 1966.*

[14] *E. T. Hall,* The Silent Language, *Fawcett, Greenwich, Conn., 1959.*

"whenever we treat lighting in purely physical, quantitative terms . . . we must constantly sit back and think where our calculations are leading us. If they lead us to a design that common sense and experience tell us will be disliked, there is no choice but to examine the design on those grounds and to reject it if it is clearly at fault."[15] Yet, despite his caveats, even Hopkinson's work has been misinterpreted and misapplied by those who make a fetish out of calculation and are afraid to trust their own judgment.

I had just begun to practice as a lighting consultant and part-time teacher in 1960 when I was asked to set down my prescriptions for good lighting in a series of articles for the *Architectural Record* entitled "Lighting for Architecture."[16] Drawing on my reading and my practical experience gained during many years spent in the design and manufacture of lamps and lighting equipment, as well as unofficial consulting on a large number of projects, I advocated lighting "for mood or atmosphere . . . to complement structure . . . for emphasis or to direct movement . . . to express intended use . . . and to modify the appearance of a space"—not merely to provide a certain quantity of task illumination, the conventional objective of contemporary lighting design. I was groping for concise formulation of the qualitative criteria which I felt to be of paramount importance. In 1965 I published a second series, "The Lighting of Cities,"[17] in the same magazine, in which I made recommendations for the design of lighting systems at the urban scale, urging that they should be organized to maximize orientation for both driver and pedestrian by giving them the greatest possible amount of useful information about the structure and hierarchy of the urban environment. I could offer no theoretical backing for my prescriptions at that time; all I had to go on was my own convictions based on personal observation, reading, and my considerable experience as a designer and consultant.

Design, however, is a team effort involving many people playing many roles, and as a consultant I grew increasingly aware of the need for a stronger basis for my recommendations than personal conviction. When making design proposals for good luminous environments stated in visual and verbal rather than numerical terms, I found that many of my clients and co-workers reacted as if "a good luminous environment," "aesthetics," and other psychological aspects of design were some sort of extravagance, to be achieved only after one had provided for "functional needs." More often than not, aesthetics were treated as icing on the architectural cake, the last thing to be added and the first thing to be dropped when the budget ran low. But are aesthetics—that elusive, essentially *qualitative* side of the visual environment—merely a matter of taste? Certainly many chapters of the history of aesthetic debate appear to support such a conviction. Aesthetic controversies have been so often arbitrary and inconclusive that one hesitates to advocate a strategy of design based on aesthetic or visual principles, however sound. Nevertheless, I now conclude that there *is* a sound, viable approach to the design of the luminous environment—a *qualitative* approach with universal validity because it is derived from fundamental human needs for visual information which are an inalienable part of man's *biological* nature.

Rene Dubos, the eminent biologist, distinguished between "the universality and the diversity in man's nature," separating out certain universal attributes shared by almost all people regardless of race, religion, or place of birth from those more limited attributes—those

[15]*R. G. Hopkinson*, Architectural Physics: Lighting, *H. M. Stationery Office, London, 1963, p. 28.*

[16]*Published in the* Architectural Record, *Vol. 127, No. 7, pp. 219–229, June 1960; Vol. 128, No. 1, pp. 170–181, July 1960; Vol. 128, No. 4, pp. 222–232, October 1960; and Vol. 129, No. 1, pp. 149–160, January 1961; also published in* Architectural Engineering, Environmental Control, *R. E. Fischer (ed.), McGraw-Hill, New York, 1964, pp. 118–164.*

[17]*Published in the* Architectural Record, *Vol. 137, No. 6, pp. 210–214, June 1965; and Vol. 138, No. 1, pp. 173–180, July 1965.*

bodies of beliefs, values, and ideals—which are held only by particular groups of human beings. I believe that a similar distinction can be drawn between those aspects of design, those attributes and qualities of environments, which are merely "cultural" in nature, and those which relate to the satisfaction of fundamental and universally shared human needs for orientation, defense, sustenance, stimulation, and survival.

I contend that as human beings we all share certain needs which I will call *biological information needs:* needs to understand the nature and structure of our immediate environment, needs which are rooted in Darwinian drives for survival and security, needs which transcend the scope of aesthetic squabbles based on personal fancy or on merely cultural distinctions between groups of human beings.

My eyes and my experience convinced me that from the analysis of such needs it would be possible to develop a new approach to the design of the luminous environment, and during my 15 years of practice and research I have formulated just such an approach. Unlike many other theorists, however, I have been presented in my work with a unique combination of challenge and opportunity: the challenge, to convince my clients and colleagues to give up preconceptions and to follow my suggestions in the search for good luminous environments; the opportunity, to test and refine my theories in a series of hundreds of projects involving several billion dollars worth of construction.

At the very heart of the approach to the design of the luminous environment which is outlined in this book lies the belief that *as human beings we evaluate an environment according to how well that environment is structured, organized, and illuminated to satisfy all of our needs for visual information. These needs derive from both the activities in which we choose to engage and the biological information needs related to the very essentials of human nature which are always present regardless of the specific activity which holds our attention at any one time.*

I call an environment which satisfies all of our needs *relevant*, and I believe that it is this quality of relevance which determines whether we judge an environment to be cheerful or gloomy, attractive or depressing, sparkling or glaring, etc. *In the relevant, appropriate luminous environment, those things which we want or need to see are clearly visible and emphasized, while those things which are distracting or unpleasant are deemphasized or hidden from sight.* The relevant environment is comfortable and reassuring—it makes us feel at ease, while helping us to do the things we do.

To design good, appropriate, relevant luminous environments, *it is not sufficient* to state vague objectives such as "create a mood" and it is counterproductive to state oversimplified objectives in purely numerical terms, such as "deliver a minimum of 70 footcandles throughout the entire building at 30 inches from the floor." There is a great need for new ways of conceptualizing and specifying performance criteria for the luminous environment which go far beyond personal taste and conventional codes based on task lighting conditions alone. Before the concepts of universal biological information needs and relevance can be usefully and widely applied, designers must develop and accept a new vocabulary and grammar of form, phrased in visual and perceptual rather than numerical terms. Until those who own, design, finance, build, regulate, and maintain our physical environments base their work on a deeper understanding of the principles of perception and of the true, total nature of human perceptual needs, they will continue to grind out bad luminous environments.

These convictions led me to write this book, to present the principles which have been the basis of my own design work, and to suggest modifications to the conventional design process which will be necessary if these principles are to receive more than lip service. I have tested them in many informal, unrecorded experiments over the years with students, clients, fellow professionals, and the users of many different kinds of luminous environments. I present them here without formal proof in the academic sense because I feel that we should all put less faith in such "proofs" and more in our own experience and in the ability which each of us has to test, to observe, and to judge for ourselves. Only by such testing and evaluation can one learn to apply the principles set forth here, actively and effectively, to one's own ends.

However, one should believe nothing blindly. Go and see for yourself. Situations and examples which illustrate all of the principles set forth in this book can be found without looking too far, if only one knows *what* to look for, and *how* to look. Above all else, the purpose of this book is to convey that particular knowledge.

William M. C. Lam
Cambridge, Mass.

Glossary

Many common terms have been included here because the conventional definition is imprecise for purposes of discussing the luminous environment. All terms in small capitals are defined in the Glossary.

Activity needs for visual information	*Needs for visual information related to specific conscious activities.*
Affective	*Having to do with the evaluation of, or emotional response to, a* STIMULUS.
Attributive	*Pertaining to the observable physical characteristics of an object or event, by which it is recognized, classified, and given meaning by the brain during the process of* PERCEPTION.
Biological needs for visual information	*Unceasing needs for visual information; not related to specific conscious activities, but rather related to the more fundamental aspects of the human relation to the environment: orientation, defense, stimulation, sustenance, and survival.*
Bright	*Perceived as being relatively high on the scale of* BRIGHTNESS.
Brightness	*The subjective description of* LUMINANCE; *a perceived characteristic of objects which does not vary directly in a simple mathematical relationship with their physical or measured brightness, which is correctly termed their* LUMINANCE. *Brightness is often misused to mean* LUMINANCE; *if so, it should be qualified as ''measured'' brightness, to distinguish between the absolute attributes (''measured'' brightness) and the perceived attributes (''apparent'' or ''subjective'' brightness) of the object in question.*
Brightness ratio	*The ratio between the* LUMINANCES *of any two elements in the visual field.*
Brilliance	*Extreme* BRIGHTNESS; *frequently, too strong to be agreeable.*
Constancies	*Characteristics of objects (especially color, size, and shape) which are perceived as remaining unchanged when the objects are seen under a wide range of conditions.*
Contrast	*The relationship between the* LUMINANCE *of an object or area of interest and that of its immediate background. Mathematically, the difference between the* LUMINANCES *divided by the* LUMINANCE *of the background.*
Dark	*Perceived as being relatively low on the scale of* BRIGHTNESS; *with reference specifically to color, one with a low* REFLECTANCE.
Dazzle	*To overpower or reduce vision by intense* LIGHT; *also, a perceptual ambiguity caused by a high-contrast pattern in which figure and background shapes are identical.*
Dim	*Appearing subdued, faintly illuminated.*
Direct lighting	*Lighting provided from a source without reflection from room surfaces.*
Disability glare	GLARE *which reduces the ability to perceive the visual information needed for a particular activity.*
Discomfort glare	GLARE *which is distracting or uncomfortable, which interferes with the perception of visual information required to satisfy* BIOLOGICAL NEEDS, *but*

	which does not significantly reduce the ability to see information needed for activities.
Dull	Uninteresting.
Footcandle	The English unit of LIGHT intensity.
Footlambert	The English unit of LUMINANCE, or measured surface brightness.
Gestalt	An environment, situation, group of objects, or combination of these elements which is perceived as an integrated whole rather than as an assemblage of unrelated parts.
Glare	An interference with visual perception caused by an uncomfortably bright LIGHT source or reflection; a form of VISUAL NOISE.
Gloomy	A condition in which desirable and expected visual information is absent, producing a sense of depression or disappointment; not necessarily DARK or DIM.
Illumination	Quantity of LIGHT per unit of surface area; the intensity or "density" of light falling on a surface. (English unit: FOOTCANDLE. Metric unit: Lux = Lumens per square meter.)
Incident light	LIGHT falling upon a surface.
Indirect lighting	Lighting provided by reflection, usually from wall and ceiling surfaces.
Light (noun)	Visually evaluated radiant energy; also, a source of ILLUMINATION such as the sun or an electric lamp, or the ILLUMINATION received from such a source.
Light (adj.)	With a high REFLECTANCE factor; with reference specifically to color, one with a high VALUE.
Luminance	The physical measure of BRIGHTNESS; luminous intensity per unit projected area of any surface, as measured from a specific direction. (English unit: FOOTLAMBERT. Metric unit: Candela per square meter.)
Luminous	Emitting LIGHT; especially, emitting self-generated LIGHT (as opposed to reflected LIGHT).
Luminous ceiling	A ceiling of back-lighted translucent material.
Luminous environment	The visually perceived environment, illuminated by natural and artificial LIGHT sources.
Matte	Having the property of diffusing reradiated INCIDENT LIGHT.
Mirror angle	In reference to the viewer and an observed surface, the angle equal and opposite to the VIEWING ANGLE.
Noise	Undesirable or disagreeable stimuli which confuse, obscure, or compete with desirable STIMULI (SIGNALS).
Normal angle	An angle perpendicular to a surface.
Perception	A meaningful impression obtained through the senses and apprehended by the mind (see SENSATION for further clarification).
Phototropic	Attracted toward or responding to a source of LIGHT.
Reflectance	That percentage of INCIDENT LIGHT upon a surface which is reradiated in the visual spectrum.
See	To perceive with the eyes; to construct a visual image in the mind.

Sensation	*The immediate result of the stimulation of the sense organs; as distinguished from* PERCEPTION *which involves the combination of incoming sensations with contextual information and past experience so that the objects or events from which the* STIMULI *arise are recognized and assigned meaning.*
Signals	*Relevant, desirable, or needed sensory information or* STIMULI.
Simultaneous contrast	*Intensification of perceived attributes of one object, especially its color or* BRIGHTNESS, *by the simultaneous perception of related attributes of other objects in the visual field.*
Solid angle	*The three-dimensional angle formed by three or more planes meeting at a point, as at the apex of a pyramid.*
Sparkle	*An attractive* BRILLIANCE.
Specular	*Having the reflective properties of a mirror.*
Stimulus	*Anything which excites a sensory receptor, causing or regarded as causing a response or* SENSATION.
Value	*An index of the lightness or darkness of a color, measured on a scale from white (high) to black (low).*
Veiling reflection	*Reflection of* INCIDENT LIGHT *that partially or totally obscures the details to be seen on a surface by reducing the* CONTRAST; *sometimes called "reflected* GLARE."*
Viewing angle	*The angle formed between the viewer's line of sight and the plane of the surface under observation.*
Visual noise	*Undesirable or disagreeable* STIMULI *from the* LUMINOUS ENVIRONMENT *which confuse, obscure, or compete with a* SIGNAL.

NASRUDIN AND THE WISE MEN

The philosophers, logicians and doctors of law were drawn up at Court to examine Nasrudin. This was a serious case, because he had admitted going from village to village saying: 'The so-called wise men are ignorant, irresolute and confused.' He was charged with undermining the security of the State.

'You may speak first,' said the King.

'Have paper and pens brought,' said the Mulla.

Paper and pens were brought.

'Give some to each of the first seven savants.'

They were distributed.

'Have them separately write an answer to this question: "What is bread?" '

This was done.

The papers were handed to the King, who read them out:

The first said: 'Bread is a food.'

The second: 'It is flour and water.'

The third: 'A gift of God.'

The fourth: 'Baked dough.'

The fifth: 'Changeable, according to how you mean "bread". '

The sixth: 'A nutritious substance.'

The seventh: 'Nobody really knows.'

'When they decide what bread is,' said Nasrudin, 'it will be possible for them to decide other things. For example, whether I am right or wrong. Can you entrust matters of assessment and judgment to people like this? Is it or is it not strange that they cannot agree about something which they eat each day, yet are unanimous that I am a heretic?'

——*The Exploits of the Incomparable Mulla Nasrudin*

1 Introduction

Light has always been recognized as one of the most powerful formgivers available to the designer, and great architects have always understood its importance as the principal medium which puts man in touch with his environment. In 1927, for instance, Le Corbusier stated that "Architecture is the masterly, correct and magnificent play of masses brought together in *light.*" Many others from the designers of the Parthenon and the craftsmen of the cathedrals to the masters of the Modern Movement have left us mute legacies of stone and steel and light which testify eloquently to their similar convictions **(Figs. 1** and **2).**

The years since Edison, however, have brought architects quite literally more light than they know what to do with. After centuries of painstakingly and often ingeniously manipulating our buildings to suit the vagaries of natural light, we find, paradoxically, that we have very little aptitude for manipulating our new wealth of artificial light to suit the vagaries of our buildings.

When all buildings were designed around a single, fixed light source—the sun—the difference between great architecture and mere building could be measured to a large degree by the skill with which that source was used. The shapes and sizes of rooms, and the materials and details in them, were determined largely by the appearance the room would take on when rendered by daylight. Light was not always simply applied to structural innovations; more often, the structures themselves were developed to make possible desired lighting and spatial effects.

Now, finally, we have artificial sources which are not only easier to control than daylight, but can also light interior spaces far more brightly. Theoretically, the possibilities for imaginative lighting are limitless. And, theoretically, our ability to create great architecture should have increased in proportion to the availability of more, and more versatile, artificial sources. Yet we have scarcely begun to scratch the surface of these "limitless" possibilities. Designers, faced with an extraordinarily rapid turnover of products and a fast, fragmented process of design and construction which has taken root in this electronic age, have yielded the control which they once exercised over the luminous environment to others: to electrical engineers, who have been primarily trained to meet minimum footcandle requirements; to building owners, who come to them with misconceived programmatic objectives; and to misguided government officials, who have been brainwashed by propaganda from the lighting and power industry into adopting and enforcing irrelevant and obstructive codes in the name of progress. This abdication of design responsibility—conscious or unconscious—by the design professions must be reversed. Lacking

THE CHILD IS FATHER TO THE MAN

 asrudin arrived at an all-comers' horse-race mounted on the slowest of oxen. Everyone laughed: an ox cannot run.

'But I have seen it, when it was only a calf, running faster than a horse,' said Nasrudin; 'so why should it not run faster, now that it is larger?'

——*The Exploits of the Incomparable Mulla Nasrudin*

1

2

an understanding of the basic principles involved, the technicians who now control our luminous environments have reduced the criteria for illumination to simple numbers, which are basically unrelated to vision, perception, comfort, or pleasure.

This blind worship of specific levels of illumination is all too often directly responsible for the defeat and compromise of good designs. If the initial design concept is stated correctly in perceptual terms, so that the type, configuration, and placement of light sources reinforce and facilitate an awareness of information required to satisfy biological needs while providing appropriate qualities of illumination for activity needs, then the actual level of light delivered becomes far less critical. Illumination levels should be a matter of design intent and budget availability and priorities, not merely a response to unjustifiable and often misconceived legal or programmatic requirements. A verbal statement of the design concept as it relates to user needs will be more complete and more likely to produce a good luminous environment than an *a priori* prescription of numbers. In the design process, determination of the levels of illumination should be the last step—it should be, figuratively, just a question of what size lamp to screw in. Once one understands that the brain analyzes and perceives the *entire* visual field, and not its individual aspects, the irrelevance of single-parameter numerical criteria such as footcandle levels is immediately apparent.

The reader will note that relatively few references are made in this book to specific quantitative levels of illumination as criteria for the good luminous environment. There are a number of reasons for this conscious omission. *Once minimal levels of illumination—on the order of 10 to 15 footcandles—have been achieved, additional light is generally not the most effective means of increasing visibility and visual comfort.* In those circumstances where further increasing the quantity of light will produce significant benefits the increase must be substantial, i.e., doubling or quadrupling the original light levels. Absolute luminance levels do have a relationship to sensations of glare and distraction, but it is the *patterns* of light sources and the nature of their *relationship* to other elements in the visual field which largely determine the overall quality of the luminous environment. It is the same with the other senses. A few wrong notes makes much more difference to one's appreciation of a piece of music than the exact volume of sound. The quantity of food one eats at a meal is much less likely to be remembered than a horrible combination of flavors or a single rotten ingredient in an otherwise delectable repast. For analogous reasons, calculation of specific *levels* of illumination is much less important in lighting design than consideration of the *quality* of illumination in terms of its distribution and characteristics, the *information* conveyed by the pattern of the sources, and the degree to which they *reinforce* or *contradict* the relationships established by the architecture and the planned activities.

Most modern buildings would provide far superior interior environments for their occupants if they had been consciously designed from the inside out. Today, unfortunately, we find ourselves surrounded by buildings which appear to have been designed primarily from the outside in. The principal intent in formgiving seems to have been the creation of environmental sculpture at the city scale, particularly in the design of working buildings such as offices, schools, libraries, and factories. Except for prestigious lobbies and a few special or public rooms, the interior luminous environments of these monuments seem to be almost an afterthought, a low-priority item in the overall hierarchy of design objectives.

Today our most comfortable, pleasant spaces are those in which the designers and users retained control over the layout and fine-tuning of the lighting: spaces such as churches and museums, stores and restaurants, in which objects of interest are appropriately emphasized by the luminous environment and set against backgrounds free from visual noise.[1] The lighting in private homes is generally satisfactory and pleasant for the same reason—it has usually been designed and adjusted by the users to suit their specific needs for visual information, not to achieve some mandatory prescribed light levels.

All spaces should be designed and lighted to satisfy specific *needs*, not just engineered to meet code requirements—different lights, as it were, for different sites.

In a good luminous environment, that which we want or need to see is emphasized and highlighted, while that which is not of interest or which would interfere with our perception of the first class of things is hidden or played down. It is an unfortunate misconception that there exists a quantitative gulf between concepts of comfort and pleasure and concepts of functionality. A comfortable, pleasant luminous environment automatically satisfies most of the visual needs of its users, yet we persist in writing specifications for our luminous environments as if "functional" task lighting were the only objective to be achieved.

Many perceptive architects have always felt that all was not well, but most have been unable to describe precisely what is wrong with the environments they dislike and what is right with the ones they love. Even those who understand and can specify the qualities which make for a good luminous environment usually encounter constant resistance from single-minded engineers, misguided clients, and well-meaning public officials with whom they must work.

If perception-based lighting design is once again to assume its proper place as a formgiver for architecture, it will not be because of the availability of cheaper glass, the introduction of more efficient light sources, or the generation of more sophisticated computer programs for calculating light levels. Innovations in each of these fields, applied indiscriminately, have already made significant contributions to the pervasive role of lighting as a *destroyer* of form. Technology, per se, is powerless to produce a good luminous environment. Concepts, not hardware, are the missing ingredients in the conventional approach to the design of the luminous environment.

To design good lighting, the designer needs to understand clearly the principles and processes of visual perception, and the nature of human needs for visual information.

We do not need more technology, nor do we need more light. What we *do* need is an understanding of how to *apply* the technology already at our disposal, which can only come from an understanding of how we see, what we look at, what we perceive, and why. Energy is no longer the unlimited resource it once appeared to be. The moment is long overdue when we must change our priorities, and design buildings which use far fewer resources to far better effect. We can no longer afford to waste space and energy so lavishly to produce

3 When Life *Magazine run this picture, their caption read: "WHAT A WONDER! WHAT A BLUNDER! Somewhere there's a ball up there . . . Sure there is, but we can't see it either."*

[1]*Visual noise refers to distracting visual stimuli (such as oncoming headlights at night) which interfere with one's ability to perceive or interpret other more desirable or needed stimuli which are relevant to the satisfaction of one's needs. The acoustic equivalent might be a foghorn in a concert hall. But distractions need not be overpowering—a neighboring and persistent popcorn-muncher in the same concert hall might be even more annoying than one blast of a foghorn, however loud, and the same principle applies to visual noise.*

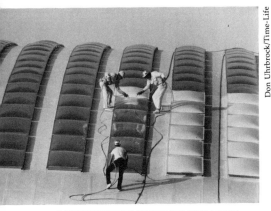

4 *"HOUSTON PAINTS ITS WAY OUT OF ITS BIG GOOF"* (caption from Life Magazine)

5

such pitiful, pitiless environments.

The reader may object to the accusation that we spend our resources today as if we had no notion of what people look at, how they see, what they perceive, and how their perceptions influence their emotional state. Yet consider, for example, the colossal fiasco at the Houston Astrodome several years ago **(Figs. 3** and **4).** Millions of dollars were spent to cover the new Houston stadium with a vast roof, a triumph of structural engineering. As soon as the first game was played, however, one critical problem became apparent.

The players were unable to see the ball against the striking patterns of black and white formed by the structure of the great roof silhouetted against the sky.

Illumination levels were high, almost as high as they were outdoors, yet the players could neither see nor catch the ball. The designers of the Astrodome had apparently never considered the fact that the powerful patterns of the silhouetted roof would make it impossible to pick out the position and trajectory of a ball in flight. The resulting signal-to-noise ratio was so low in the Astrodome that the noble game of baseball was reduced to a comedy of errors.

Since the power of the signal could not be increased (assuming that luminous baseballs remain out of fashion) the only thing that could be done was to reduce the power of the background noise. To correct the situation, the acres of expensive translucent plastic skylights were painted out. The grass died, and was replaced with Astroturf. The artificial lights must now be used for every game.

Unable to think of the requisite luminous environment in terms of quality rather than quantity, many people rationalized that since the skylights had to be painted out at Houston, there must have been *too much* light. That seems like an eminently reasonable argument, until one considers that the game has been played outdoors under even higher levels of illumination ever since its invention, and baseball players have always been able to see a fly ball silhouetted against the featureless vault of the sky. Had the critics and designers of the Astrodome been thinking in terms of information transfer (too much competing pattern) rather than quantity of sensation (too much light), they would have realized that a structure with less inherent pattern, such as an air-inflated bubble **(Fig. 5)** of the same dimensions as the original dome, could have been equally bright without interfering in the least with perception of the ball in flight. It is this kind of unclear thinking which we must all learn to avoid. If the problems to be solved in the design of an appropriate luminous environment for the game of baseball had been correctly stated in perceptual terms from the inception of the design process, it is unlikely that the Astrodome would have had such a nasty surprise in store for its owners and designers.

If the perception process, the nature of people's needs for visual information, and the characteristics of a good luminous environment are clearly understood, the need for new design criteria and a new design process becomes equally clear. Hopefully, "lighting design" will eventually cease to exist as a separate discipline. The current state of affairs bears mute witness to the alienation of one of the architect's most useful and potent design tools. The design of human environments is, in effect, the design of human sensory experience; all visual design is *de facto* also lighting design, and the sooner this is acknowledged in the design process, the better.

2 Environmental Objectives and Human Needs

A good luminous environment helps us to do what we want to do and makes us feel good while we do it. Although it may seem simplistic, this statement summarizes the real objectives of lighting design—to provide a comfortable, pleasant, reassuring, interesting, and functional space for the people who will inhabit it.

We are comfortable when we are free to focus our attention on what we want or need to see, when the information we seek is clearly visible and confirms our desires and our expectations, and when the background does not compete for our attention in a distracting way. When these conditions are satisfied, we consider that a space is attractive and has an appropriate focus. We are distracted and made uncomfortable when the visual information is irrelevant or confuses our understanding of the environment. Our discomfort is increased when visual noise—irrelevant or confusing signals—dominates the field of vision and interferes with the ability to perceive relevant, useful facts about the nature of the environment or the progress of activities.

Activity needs for visual information

Almost every built environment is created to house some form of human activity. To perform almost any task, to engage successfully in almost any activity, one needs certain definable types of visual information. When reading, one needs to be able to see the words on the page clearly; when carving wood, one needs to be able to see and judge the progress of the work. A luminous environment which yields the required information easily will obviously be more satisfactory than one which does not.

When approaching the design of any luminous environment, therefore, it is important to analyze first the activities which will take place, to list them according to their various characteristics, to determine the needs for visual information associated with each activity, and to assign them priorities. Each activity can be ranked according to its frequency, its relative importance, its location, the people who will participate in it, and whether or not it takes place simultaneously with other activities in the same space. It is important to define visual tasks and activities as carefully and completely as possible before attempting to design a lighting system. The designer must ask such questions as: "What are the tasks? How frequently are they performed? Where? Are they vertical or horizontal? Two or three dimensional? Pencil, ink, or printed? Colored or black and white?

Would the presence of daylight help or hinder the perception process?'' The answers to questions such as these provide the only meaningful basis for the formulation of design objectives and performance criteria for the luminous environment.

Unlike biological needs, activity or "task" needs have always been recognized as objectives for lighting — too often, unfortunately, as the *only* objectives. Even so, optimum lighting conditions for tasks are seldom achieved, because quantity rather than quality of light is the common method of specification. Increasing the illumination on a task or an object can increase its visibility *or it can decrease it*, depending on the qualities of the illumination far more than on the quantity of light provided. The direction of the light, its source concentration, its color, and its other qualities must be appropriate to the specific nature of the information required and the characteristics of the object being viewed.

For each activity or task there are optimal luminous conditions under which we would ideally like to operate, and which would most facilitate the performance of the task or activity. The typical approach to lighting, however, starts with the isolation of one "most difficult task," such as reading smudged fifth carbon copies, which is then taken as the basis for lighting levels *everywhere* in a space, with no regard for how often and where within the space that task is likely to take place. Although they may demand different and even conflicting qualities or quantities of light, all other tasks and activities which take place in the same space are not considered. Biological needs are never mentioned.

This "shotgun" approach is directly responsible for most of the bad aspects of our luminous environments. It is ridiculous that a committee in New York or Washington should have the power to specify inflexible lighting criteria based on abstract "most difficult tasks," for all offices across the continent or all classrooms from kindergarten to university, when they have no knowledge of the actual tasks, their mix, and their frequency of occurrence. One would never argue that since lumberjacks require 5000 calories per day, *everyone* should eat 5000 calories per day. Light, like diet, must be balanced and related to the unique needs of each person's physiology and the activities in which each engages. This is the reason why we advocate a "rifle" approach to task lighting, rather than the conventional, wasteful, and often counterproductive "shotgun" approach which calls for every corner of a space to be drowned in enough light to accommodate the most demanding sort of task, regardless of its probable location or frequency of occurrence — different watts for different spots. As I type these words, the illumination on my desk is less than one-fifth of the current United States recommended level for an office environment, yet in my office that is all the light I need for most of my activities. When I need more light, or a special kind of light for a special activity such as viewing slides, I push a switch and adapt the luminous environment selectively to meet my particular needs of the moment. Flexibility and quality, not sheer quantity, are the essentials of a good multiuse luminous environment.

It is unfortunate that very little useful research has been done to generate statistical data on typical activity patterns and durations in common types of spaces. Such applied research would be very helpful for the designer who must frequently work from an incomplete program, often for a building type with which he or she is relatively unfamiliar. Most lighting codes which establish minimum illumination levels for different types of space incorporate implicit assumptions about the nature of activities which are expected to take place, and yet research often proves these assumptions to be highly erroneous. For instance, reading and writing are the visual tasks which are most commonly used as the basis for illumination codes. The implicit assumption is that reading and writing are sufficiently important and frequent activities that the overall luminous environment should be adjusted to suit the exigencies of these particular tasks. But are reading and writing important and frequent activities in most spaces? At the suggestion of the author, the M. I. T. planning office conducted a survey in 1967 of visual activities in typical classrooms at M. I. T.; the results are presented in Table II–1. This study revealed that reading and writing constituted less than 20 percent of the activities in the surveyed spaces, and that *none* of the activities recorded involved *pencil* handwriting—the task on which the illumination recommendations of the lighting industry are based. Note that these surveys were conducted in *academic* spaces, in which one would expect to find a higher proportion of time spent on reading and

Table II–1. RESULTS OF PILOT PHOTOGRAPHIC STUDY BY M.I.T. PLANNING OFFICE IN 1967

This study was carried out by photographing spaces and their occupants from the front corner of the room. The photographs were then analyzed to determine the exact visual task of each person in the scenes. Each person photographed constitutes "one observation."

Visual Activity	Classroom Observations		Lecture Hall Observations	
	Number	Total, %	Number	Total, %
None				
Gazing	30	11.7	278	12.8
Lecturer or conversation	64	25.0		
Horizontal				
Reading (continuous):				
pencil				
ink				
typewritten duplicate				
printing				
other (name)				
Writing (includes reviewing):				
continuous				
notes	62	24.2	395	18.2
drafting				
Vertical				
Chalkboard	100	38.1	1,294*	59.5
Displays				
Projection: transparency			207	9.5
opaque				
Three dimensional				
TOTAL NONTASK ORIENTED	94	36.7	278	12.8
TOTAL TASK ORIENTED	162	63.3	1,896	87.2
TOTAL	256	100.0%	2,174	100.0%

*Chalkboard or lecturer: It is not possible to distinguish from photographs in large lecture halls exact visual activities without the type of apparatus used by Mackworth. The chalkboard test is a conservative estimate; classroom observations indicate that a more accurate study would show a substantial number of observations of the lecturer.

writing than in other types of spaces. The conclusion should be obvious: it is not reasonable to tailor the luminous environment to suit the special needs of an activity which is neither frequent nor of long duration.

Further surveys should be conducted in other types of spaces to check the validity of this and other implicit assumptions which have been built into most contemporary lighting codes.

Biological needs for visual information: new criteria for design

Human perception is an active, information-seeking process which involves many mechanisms in the eye and the brain, some conscious and others unconscious. William James underlined the *selective* nature of perception when he wrote:

> Millions of items of the outward order are present to my senses which never properly enter into my experience. Why? Because they have no *interest* for me. *My experience is what I agree to attend to.* Only those items which I *notice* shape my mind—without selective interest, experience is an utter chaos. Interest alone gives accent and emphasis, light and shade, background and foreground—intelligible perspective, in a word. It varies in every creature, but without it the consciousness of every creature would be a grey chaotic indiscriminateness, impossible for us even to conceive.[1]

We direct our voluntary attention to elements of the visual environment which provide information we need to perform our conscious activities. As James put it, "our voluntary attention is always *derived;* we never make an effort to attend to an object except for the sake of some interest which the effort will serve."[2] One criterion for a good luminous environment is therefore obvious: *it should make readily perceptible the information which we require for our conscious and voluntary activities.* In the following discussion, we will refer to needs for such activity-related visual environmental information as *activity needs.*

In much oversimplified form, activity needs are often misused to justify the illumination minima specified in lighting codes. But activity needs are not the only needs which must be satisfied by the luminous environment, nor are they necessarily the most important. In the same passage, William James went on to write:

> But both sensorial and intellectual attention may be either passive or voluntary.
>
> In *involuntary attention* of the *immediate sensorial* sort, the stimulus is either a sense-impression, very intense, voluminous, or sudden, . . . or else it is an instinctive stimulus, a perception which by reason of its nature rather than mere force, appeals to some one of our normal congenital impulses and has a directly exciting quality . . . we shall see how these stimuli differ from one animal to another, and what most of them are in man: strange things, moving things, wild animals, bright things, pretty things, metallic things, words, blows, blood, etc., etc., etc.[3]

Classifying the objects of involuntary attention cited by James into broader categories, and extending the *et cetera*, I suggest that these "normal congenital impulses" relate directly and logically to the essence of human beings as biological organisms—to their safety and security, sustenance and stimulation. I propose that we call James's "normal congenital impulses" *biological information needs*, because they

[1]*William James*, The Principles of Psychology, *Henry Holt and Company, Inc., New York, 1890, vol. 1, p. 402.*

[2]*Ibid., p. 416.*

[3]*Ibid., pp. 416–417.*

derive directly from *the biological* nature of the human being.

Such information is required by everyone, everywhere, everywhen, regardless of their immediate state of activity or inactivity. The intensity of the various biological information needs is conditioned to a certain degree by the experience and cultural background of each individual, and by the nature of the particular circumstances in question. Yet underneath the diverse aspects of human individuality, there lie more fundamental, universally shared characteristics—the basics of human nature. Rene Dubos, in *So Human an Animal*, wrote:

> While civilization obviously conditions what man becomes, it does not significantly affect his biological nature; what changes is his social milieu. . . . as the English historian Arnold Toynbee wrote: "Scratch the surface and efface what we receive from an education which never ceases and we shall discover something very like primitive humanity in the depths of our nature." This is true not only for social behavior but also for biological and emotional needs.[4]

When fully concentrated on a demanding task, we become relatively unconscious and unconcerned about anything else, and any irrelevant visual information may be an undesirable distraction. As formal tasks demand less focus, or as our attention strays, the focus of perception turns to the search for information related to the satisfaction of biological needs. We seek facts of orientation: where we are, the shape and structure of the space, the nature and quality of furnishings and finishes, the identity of our neighbors, who they are and what they are doing, the time of day, and the weather. Our senses are constantly monitoring the environment for signs of change; all the senses take part in this biological Distant Early Warning system. In his book *Perception through Experience*, M. C. Vernon states that "The type of motivation to which perception is mostly directly related is the necessity of maintaining contact with the environment and adapting behavior to environmental change. . . . the perceptual capacities seem to function in such a manner as to produce rapid reaction to change, whereas in an unchanging environment they may cease to operate effectively."[5] When we have no specific activity to occupy our attention, the monitoring of biological information may *become* our conscious activity.

As James points out, "figure" objects, which are often relatively bright or strongly patterned with regard to their visual background or context, automatically attract our involuntary attention. If these automatic foci give us desired or needed information we are likely to find them satisfying and reassuring; an example would be a well-placed illuminated EXIT sign, bright enough so that we are aware of it but not so bright as to interfere with our other perceptions. However, if bright or strongly patterned stimuli which trigger our involuntary attention are informationless, ambiguous, or distracting, we find them annoying. Luminous environments in which biologically necessary information is unavailable, distorted, confused, or overpowered provoke feelings of dissatisfaction and discomfort, unless there is clear evidence that this deprivation was consciously intended to call forth some agreeable or exciting response. Planned distortions of biologically necessary information can be exciting in the context of a funhouse, but they have no place in most environments.

In considering James's comments on the nature of involuntary visual attention, one must always bear in mind that visual perception

[4]*Rene Dubos*, So Human an Animal, *Scribner, New York, 1968, p. 40.*

[5]*M. C. Vernon*, Perception through Experience, *Methuen, London, 1970, p. 201.*

is a process which involves much more than the eye alone. It cannot be analyzed as a simple stimulus-response system, because *seeing* involves the brain as well as the eye, and through prior experience the brain plays a major role in determining which characteristics of objects make them worthy of attention—figures seen against a background of visual context. Since the brain is constantly monitoring the visual environment for new information which might be of significance with regard to biological or activity needs, things which are unexpected or which contrast with their visual backgrounds because of some unusual quality are likely to be treated as figures by the visual-processing system, attracting the attention of the beholder. Note that it is not necessarily the strength of a particular quality such as brightness or movement which attracts the attention; depending on the nature of the context, it might be that an absence of a particular quality such as color or movement might establish a figure/background relationship demanding the visual attention. A face drained of color, a motionless figure lying on the ground, a sudden darkness overhead can all trigger the attention of the viewer. The key here is contrast with context or expectation, not necessarily the simple strength of the stimulus.

Consider 10 fans of an identical model, all gray except one which is painted red. The attention is drawn to the red one because of its color contrast with the others. If nine had been red, and one gray, the gray one would have attracted the visual attention because the very neutrality of its color made it a figure against a red background. Suddenly one fan starts to turn. Immediately the eye is drawn to it, since its new quality of movement distinguishes it from all the others. Then all the rest start. The eye wanders; all are now the same, in motion. There is no figure, no background. But if one slows down and stops, the eye will be drawn to it by its *lack* of motion, a new figure quality which distinguishes that fan from all the others. Clearly contrast and context, prior experience and expectations all influence the operation of the involuntary attention, and a quality which distinguishes a focus for the attention one minute may quickly be supplanted by its opposite.

If they want the environments which they design to respond effectively to all the needs of the user, designers must understand the workings of these innate, automatic perceptual mechanisms related to the satisfaction of biological needs.

It should be obvious that biological needs for environmental information are extremely important, yet in lighting codes and in the normal processes of programming and design, these needs are given no explicit recognition whatsoever. There can be no question that our luminous environments should be structured to facilitate the perception of biologically necessary information, but until these needs can be articulately and concisely expressed, they will be given lip service in principle and ignored in practice, as they have been in the past. We must be able to state more precise environmental objectives than "create a mood" or "create an attractive space."

Table II–2 summarizes briefly a number of important biological needs, and lists perception-based criteria for the design of relevant, appropriate luminous environments. Characteristics of good hardware systems and lighting appropriate to the satisfaction of various biological needs are also suggested, although the selection of hardware should always be held in abeyance until all needs have been analyzed

Table II–2. SPECIFIC BIOLOGICAL NEEDS FOR VISUAL INFORMATION AND THEIR IMPLICATIONS FOR THE LUMINOUS ENVIRONMENT AND FOR THE SELECTION OF HARDWARE SYSTEMS

Biological Need for Visual Information	Critical Time or Situation	Visual Information Required	Implications for the Luminous Environment and Hardware Systems: Desirable Qualities	Qualities to be Avoided
Orientation	At all times; maximum when moving	Level horizontal reference clues	Use material joints (e.g., in masonry), moldings, expansion joints, mullions, etc., to establish clear horizontal orientation	Avoid inclined floors without clear visual information defining the nature of the incline; avoid spaces defined by irregular or curvilinear enclosing surfaces without clear horizon clues
		Definition of ground surface contours, enclosing boundaries, level changes	Define level changes and edges with high-lighting, consistent lighting (color, surface, or reflectance)	Avoid distracting elements in the visual field at level changes; avoid confusing elements such as inconsistent shadows or carpet patterns which tend to obscure rather than to emphasize level changes
		Location relative to destinations and exits	Articulate the building layout and circulation system by a clear differentiation of circulation nodes and destinations with distinctive patterns of decorative light sources or by selective highlighting of elements such as elevator cores, etc.; corridors should be differentiated from work spaces, and different types of corridors should be treated differently; good graphics should be used, particularly at decision points such as corridors and intersections	Avoid undifferentiated lighting schemes which apply the same design to functionally disparate spaces, providing no visual guidance information to the users of the spaces location
				Avoid backlighted signs with opaque lettering, in which the shape of the background typically dominates the intended message
Physical security	When danger is expected from people or animals	Location of potential threats; the nature of the surrounding enclosure	Eliminate unlighted areas and sources of glare which might conceal danger; clarify the nature of the surrounding enclosure—structure, possible exits, etc.	
	When danger is expected because structure could be perceived as threatening	Comprehensible structure with clear continuity and visual logic	Use forms consistent with the expectations of the viewer; use light gradients consistent with the forms of the structure which they illuminate	Avoid flimsy structural forms such as the typical luminous ceiling; avoid obscuring structural elements with unshielded light sources; avoid using sources inconsistently (different sources to light identical surfaces)
	When danger is expected from fire	Location of control and prevention equipment; escape routes clearly visible	Use lighting to articulate circulation paths and exits; use color-coded fire extinguishers and clear EXIT signs	Avoid unevenly illuminated EXIT signs and EXIT signs which do not dominate their surroundings sufficiently to be clearly visible; eliminate other signs in the vicinity of EXIT signs which would compete for the visual attention; avoid overly bright EXIT signs, on the other hand, in dark environments such as theaters
	When danger may be caused by intense light or glare		Use proper glare shields or other control devices on luminaires so that sources do not achieve an undesired prominence or create disability glare conditions while providing required illumination for tasks or biological needs	
	When danger might be anticipated due to unsanitary conditions	Maximum evidence of high sanitation standards	Emphasize clean work areas in kitchens, labs, etc.	Avoid highlighting areas such as dirty dish conveyors or garbage collection areas
Relaxation of the body and mind	During sleep	Only that required to maintain the sensation of security; uniform conditions of light, sound and temperature desirable	Provide night lights as required for security; switching hardware should be readily accessible	Minimize the number of obtrusive luminous signs visible from sleeping areas; avoid street lighting with poor glare control
	During work	Interesting visual rest centers desirable	Provide visual foci such as views, artwork, positive expression of structural form, decorative or orientation-related patterns of light sources (chandeliers, graphics, illuminated sculpture)	Eliminate competing sources of visual noise such as glaring fixtures
	While awake but waiting or idle	Interesting visual environment	Provide visual foci as above; evidence of sunlight, plants, water elements such as pools or fountains, etc.	Minimize unsightly, unpleasant, or irrelevant elements of the visual environment, since their negative impact will be greatest when the viewer has no conscious preoccupation
Adjustment of the biological clock (time orientation)	Continuous need, particularly strong in unfamiliar situations	Awareness of the state of the diurnal cycle, since luminous conditions in interiors are evaluated with reference to external conditions	Views of exterior conditions should be possible via clear windows or clear skylights	Do not design windowless spaces unless the justification is clear and the omission serves some other need: i.e., in a museum or theater; wherever possible, give a view of more than just sky
Contact with nature, sunlight, and with other living beings	Interior environments	Evidence of sunlight in every space or in nearby and accessible spaces	Visible daylit or sunlit surfaces such as plant material or window reveals; also daylit or sunlit surfaces such as meaningful translucent glass or colored glass block	Avoid excessive direct sunlight on work surfaces; avoid information-less surfaces such as translucent windows and skylights; sun control devices if required should create minimum visual noise and figure/background conflict with the view (i.e., large-scale louvers or fine-mesh screening rather than intermediate-scale egg crates or blinds with no inherent visual interest)
Definition of personal territory	Particularly in public or work environments	Visible evidence of personal control and occupation of territory	Provide local lighting which can be controlled by users; provide distinctive or large-scale organization of the visual environment which can be used to locate and identify personal territory from a distance	Avoid public or work environments with no inherent means for personalization of space by the users

and evaluated for their visual implications. The table is not intended to be complete or definitive; introspection will reveal other biological needs which deserve consideration in the design of luminous environments.

Among the most important biological needs for environmental information, we may list an awareness of the following:

- *Location*, with regard to water, heat, food, sunlight, escape routes, destination, etc.
- *Time*, and environmental conditions which relate to our innate biological clocks
- *Weather*, as it relates to the need for clothing and heating or cooling, the need for shelter, opportunities to bask in the beneficial rays of the sun, etc.
- *Enclosure*, the safety of the structure, the location and nature of environmental controls, protection from cold, heat, rain, etc.
- *The presence of other living things*, plants, animals, and people
- *Territory*, its boundaries and the means available within a given environment for the personalization of space
- *Opportunities for relaxation and stimulation* of the mind, body, and senses
- *Places of refuge*, shelter in time of perceived danger

Changes in the perceived status of these important aspects of the environment trigger warning signals in the brain, demanding attention. We pay more attention—conscious and unconscious—to biologically important factors than we do to other sensory data which are less relevant to our physical, intellectual, and emotional well-being.

If the incoming sensory data are ambiguous, so that we are unsure about the definite status of biologically important elements of the environment, we become uneasy and uncomfortable. If the incoming data are unambiguous and if the perceived facts indicate that everything is as expected and under control, we relax. On the other hand, if the facts indicate danger, we feel tense and wary. We react negatively to informationless environments such as a dark alley or a window at night through which we can be seen but cannot see, because that which we can neither comprehend nor classify might contain danger.

The need for orientation

For protection of the body, an awareness of its location, movement, and state is necessary at all times. Our sensory monitors which provide the necessary environmental information for such orientation operate continuously, even during sleep. High-quality continuous visual information is required for all physical activities, such as walking, running, jumping or working.

When we are walking and even when we are seated, awareness of the horizontal is important. The human mind can cope with a horizon which is unclear because of low contrast. But our biological need for horizon orientation makes us uncomfortable when the horizon is completely obscured, as in **Fig. 6.** If the fog obscures the crisp edge between sky and sea, for instance, while eliminating orientation clues normally provided by the directional quality of sunlight, we may become disoriented and uneasy.

The example in **Fig. 6** may seem somewhat irrelevant to most architectural situations—fog is after all relatively infrequent inside most buildings—but the *principle* involved remains valid. Inside buildings, we normally use other visual clues besides the physical horizon to give us orientation to the horizontal; when these clues are distorted or absent, the effect can be very disturbing. One such disorienting space can be found in the TWA terminal at Kennedy Airport in New York **(Fig. 7)**. The corridors which lead from the main lobby to the departure lounges have sloping floors and smooth, featureless, nonvertical walls—an environment which gives the beholder no clues whatsoever as to the true vertical and horizontal. This disorienting effect is heightened when there are no other people in the corridor who can be used as references. Vertical pictures, graphics, or visible expansion joints which would create reference planes would alleviate the unpleasant sensation of disorientation.

Another well-known example of a disorienting space is the spiral exhibition gallery in the Guggenheim Museum in New York **(Fig. 8)**. Many people are somewhat uncomfortable in this space because they cannot tell whether to stand perpendicular to the gently sloping floor or parallel to the pictures which are hung on a true horizontal. Although the pictures do give reference lines indicating the true horizontal, the incoming sensory data are sufficiently ambiguous so that one becomes uneasy—though the untrained observer may be unable to articulate the source of his or her distress.

Orientation as affected by expectations and prior experience[6]

The phenomenon of disorientation in ambiguous interior spaces brings up an important aspect of the process of perception. As James pointed out, our senses are constantly bombarded by a flood of impressions—incoming raw sensory data—which is sorted and processed by the mind and the sense organs themselves so that only relevant information is brought to the conscious attention. However, the incoming stimuli are not evaluated solely according to their quantitative characteristics—strength, duration, information content, etc. The *meaning* which they are given, the importance which is attached to them during the actual process of perception formation, is conditioned almost exclusively by prior experience with other, similar or related stimuli. The interpretive mechanism of the mind's eye operates according to the basic principle that similar causes will produce similar effects; we can survive and function only because the world usually behaves and appears as we *expect* it to.

Obviously, expectations play an indispensable role in the process of physical orientation. We *expect* floors to be flat, because the vast majority of floors which we experience *are* flat. When we encounter a sloping floor, without clear visual signals that it is in fact sloping, our expectations tell us that the floor is probably flat, while the inner ear tells us something quite different. The inner conflicts which such perceptually ambiguous situations set up can be profoundly disturbing.

Expectations affect our emotional response to different

6 *Loss of horizon orientation.*

7 *Corridor, TWA Terminal at Kennedy Airport, New York (Eero Saarinen/ Architect).*

8 *Gallery, Guggenheim Museum, New York (Frank Lloyd Wright/Architect).*

[6]*The roles played by expectation and prior experience in the process of perception are analyzed in considerable detail in Chapter Three.*

9 *Handball court—scallops confusing.*

10 *Squash court—scallops painted out.*

[7]*For a fascinating discussion of these biorhythms, see Michel Gauquelin,* The Cosmic Clocks, *Peter Owen, London, 1965.*

environments in a number of ways. In particular, they condition our response to the presence or absence of biologically necessary information. Our evaluation of any environment is colored by the memory of prior experience in analogous situations. In the seashore example, we know that under other circumstances we would be able to see the horizon; if we cannot see it, there is less biologically relevant orientation information available than there once was. The brain, consciously or unconsciously, is aware of the lack, and makes us uneasy. If we were flying or sailing, we would be acutely conscious of a lack of visible horizon; in fact, airplane instrument panels have artificial horizons for such occasions. On the other hand, in a basement or a coal mine shaft far under the surface of the earth, we would not expect to see the horizon; we have never seen it under such circumstances, and therefore its absence seems perfectly natural.

One must avoid making careless generalizations regarding biologically required information for orientation: under different circumstances, different types of information become necessary and appropriate. In certain sports, for instance, awareness of the horizon is relatively unimportant, and other orientation clues assume top priority according to the particular nature of the game. The luminous environment should provide appropriate information to meet these special needs. For instance, the handball player plays against the ceiling as well as the walls. The poor definition of the junction between wall and ceiling in **Fig. 9** caused by the strong pattern of scallops on the walls is distracting and confusing. In the squash court in **Fig. 10,** the ceiling is not a playing surface; therefore good definition of that junction is less important to the players and the disturbing scallops were simply painted out. The same lighting fixtures which were inappropriate to the handball court are more satisfactory in the squash court in **Fig. 10.**

The need for time orientation

Time orientation is another important biological need for which we require types of visual information about the environment. Human beings, like most other organisms, possess inherent biological mechanisms which act as clocks of different sorts, to keep track of the rhythm of day and night as well as other biologically important cycles.[7] As the seasons lengthen and shorten the hours of daylight, our internal clocks respond accordingly. This continually recalibrated time orientation gives us definite expectations of how light or dark it should be outside, and these expectations play a major role in our evaluation of any luminous environment, by establishing reference levels in the brain against which we evaluate incoming sensory data about the apparent brightness of the immediate environment. It is upsetting to go outdoors at noon and find it overcast and gloomy, because we *expect* it to be bright and sunny. We would be even more upset to walk outside at midnight and find it "bright as day"!

It should come as no surprise that expectation and time orientation play a major role in the evaluation of exterior environments; yet it is less well known that expectation and time orientation play an equally critical role in the evaluation of *interior* luminous environments. Because of time orientation, during the day we subconsciously expect it to be brighter outside buildings than inside, as in **Fig. 11.** At night, we expect it to be darker outside than

Ripman

Ripman

Lam

11 *Normal daytime orientation—exterior brighter.*

12 *Normal nighttime orientation—interior brighter.*

13 *The sensation of visual gloom results from contradiction of time orientation (for instance, when an interior is brighter than the scene outside during the daytime).*

inside **(Fig. 12).** During the day, we generally expect bright interior conditions, with walls and ceilings cheerfully illuminated, since they take the place of the sky and sunlit surroundings. At night, we expect the environment to be less bright, and luminance levels in the same space can be far below those appropriate during the daytime without making the space feel dark or generating feelings of gloom or sensory deprivation. Our eyes adapt to gradually changing luminous conditions during the cycle of the day and night, so that at night a candlelit room may be perceived as being brilliantly illuminated. The apparent brightness is high, even though the measured brightness or luminance is very low.

Sensations of gloom are likely to be caused not by low luminance levels, but by the contradiction from incoming sensory data of expectations based on time orientation. This happens frequently at dusk and on overcast days, as in **Fig. 13,** when the outside world seems to be darker than the inside. The length of this unpleasant period is extended by the use of low-transmission glass, which affects our perception of the relative brightness of interior and exterior conditions. If, due to the use of low-transmission glass, our eyes tell us that the outside world is darker than our time orientation tells us to expect, the effect is unpleasant because our time orientation is being fed distorted and unexpected data.

The need for consistency between lighting gradients and structural forms

For hundreds of thousands of years, people perceived the world around them illuminated by a single, directional light source—the sun. Whether because of species conditioning or because of each individual's childhood experiences while learning to see, we have definite expectations of how three-dimensional objects should appear. We perceive the third dimension not only through our stereoscopic vision, but also by observation of the light gradients and shadows which define volume and form. We have definite expectations of how most things—including structural elements such as flat walls, floors, and beams—should look when rendered in light. Uneven gradients of light which define the shape of three-dimensional solids seem pleasant and natural when consistent with our expectations **(Fig. 1),** but they can be disturbing, unnatural, and distracting when, for instance, a uniform flat surface is illuminated unevenly for no apparent reason **(Fig. 15).** Contradiction by the senses of biologically important expectations concerning the nature and form of structure is usually disquieting and should be avoided whenever possible.[8]

The ambiguous and irrelevant nature of most luminous ceilings

[8]*A more detailed discussion of how we perceive and interpret light gradients is given in Chapter Three, in the section "Luminance Gradients, the Perception of Brightness and Three-Dimensional Form."*

14 *Typical luminous ceiling.*   **15**   **16**

(Figs. 14, 67) is unpleasant because most luminous ceilings conceal the real structure while substituting a flimsy, uneven, shoddy, ambiguous surface with badly finished joints. Rows of glaring fixtures which relate neither to any perceptible structure nor to the activities which they illuminate are likely to be found unpleasant for similar reasons: such fixtures confuse the comprehension of structure and give little evidence of the work of the concerned hand of the designer to tailor space to the use of its occupants.

The need for contact with sunlight

Visible evidence of the presence of sunlight satisfies a basic biological need, providing important clues about three-dimensional form and orientation in addition to indicating the state of the weather. For some activities, such as relaxing on a beach, sunlight may be entirely positive. But while we all enjoy seeing signs of the sun's presence, being in the sunlight itself may be unpleasant if the light or heat interferes with what we want to see or do **(Fig. 16).**

As long as it does not interfere with our activities we welcome sunlight inside buildings. Direct sunlight on a desk or work area, however, can be extremely bothersome, particularly if the condition persists for a long time, and if one is unable to control it or move away.

Even a small patch of sunlight is adequate to satisfy this particular biological need—a minimal area of clear glazing overhead can add more dramatic life and vitality to a space than acres of translucent glazing, which tend to contribute only unbearable glare and unpleasant solar heat (consider the Pantheon and compare it to a greenhouse with walls and roof of corrugated translucent plastic). The small areas of direct sunlight in **Fig. 17** interfere with activities in only a small portion of each space; since the occupants are free to move about, no one is inconvenienced by these biologically satisfying shafts of sunlight. Analogous conditions may be seen in **Figs. B4-4 and H2-8.** It is important to note that light fixtures of equivalent size and brightness, if substituted for the patches of sunlight, would make most people feel uncomfortable. Unlike the sunlight, the light fixtures would seem arbitrary and out of place, distracting, glaring, and informationless rather than pleasing—one more piece of evidence that it is the *meaning* of bright sources in the visual field, and not merely their surface luminance or size, which determines our emotional response to them.

We react negatively to being deprived of desirable sensory information without some compensation. Obscured or pebbled glass windows are disturbing for this reason. We react favorably to stained-glass windows, on the other hand, because they substitute another desirable form of positive visual experience for the view which they replace. If translucent panels are given a definite color or are overlaid with some pattern of interesting information, such as the maps in **Fig. 19,** they are at least more interesting to view.

Translucent panels give us no pleasure when backlit as they are in **Fig. 18.** As large, bright area sources they demand attention, yet because they are informationless they are more frustrating than pleasurable, whereas a window of comparable dimensions and luminance which framed a view would make a positive contribution to the space. We react negatively to informationless translucent panels backlit by the sun, not only because they are ambiguous, but also because the presence of sunlight tells us that we might have been able to have a view as well. Evaluation of the luminous environment is always comparative, never absolute: *that which might be* is always a factor in the evaluation of *that which is.*

The need for view

Manning[9] has demonstrated that daylight is desirable, not only because of its illumination and spectral qualities, but because of the view which is usually associated with the daylight. Since people enjoy looking at sunlight falling outdoors as well as inside interior spaces, clear windows are desirable. North-facing clear windows are particularly valuable in this respect because they require no solar-control devices, which often destroy the view that the window was intended to provide in the first place. The view through many types of sunscreens, heavily mullioned windows, or Venetian blinds is uncomfortable because of the undesirable competition between the elements of the glazing plane and the view beyond. Such solar-control structures can generate substantial annoying visual noise which detracts from the pleasure of the view. The high brightness and prominent joint pattern of glass block walls attract the attention of the viewer, but the distorted irregular light pattern from the glass prisms is often difficult to understand and ambiguous, hence biologically unsatisfying.

When applied to fenestration, the characteristic American attitude that "more is better" (or, perhaps, "more is cheaper") has brought us more curses than blessings. Anyone who has had to work in a glass curtain-walled building with no provision for solar control will be familiar with the problems of excessive solar heat loads in summer, unpleasant radiant cooling in winter, excessive sky glare and shadows, etc. Technical solutions such as mirrored glass can mitigate these problems but not solve them completely.

The role of the window in modern architecture needs reexamination. With today's means for artificial illumination, the size, shape, and placement of windows should be chosen primarily to optimize the view. A horizontal view such as a skyline or shoreline should call forth horizontal windows—the *fenêtre-en-longeur* so beloved of the Modern Movement. When the view is all below eye level, window sills should be low, and there is no need for large areas of glazing well *above* eye height. High windows extending to the ceiling line are good in low buildings with interesting surroundings such as trees, other buildings, etc., especially if these surroundings protect the windows from the ravages of the summer sun. In high-rise

Steve Rosenthal

17 (*From* **Case Study D3.**)

Ripman

18 *Ambiguous translucent windows.*

Ripman

19 *Interest added to an otherwise ambiguous and uninteresting translucent panel by an information overlay.*

[9]P. Manning (ed.), Office Design: A Study of Environment, *The Pilkington Research Unit, Liverpool, England, 1967.*

buildings, on the other hand, where little of interest can be seen above eye height, limitation of window heights reduces sky glare, excessive energy consumption, and problem sunlight control while sacrificing none of the interesting elements of the view **(Fig. 20;** compare with **Fig. 78).** When the most interesting mix of visual information is vertical, then vertical windows should be used. These are particularly appropriate when internal wall space is needed for other purposes such as teaching surfaces.[10]

The view through skylights and high clerestories is pleasant when the glazing is clear and uncomplicated. Otherwise, skylights should be baffled by a skylight well, which reads as an interesting, understandable surface providing desirable structural information. Under normal circumstances, one should never place a translucent diffuser at the bottom of a skylight well as in **Fig. 21,** because this has the same effect as obscuring a window: it reduces the meaningful character of the skylight to that of a light-fixture surface, increasing the amount of discomfort glare which is experienced by the viewer.

A note on signs and other directional clues

Our environments are extremely complex. To find our way around in them, we rely primarily on the memory, in which are stored meaningful, recognizable patterns of visual information which are used by the mind in its continuous search for physical orientation and direction. The interstate highway sign with its distinctive profile, the yellow-striped crosswalk, and the crescent moon on a door all provide equally meaningful guidance to those who have encountered them before. All such orientation clues must be *learned;* they do not come built into the visual memory at birth.

It is important to remember that every environment contains more visual information than we can either comprehend or use. Out of this, we must be able to pick the particular patterns which will enable us to find our way around. Some of these directional signals are standardized: the red EXIT sign is a familiar example. However, we normally find our way by means of much subtler patterns of visual information, which may never reach the level of conscious awareness.

In an unfamiliar environment it is helpful if the perceptible patternings of visual information are sufficiently consistent that they may easily be used for orientation and guidance. One simple form of this sort of consistency in the luminous environment is the differentiation of public and private corridors with various kinds of lighting systems, colors, and materials. Another is the distinctive illumination of the walls of service cores and vertical circulation elements. A third is the use of decorative light fixtures to call attention to circulation nodes and important destinations.

Good graphics are indispensable in any complex environment; shopping streets, government buildings, office buildings, and universities would be incomprehensible without them. Yet graphics and other information systems, though critical, are often poorly designed with regard to the principles of visual perception. We frequently encounter backlighted signs in which the large, brightly illuminated, geometric shape of the background dominates the actual message which it sets off **(Fig. 22).** Failure to apply the principles of perception to the problem of information transfer defeats the purpose of such signs, or at least undermines their effectiveness.

Ripman

20 *The uninteresting portion of the view in this space has been eliminated by the chamfered ceiling. Compare with* **Fig. 78.**

Steve Rosenthal

21 *Skylight, or fluorescent fixtures over the central well? Hard to tell—and yet there is a skylight above the diffusers.*

[10]*See, for instance,* **Case Studies E9** *(the Pierrefonds Comprehensive High School) and* **G5** *(Governors State University).*

This is a classic case of counterproductive visual noise, a mistake that can easily be avoided by using illuminated letters against opaque backgrounds, which maximizes the visibility of the desirable signal by effectively eliminating the background as a competitor for visual attention **(Fig. 23)**.

In the design of visual guidance systems, consideration of the principles of perception and visual noise is especially important. In the high-speed environment of the highway, safety and driving pleasure can be enhanced considerably by the clear definition of roadway alignments and intersections with consistent and comprehensible patterns of lighting, so that drivers need not rely solely on conventional signage for directional information. The clear and consistent use of distinctly different fixture types and mounting heights can be of invaluable assistance to both pedestrian and driver in terms of providing orientation to the hierarchy of city streets.

22 *Background shape dominates the intended message.*

The need for focus on activities

Although we readily acknowledge the need for orientation and visual guidance clues in complicated, specialized, multiuse spaces, the conventional wisdom of lighting design gives no recognition to the equal desirability of creating an appropriate hierarchy of foci on activities in a general work space. Lighting can and should be used to create order and relevance in our work environments, instead of simply adding glaring, informationless, and distracting patterns of visual noise as it so often does. Elements of the visual field which are of interest or which provide visual information related to the satisfaction of activity or biological needs should be highlighted. As a general rule, spaces which enclose a strongly directed activity should create a strong luminous focus on that activity. Spaces with varying, multiple activities, on the other hand, should not create a dominant focus on any one specific activity, but should provide understandable backgrounds which allow the user to choose a focus and concentrate on it without distraction. Illumination should be of adequate quality and quantity for each activity. For relaxation, which is an important and often ignored aspect of every human environment, there should be obvious points of interest—featured works of art, for instance, or views which bring satisfaction to all. Relaxation and comfort will be enhanced by clarity of biologically important information such as circulation patterns, the nature of structure, views, evidence of sunlight, etc.

The definition of appropriate, visually defined foci in the luminous environment simplifies tasks and facilitates concentration. It can also save an enormous amount of costly, scarce energy which would otherwise be wasted in providing unnecessary levels of illumination throughout entire spaces, regardless of needs. *It makes no sense whatsoever to illuminate that which we neither want nor need to see.* Obviously, however, this sort of qualitative objective is alien to the conventional approach to lighting design, which defines good lighting only in terms of providing specified minimum footcandle levels *everywhere* in a space, with no premium assigned to the selective emphasis of that which we want or need to see, or to the concealment of that which we would rather not (or do not need) to see.

Two spaces in which positive focus has been achieved through

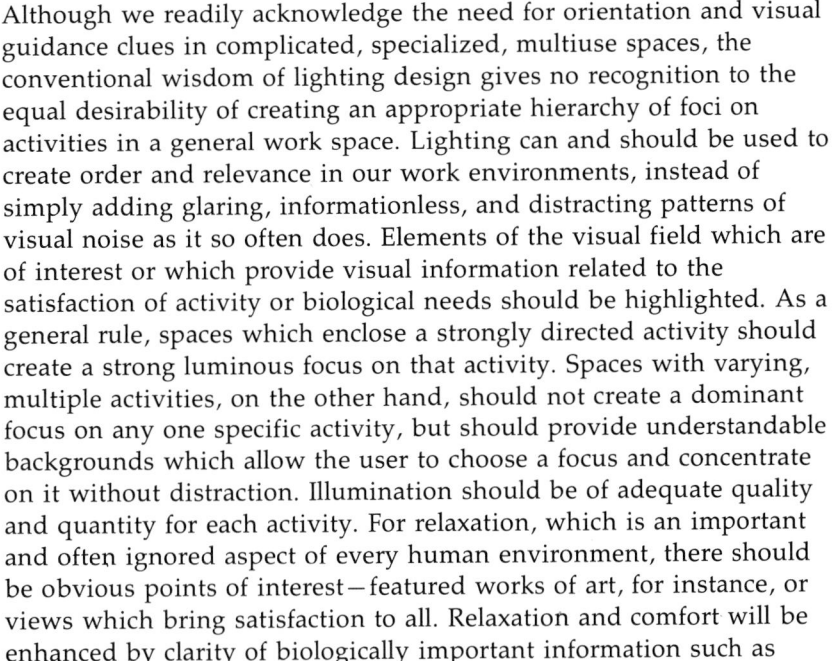

24 *IBM Dining Hall, Endicott, New York* (Sherwood, Mills & Smith/Architects; William Lam Associates/Lighting Consultants).

26 *Library, Rochester Institute of Technology* (Harry Weese & Associates/ Architects; William Lam Associates/ Lighting Consultants).

23 *Message dominates as intended (from* **Case Study H5;** *see also* **Fig. C5-8).**

25 *Grafton County Courthouse, Grafton, New Hampshire* (Johnson-Hotvedt & Associates/Architects; William Lam Associates/Lighting Consultants).

27 *Local lighting.*

appropriate coordination of lighting systems and architectural elements are shown in **Figs. 24** and **25.** The usual complex clutter of light fixtures has been eliminated in the kitchen **(Fig. 24).** The space has been organized by arranging nonglaring indirect lighting around the hood islands. The illuminated ceiling conveys a cheerful sense of spaciousness and helps to eliminate feelings of gloom during the day, when time orientation and expectations demand a bright ''sky'' overhead. The lighting in the courtroom **(Fig. 25)** was carefully conceived and coordinated with the architecture to create an appropriate setting and focus for trial proceedings. In both spaces, the positive focus achieved increases the relevance of the luminous environment.

The need for definition and personalization of territory

Wherever they go and whatever they do, people show a clear tendency to personalize the spaces in which they live and work. This biological need to define territory and to personalize private space has strong implications for the design of the luminous environment. In public spaces such as libraries, control over local lighting and furniture arrangement may be the only available means by which the user can carve a personal niche out of the general public turf. Provision of such simple and inexpensive devices as Luxo lamps or individual carrel lights can make a tremendous difference in the extent to which people feel at home and in control of the public spaces they use **(Fig. 26).**

In large, open office landscapes, people generally seek ways to define and identify their particular location—their *place.* If the structure of a building and the organization of its luminous environment provide large-scale elements such as major ceiling coffers or columns, to which the inhabitants can relate their sense of place, the environment is likely to be more satisfactory in this respect than if the only architectural elements available for place identification are an endless sea of featureless acoustic ceiling tiles punctuated at regular intervals by an equally endless array of closely spaced light fixtures (see, for instance, **Fig. 30).** The scale and arrangement of such fixtures add nothing to one's ability to relocate elements in the visual field.

A brief comparison of the spaces in **Case Studies E8 (Fig. 30), G5,** and **H5 (Figs. 28, 29)** with those in **Case Studies E2, E3,** and **F1** will reveal the generic difference between the two ways of organizing the luminous environment. Readers can judge for themselves in which type of space they would find it easier to orient themselves.

A note on exterior spaces

The typical activities in most outdoor spaces—circulation, congregation, etc.—have lighting needs which are primarily biological in nature; appropriate lighting for such spaces must therefore reveal and emphasize that environmental information which satisfies the biological needs for safe movement, orientation, security, pleasure, relaxation, stimulation, etc.

In daylight, all is revealed. Usually, the amount of light in no way limits the visual information available to the user of an exterior space. Good environmental design for daylight conditions creates a positive focus on information relevant to activities and biological needs. While it is desirable to obscure irrelevant or distracting visual information, this is usually difficult to achieve during daylight hours because of the high overall light levels and their general, unselective distribution. At night, however, the physical and financial constraints which preclude the simulation of daylight levels and distribution can be used to advantage to selectively reinforce the relevant and obscure the irrelevant.

It should be emphasized that attainment of high illumination levels along circulation paths is not the primary design problem involved in the lighting of exterior spaces. If clear and undistorted orientation information is provided for the user, while other biological information needs are satisfied, very low light levels on the order of one-tenth of a footcandle may be perfectly adequate for safe circulation.

In exterior spaces as in buildings there should usually be a well-defined sense of "background" and "foreground." Background spaces should be illuminated as unobtrusively as possible to meet the functional needs of safe circulation, protection of persons and property, etc. Whenever possible, those needs should be taken care of with "spill" light from the positive delineation of circulation spines and nodes, signage and displays, entrances, and other focal elements relevant to the definition of circulation. Foreground spaces, on the other hand, are the major spaces in a city—focal points for orientation or special places of congregation—and should be treated accordingly.

A number of the case study projects which are presented in the second half of this book play foreground space roles in their communities. In each case, the exterior lighting of the buildings themselves and of their extensions such as billboard kiosks, stairs, and terraces provides illumination and definition for the surrounding spaces. The National Arts Centre of Canada **(Case Study H1)** and the Quebec Government Center, Complex "G" **(Case Study H5)** are excellent examples of this approach to exterior lighting.

28 (From **Case Study H5**).

29 (From **Case Study H5**).

30 (From **Case Study F1**).

Summary

A good luminous environment is simultaneously comfortable, pleasant, relevant, and appropriate for its intended uses. The definition of the terms *comfortable, pleasant, relevant,*[11] and *appropriate* need no longer be left to the vagaries of "artistry"; they can be defined much more specifically. A good luminous environment satisfies as many of the needs of its users as possible, and must provide the specific qualities and quantities of visual information which are required for the activities that take place within it. But in addition to activity needs for visual information there are always biological needs which must also be satisfied, and which may be even more important than the activity needs. Designers who give these biological needs for visual information the priority they deserve in the process of programming and design will find that *in most spaces, lighting which provides well for biological needs simultaneously takes care of most activity needs.*

[11]*The relevance of a given luminous environment and its correlation to user satisfaction can be empirically measured. In 1969, the author, together with David Canter (then environmental psychologist from the University of Strathclyde, Glasgow), conducted a pilot experiment in two spaces: a lecture hall and a corridor at M.I.T. Students who used the spaces were asked to rate (1) the desirability of seeing various elements of the visual environment related to activity and biological needs (such as the lecturer, the blackboard, other students, walls, ceilings, light fixtures, view); (2) the extent to which the luminous environment created an emphasis on those elements; and (3) their evaluation of the overall environment on a semantic scale: pleasant or unpleasant, comfortable or uncomfortable, etc. Evaluations in the third category were compared with the match revealed by the first two questions between the desired hierarchy of information in the visual environment and the actual hierarchy. A good match between the desired and actual hierarchy of visual information produced a statistically significant correlation with a positive evaluation; a bad match produced an equally significant correlation with a negative evaluation.*

3 The Process of Visual Perception

SALT IS NOT WOOL

One day the Mulla was taking a donkey-load of salt to market, and drove the ass through a stream. The salt was dissolved. The Mulla was angry at the loss of this load. The ass was frisky with relief.

Next time he passed that way he had a load of wool. After the animal had passed through the stream, the wool was thoroughly soaked, and very heavy. The donkey staggered under the soggy load.

'Ha!' shouted the Mulla, 'you thought you would get off lightly every time you went through water, didn't you?'

——The Exploits of the Incomparable
Mulla Nasrudin

[1]*In the following discussion, we have tried wherever possible to use simple, everyday terminology rather than the often unfamiliar (but sometimes more precise) terminology from the contemporary literature of perceptual psychology. The intent of the discussion is to present the fundamentals of visual perception as they relate to the design and analysis of luminous environments, not to present an exhaustive review of the state of knowledge concerning perception. For further, more detailed analysis of the various components of perception, the reader is referred to the section "The Psychology of Perception" in the Bibliography.*

[2]*The mechanisms that determine which of the many possible stimuli is selected as the object of attention are dealt with later in this chapter in the section "What Do We Look At?"*

The process of perception

The world around us is constantly changing. Autonomous events and processes produce changes in the environment over which we have no control; in addition, every time we move or act, we change the way the world around us appears. As a result, the patterns of sensory stimuli which are recorded by our senses and reported to the brain are also in a continuous state of flux.

The stimuli which bombard our organs of perception at every instant are substantially greater than can be assimilated consciously at any moment; therefore, during the process of perception the brain must actively sort, classify, and interpret the incoming flood of raw sensory data, distinguishing between those stimuli which are relevant to current needs and those which are not. Irrelevant information is shunted directly into the memory, from which it may later be recalled; this usually takes place without engaging the conscious attention of the perceiver. Relevant information, on the other hand, is incorporated immediately into the consciousness of the perceiver, where it is used to satisfy the needs which initiated the search for it.

Perception is not simply a passive recording process which receives and processes all incoming sensory stimuli indiscriminately. If this were the case, our minds would have no time at all for consciously directed activity; we would be continuously enmeshed in a wild unceasing flood of sense impressions, without hope of rest or relief. We would be unable to think, to direct our attention at will, to act usefully and meaningfully. There is simply not enough time for the conscious mind to analyze and respond to every new impression, every change in the state of the world which is registered by our sense organs. The unconscious biological mechanisms of perception handle most of this sorting and selecting automatically, although they require time and experience to learn how to do so. Visual perception is an amazingly complicated and sophisticated process, yet it functions by and large without requiring the intervention or even the attention of the conscious mind.[1]

Let us trace in a somewhat idealized and simplified form what happens to a visual stimulus as it is received by the eye and converted into a perception.[2] A pattern of light passes through the lens of the eye, which focuses the image on the nerve cells that make up the retina. In and of itself, the pattern of light and dark and color has no inherent *meaning* despite the fact that it could be quantified, measured, and described—so much light of such and such wavelength here, a darker area of such and such a size there, etc. The cells of the retina convert the pattern into raw sensory data—a complex matrix of electrical charges of various strengths—and send them coursing along the pathways of the optic nervous system to the brain.

The attributive stage of perception

During the next stage of perception the raw data from the eye are interpreted, classified, and given *meaning* by association. The patterns of information which have been encoded in electrical impulses, patterns which describe objects or other elements in the visual field, are sorted and classified by what we will call the *experience filter:* that part of the unconscious memory which stores data about all past experience. Incoming stimuli are classified according to their characteristics and associated with other, prior, analogous situations or objects which have already been filed in the experience filter. These linkages to prior experience, established by subconscious mechanism which matches or "recognizes" analogous items in the experience filter, are essential to the assignment of meaning to the incoming data. In the terminology of perceptual psychology, this process of matching patterns and classification of stimuli is called the *attributive* component of perception, since it involves the *attribution of meaning* to the incoming stimuli. Attributive classification involves the simplification of incoming data, by classifying it according to the highest recognizable level of order which can be found in the experience filter. In **Fig. 31,** for instance, we see 15 dots, but we also see the circle they form, and the circle is generally perceived before the mind registers that there are in fact 15 dots. The attributive stage of perception seeks to find the general among the particulars, the highest level of organization—in this instance, the circle—which can be perceived and recognized in any given visual field.

To examine the attributive phase of perception in a little greater depth, look at the two images in **Figs. 32** and **33.** As each image falls on the retina, it is converted into patterns of electrical energy, as yet devoid of meaning. Because of past experience, most readers will be able unconsciously and instantaneously to classify **Fig. 32** as a photograph of some vegetables, specifically, five leeks. **Fig. 33,** however, may prove more difficult to interpret. The average experience filter does not contain a sufficient store of analogous patterns which would permit the classification of the image. The picture is unclassifiable, and arouses curiosity.

This raises a key aspect of the attributive process of classification, one which will be of considerable importance later on during the discussion of ambiguous elements in the visual field. When there is no "file" of relevant, analogous information in the visual memory to which the incoming stimulus may be successfully compared and assigned—i.e., given meaning—the attention is drawn to the unclassifiable element of the visual field. The unclassifiable is intrinsically fascinating, partly because it is unfamiliar (novelty excites curiosity) and partly because the unfamiliar may be dangerous. When one encounters the unfamiliar, biological defense mechanisms are set off which heighten awareness until the new element has been classified. An image such as **Fig. 33** excites curiosity only, since we know that it cannot be dangerous. But it is important to remember that unclassifiable or ambiguous visual stimuli demand further visual attention. This explains why featureless, translucent windows

31 *Which do you perceive first—a circle or 15 dots?*

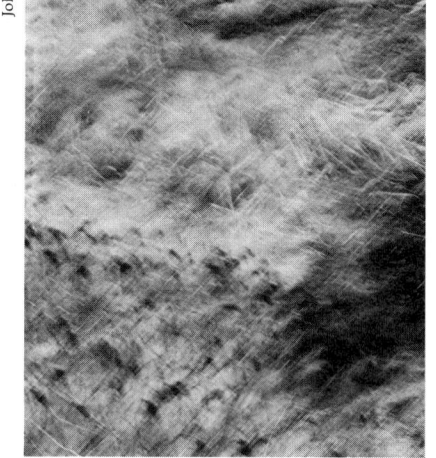

32

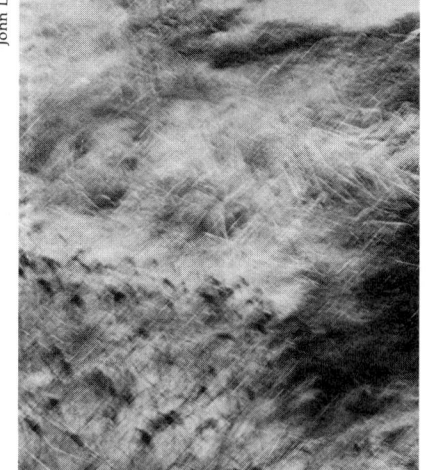

33

are distracting and should be avoided.

The process of attributive classification of incoming stimuli does not depend solely on the characteristics and patterns of the individual stimulus which is the immediate object of the visual attention. All elements of the visual field are simultaneously evaluated as context, and the context plays an important role in the attribution of the stimulus to a particular "file" in the experience filter. *Meaning* is determined as much by the perceived context as by the unique, individual characteristics of the particular stimulus itself. Contextual information is an essential part of the "index" system of the experience filter.

To see the importance of context in the attributive process of classification and interpretation, turn to the next page and look at **Fig. 34.** You will recognize **Fig. 33** as the outlined portion of **Fig. 34,** but now you should be able to interpret both—a blurred photograph of long grass, a pond with the reflection of a tall smokestack and several trees. Although the same information concerning the outlined area is available in both figures, with the additional information of the context in **Fig. 34** you can successfully classify and interpret the outlined area **(Fig. 33).** This simple experiment graphically demonstrates the importance of contextual information as a factor which conditions the classification and interpretation of sensory stimuli. In a process which involves the brain as well as the eye, we see a complete visual world, and we make reference to as much of it as is required to classify any specific stimulus. In a laboratory experiment involving perception, subjects may not be able to interpret definitively what they see because they are deprived of essential context information.[3] In real life, the context is usually available. It is often an unrealistic lack of contextual information which destroys the usefulness of a number of otherwise interesting psychological experiments as possible sources of design criteria for the luminous environment.

One aspect of the attributive process of classification deserves brief discussion in passing because it is critical to the design of the luminous environment. It might seem logical that the impact of a stimulus—attributive, expectant, and affective—would be in proportion to the absolute (measured) magnitude of the dimensions of the stimulus itself: brightness, color, size, etc. This is the tacit assumption which underlies the "more is better" approach to lighting design. However, consideration of the entire mechanism of perception reveals that the magnitude of a stimulus is not necessarily the most important factor: the immediate awareness of a stimulus is largely a function of the *associations* which can be made in the experience filter, and of the *relevance* of the stimulus to current needs for environmental information. It is the interpretation and the relevance—the *meaning*—of the stimulus which determines the relative importance which it will be assigned during the process of perception, and whether it will be perceived as useful signal or as counterproductive visual noise.

Expectations in the process of perception

In our simplified model of visual perception, once the incoming data have been sorted and classified the second component of the process—*expectation*—comes into play. Whereas the attributive stage involves the classification by association of momentary stimuli, the expectant

[3] *It has been demonstrated, for instance, that subjects may be unable to tell under certain conditions whether they are seeing a red plate illuminated by white light, or a white plate under red light. However, under normal conditions one could see the source, or at least the effect of the light it casts on other, familiar objects; from this information, one could easily determine whether it was the plate or the light which was red. For further discussion, see Leo M. Hurvich and Dorothea Jameson,* The Perception of Brightness and Darkness, *Allyn and Bacon, Boston, 1966, p. 86: the Gelb Effect.*

phase establishes associations with *sequences* of events.

The importance of expectations in connection with the design of the luminous environment should be obvious for such mundane activities as finding one's way around. If one is lost in a city, one expects that the streets will be arranged in some rational order and that the houses will be numbered consecutively. Prior experience tells us that signs of a certain shape located on poles of a certain height will probably be helpful directional indicators; the scanning pattern of our eyes is directed accordingly. Thus expectations are not only outputs of the process of perception, but they also influence the subsequent selection of sensory inputs by redirecting the attention, controlling eye movements and scanning patterns, and determining the attributive files in the experience filter against which the incoming data are likely to be checked in the process of attributive classification. Expectations allow us to create extensions of the visible world in our minds: we *expect* that a red sign inside a building which manifests the visual pattern "EXIT" indicates a means of egress in time of danger. This kind of consistently used design element plays an indispensable role in the successful satisfaction of the biological need for orientation and security in both interior *and* exterior environments.

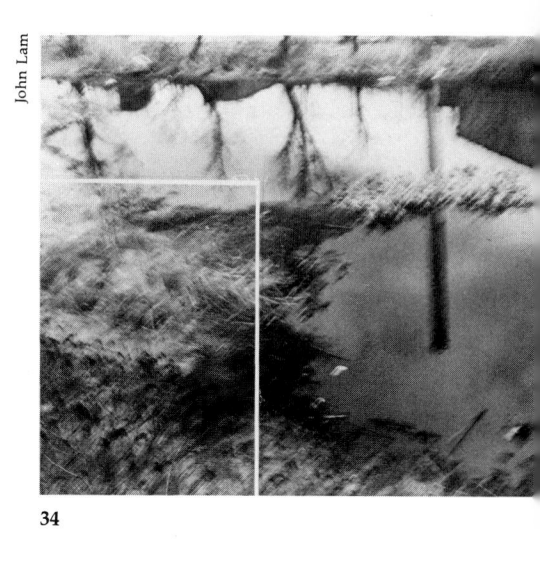

34

The affective component of perception

The third fundamental component of the perception process is called the *affective* because it is concerned with how each stimulus *affects* our emotional or evaluative responses to stimuli. The attributive classification to which a stimulus is assigned and the expectations which are activated by that classification trigger emotional responses which in the aggregate determine how we feel in a given situation or environment. This in turn influences the amount of attention which is paid to any element of the visual field: an interesting or pleasurable stimulus may be made the focus of visual attention and examined in great detail, while an uninteresting or irrelevant stimulus may be passed over and filed without further ado in the visual memory. The affective response generated by a stimulus also determines to some extent *where* in the memory—in which attributive "files" in the experience filter—the incoming stimuli will eventually be filed.

When the environment appears and behaves as expected, i.e., when the luminance levels, gradients, patterns, and colors in the visual field are relevant to needs and are as expected, the associative links established by prior experience in the experience filter are confirmed. This generally produces a positive emotional response in the perceiver (assuming of course that the expectation was for a pleasurable, comfortable environment).

All three aspects of perception—the attributive, the expectant, and the affective—are inextricably interwoven in real life. We have pulled them apart for purposes of analysis, yet in fact they are so intimately interrelated that they cannot really be separated. The attributive establishes links to prior experience, activating expectations and provoking emotional responses. Expectations in turn influence what will be chosen as the next object of sensory attention, and can trigger any emotion from joy to fear to apathy depending on the nature of the anticipated developments. The affective qualities of a perception determine the importance which we give it, which in turn influences what impact it has in terms of recalibrating the experience.

The entire, complex mechanism of the experience filter is constantly being updated as new stimuli are classified, activate expectations and emotions, suggest new foci for the attention, and are finally filed in the visual memory. If the environment behaves as expected, the web of associative relationships which constitute the experience filter will remain essentially unchanged; the relevant associations will merely be strengthened by confirmation, and will be correspondingly stronger the next time they are called into play. If, however, the world behaves in some unexpected way, the validity of established associations is called into question, and the inferential relationships which underlay the initial set of expectations will be reevaluated. The experience filter is modified in the process; subsequently, an identical stimulus may call forth a different set of expectations and emotional responses.

Suppose, for example, that I see my best friend, and without warning he punches me in the nose. The next time I see him, I will be much more cautious and suspicious. My experience filter—specifically, my image of my friend—has been drastically modified by my recent experience. From now on, I will respond differently to the sight of his approach!

If, on the other hand, my friend behaves as expected and greets me warmly, it will be a pleasant encounter and I will look forward to our next meeting.

Likewise, an environment in which there is a good match between positive expectations and the perceived reality of the situation will evoke a positive affective response. The environment will seem friendly, attractive, appropriate, and pleasant and I will feel good about it. But if the environment contradicts my positive expectations or confirms my negative expectations, it will provoke a negative affective response. I may perceive it is unfriendly, ugly, inappropriate, or unpleasant, depending on the nature of the contradiction or confirmation.

We always have conscious and unconscious expectations about the nature of the immediate environment, and designers must realize that the success of an environment is directly dependent on how well they anticipate and then consistently confirm the positive expectations of the user. Evaluation is always dependent on expectations.

Summary

Seeing is not a passive response to patterns of light; rather, it is an active information-seeking process directed and interpreted by the brain. Visual sensory data are coordinated with incoming contextual information from the other senses related to past experiences of a comparable nature, and given attention or not depending on whether the incoming stimulus is classified as signal or noise. It is the information content and context of a stimulus, not its absolute magnitude, which generally determines its relevance and, finally, its importance. This in turn largely determines *what we look at* and *what we perceive*.

What do we look at?

Close your eyes for a minute. When you open them again, look around the room. Note carefully the first thing you look at in the visual field, then the second, etc. Unless you were looking for something specific, it is very likely that the first thing to attract your undirected visual attention was either bright, fast moving, strongly colored, of high contrast, strongly patterned, or a combination of two or more of these characteristics. Some unusual quality caused it to contrast with its visual context, making it a figure. The eye searches the visual environment automatically for signals which supply information relevant to the satisfaction of activity or biological needs, and "figure" objects with these characteristics tend to attract the visual attention automatically.

The focus selector

Through what we will call a *focus selector*, the brain dictates the scanning pattern of the eye. Whenever the eye is not under conscious control, it monitors the general luminous environment, checking that no significant changes have occurred which would require conscious attention. During this scanning, undirected by the conscious mind, the focus selector is likely to pick out stimuli which relate to William James's "normal congenital impulses"—i.e., to biological needs for information.

As noted in the previous section, both the experience filter and current expectations play important roles in dictating the pattern of eye movements. The choice of specific elements in the visual field by the focus selector is influenced by various aspects of the experience filter including (1) stored past information in the form of attributive files; (2) personal habits and expectations; and (3) the current state of the perceiver—rushed or at leisure, happy or depressed, friendly or irritable, sick or well. The nature of the activities in which the perceiver is currently engaged also affects the operation of the focus selector in proportion to the amount of uninterrupted attention required by the task at hand.

Central versus peripheral vision

When open, our eyes produce two different kinds of stimuli, due to the physical construction of the eye itself. Visual acuity[4] is highest in a very small area of the retina, called the *fovea*. Under normal conditions, patterns of light falling on the fovea are reported to the brain in much finer detail than the visual information falling on other parts of the retina. This innate differentiation of the visual receptor itself produces a functional differentiation between *central* and *peripheral* vision. In effect, the central vision (generated by the fovea) scans the luminous environment, gathering detailed information about elements of the visual field to which it is directed by the focus selector; simultaneously, the peripheral vision (produced by the rest of the retina) monitors the remainder of the environment for changes which might be of sufficient biological significance to warrant the attention of the central vision.

Routine control of eye movements by the conscious brain is sometimes interrupted by seemingly involuntary movements of the eye toward stimuli which the peripheral vision has detected and which the focus selector, in conjunction with the experience filter, has determined to be of relevance to biological needs.

[4]*Visual acuity refers to the sharpness of vision, in terms of the size of detail which can be detected by the eye at a given distance. The standard alphabetical optometrist's chart is one method of measuring acuity.*

35 *Adaptation of the eye: With a focus on the face, the view momentarily becomes visual noise.*

36 *Focus on the view.*

The role of the experience filter

Although it is inherently phototropic (i.e., attracted to light), the focus selector is profoundly influenced by the relevance assigned to incoming stimuli by the experience filter. Irrelevant or undesirable signals (visual noise) are rejected as possible centers of visual attention in favor of signals related to what we want or need to see, even if what we want or need to see is not the brightest element in the visual field. As pointed out in the last section, the absolute luminance of a stimulus is not as important as its information content from the point of view of the focus selector. For instance, if we are looking for a friend in **Fig. 35,** the bright landscape is perceived as a background, and the focus selector directs the visual attention to the silhouetted figure, despite the fact that the landscape is hundreds of times brighter than the figure. On the other hand, if we are only concerned about walking down the stairs, the focus selector concentrates on gathering information required for physical orientation: the railing, the height of the stair risers, the landing, the horizon line, the people in the distance, the weather, and so forth **(Fig. 36).**

Even if the person is the object of focus, however, the peripheral vision still registers useful facts about the background, partly to provide contextual information for attributive classification (identification) of the oncoming figure, and partly to satisfy the continuous biological need for orientation information. In addition, the high luminance (brightness) of the background tends to dominate the visual field, causing the eye to reduce the amount of light which it lets fall onto the retina, thus interfering with the perception of the person.

Ferris wheels, fire engines, neon signs, and traffic signals all owe their success as attractors of the visual attention to the fact that they take full advantage of the innate phototropic tendencies of the focus selector (tendencies which derive directly from biological needs) while providing useful or pleasurable visual information which makes them desirable foci in the luminous environment.

Distraction

When the focus selector interrupts the normal sequence of consciously directed eye movements, we say we have been *distracted.* The new stimulus is processed through the experience filter, which decides whether the new information is of sufficient importance to call for a redirection of the conscious attention. If it is not, the focus selector returns to the initial focus, unless the distracting stimulus is so close to the initial focus and so overwhelming in luminance or strength of pattern that the mind's eye cannot ignore it.

Distractions may relate either to activities or to biological needs. Activity-related distractions can be very useful; they bring to our attention changes in our activities which are likely to make them more productive or satisfying. For example, suppose that while hammering a nail you suddenly notice that the board is too short or cracked or discolored. This functional distraction will bring the hammering to a halt if you care about the appearance of the finished product. To give another example: if my peripheral vision registers a sparkling stimulus on the pavement as I walk down the street, the distraction causes me to pause and reorient my attention, since the signal might indicate a dangerous piece of broken glass—or a silver dollar!

The last example can also be considered a distraction of biological importance, since it is relevant to the protection of the body. Distractions of biological importance may be due to potential danger, an undesirable or repulsive situation, or an ambiguous stimulus in the visual field. An unusually dark shadow at night or a sparkling object on the ground may indicate danger, causing the focus selector to redirect the attention in order to evaluate the situation. A dirty windshield illuminated by oncoming headlights causes undesirable distractions, interfering with our ability to perceive necessary information about the environment. Ambiguous signals often distract us for longer periods of time. Due to our inability to classify them attributively, we are unsure of their functional implications. In the discussion of biological needs, it was pointed out that glazed surfaces can be somewhat ambiguous if nothing recognizable can be seen through them. Windows are more comfortable to look at and less distracting if familiar elements—clouds, trees, buildings, etc.—are visible on the far side. In a tall building, where the ground plane may be well below the field of view, the presence of some structural element such as a window reveal or a roof overhang beyond the glazing plane reduces the irritating ambiguity which can be distracting on overcast days. The most ambiguous and unpleasant type of window is one glazed with white translucent patternless glass, since it is very difficult for the experience filter to differentiate such glazing from a uniformly overcast sky.

Distraction caused by luminance dominance

When distraction is caused by an extremely bright source (dominance of luminance), the eye responds by constricting the iris, reducing the amount of light which falls on the retina. This simultaneously reduces the visibility of other objects in the visual field, which can be dangerous under some circumstances—the difficulty of driving into the setting sun will be familiar to most readers. Anyone who has been blinded by oncoming headlights when driving at night is familiar with a classic example of dangerous visual noise, but few people realize that the same phenomenon occurs to a lesser degree each time they look up in the typical office or classroom, and their eyes are assaulted by glaring light fixtures. Direct light sources, which typically have a high surface luminance, produce a defensive response on the part of the eye. If the light sources themselves are of no inherent interest, and serve no useful function in terms of satisfying biological needs, the mind usually evaluates them as glaring and unpleasant regardless of their actual luminance.

Unexpected bright elements in the visual field, particularly if they are distorted, demand the attention of the focus selector, causing distraction. The uneven illumination of the planar structural surfaces in **Fig. 37** distorts their apparent form, commanding attention and forcing viewers to make sure that the structure is not in fact the irregular shape which the patterns and gradients of incident illumination seem to suggest it is. This sort of distracting distortion is annoying and should be avoided whenever possible.

Despite its tremendously high luminance, the sun is not distracting, unless it lies close to our line of sight, because we expect it to be in the sky. We know what it is, it always behaves consistently

37 *Perceptual distortion of structural form because of poorly coordinated light gradients.*

38

39

with our expectations, and the highlights and shadows which it causes give us continuous orientation to its location. There is no confusion or distortion in the scene in **Fig 38,** although the brightness ratios between the sunlit surfaces and those in shadow are on the order of several hundred to one, and the luminance of the pavement is probably several thousand footlamberts. On the other hand, the lens of a fluorescent fixture of comparable luminance is perceived as ambiguous, unnatural, and unpleasant, and the focus selector is drawn to it again and again to investigate it further. This is tiring and annoying for the viewer, even though it may proceed at a totally unconscious level.

Distraction caused by pattern dominance

Strong patterns of visual information can also dominate the visual field, demanding the attention of the focus selector. The problems of visual noise at the Houston Astrodome can be traced directly to this type of distraction. The strong pattern of the structure completely drowned out the relatively weak signal of the ball. But it is important to realize that the same phenomenon is at work in every office with a regular grid of high-brightness fluorescent troffers: this type of lighting produces an identical form of distraction, due to the strength of the inherently arbitrary and therefore meaningless pattern of fixtures in the visual field. This problem can be eliminated by the use of indirect lighting systems, which deliver light to the room by reflection from room surfaces, which are intrinsically interesting to look at. These bright room surfaces satisfy biological needs for structural clarity and for a bright, cheerful environment. Compare the offices in **Figs. 28** and **30;** the photographic medium cannot capture the real brightness relationships of the actual environments, but the difference should be quite obvious.

When glass planes are incorporated into interior partitions above eye height in such a way that they reflect patterns of direct fixtures, still another distracting form of visual noise is introduced into the luminous environment which further compounds the undesirable qualities of this type of lighting (see **Fig. 39**). When the glass runs at an angle to the lines of fixtures, the reflections are even more confusing. A similar unpleasant effect is usually produced when mirrored glass is used in exterior windows: during the day, the glass reflects patterns of interior fixtures, overlaying them on the view outside, confusing the mind's eye and distracting the focus selector. The negative emotional response generated by this kind of visual noise is intensified if the patterns of glaring fixtures seem to show no relation whatsoever to the activity patterns within the space. Irrelevance intensifies annoyance.

Summary

We look at what we want or need to see, unless our visual attention is redirected by the focus selector to a distracting stimulus in the visual field. Such a stimulus need not be the brightest thing in view: the information content of the stimulus is also important in determining its relevance and consequently its inherent attractiveness to the mind's eye. When brightly illuminated elements of the visual field are unrelated to our needs, they distract us from our conscious activities, which can be both annoying and dangerous. When driving at night, for example, we may hit another car or drive off the road, not because we were unable to see the other car or the edges of the road, but because we were momentarily distracted by the brightness of oncoming headlights or misguided by a pattern of poorly placed street lights. We are comfortable when we are free to look at what we want or need to see, and uncomfortable when the luminous environment itself interferes with our freedom to do so.

Attributive classification of visual stimuli: assignment of meaning

We know now that our visual system is far more than an assembly of passive gauges, capable only of measuring and recording luminance levels, visual size, and spectral color. We do not "see" the separate attributes of shape, color, or brightness as abstract, independent qualities: the synthesizing function of the perceptual system delivers complete perceptions to the conscious mind—we see a ball in flight, a man walking, a rose in bloom, and so forth. Each set of stimuli can only be given one holistic interpretation at a given moment; consider for example the classic ambiguous drawing in **Fig. 40** by the Danish psychologist Rubins. We perceive *either* two faces silhouetted against a white background, *or* a vase against a black background. Each perception is a whole and independent of the other; in fact, it is impossible to perceive both vase and faces simultaneously, because the conscious mind cannot simultaneously assign two distinct and unrelated interpretations to the same stimulus. In viewing the Rubins figure, we do not perceive a series of curves and lines, and then add these up laboriously in the conscious mind to create meaningful combinations, unless we are consciously trying to follow and analyze the perception process itself. Normally, the synthesis of related stimuli into holistic, meaningful images is performed unconsciously by the apparatus of perception itself.

In the same way, we perceive objects and their individual attributes *in context*—in relation to their use, feel, odor, intent, etc. Precise measurements of only one aspect of an object, such as its color or luminance, cannot yield a meaningful or accurate index of how that object will be perceived by an observer. In and of itself, the measured surface luminance of an object does not determine per se how bright the object will appear as perceived by the conscious mind. That perception, like any other, is influenced by a host of related factors, all of which combine to determine the *perceived* brightness of the object. This is why the specification of single-valued numerical criteria for the luminous environment, such as minimum footcandle levels, gives no guarantee whatsoever that the resulting environment will be perceived as bright or cheerful, pleasant or appropriate. All such judgments are based on holistic, *complete* perceptions involving the entire visual field, as well as expectations and prior experience.

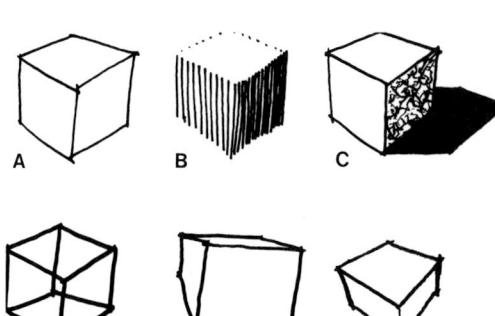

40 *Rubins' ambiguous figure.*

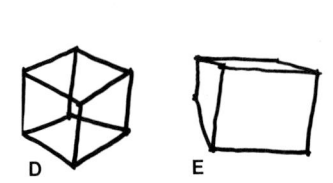

A B C

D E F

41

The unconscious search for order in the visual field

During the attributive phase of perception, the unconscious mind seeks to classify what we see acording to the highest level of recognizable organization. Thus in **Fig. 31** we saw a circle before we were aware of the 15 individual dots. Since the mind can only formulate one complete perception at a time from a given set of

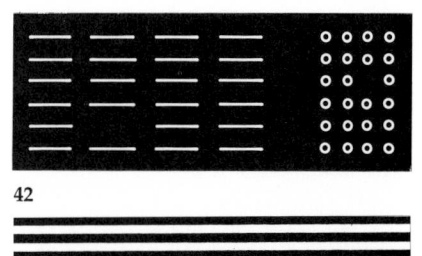

42

43 *Figure/background ambiguity.*

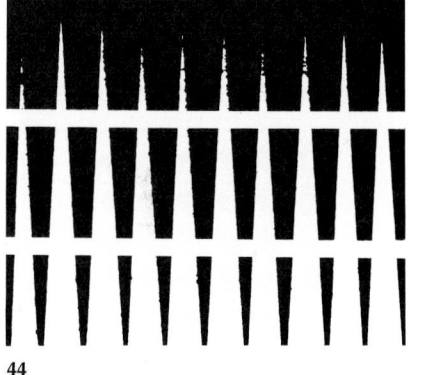

44

45

Ripman

46

Ripman

stimuli (remember the Rubins drawing, **Fig. 40**), this quality of classification according to the highest perceptible form of organization allows us to comprehend several objects simultaneously when all are clearly interrelated and form a single message or gestalt. We perceive a circle instead of 15 dots, a colonnade instead of a number of columns, etc. Very complex visual environments are easily comprehended if all the available information is interrelated and clearly synthesized, giving evidence of a coordinating intent: for example, an extremely complex Gothic portal is neither confusing nor difficult to understand, because of the clarity of its overall organization.

The effect of perceptible order in the visual environment

Discomfort and distraction are largely but not entirely interdependent. It is quite possible to have a situation that is distracting but not positively uncomfortable. An increase in the perceptible order of the visual environment may reduce its distracting quality. For instance, a disorderly layout of light fixtures can be made less distracting by rearranging them into more orderly and understandable pattern, or by clearly relating the fixtures in a consistent fashion to other elements of the architecture—structure, the partition module, window mullions, furniture, etc. The perception process always attempts to extract meaning out of apparent chaos (documented by the Gestalt psychologists' principle of closure). This has obvious implications for the design of the luminous environment.

Pattern, perceived order, and expectation

When bright light sources are directly visible, or when their images can be seen reflected from some specular surface such as a piece of glass or a wet roadway, *pattern* becomes even more important than usual as a signal. Pattern is an easily perceptible form of order, and triggers expectations of completeness and consistency. As pointed out in the previous chapter, expectations and a patterned context draw the eye to an omitted element of the pattern, which becomes a *de facto* focus, whether intended or not **(Fig. 42)**. Here we have yet another example of the role of expectations as they influence our evaluation of the luminous environment.

Figure/background effects

In the attributive phase of perception, a signal is always selected from its background according to the needs which currently control the focus selector and influence the experience filter, unless there is a perceptual ambiguity—i.e., a signal which cannot be classified as either figure or background (signal or noise). Upon encountering an ambiguous stimulus of this sort, the focus selector shifts back and forth at some expense in effort and discomfort. The attributive category to which the stimulus is finally assigned is initially influenced by current needs, subsequently by which of the two options has a higher information content (and is therefore more understandable and interesting). If one looks at black and white stripes of uniform width such as the ones in **Fig. 43,** it is difficult to select one set of stripes as figure over the other as background, since neither relates to any immediate need and both contain effectively equal qualities and quantities of information. The same difficulty is encountered with a different configuration such as **Fig. 44.** Compare either the top or the bottom portion of the figure with the middle section; clearly it is most difficult to separate figure and ground in the center section, where the two possibilities most closely resemble each other.

Good camouflage patterns and much of the graphic work of Maurits Escher are successful because they cunningly manipulate figure/background ambiguities.[5]

Venetian blinds **(Fig. 46)** frequently create a figure/background conflict similar to that of **Fig. 43,** although the intensity of the ambiguity is reduced because one set of stripes — the view — is more interesting than the other. Nevertheless, it should be recognized that other types of sun-control devices are less distracting because they introduce less of a figure/background ambiguity into the visual field. For this reason, very fine sun screens of an even texture and large-scale sun-control devices are generally preferable to solar-control systems such as Venetian blinds.

The conflict between figure and background is increased further when the shapes are all similar. Note the dazzle effect in **Fig. III – 48:** when the shapes are similar and the black and white areas are equal in size, the experience filter examines the arrangement to try and discern some form of intelligible order and relation to context in an attempt to distinguish between intended figure and intended background. Alternating dark and illuminated panels or ceiling coffers **(Fig. III – 49)** often create similar dazzle effects and should be avoided.

Constancies in the process of visual perception

Everything we see is interpreted during the process of perception in relation to reference files in the experience filter, which means that all conscious visual perceptions — brightness, color, distance, size, movement, perspective, solidity, etc. — are determined in part by prior experience. These files are not all present at birth; most must be learned. Fortunately, an incoming stimulus need not be identical to a prior stimulus in order for attributive classification to be possible. Through the experience filter, the brain is capable of association involving generalization and abstraction; in other words, it can recognize new and different views of a familiar object. This ability is dependent on sufficient prior experience with the object in question. The experience filter must contain adequate information concerning the expected appearance of the object when viewed under different conditions of light, from different angles and from different distances, etc. A person who has been blind from birth and is suddenly given the ability to see by surgery cannot make this sort of associative visual generalization.[6]

This translational associative ability, which involves what are called *constancies* in the terminology of perceptual psychology, enables us to separate functionally important changes in the visual environment from changes in incoming stimuli which are only caused by movements of the head or the body or by changes in the nature of the incident illumination. Constancies involve the ability of the brain to recognize objects and their characteristics under different conditions, so that although the actual measured stimuli which fall on the receptors of the eye may be quite different under different

47 *Background shapes different from figure.*

48 *Background shapes similar to figure.*

49

Joseph W. Molitor

[5]*For an excellent discussion of the graphic work of Escher which is highly relevant to the present analysis of the process of visual perception, see Marianne L. Lamber, "Sources of Ambiguity in the Prints of Maurits C. Escher," Scientific American, vol. 231, no. 1, pp. 90–104, July 1974.*

[6]*J. Z. Young, Doubt and Certainty in Science, The BBC Reith Lectures, 1959, Oxford, 1951, pp. 61ff.*

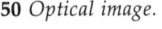

50 *Optical image.*

51 *Mental image.*

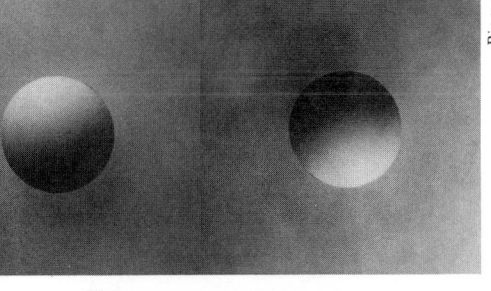

52

53

54

circumstances, the experience filter learns to disregard differences caused solely by changes in lighting conditions or by shifts in the viewpoint of the perceiver. Nevertheless, lighting should reinforce rather than contradict established constancies.

We are all totally dependent on constancies to find our way around in the built environment. This fact underscores the importance of consistency and clarity in the design of the luminous environment to provide orientation and visual guidance for its users. Such orientation can be relatively unsophisticated—systems of directional signage, for instance—or it can be quite subtle, operating below the level of the conscious mind, and involving the careful differentiation and consistent application throughout a project of different types of lighting to each element of a circulation system, such as elevator cores, fire stairs, reception and information nodes, public corridors, private corridors, lounge areas, etc.

Constancies enable us to make cognitive leaps in the experience filter, associating the same meaning with quite different patterns of visual stimuli. Although they are far from identical, the six sketches in **Fig. 41** are all recognizable as representing a cube because constancies of form and shape tell us that each probably represents a topological form which is conventionally called *cube*. Constancies exist for all aspects of visual perception—brightness, color, shape, size, pattern, etc.—and they play important roles in our interpretation of the luminous environment, which will be examined in some detail in the remainder of this section.

Shape constancy

Shape constancy simply means that we can recognize the shape of an object or pattern even though it may be modified by a change in viewpoint, illumination, or distance from the eye. When viewed from across a room, a rectangular table is understood to be rectangular even though its optical image (as it would be traced from a photograph) is a trapezoid. Objects and two-dimensional images are seen in context, which establishes a frame of reference in the form of a common perspective; this in turn influences the types of possible associative patterns in the experience filter to which incoming stimuli will be compared for classification. If we could not make this kind of automatic adjustment for perspective distortion, we might interpret a plate seen from an angle as an ellipse **(Fig. 50)** rather than a circle.

Shape perception and interpretation are also influenced by *expectations*; indeed, constancies are a form of subconscious expectations. Expectation enables us to project the curve of the street beyond the corner in **Fig. 52,** despite the fact that we cannot actually *see* what happens beyond a certain point.

Shape constancy also enables us to recognize the drawings in **Figs. 41e** and **41f** as cubes, even though the two-dimensional images are quite different from each other.

When faced with situations involving the perception of three-dimensional objects in which there is no evidence of the direction of the light source, we usually base our interpretation of shape on the unconscious assumption that the light comes from above—the normal direction of daylight. In a laboratory setting, the brain can be confused, leading to misinterpretation. (In **Fig. 53** the mind assumes a single light source, and reads the right figure as a hole and the left one as a bump in the surface, whereas both are in fact bumps, the right one illuminated from below and the left one from above). In the real world, however, the location of the source is usually obvious, as in **Fig. 54,** and the mind compensates automatically for any unusual directional qualities of the light.

Size constancy

Perception of size is influenced more by context than by optical size (which is measured as a solid angle from the eye to the object). By itself, the parallax factor of our stereoscopic vision is not particularly helpful for judging size, once an object is more than about 15 feet away. Without a context, we cannot tell whether we are looking at a small object a few feet away or a larger object of similar proportions and coloration at a considerable distance. We usually judge the size of an object by how it relates to the optical size of other known objects in the visual field and to the memory of the relative size of the various objects. A given plate appears smaller on a large table than on a small table of the same color and shape **(Figs. 55 and 56),** particularly when seen from a distance or in a photograph. But if other, familiar reference objects of known size are present, as in **Fig. 50,** then the perceived size of the plate will be less affected by the size of the table. An open-ended line appears to be longer than a closed one of the same length **(Fig. 57),** due to the distorting effect of its context — the terminal arrowheads.

Is the object in the center of **Fig. 58** a Ping-Pong ball or a beach ball? The way it is perceived and the size which we judge it to be will be determined by which of its contextual neighbors the mind's eye chooses to relate it to. On the other hand, if we know how big the ball actually is, we can use that information to judge how far away the hand and the figure must be.

When deprived of all other contextual information which would reveal the absolute size and distance of several objects, the brain may still be able to determine at least their relative distance by comparing their relative size **(Fig. 59),** or how they overlap **(Fig. 60)** and particularly how they overlap when the observer is moving with relation to them. Note that the larger tree seems nearer in **Fig. 59,** while the smaller is clearly nearer in **Fig. 60.**

The perception and accurate judgment of color

From the point of view of the physicist, the color of an object can be accurately described by quantitative analysis of the amount of energy which it radiates at each wavelength in the visual spectrum. The stimuli which fall on the retina of the eye are produced by the interaction of *light* and *surface*. The *perception* of color, on the other hand, is influenced by many other factors. Light itself consists of various quantities of energy at various wavelengths. The surface of an illuminated object selectively absorbs and reflects different parts of the spectrum of the light falling upon it, which explains why beams of light from sources with different spectral qualities may produce different colors when reradiated from the surface of a given object.

The accurate judgment of color requires full-spectrum light:[7] light which is produced by heated "black body" sources such as an incandescent lamp filament or the sun. In order for two objects to be

55 *Plate on a large table*

56 *The same plate on a small table.*

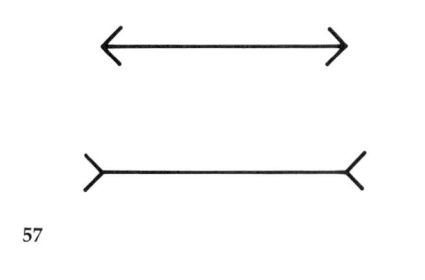

57

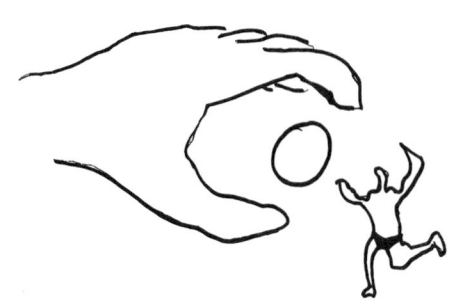

58 *Beach ball, or Ping-Pong ball?*

[7]*White, or full-spectrum, light contains energy at all wavelengths of the visible spectrum.*

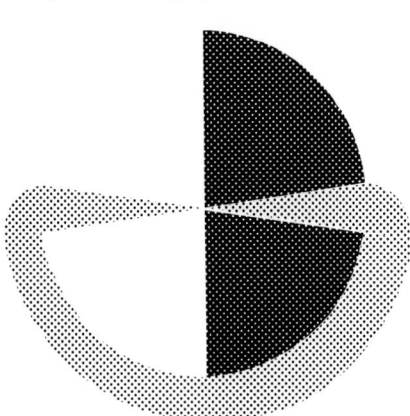

59 *Which tree seems closer?*

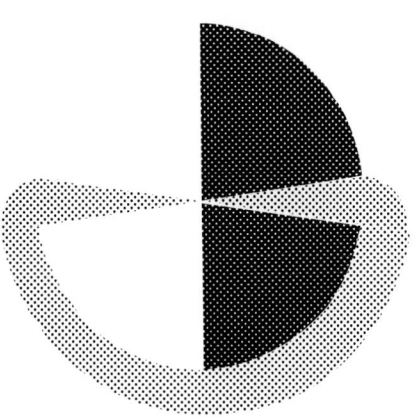

60 *Which tree is closer?*

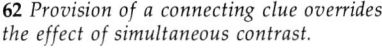

61 *Simultaneous contrast: Are the two small triangles the same grey?*

62 *Provision of a connecting clue overrides the effect of simultaneous contrast.*

perceived as having the same color under a wide range of different spectral qualities of illumination, the two objects must contain proportionate amounts of the same colors, i.e., their surfaces must absorb and reflect different wavelengths of light in a similar manner. To ensure this sort of perfect match, the illuminant under which they are compared must contain the entire spectrum of light, without any frequency bands omitted or accentuated. Such accurate color judgment is required for matching paints, for instance.

For most purposes, however, we do not need such exacting qualities of illumination to perceive colors accurately, due to the existence of *color constancies* in the process of color perception.

If the eye worked like a camera, objects would appear very different under different qualities of light. Luckily, we do not need to "change films" in the eye every time we encounter a different quality of light; the unconscious processing mechanisms of perception perform the adjustment automatically. The brain usually compensates for the color of light in making color judgments. This color constancy also affects our perception of apparent brightness: a light-colored object, dimly illuminated, is perceived as such, not as a dark-*colored* object. Given sufficient contextual information—familiar objects seen under the same light—we can judge the light to be dim because we know from prior experience that this must be the case. Without prior experience, we may be unable to make this distinction. To interpret color correctly, the experience filter requires information concerning the selective reflectance properties of the surface of the material in question and the spectral characteristics of the light. Both types of information can usually be found in the visible context.

Perception of color is definitely influenced by certain conditions of background and illumination. This phenomenon—the modification of perceived color by context—is called *simultaneous contrast*. Simultaneous contrast affects all aspects of color perception: *hue* or chroma (judgment of color as red, green, blue, yellow, etc.); *value* (the relative lightness of darkness of a color, measured by reference to a scale from white to black); and *intensity* or saturation (the purity of a color of any given hue, which increases from a neutral gray to reach a maximum at the pure hue).

Color constancy prevails over simultaneous contrast in the formation of color perceptions as soon as the eye is given a connecting clue. **Figs. 61** and **62** demonstrate this effect with regard to value.

The mind perceives what it expects to perceive due to color constancy, and is swayed little by the specifics of the incoming stimuli as long as it has prior experience on which to form its expectations and sufficient contextual information for correct orientation. Color constancy makes us perceive our friends as we expect them to appear. We do not perceive people as being of significantly different colors under direct sunlight, in the shade, under an overcast sky, or indoors under fluorescent or incandescent lighting, despite the fact that if they were photographed in these situations with the same film and no color-correction filters, they would appear to be quite different colors. If, however, the incident illumination on a scene changes color rapidly or drastically, people are seen as being "tinted" by a colored light. This effect will be familiar to anyone who has stood under a flashing neon sign with alternating colors. Such tinting may or may not be disturbing, depending on our expectations; in a discotheque, a funhouse, or a theater, it may seem perfectly natural. In an interior corridor lit with a sequence of fluorescent tubes of different types, on the other hand, the effect may be very annoying if there is no perceptible reason for the inconsistency. Color constancy is an adaptive process which requires time to come into play; when color changes are too rapid, or when sources of radically different qualities are visible simultaneously, color constancy cannot compensate effectively.

The importance of consistent use of colored sources in the visual field

Each type of light source—the sun, an incandescent light bulb, a fluorescent tube, a metal halide lamp, an arc lamp, etc.—has its own unique and typical spectral characteristics, and each therefore has the potential to produce different colors from a given surface. When the color quality of illumination in a visual field is consistent (i.e., all objects are illuminated by the same kind of light), there is relatively little color distortion. Surfaces of similar materials are perceived as similar, and the average person is unaware of any distortion. If part of a continuous surface is illuminated by daylight, however, and part by incandescent light, the area under incandescent illumination appears yellowish by comparison. When the daylight is gone, the surface which previously appeared yellow now appears to be white. The mind can and does compensate, due to color constancy. Expecting white light, the mind perceives things as if they were illuminated by white light unless some evidence in the visual field indicates that this is not the case. If different types of sources are used the effect will not be disturbing as long as the different source types are carefully and consistently coordinated with different classes of objects in the visual field. Suppose that the brick walls of a space are illuminated by incandescent sources, while the floor is lighted by fluorescent lamps. The different color characteristics of the two kinds of light may not be noticed at all. On a continuous surface such as a plaster wall, however, intermittent or inconsistent illumination from different types of sources would be immediately apparent and disturbing unless the mind's eye could discern some reason for the difference. For instance, if there are paintings displayed on the wall, which are illuminated brightly by incandescent spotlights while the wall itself is evenly illuminated by daylight or by a continuous fluorescent fixture concealed at the top of the wall, the mechanism of perception disregards the gradations of color on the wall because of the obvious intended focus. The wall is perceived as a continuous white surface.

The mind responds quite negatively to the inconsistent use of different source types with no apparent justification. The mind's eye has no inherent objection to the use of different *types* of source, however, only to their *inconsistent* and *arbitrary* use. Positive, consistent differentiation of elements in the visual field by the use of different types of sources can provide extremely useful information which helps to satisfy biological needs for orientation.

A note on the use of tinted glass

Since mirrored, tinted, and low-transmission glass all modify the spectral characteristics and the intensity of the light which passes through them, they alter the qualitative characteristics of the light

which influence color vision. This effect will be offset by color constancies as long as there is no comparable, correctly colored scene visible against which the mind's eye can compare the altered stimuli. In other words, the color of the tinted glass will be noticeable and disturbing *if* the viewer can simultaneously see another view of accurate color and brightness as in **Fig. III–32.** When there is such a basis for comparison, the view through the tinted glass is perceived as distorted and gloomy, because a more pleasing alternative is visible. This situation leads to feelings of deprivation and annoyance. If there is no reference view available, on the other hand, color constancy assumes dominance of the perception process, reducing somewhat the unpleasant effect of the tinted glass.

63

The perception of brightness

The visual system is capable of detecting objects over an extraordinarily large range of surface luminance. An object in direct sunlight may be as much as 1 million times brighter than the same object illuminated by moonlight, but the human eye can perceive both **(Fig. 64).**

COMMONLY EXPERIENCED BRIGHTNESS LEVELS

incandescent lamps—over 10,000FL
lawn or dark road, sunny day—1600FL
clear sky—700-1500FL
overcast or hazy sky—500-4500FL
snow, sunny day— 6800FL
snow, overcast day—850FL

.01   .05 .1   .5   1   5 10   50 100   1000   10,000

book, one candle—.3FL   surface 50FC
luminous ceiling—50FL
lawn or dark road, streetlight—.03FL   lawn or dark road, overcast day—220-400FL
snow, moonlight—.015FL
sidewalk, moonlight—.01FL   concrete pavement, overcast day—550FL
night vision-below—.001FL   surface fluorescent lamp—2500FL
concrete pavement, sunny day—4400FL

64

Such ratios can be measured in the laboratory, but they have little relation to the *subjective* perception of relative brightness. Subjects' descriptions of the perceived luminance or brightness of objects in the field of view do not vary directly in arithmetic ratio with the measurements of the absolute luminance of the objects. This is an important fact for the lighting designer to understand: it means that doubling the amount of light in a space will *not* make it seem twice as bright (although it *will* consume twice as much energy). One must be wary, therefore, not to make simplistic cost-benefit analyses about lighting which fail to take account of the fact that each additional doubling of the light level produces a much smaller increment in the perceived brightness of the scene. In fact, doubling light levels produces what experimental subjects typically describe as a "just noticeable difference." The perception of brightness, just like the perception of shape or color, is influenced by a host of other factors besides the absolute intensity of the stimulus in question. Context plays a role, as do expectations, so that we may meaningfully describe a "bright moonlit night" or a "dark overcast day" even though the latter scene may have an average luminance thousands of times greater than the former.

A research group at the Pratt Institute[8] found no correlation between their observations of apparent (perceived) brightness in a number of buildings and the actual measured footcandle levels. This is as we should expect, because the colors and reflectances of the room

[8]*See* Performance Criteria: Lighting, *Preliminary Report, October, 1965, prepared by the Pratt Institute for the State University Construction Fund, State of New York.*

surfaces, the use of the space, time orientation, and other factors, all have an important bearing on the perception of brightness—a bearing which is not taken into account at all by direct footcandle measurements. Measured physical brightness, therefore, does not determine perceived brightness in a simple, one-to-one manner. This fact underlines the need to consider relative, not absolute, luminance levels during the process of lighting design, and points up one of the conceptual fallacies behind many quantitative lighting codes.

As noted in the Preface, limits to brightness ratios have been proposed as meaningful qualitative criteria for interior luminous environments. Contrary to most current thinking in the field of lighting, high brightness ratios are not inherently undesirable, as long as the eye can perceive and justify the cause of the high brightness ratio. A brilliantly illuminated crystal chandelier is a pleasure to behold, regardless of the high brightness ratios which it may engender in a space.

Adaptation and the perception of brightness

In the preceding sections we have discussed at several points the effects of bright sources in the visual field. Bright sources cause the iris of the eye to contract, reducing the amount of light which falls on the retina. This phenomenon of adaptation profoundly influences the perception of brightness. As Hopkinson describes the process:

> In any given scene, the eye sensitivity settles down to a general average state of adaptation. This acts as a "reference standard" such that individual items of the scene which have a higher physical luminance than this reference level "look bright," and those with a lower luminance "look dark." The brilliance of the highlights and the murkiness of the shadows consequently depend not only on their intrinsic physical luminance, but also on the state of adaptation to the eye. Raise the adaptation and the shadows look darker. Lower the adaptation (screen the window with your hand) and the shadows look brighter. So do the highlights. Thus a surface with a luminance of 100 footlamberts has an apparent brightness of 100 when one's eye is adapted to 100 footlamberts, but the same surface would have an apparent brightness of 230 when one's eye was adapted to 10 footlamberts.[9]

This extremely important process of adaptation explains why a room may appear gloomy and dimly lit during the day but bright and cheerful at night. At night, there are no bright windows or direct sunlight in the space which would cause the eye to adapt, reducing the apparent brightness of other surfaces in the space. Because of adaptation and expectation, we need more artificial light in many interior spaces during the day than at night, to balance the higher daytime levels so that the interior does not appear dim and gloomy.

It is also clearly wasteful, therefore, to run interior lighting at full intensity at night, when artificial sources no longer have to compete with daylight illumination. Switching, dimming, or multilevel ballasts should be provided so that light levels can be reduced at night when the eye needs less light to see well and to interpret a space as appearing bright. If there must be lighting codes, they should incorporate requirements for the provision of such control devices, both to conserve energy and to increase the comfort and quality of the luminous environment, rather than concentrating on specifying

[9]*R. G. Hopkinson and J. D. Kay, The Lighting of Buildings, Praeger, New York, 1960, p. 46.*

arbitrary minima to be met at all hours of the day or night, with no regard for what is really appropriate and necessary.

The influence of simultaneous contrast on brightness perception

The perception of brightness, as well as color, is influenced by simultaneous contrast. Objects of the same surface luminance will be perceived as brighter or darker depending on the relative luminance of their context. Only displayed objects are highlighted in **Fig. 65;** they seem considerably brighter than they would appear if placed in a brightly illuminated room, even if the surface brightness of the objects themselves was kept constant. The illumination level on the painting in **Fig. 66** is kept intentionally low for reasons of preservation, yet the painting seems much brighter than the paintings in **Fig. 67,** which receive 10 times as much light from a glaring luminous ceiling. The painting in **Fig. 66** would appear still brighter if the surrounding walls were dark colored or unlit.

Comparative brightness judgments

Assessment of the relative brightness of objects which are not simultaneously visible involves the entire perception mechanism. If, in a laboratory, a white disk is illuminated to various luminance levels, a doubling of the luminance produces a "just noticeable difference" to the eye. If the disk is completely darkened for a minute before it is reilluminated to a higher level, the eye may be unable to detect any difference at all. In our daily experience, however, context, experience, and expectations all come into play as the eye adapts to each scene. These factors influence the perception of brightness, and color our judgment as to whether an object is dark or light, too bright or too dim. They may make a totally enclosed interior space seem brighter than a sunlit exterior, even though the measured luminance levels may be a thousand times greater outside.

It is most instructive to buy or borrow an inexpensive footcandle meter and measure the illumination levels in various spaces, subsequently comparing them with one's judgment of the "brightness" of the space. A "bright" cocktail lounge will generally have substantially lower measured light levels, for instance, than a cafeteria which is perceived as equally bright. Compare your response to sunlight on a windowsill and to a light fixture which seems to be equally bright; then measure the actual surface brightnesses. You will probably find that the light fixture seems much brighter than it actually is, because it is not so pleasant to look at. Compare your evaluation of the light levels in an exterior corridor with a window at the end by day and by night. When does the space seem brightest? Usually, the corridor will seem brighter at night, because the eye is adapted to nighttime brightness levels; during the day, the bright sky dominates the field of vision, forcing the perception mechanism to evaluate the corridor as relatively dark, even though it may be far brighter in terms of measured luminance than at night.

Easy experiments such as these will soon convince anyone with normal perception that measured and perceived brightness levels do not interrelate in a simple, mechanical way. This, in turn, should lead one to question the validity of brightness ratios, footcandle levels, and other conventional criteria as useful tools for the design of the luminous environment.

65 (From **Case Study D4.**)

66

67

Luminance gradients, three-dimensional form, and the perception of brightness

One effect of the adaptive ability of the perceptive mechanism is that we do not necessarily perceive unevenly lighted surfaces as being unevenly lighted. Expectations and constancies of shape also influence the interpretation of brightness gradients in the visual field, so that surfaces are perceived as continuous and evenly lighted as long as the luminance *gradients* (the *rate of change* of luminance, not the absolute luminance) seem natural and appropriate for the shape of the surface. The various planes of the monitor skylight in **Fig. 68,** for instance, appear evenly illuminated because the brightness gradients fall off consistently and evenly, in a natural and comprehensible way. Hurvich and Jameson state that brightness will appear to be more or less uniform throughout an area where the luminance gradient is constant.[10] Adaptation, expectation, and the perceived relevance of brightness gradients to the forms which they define are all important determinants of the final perception. The key factors are relative luminance levels and their rate of change, not the absolute intensity of the illumination at any given point.

A ceiling, for example, appears to be flat, evenly lighted, and of one consistent color when the luminance gradient is constant across the entire surface. When there is an exterior window in the room, as in **Fig. 68,** the surface brightness of the ceiling by the window may be 20 times the brightness near the interior wall, yet the ceiling still appears to be quite evenly illuminated.

A variation in the rate of change of luminance implies a change of shape to the mind's eye. A change in luminance gradient is particularly noticeable if the shape on which it occurs is obviously flat (see, for instance, **Fig. 37**), and does not in fact change shape as the luminance gradients suggest. This effect will be disturbing unless the justification for the confusing gradient is apparent to the eye: for instance, scallops of light caused by point-source fixtures are less noticeable if they are obviously coordinated with some modular architectural element such as columns, reveals, or panels **(Fig. 69).** If, however, similar scallops are seen on an otherwise flat wall they are much more disturbing and distracting **(Fig. 15)** because the gradients which they generate contradict the actual planarity of the wall for no apparent reason.

Note that scallops of light on a flat wall may be perceived as appropriate if the strong highlights they cause serve to create an obviously intended focus on some element of the design **(Fig. 70).** Conversely, the unpleasantness of a poorly coordinated, unnatural effect will be heightened if the fixtures which produce the uneven gradients were obviously not intended to serve as focal decorative elements **(Fig. 15).**

If the continuity of a planar surface is clearly interrupted by a beam or a stripe, the two areas thus defined may be perceived as having different colors or luminances, even though the luminance gradient is constant over the entire surface and the overall illumination has identical color characteristics. The eye "averages out" the gradient in a defined, bounded area which is perceptibly continuous and planar; subdivision of one area into several smaller areas can lead to the perception of a different "average" brightness in each area due to the localized averaging process.

This phenomenon can be utilized to reduce the perceptual

68 *Colby College Art Center, Waterville, Maine* (Johnson-Hotvedt & Associates/ Architects; William Lam Associates/ Lighting Consultants).

69

70 *(From* **Case Study D1.***)*

[10]*Hurvich and Jameson, op. cit.; p. 108.*

Lam

distortion of structure resulting from sharp brightness gradients: the distorting effect will be diminished if the designer can locate a color change (**Fig. 10**) or a prominent joint line where a drastic rate change in brightness gradients is unavoidable due to the geometry of the situation.

Flat, uniform surfaces are expected to appear that way; uneven gradients are much more noticeable on a flat ceiling (**Fig. 71**) than on an articulated (three-dimensional) one (**Fig. 72**) where the shape of the ceiling itself helps to justify the gradients to the mind's eye as long as the relation between shape and gradient is consistent throughout the visual field. One of the disturbing aspects of the lighting scheme in **Fig. 37** is the inconsistency and incompatibility of the relationship between structural form and luminance gradients.

71 *Will Ross Factory, Jackson, Wisconsin (William Lam Associates/Lighting Consultants).*

Expectation as a component of the process of perception

Larry Day

The expectations which are triggered during the process of perception influence both the activity and emotional state of the perceiver. They also govern the operation of the focus selector. Expectations condition the attributive classification of stimuli by preselecting categories in the experience filter against which the incoming stimuli are most likely to be matched in the process of associative assignment of meaning. Expectations establish frameworks for comparative judgment and evaluation: they make a white rabbit seem perfectly normal, while a white tiger or a white lobster (both of which exist) seem extraordinary. The intensity of the whiteness is obviously not the most important factor in these evaluations; it merely raises the curtain, as it were, for a drama whose script has already been written in the unconscious mind by the expectations.

Because they establish standards of comparison, expectations affect every evaluative reaction to the luminous environment: *too bright* and *too dim* both imply comparison with some standard or reference. Expectations have been covered in considerable detail elsewhere in this chapter; therefore, only one additional aspect—the relation between expectations and the color temperature of light—will be discussed briefly here.

72 *(From **Case Study E1**.)*

[11] *The color temperature of light refers to the temperature to which one would have to heat a "black body" source to produce light of similar spectral characteristics. Low color temperature implies warmer (more yellow) light while high color temperature implies a colder (more blue) light.*

[12] *As reported by Faber Birren, in his Light, Color and Environment, Van Nostrand, New York, 1969, p. 68.*

[13] *In general practice, there are three main reasons why distortion of the color-rendering qualities of an artificial lighting system toward the warm-white is preferable (assuming that the color-rendering properties of the system cannot be controlled at will by dimmers, etc.): (1) when daylight comes from an overcast sky, an association with warmth is welcome in interior spaces; (2) for a given brightness level, people experience less glare from a warm-white source than they do from a cool-white source; (3) at night, warm-white fluorescent color seems most appropriate and natural because of adaptation to low brightness levels.*

Expectation and the color temperature of light

Expectation based on the time of day influences the evaluation of the color temperature[11] of artificial light as appropriate or inappropriate. We expect illumination to be of a high color temperature (relatively blue) when luminance levels are high because we refer them unconsciously to daylight, which has a relatively high color temperature. We expect low color temperatures (i.e., a warmer quality of light) when luminance levels are low—perhaps by association with firelight, candlelight, and so forth. Kruithof[12] had measured the range of color temperature under which objects appear "natural" and pleasant at different levels of luminance. His results (**Fig. 73**) substantiate the conclusions just presented, which were derived from the principles of perception. These conclusions support the general use of light sources with relatively low color temperature in interior environments[13], particularly at night.

The affective component of perception

Perceptions of the luminous environment always include an affective component: an evaluative or emotional response to the perceived state of affairs. Typical pairs of opposed terms which we use in verbalizing affective judgments are:

Distraction / Positive Focus
Glare / Sparkle or Glitter
Gloomy / Cheerful
Dull / Dramatic or Interesting
Chaotic / Ordered
Public / Intimate
Unpleasant / Pleasant
Unfriendly / Friendly
Inappropriate / Appropriate

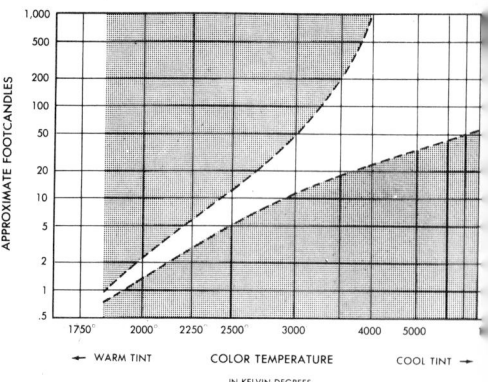

73 *Preferred Color Temperature Chart (after Kruithof).*

Obviously, such judgments tend to be qualitative rather than quantitative. For instance, we say that a space is glaring and uncomfortable, not that it has a brightness ratio of 30 to 1 and an average luminance of 200 footlamberts.

Our evaluation of a space depends on how well it meets our expectations. We base our judgment of whether a space is "light" or "dark" not on the actual luminance levels in the space but on whether or not the luminous environment meets our expectations and satisfies our needs for visual information by emphasizing what we want or need to see. Relevance and appropriateness are the key concepts here. An unhighlighted mural which is located as an obvious focal point for a room would be judged "inappropriately dark" regardless of its actual measured luminance because one expects that it was intended to be featured. Highlighting a dirty wastebasket, on the other hand, would create a scene described by most people as "too bright." The janitor, however, might find such highlighting useful.

Elements in the visual field are typically judged to be "too bright" when there is no perceptible reason for them to be brightly illuminated or when they interfere with our ability to perceive information required for the satisfaction of activity or biological needs. An evenly overcast sky, for instance, is evaluated as "unpleasantly bright" because it competes with our perception of the landscape, which is of greater interest and importance. During a performance in a theater, a lighted chandelier will always be perceived as too bright (even if only barely illuminated) because it is distracting. During intermission, on the other hand, the same chandelier brilliantly illuminated will be evaluated as beautiful and sparkling rather than glaring, annoying, distracting, or too bright.

When the largest, brightest, and most colorful elements within a space are the intended objects of attention, a positive focus exists which is likely to satisfy and please the users of the space. If, on the other hand, such objects are not the intended focus of attention, they will be perceived as annoying distractions, which may lead to a judgment of the entire space as unpleasant. This often happens when direct high-brightness fixtures are used; the standard lensed fluorescent troffer is particularly offensive in this respect.

Sparkle versus glare

Sparkle is defined in Webster's Dictionary as "an attractive brilliance."

Something which is perceived as sparkling is in and of itself attractive, a desirable and natural focus for a space. Its brightness may interfere with the perception of other elements of the visual environment, but because the source itself is attractive this does not cause an annoying distraction. Sparkle ought to be perceived as the result of a design intent. A bright element in the visual field is evaluated as sparkling if it is the desired object of perception — a chandelier, a view, or a patch of sunlight — but the same element would be evaluated as *glaring* if it merely caused a distraction without satisfying any activity or biological need for visual information. *Glare* is dazzling light which interferes with the perception of what we want or need to see — i.e., visual noise. Thus the relevance or irrelevance of a stimulus can play a more important role in causing the sensation of "glare" than abstract considerations such as luminance levels or brightness ratios.

In his study of artificial light sources of large areas, Hopkinson[14] concluded that glare is just acceptable at 150 footlamberts, and that the sensation of glare is relatively independent of the size of the glare source. He also points out in a note that these conclusions are inconsistent with our everyday experience with daylight: it is not visually uncomfortable to walk about outdoors on a sunny day, even though everything in sight may be many times brighter than 150 footlamberts. Nor does it cause discomfort to look out of a window at a daylight scene, even when the eye has adapted to moderate interior brightness levels. The explanation of these discrepancies between psychophysical experiments in the laboratory and real-world observations may be the key to understanding the true determinants of visual comfort in the luminous environment: *relevance* and *appropriateness.*

For a meaningless, informationless, and uninteresting surface such as a translucent diffuser on a fluorescent fixture or a typical luminous ceiling, a surface brightness of considerably less than 150 footlamberts will generally be perceived as unpleasant — "too bright" — whereas a more interesting or relevant feature of the visual environment might be 10 times as bright without causing any discomfort or displeasure. Relevance and interest, not the measured surface brightness, are the critical factors; yet these factors, being very difficult to quantify, are almost always omitted from experimental research on glare and from conventional lighting criteria. Such omission effectively invalidates the results of such research as useful criteria for the design of the luminous environment.

The sensation of visual gloom

The sensation of *visual gloom* is usually caused by the lack of some expected and desirable quality in the luminous environment — a lack of information or a lack of appropriate focal points aggravated by the awareness of a more satisfactory alternative.

A space may be perceived as "gloomy" if inadequate or inappropriate lighting makes it difficult to perform activities. This can happen, for example, when there is not enough light to perceive a visual task accurately, or when a focal object is obscured by shadows, bathed in light of an unnatural color or silhouetted rather than highlighted, or when distracting glare sources or veiling reflections interfere with one's ability to perceive desired signals.

However, frustration of biological needs for environmental

[14]R. G. Hopkinson, P. Petherbridge, and J. Longmore, Daylighting, Heinemann, London, 1966, p. xxxiii.

information is far more likely to be the cause of feelings of gloom. If, for instance, the design of an interior space cuts one off from contact with sunlight or deprives one of a view of the outdoors, the space will feel gloomy (except, of course, when there is a clear justification for the deprivation, as in a photographic darkroom or a movie theater).

When the perceived brightness of a space does not meet our expectations we may feel that the space is gloomy regardless of the actual ambient light levels. Unless dim lighting seems called for (as it might in an intimate dinner club), a dimly lit space will be perceived as gloomy during the day because our biological clocks are oriented to daytime and our eyes are adapted to high daytime luminance levels. Generally speaking, we expect interior spaces to be bright during the day, while dimly lit spaces seem perfectly natural at night because of adaptation and orientation to the nighttime environment with its typically low light levels. Thus a dark cocktail lounge will never seem gloomy at night because of a *lack of light* (although it may feel depressing because of drab decorations or a morose clientele).

The sensation of visual gloom can also be caused by inappropriate focal points in the luminous environment which draw attention away from what we want or need to see. For example, consider the scene in **Fig. 74.** The ground objects are dark in comparison with the overcast sky. A uniformly overcast sky is always the brightest element in the visual field. Because we usually want to focus on the ground objects which are more visually interesting and more relevant to our needs than the brighter but informationless sky, the overcast sky makes the entire scene seem gloomy despite its high ambient light levels (which may be as high as 5,000 footcandles). We judge the scene to be gloomy partly because the luminous environment emphasizes the uninteresting sky and partly because the diffuse light from the overcast sky robs the scene of the visual richness which comes from the play of highlight and shadow. Note that a sky full of billowing clouds, while casting no shadows, seems exciting rather than gloomy because there is still drama and visual interest in the scene.

On a sunny day **(Fig. 75)** ground objects are typically brighter than the blue sky vault while shadows define and emphasize the three-dimensional aspects of form. The scene feels "right"— bright and cheerful.

At night we judge a street scene such as the one in **Fig. 76** to be "brightly illuminated" because the focus in the luminous environment is on the building facades where it belongs. Although the sky overhead is pitch black and luminance levels are perhaps a thousand times lower than in the daylit scene of **Fig. 74,** the positive focus in the night scene eliminates any sense of dimness or visual gloom.

A glaring direct light fixture, translucent window or luminous ceiling which is allowed to dominate the visual field will always be perceived as an inappropriate focus for the luminous environment. The typical luminous ceiling **(Figs. 67** and **A4—6)** is directly analogous to the overcast sky in the preceding examples: it makes the interior "landscape" which it illuminates seem gloomy for the same reasons. This unpleasant attribute of luminous ceilings is hardly helped by the fact that the typical luminous ceiling appears cheap and flimsy, highlighting only construction flaws, manufacturing defects, and maintenance problems. These characteristics disappoint our

74

75 *(From **Case Study A7**.)*

76

77

biological need for structural security and comprehensibility.

Although most designers pay a good deal of attention to lighting those surfaces and objects which they have decided to emphasize as focal points, relatively few designers pay equal attention to what *not* to light. Just as a bright but uninteresting light fixture is always offensive when it becomes the dominant visual focus of a space, so a highlighted dish return area in an adjacent kitchen would be an inappropriate focus for the luminous environment of a dining hall and would probably cause the viewer to condemn the entire space as unpleasant and gloomy.

It is important to realize that where a positive focus is obviously called for, the absence of such a focus can generate equally strong negative feelings about a design as can an inappropriate focus.

In summary, far more spaces are unpleasant because they are visually gloomy than because they are inadequately lighted. In most spaces improvement of the luminous environment may simply call for the use of *less* light, distributed in a more relevant manner to upgrade the overall appearance of the space and to bring it into line with subconscious expectations and needs.

Dull versus interesting

A subject or space of great interest is seldom described as visually *dull*. However, something which is inherently dull cannot be made more interesting by merely increasing its surface luminance. An inherently dull environment can only be made more interesting by the addition of color, more relevant or appropriate foci for the visual attention, shadows from directional light which emphasize the nature of its three-dimensional forms, or by the use of dramatic luminance gradients (such as the effect created at night by pools of light along a path in a pleasant garden). A brightly lit scene, however, may appear dull and uninteresting if intended or desirable objects of attention are dominated by inherently dull or informationless elements such as an overcast sky or a luminous ceiling.

Order in the visual environment

Evidence of order in the visual environment is usually pleasing to the beholder. Observable order and organization set up strong expectations, and when these expectations of consistency are not fulfilled, the environment may be perceived as disorderly and chaotic. The office landscape in **Fig. 77,** for example, appears busy and disorganized because it fails to respond to the highly directional geometries of the background context. The angled buildings in **Fig. 74,** on the other hand, do not seem disorderly because the contextual background of sky and river and woods is inherently directionless, but in a more ordered context they too might appear annoyingly disorganized.

One aspect of order in the visual field which is commonly overlooked concerns the design of lighting for symmetrical buildings. When the plan is square and both structure and glazing are treated identically on both axes, one expects interior elements such as the ceiling module and the patterns and shapes of light fixtures to show an equally clear and consistent symmetry. Rectangular light fixtures look out of place in an otherwise symmetrical interior. (The standard 2×4 fluorescent troffer is often misused in this way.) If, on the other hand, the lighting has been clearly and consistently related to the disposition of furnishings or walls, rather than to some overall pattern derived from the entire building, there will be no expectation that lighting fixtures should align with window or structural module, or that the lighting module should be regular if the furnishing layout is irregular.

Security and insecurity

Two emotional states which are directly conditioned by expectations are *security* and *insecurity*. It is common knowledge that the unfamiliar breeds fear; we are afraid of the dark at least partly because it is inherently informationless. Turning off the lights in your living room does not create tension because you know the environment too well; you have sufficient experience on file to enable you to find your way around without the aid of your eyes—and you know where potential sources of danger are located. If the lights go out suddenly and unexpectedly in an urban park, however, the unfamiliar, unpredictable, and now invisible environment generates immediate apprehension and fear of danger. The dominant message is that there may be danger in this "dark" park—an expectation—and one focuses possible sources of danger and tries to find a safe escape route. When no danger is expected, such as during an evening walk on a pleasant country lane, identical luminance levels might be perceived as intimate or romantic, rather than dark and threatening.

In designing lighting which is intended to engender a feeling of security, the expectations of the users must always be one of the most important inputs to the design process. User studies have clearly indicated that where there is fear of crime on a street, every shadow is perceived as potentially threatening. On this type of street, relatively low intensity light sources on short, closely spaced poles (a geometry which produces minimum shadows) were judged to provide a greater sense of security than much more powerful luminaries mounted farther apart on higher poles (which inherently tend to produce extensive shadows). The fact that the more powerful luminaires also produce 20 times as much light on the road did not offset the sense of increased danger due to the more extensive shadows. In this example, shadows, not light levels, were the problems in the street environment, and the traditional strategy of simply increasing light levels fails to address that problem.

The feeling of intimacy

Expectation, visual order, and the appropriateness of the inherent hierarchy of foci in the luminous environment all influence our affective evaluation of a space as intimate or public. Intimate spaces are generally perceived as private, closely personal, or cozy, but they need not necessarily be *dark*. An intimate environment can be created in a dining room, for instance, by creating separate pools of light, as well as by physically separating booths or by using plant materials as screens. Sparkling screens of brightly illuminated reflective materials which effectively block off weaker visual signals from other tables can also be used to create the sense of intimate, private space.

How well do we see?

The higher the strength, quality, and information content of a visual stimulus, and the higher the signal-to-noise ratio in the visual environment, the better we can see, in the sense of being able to form useful, meaningful perceptions related to our needs for visual information. All of these factors are influenced in turn by the surface characteristics of the object of interest and the state of the observer, as well as by the source characteristics, quality, and quantity of illumination. Among the factors which must be considered in an analysis of the quality of human visual perception, therefore, we must list:

- The experience and attention of the observer
- The characteristics of the object: form, optical size, inherent contrast, color, texture, specularity, reflectance, etc.
- Simultaneous contrast
- Context: information content, patterns, figure/background separation, etc.
- Adaptation
- Illumination qualities: geometry, dispersion characteristics, directionality, spectral type, quantity, polarization, number and type of sources, consistency of directional characteristics and color-rendering effect, etc.
- Presence or absence of focus or distraction in the luminous environment.

The quantity of light is obviously only one of the factors which determine how well we see, and although it may seem surprising, it is usually a relatively unimportant factor. Each viewer has specific information needs and each object has specific characteristics. The quality of the luminous environment depends entirely on how well it responds to both.

Attention and experience

The first factor which influences how well we see something is the degree to which it stands out as a natural focus of the luminous environment. Strong simultaneous signals which compete for the observer's attention can either detract from or emphasize focal qualities of the object of interest. If they obscure or confuse the desired signal, we call them distractions or visual noise (as in the ceiling of the Houston Astrodome). If they help to create a positive attraction to the intended focus (such as an EXIT sign) we say that they emphasize the signal, intensifying the existing focus.

The more the distraction, the harder it is for the observer to maintain a focus of visual attention on the signal; the stronger the focus, the less effort it requires. The motivation and mood of the perceiver determine the length of the attention span, as well as the willingness to concentrate and to follow through with activities.

As a general rule, unfamiliar tasks demand a higher quality and/or quantity of light, if performance is to be as high as it would be in a familiar task. Experienced observers need less visual information to form meaningful perceptions. Given the same amount of information, they tend to perceive familiar objects more accurately than inexperienced observers, because they know what to look for. For example, a person who has never hunted can only find animals in the woods with great difficulty, no matter how brightly illuminated the woods may be, while a trained hunter takes full advantage of all relevant signals, because his experience filter has been conditioned by prior experience to recognize them at once.

The form and surface characteristics of objects

The clarity of object characteristics—form, surface texture, color, inherent contrast, etc.—has a great influence on how well we can see at various levels of illumination. Different types of objects call for different types of lighting, and a summary listing of typical information needs, related object characteristics, and the corresponding illumination qualities which will maximize the visibility of the desired information is given in Table III–1.

The information content and strength of a signal are a function of the optical size and inherent contrast of the object of interest. A zebra has high inherent contrast; a smudged fifth carbon copy has relatively low inherent contrast. If optical size cannot be changed (the object cannot be brought closer to the eye or magnified in some way) the information provided by contrast becomes the prime determinant of the quality of a signal. The amount of contrast produced by an object is dependent on its form and surface characteristics as well as on the quality and quantity of available light to make the contrast visible to the eye. Color perception is dependent on the spectral qualities of the light; perception of texture and form depends on the direction and relative concentration of the illumination. Different types of sources disperse the light they produce in different ways. Point sources such as incandescent lamps, metal halide lamps, and arc sources disperse light more or less evenly in all directions. This light then decreases in intensity according to the inverse square law. Line sources such as fluorescent sources disperse light in a cylindrical distribution the intensity of which decreases in direct proportion to the distance from the source. Area sources such as luminous ceilings, an overcast sky, indirectly illuminated walls or ceilings, and large translucent panels disperse light in different directions as a function of the solid angle and surface brightness of the source in each direction. Fixture characteristics can modify the original source distribution through the use of lenses, reflectors, and/or baffles. Obviously, the extent to which the inherent characteristics of the objects viewed will be enhanced or obscured by a given lighting system is dependent not only on the quality and spectral characteristics of the light but also on the directional characteristics of the light sources themselves, as well as their location with relation to both object and viewer.

Context

The clarity with which an object is perceived is influenced by its context. One aspect of context is its information content: the shape of a wire sculpture, for instance, can be clarified by a single set of shadows thrown against a flat, featureless background surface. Multiple shadows, shadows thrown onto a complex background, or a visually noisy background, on the other hand, will confuse the

Ripman

78

perception of the same sculpture. The confusion will be redoubled if the sculpture is complex and the location of the sources is not evident. Clearly, care must be exercised during the design of lighting systems incorporating directional sources to avoid this sort of counterproductive confusion.

Other aspects of context which influence the quality of perception are *phototropic effect, simultaneous contrast,* and *color.* Phototropic effect—a term which comes from the Greek words "to seek light"— refers to the automatic attraction exerted on the focus selector by bright sources in the visual field. Bright sources which are not the intended focus of attention cause the eye to adapt to a high average brightness level, reducing the perceived strength and quality of the desired signal. We react defensively when such sources cannot be excluded from the field of vision **(Fig. 78).** When the competing background is of a higher luminance than the signal, the clarity of the signal is reduced. The effect is greatest when the offending background elements are located close to (or surround) the signal. A glossy table top can be an annoying source of reflected glare if overhead fixtures fall into the mirror angle.[15] Competing glare from work surfaces can be reduced by locating light sources outside the mirror angle. Simultaneous contrast—the contrast between figure and background—can enhance the distinctive qualities of the signal. The relation between the color characteristics of the desired focus and of the background can either reinforce the signal or effectively camouflage it. The characteristics of one particular ruby, for instance, can best be seen against a featureless black or dark green background, as any jeweler knows. If the same stone were to be seen lying on a heap of other rubies, simultaneous contrast and color contrast would be minimized.

Signal quality as a function of the quantity of illumination

It has already been emphasized that using relevant and appropriate qualities of light, rather than indefinitely increasing the quantity of incident light, is usually the most effective way to maximize the visibility of desired or needed information. Above levels of luminance on the order of 10 footlamberts, the geometry of light source and objects viewed becomes far more important as a determinant of signal quality than the absolute quantity of light.

To increase visibility by brute strength (additional footcandles) rather than skill (fewer footcandles used to better effect) is not only grossly wasteful; it is likely to have undesirable and counterproductive side effects in the form of glare. When a space is sufficiently well illuminated to satisfy biological information needs, and a shortage of light is still the operative constraint on the visibility of a task, the task is usually so demanding that it should be given a special focus in the overall luminous environment. The most effective way to satisfy such special needs is via *local lighting* (see below) rather than by increasing the lighting throughout a space to the levels required for one highly demanding and probably localized task.

Visual capacity is often thought of as limited primarily by the strength of the task luminance, which suggests that better vision is simply a matter of increasing the incident illumination. However, the visibility of a task may be limited by either visual acuity or contrast sensitivity, both of which vary with task luminance. The relationships between task luminance, visual acuity, and contrast sensitivity are

[15]*The concept of a* mirror angle *can be most easily understood by the use of a mirror. If a mirror was located flat on the desk in question, a portion of the ceiling could be seen reflected in it. This portion is said to lie within the mirror angle for that particular desk surface.*

Table III–1. VISUAL INFORMATION NEEDS, OBJECT SURFACE CHARACTERISTICS, AND ILLUMINATION QUALITIES MOST LIKELY TO REVEAL AND OBSCURE THE NEEDED INFORMATION)

Information Need	Object Surface Characteristics	Positive Lighting Qualities	Lighting Qualities to Avoid
Maximum surface brightness	Totally matte surface (carpet)	Illumination normal to the surface; the surface should be of maximum reflectance	
	Totally glossy surface (glossy paint; mirror)	Illumination at the mirror angle (particularly for mirrorlike surfaces with no inherent color which can only gain surface luminance by reflecting a source or illuminated surface at the mirror angle)	
Brightness contrast from surfaces of varying reflectance	Totally matte surface (carpet)	Illumination normal to the surface	
	Totally glossy surface (glossy photo)	Illumination from other than the mirror angle	Illumination from a source within the mirror angle; if such sources cannot be avoided, the negative effects of mirror reflections can be minimized by using sources of maximum size and minimum luminance
	Dark glossy surface on a light matte background (dark printing on white matte paper)	Illumination from other than the mirror angle	Illumination from a source within the mirror angle
	Light glossy surface on a dark matte background (white printing on black matte paper)	Illumination from a uniform source of maximum size at the mirror angle	
	Dark matte surface or a raised projection on a glossy background (matte paint or raised lettering on glass)	Illumination from a uniform source of maximum size at the mirror angle	Illumination from a concentrated source at the mirror angle
	Dark matte surface or an indentation on a glossy background (grout joints in tile work)	Illumination from a uniform source of maximum size at the mirror angle, or from a concentrated source from the viewing angle	Illumination from a concentrated source at the mirror angle
	Metallic glossy surface on a dark matte background (gold or silver printing on a dark matte book binding)	Illumination from a uniform source at the mirror angle	Any illumination from outside the mirror angle
Color contrast		Same as above except that a full spectrum source should be used for discrimination between a full range of colors; a limited spectrum source may be acceptable for discrimination between a limited range of colors	
Brightness contrast from variation in light transmission characteristics	Transparent surface (stained glass and glassware)	Backlighting from a uniform source	Backlighting from a concentrated source directly behind the transparent surface or object
	Projected image	Projection onto an opaque nonspecular surface	Stray light from other sources falling on the screen from any angle
	Translucent surface (white glass)	Backlighting; a concentrated source is acceptable if located some distance behind the translucent surface, unless the surface is closer to transparent than translucent	

Information Need	Object Surface Characteristics	Positive Lighting Qualities	Lighting Qualities to Avoid
Shape	Simple closed solid (ball)	Illumination from a single concentrated source, or diffused illumination with a dominant direction somewhat displaced from the viewing angle	
	Closed solid with surface detail (sculpture, face)	Illumination from a single concentrated source, or diffused illumination with a dominant direction somewhat displaced from the viewing angle	Overlapping shadows from several concentrated sources
	Solid object related to other surfaces by cast shadows (ball in the air, steps in sunlight)	Illumination which creates a single sharp shadow	Illumination which creates multiple shadows, particularly if the shadows are cast from several different directions
	Simple open object understandable in silhouette (picket fence)	Illumination with a dominant direction; multiple shadows are usually acceptable	
	Complex open object (wire sculpture)	Single sharp shadow cast by a source located away from the viewing angle	Multiple shadows
	Dark raised solid (dark raised letters)	Concentrated or diffuse illumination from the viewing angle	Illumination from a concentrated source at other than the viewing angle, particularly at grazing angles
	Light raised solid (light raised letters)	Illumination from any angle which produces consistent sharp shadows	
	Totally glossy solid with no inherent color (polished metal sculpture)	Illumination from a large uniform source at the mirror angles	Illumination from a diffuse source surrounding the object; supplementary concentrated illumination can be used to create highlights, reducing the negative effects of a large uniform enveloping source
	Moving solid (runner)	Illumination with a dominant vector from the viewing angle such that it creates shadow gradients on the object; best seen against a uniform contrasting background	Visual noise in the background; minimize by locating potential sources of distraction such as light sources as far from the line-of-sight as possible
	Surrounding enclosure (room, courtyard)	Illumination which defines planes of enclosure with even light gradients	Illumination which upsets or destroys the visible form of surrounding surfaces, with confusing or distracting illumination gradients which are inconsistent with the true form of the surfaces
Texture	Simple rough texture (brick wall)	Illumination from a single concentrated source or from diffused sources at grazing angles	
	Complex rough texture (electrical circuits)	Illumination from diffuse sources at grazing angles or from a concentrated source at neither grazing nor normal angles	

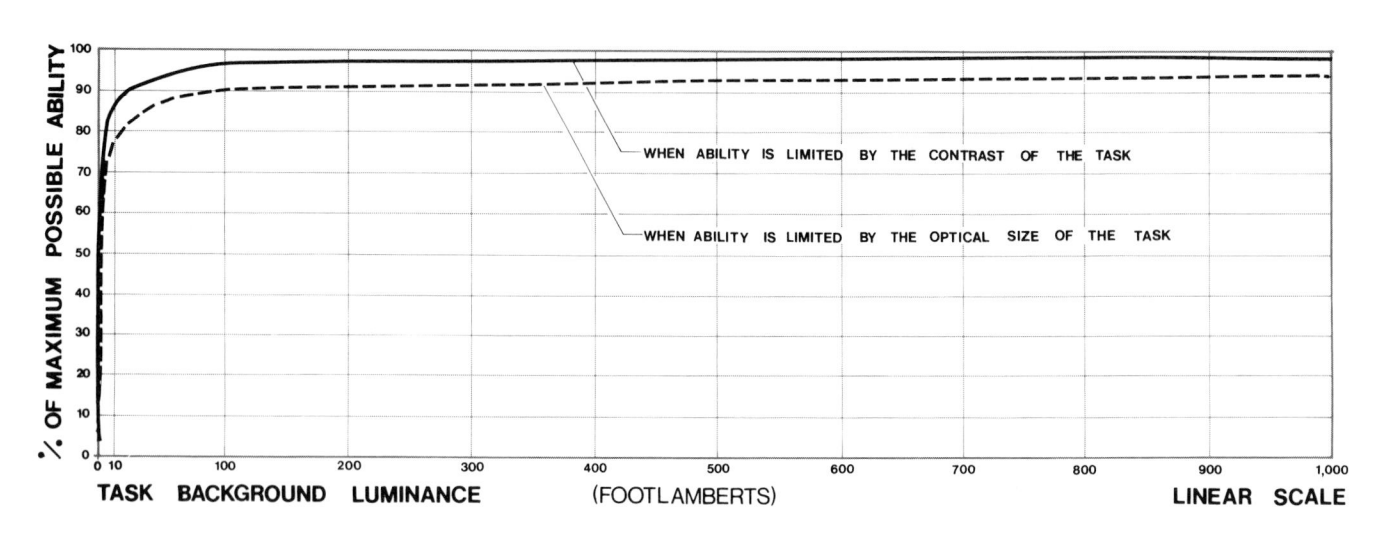

VISUAL ABILITY AS A FUNCTION OF TASK LUMINANCE

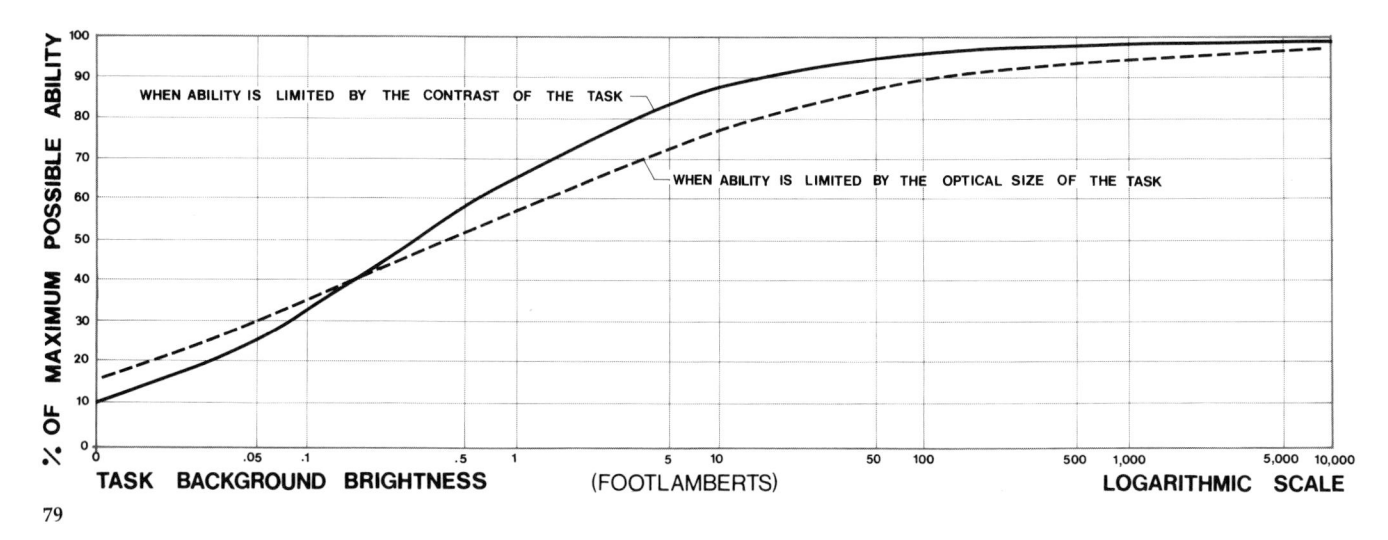

summarized in **Fig. 79.** As the luminance of the task increases, visibility also increases up to a point, but both curves very rapidly reach a point of diminishing returns above which very large increases in background luminance are required to produce even small increases in visibility.

The operation of the law of diminishing returns can easily be seen in the relation between visual acuity and surface luminance of a task. Visual acuity means the sharpness of vision, measured by the smallest size of detail which can be seen at a given distance. Our visual acuity is at 57 percent of maximum when the object of interest has a surface luminance of only *1* footlambert. At 10 footlamberts, acuity has reached 78 percent of maximum. When luminance is doubled from 10 to 20 footlamberts, visual acuity is increased by only another 3 percent;

80

from 50 to 60 footlamberts, the increase produced in visual acuity is only 1 percent; and when the increase is from 100 to 110 footlamberts, the increase is a minuscule 0.1 percent—effectively undetectable. If this is so, one may well ask why lighting codes recommend such high levels of illumination—levels which require expensive investment in fixtures, levels which mean high operating cost and wasteful energy consumption while contributing almost nothing to our ability to see. For viewing small objects (when visual acuity is the limitation on visibility) a minor increase in the optical size of the object is worth more than an *infinite* increase in the quantity of illumination. A lens or a watchmaker's eyepiece can increase task visibility far more effectively under these conditions than pouring on more footcandles **(Fig. 80).**

When a chalkboard is to be viewed, for instance, a 25 percent decrease in viewing distance produces an improvement in visual acuity equal to increasing the amount of light 100 times (from 10 to 1,000 footcandles). When visual acuity is the limitation, the solution is for the teacher to write larger and for the visually handicapped to sit in the front of the room. However, acuity is limited more often by lack of contrast than by an absence of light.

The ability to perceive luminance differences between adjacent areas of the visual field is called *contrast sensitivity.*[16] For contrast sensitivity, a relationship exists between luminance levels and visibility similar to that for visual acuity. Contrast sensitivity plays an important role in determining how well we can see: the higher the contrast, the less contrast sensitivity will be required to perceive a given visual task accurately. If it is necessary to detect subtle differences in contrast, high illumination levels will be required. Visual tasks which have little inherent contrast, such as reading smudged fifth carbon copies or light pencil handwriting, are often used as the justification for demanding high levels of illumination in work spaces such as offices or schools. However, it is usually more effective and less expensive to improve visual performance by increasing the contrast of the task than by increasing the illumination on the task severalfold. Increased contrast can be achieved at low cost, for instance, by using softer pencils or better duplicating processes.

The qualities of illumination—source concentration, direction, and polarization, for example—can greatly enhance or reduce the visibility of an object or task; therefore, they also influence the required contrast sensitivity. For instance, only 1 footcandle of concentrated directional grazing illumination[17] might be required to make a chip in wood grain or the texture of board-formed concrete visible to the same degree as would 1,000 footcandles of diffuse illumination from a direction normal to the surface being observed.

For a given quality of task illumination, the required contrast sensitivity for a given level of performance of a given visual task is a non-linear function of the task luminance (and therefore, of the quantity of incident illumination) as shown in **Fig. 79.**

At a recent, government-sponsored symposium held in Cincinnati, lighting expert Dr. H. Richard Blackwell underlined the greater sensitivity of the visual system to changes in contrast than to changes in illumination levels, when he commented

> back in the 1930's . . . people thought that they knew what was good light, namely, indirect light. We discovered that, when we switched over from indirect lighting with very low levels to direct

[16]Contrast *is defined mathematically as the luminance of the background of a task, less the luminance of the detail, divided by the luminance of the background (it assumes a dark task such as printed text on a lighter background such as white paper).*

[17]Grazing illumination *is directional light oriented almost parallel to the surface under observation, causing any irregularities in the surface to pick up highlights and cast shadows.*

lighting with the new fluorescent tube and increased light levels by three times perhaps, we did not really change or improve vision at all. Although the light went up by three, the contrast, generally speaking, went down . . . In many cases, you are worse off than before; and every architect in the business always thought this was true. But now science has finally caught up with common sense and we know why. It is because the eye cares linearly about contrast and non-linearly about the amount of light.[18]

Contrast must reveal characteristics, not confuse or obscure them. For instance, high contrast caused by specular reflection of the light source from the surface of an object often hinders the perception of the object more than it enhances it. This problem is frequently encountered in the lighting of textured oil paintings—high light levels combined with bad reflections can do more to obscure a work of art than to make it visible.

It should be apparent by now that the nature and quality of perceived contrast are an important design variable, to be manipulated rather than taken for granted in the design of appropriate, relevant luminous environments. Successful design to maximize the perception of contrast is far more dependent on the geometry of lighting than on the quantity of task illumination provided.

Local lighting

Local lighting produces maximum focus and minimum distraction as long as the light source itself is baffled from view. The Luxo lamp is a familiar example of a highly flexible local lighting fixture. Using this type of fixture, objects of interest and tasks can be brightly illuminated while the background produces only minimal distraction because of its much lower brightness levels and the absence of glare.

Local lighting can be arranged to deliver a given quantity of light with maximum effectiveness, without simultaneously inflicting glare or intense heat on other persons in the room. There are many ways of delivering local lighting: for example, it can be "piped" through acrylic rods. Local lighting combined with magnification of the task can be more effective in increasing signal quality than an infinite increase in general illumination without magnification **(Fig. 81)**.

Examples of object types and relevant lighting characteristics

This section contains a series of photographs which illustrate different object characteristics in various contexts, illuminated to various luminance levels by appropriate (and inappropriate) qualities of light. These examples demonstrate the importance of relevant lighting qualities: geometry, dispersion and directional characteristics, degree of diffusion, spectral type, number and consistency of sources, etc.

A light source at the mirror angle is shown in **Fig. 82. Figs. 83** and **84** show a totally glossy object—a photograph—and totally glossy background—the surrounding pane of glass. The illumination is modest, the position of the source is proper relative to the specular surfaces (i.e., away from the mirror angle for those surfaces). Frame shadows have been eliminated by using shallow frames and by avoiding illuminating the display from a grazing angle.

Fig. 85 illustrates a totally glossy object with inherent color— the wet swimmer—as well as a solid object seen against a glossy

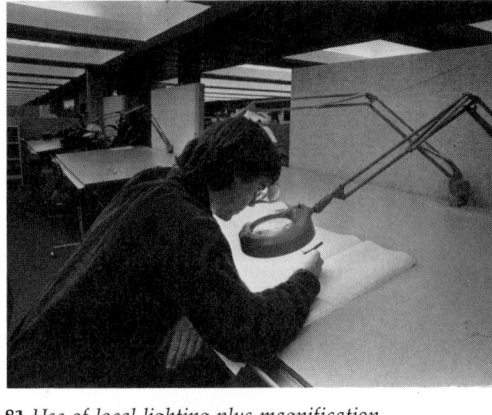
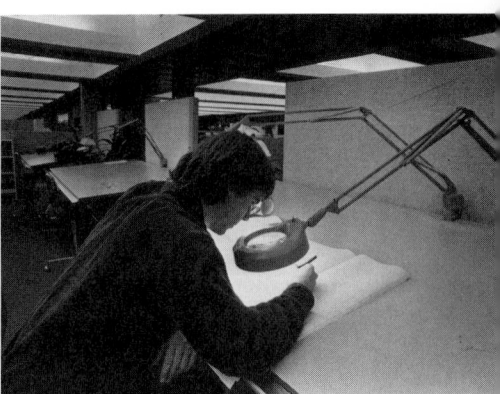

81 *Use of local lighting plus magnification.*

82 *Unpleasant veiling reflections on the glass over the print on the wall.*

[18]H. R. Blackwell, *The Occupational Safety and Health Effects Associated with Reduced Levels of Illumination: Proceedings of a Symposium,* U.S. Department of Health, Education and Welfare (National Institute for Occupational Safety and Health); HEW Publication No. (NIOSH) 75–142, p. 65.

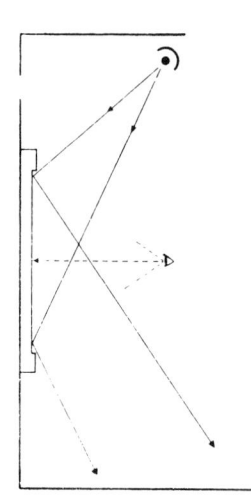

83

85

86

87

85 *Surface reflections interfere with perception of swimmer.*
86 *Diffuse daylight from behind the observer improves the visibility of swimmers.*
87 *Underwater lighting plus lighting concealed above the spectator gallery produces almost perfect visibility at the Johns Hopkins Athletic Center, Baltimore (Meyer, Ayers and Saint/Architects; William Lam Associates/Lighting Consultants).*

83-84 *Appropriate lighting geometry for a flat, totally glossy object, such as photographs under glass.*

background—the swimmer seen against the surface of the water. The reflected image of the window creates complex veiling reflections on the surface of the water which make it impossible to see the swimmer under water unless the pool receives additional light from other than the mirror angle. This can be accomplished by the introduction of diffuse (north or reflected) daylight, indirect illumination of the ceiling, or the introduction of supplementary underwater lighting as in **Fig. 87. Fig. 86** was taken in the same pool as **Fig. 85,** but facing the other way—away from the major window. Comparison of the two makes immediately obvious the importance of correct orientation of light sources with respect to the surfaces and objects which they are intended to illuminate.

Surfaces are classified as *matte* or *specular* depending on the directional qualities which they impart to the light which they reflect. A matte surface diffuses the light falling upon it, reradiating it in all directions: ''flat'' paint and Persian carpets are good examples of matte surfaces. At the other extreme is the perfect mirror, a flat specular surface which reflects incident light without changing in any way its degree of angular dispersion. Most surfaces fall between these two extremes, diffusing somewhat but maintaining the general directional qualities of the incident light: a polished table top and a piece of white Formica are both semimatte surfaces.

Specular surfaces require special kinds of illumination. Details of a specular surface can best be brought out by either grazing light or by a large uniform source at the mirror angle. Mirrors and polished metallic surfaces can only gain luminance from a mirror reflection, since their perceived brightness is determined almost entirely by the brightness of what they reflect. This explains why polished metal buildings are particularly difficult to light at night—they simply reflect light from sources on the ground up into the sky; if the sources are placed high up, they are seen as points of light on the side of the building. If the surface of the metal is not perfectly polished—for instance, if it has a brushed or sand-blasted finish—it will diffuse the light to a certain degree, alleviating this problem. Flat polished metal letters seen against a dark background are equally tricky to illuminate well. They may appear brighter than the background during the day because they reflect the sky or other bright elements of the surroundings; at night, however, they can only be illuminated from the mirror angle if they are to appear bright.

The series of photographs in **Figs. 88, 89, 90** illustrate the unusual difficulties inherent in the proper illumination of certain types of book titles. Visibility of dark, glossy titles on light-colored bindings is maximized by exactly the opposite lighting qualities which would maximize the visibility of silver and gold (specular) titles on dark bindings. Probably the most difficult book titles to read are those printed in silver or gold which act as mirrors and appear bright only if there is a bright surface at the mirror angle which they can reflect—the same problem encountered with the illumination of flat polished metal letters.

Visibility of specular titles is maximized by increasing the contrast between them and the background binding. This can be done by increasing the illumination at the mirror angle (which will be reflected most effectively by the specular type) relative to illumination from other angles (which will be reradiated more effectively to the eye by the bindings). However, this is difficult to accomplish in conventional library stack geometries, for obvious reasons.

88 89 90

Tilting a book up maximizes specular reflection from reflective type if the ceiling surface is brightly and evenly illuminated. Tilting the book down greatly decreases the brightness of the binding, but legibility will be increased if the brightness of the binding decreases faster than that of the reflective printing. The same effect can be achieved by shielding the binding with one's hand.

Either of these steps is more effective than simply increasing the overall illumination levels substantially without changing the geometry. Correct lighting geometry is far more important in the proper illumination of specular materials than the absolute illumination level. For most library conditions, a large area source overhead such as an indirectly illuminated ceiling **(Fig 88)** combined with a light-colored floor material will maximize the visibility of the required information. Although the direct sources in **Figs. 89** and **90** produce an *identical* quantity of vertical footcandles on the bindings as the indirect source in **Fig. 88,** the difference in legibility is immediately apparent.

The clarity of raised objects, such as letters, is particularly affected by the contrast between the letters themselves and their background. A shadow from a dark raised letter on a light-colored background reduces clarity because the shadow resembles the tone of the letter, confusing the outline of the letter itself. Spacing the letter from the background reduces the confusion somewhat, by increasing the separation between the two dark images—letter and shadow. Dark letters are better when flat or recessed, so that shadows either do not exist or fall within the letter itself. On the other hand, shadows are helpful in the perception of light-colored raised letters, because they increase rather than decrease the amount of useful information available to the eye. When light letters are recessed, shadows reduce both the clarity of the image and the contrast between signal (letters) and background. **Fig. 91** illustrates these various conditions.

Transparent objects such as glassware are best illuminated by backlighting **(Fig. 92).** In the laboratory, for instance, titrations are often more visible when seen in silhouette against the background of a well-lighted featureless white wall than when the illumination falls directly on the equipment itself—a lighting geometry which is likely to cause distracting ceiling reflections and glare.

For the perception of three-dimensional objects, the geometry of light sources is extremely important. Most of our ability to perceive volumetric form comes not from the contrast inherent in the object itself but from the gradients of light and shadows produced by the illumination which falls on the object. Shadows are poorly rendered by uniform diffuse lighting such as that produced by an evenly overcast hemispheric sky. Under such circumstances, when we are deprived of the information provided by modeling and shadows, we must rely more on outline, color, and other information for the perception of shape and form. At the other extreme of the scale, light from a single concentrated source produces maximum shadows and modeling, but much useful information may be hidden in the shadows themselves.

A simple three-dimensional object such as a cube illuminated by several concentrated sources may still be comprehensible, because the perceptual process compensates for some inconsistency in gradients and shadows as long as the nature and location of the sources are also comprehensible. However, when several complex objects are viewed

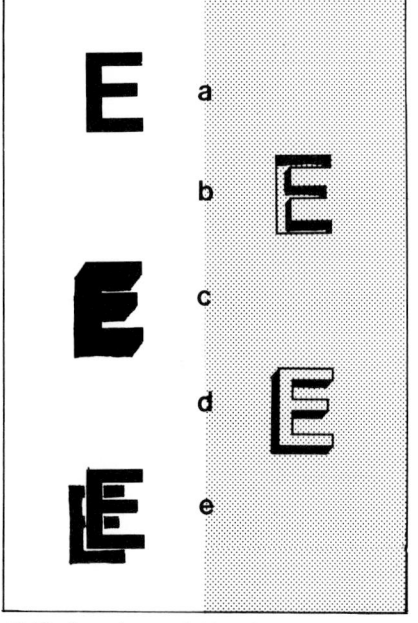

91 *Shadows from raised and recessed letters —help or hindrance?*

92 *Backlighting.*

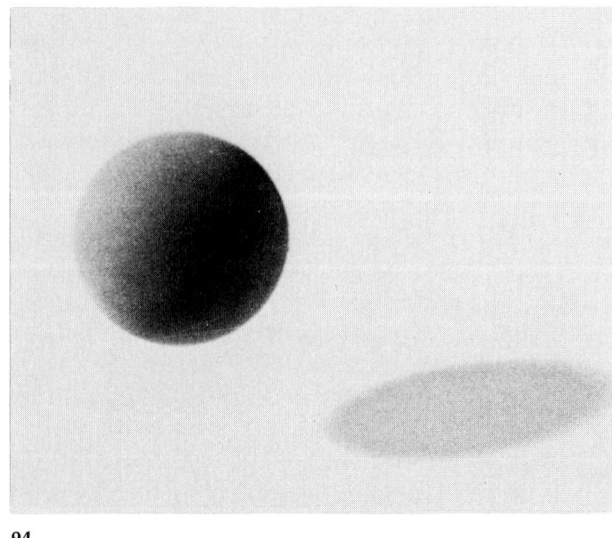

93 94 95

simultaneously, multiple gradients and inconsistent shadows can be thoroughly confusing.

If there are no other reference clues to the size and position of an object in its context, the shape of a shadow and the sharpness of its edges can provide enough information to establish its relative position **(Figs. 93, 94,** and **95).**

The best condition of illumination for most three-dimensional objects corresponds to the condition we encounter outdoors: a combination of directional sunlight and diffuse skylight, which produces consistent, sharp shadows, all from the same angle, as well as sufficient light from other directions to fill in detail in the shadows. Indoors, lighting from a window produces soft shadows with a coherent grading (the window can be regarded as a uniform area source). The equivalent in interior lighting to the sunlight condition would be a combination of overall diffused lighting supplemented by a directional component from a point source (or a set of consistently directional sources). Artificial diffused lighting with a dominance in one direction can produce the same desirable modeling effect as interior daylighting from windows on one side of a space.

The characteristics of illumination which are most relevant to the perception of closed solid objects with detail, such as a typewriter or a camera, can best be understood by considering the qualities of lighting which are most appropriate for the perception of *faces.* High-quality perception of three-dimensional objects such as faces requires visibility of detail and color as well as overall form. Illumination should have a dominant direction (vector) neither coinciding with the viewing direction (i.e., from behind the observer, which produces minimum modeling), nor perpendicular to the viewing direction (which produces maximum modeling). When the direction of the lighting is poor, the ratio between maximum and minimum illumination should be low, particularly for viewing faces: the optimum brightness ratio would be less than 10 to 1, ideally between 2 to 1 and 5 to 1. For illuminated faces with a low brightness ratio, the direction of the light is not so critical **(Fig. 96),** whereas with a high brightness ratio, sidelighting is much better than light from overhead. If the direction is good, of course, the brightness ratio can be much higher than 10 to 1. Such ratios, and good object visibility, can be achieved with a combination of directional and diffused

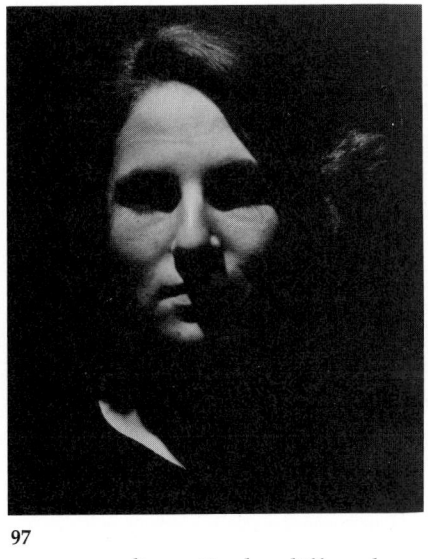

Ripman

96

97

98

sources; alternatively, diffused sources of varying strengths can be used, which in combination produce light with a dominant vector, like that from a window. The diffuse sources need not necessarily be light fixtures: illuminated walls, floors, table tops, and other room and furniture surfaces can serve as general sources of diffuse light. This sort of moderately directional light is preferable to that produced by a large uniform area source overhead such as an overcast sky or a luminous ceiling. Multiple point sources are likely to cause multiple and confusing shadows.

Shading and shadows should be neither excessively dense nor confusing. Dense shadows from the side are better than those from above or below because faces are more symmetrical about the vertical axis. Shadows from the side emphasize individual characteristics **(Fig. 98),** while those from above or below tend merely to emphasize the symmetry **(Fig. 97).**

Summary

Visual perception involves far more than a passive and mechanistic response to patterns of light: it is a complex, active process of information selection, filtering, interpretation, and storage in which context, prior experience, and expectations are combined with incoming sensory data to create meaningful perceptions. Unless distracted, we look at what we want or need to see, as dictated by activity and biological needs for visual information. The visual attention is automatically directed by the focus selector to elements of the visual field which will provide the needed information. A distracting stimulus may cause the focus selector to redirect the visual attention. Such a stimulus need not be the brightest thing in view. The information content and context of stimulus also play important roles in determining its perceived relevance and importance. The eye adapts to general illumination levels over a very wide range, which explains in part why it is the relative *apparent* brightness of a stimulus and its context, and not the actual measured luminance levels, which determine its attractiveness to the mind's eye.

We are comfortable when we are free to look at what we want or need to see; we are uncomfortable when the luminous environment itself interferes with our freedom and ability to do so. The higher the strength, quality, and information content of desirable visual stimuli, and the higher the signal-to-noise ratio in the visual environment, the better we can see. These factors are influenced by the surface characteristics of the objects of interest, as well as by the source characteristics, quality, and quantity of the incident illumination. The experience and attention of the viewer, the nature of the visual context, adaptation, and the presence of positive focus or distracting signals in the visual field also affect the quality of human vision. Clearly, all these factors must be considered in the design of successful, relevant luminous environments.

There is no simple one-to-one relationship between measured luminance levels and the apparent brightness of objects as they are perceived by the viewer. Similarly, one cannot derive any simple quantitative formula to predict either the meaning which will be given to a particular stimulus or the emotional and evaluative responses which it will trigger. People perceive information and visual relationships, not absolute intensity levels of light. The final impression which will be lodged in the brain is principally determined by whether the stimulus is meaningful or meaningless, clear or ambiguous, relevant or irrelevant, expected or unexpected. These are the real questions which must be decided in the course of lighting design.

Considerations such as these explain why a pattern of light fixtures or a luminous ceiling may be perceived as glaring and annoying while a chandelier or a window view of even greater luminance may be judged to be sparkling and enjoyable, and why a well-lighted dirty concrete floor seems dull while a Bokhara carpet with much less light on it can be interesting and even exciting, and why a moonlit urban park may be seen as "dark" while a beach or a safe patio in suburbia with similar light levels would probably be judged as "unpleasantly bright." In all of its complex aspects, visual perception is a thoroughly relativistic process.

Since the optimum lighting for different activities may vary greatly in qualitative terms, designers must know the surface characteristics of the objects to be seen, and must understand which illumination characteristics and geometries will enhance the relevant desired information and which will obscure it. At any level of illumination, the desired information which can be extracted from the task object can be enhanced or obscured according to the qualitative characteristics of the incident illumination. A small quantity of the right kind of light can produce far better task visibility than much larger quantities of an inappropriate kind. The designer must also recognize that the law of diminishing returns applies to the productivity associated with increasing light levels, and that for most tasks a level of illumination is soon reached at which the *quantity* of incident illumination ceases to be the effective constraint on the quality and speed of visual perception.

Knowing what information one wishes the luminous environment to convey is therefore far more important than specifying arbitrary general light levels. The eye adapts to light levels automatically; the *mind* responds to *information*. This simple premise lies at the heart of the design process proposed in the following chapter, and served as the conceptual point of departure for the design of the projects presented as case studies later in this book.

4 The Design of the Luminous Environment

The conventional contemporary process of lighting design

Today, the process of design has become fragmented and compartmentalized, so that the original design concept, no matter how strong, is almost inevitably subjected to sequential erosion. Decisions are typically made one at a time—first planning, then structure, then mechanical systems, then lighting, then detailing, then finishes—with each stage in the decision-making process more or less isolated from and constrained by its predecessors. Irreversible decisions made in the early phases of such a linear, sequential process inevitably restrict the range of options which are open to the design team in subsequent stages. Some designers seem to believe that no joint decisions are possible—that each design phase must be a separate layer. The results of this line-of-least-resistance approach are usually boringly repetitive, wasteful, and frequently even confusing. All too often, the resulting luminous environment shows little or no variation throughout a project, even though the activities and needs in different areas may be quite different. In terms of effectively meeting the biological and activity needs for environmental information discussed in the previous chapters, far too many new working buildings fail miserably; responsibility for the generally low quality of these luminous environments can be attributed at least in part to the typical sequential, compartmentalized process of design. Let us run briefly through a typical design sequence.

Our hypothetical architect begins his or her design with no further consideration of artificial lighting than to make brief programmatic statements such as "downlighting" or "recessed fluorescent lighting, 70 footcandles." Late in the design development stage, or at the beginning of contract documentation, lighting design proper begins. The electrical engineer is given responsibility for the lighting, and follows the "lumen method" throughout the building except for a few, special spaces such as the lobby or the executive floor which receive more attention and thought. The steps in the lumen method are as follows:

1. From the IES Handbook, from government codes, or from the client's specifications, determine the required average level of horizontal footcandles for the project. A single level may be specified for the entire building, or various levels may be

THERE IS MORE LIGHT HERE

Someone saw Nasrudin searching for something on the ground.
'What have you lost, Mulla?' he asked. 'My key,' said the Mulla. So they both went down on their knees and looked for it.
After a time the other man asked: 'Where exactly did you drop it?'
'In my own house.'
'Then why are you looking here?'
'There is more light here than inside my own house.'

——*The Exploits of the Incomparable Mulla Nasrudin*

established for different types of space: office, classroom, corridor, etc.

2. Select a lighting fixture or fixtures suitable for mounting in the preselected ceiling system, which uses the most economical lamps available and has the highest fixture efficiency in terms of producing illumination on the horizontal plane at desk level. The shape of the fixture relative to that of the room is usually considered to be of secondary importance, if it is considered at all. Some consideration is given to quality of the lighting system by limiting direct glare; generally, however, low-brightness fixtures will not be selected if they cost more per footcandle delivered on the work plane.

3. Calculate the number of fixtures required to achieve the average illumination level or levels determined in step 1.

4. Find a layout for the required number of fixtures which distributes the light uniformly over the room as measured at the work plane.

Conventional "qualitative" criteria and their limitations

Some variations on this standard procedure do take place. Additional qualitative restrictions may be imposed by the government or by the client. Such requirements are frequently stated in terms of maximum permissible brightness ratios. The deficiencies of brightness ratios as indices of quality have already been pointed out: they simply fail to take into account the *desirability* of seeing the source in question, which is an important determinant of the viewer's reaction.

Although brightness restrictions are not sufficiently stringent to eliminate undesirable visual noise such as glaring patterns of meaningless light fixtures, they are often *too* restrictive to allow desirable, relevant high-brightness elements such as pleasant window views. Brightness restrictions have been misused to eliminate windows from school designs, and to lower the transmission value of window glass to such a degree that even sunny days appear dull and gloomy from inside the building. Abstract numerical criteria such as these cannot distinguish between objects we like to look at and those we do not; as a result, people are deprived of desirable and biologically necessary information in the name of their own comfort.

The Visual Comfort Probability Index (VCP) is representative of another type of qualitative restriction which may be imposed on a lighting design. Indices such as VCP attempt to rate various arrangements of fixtures according to the proportion of viewers who would find the arrangement in question *tolerable* from the point of view of glare. Incorporation of VCP requirements into design criteria has the unfortunate side effect of restricting fixture options to those which have been listed by the manufacturer as meeting VCP minima for the contemplated fixture arrangement, room size, and proportions. Since only regular arrangements are listed, the designer's options are quite restricted from the start. We have seen that optimal luminous environments are likely to call for irregular fixture layouts and selectively illuminated room surfaces, or for low general illumination combined with supplementary local lighting on demanding tasks. Faced with glare limits stated in terms of VCP however, a designer trying to achieve the optimum luminous environment is handicapped by the necessity of using rated fixtures in regular patterns. Indirect lighting cannot be considered, since there are no published tables from which the designer could derive meaningful VCP ratings for the illuminated room surfaces which serve as sources of light. The only alternative involves the expense of carrying out either complicated calculations or a full-scale testing program for each design option—an operation for which the average designer has neither the requisite funds, experience, nor equipment.

Much better results can be achieved if the design team and building committee use mock-ups or even realistic model studies of alternative designs—including those which can be assigned VCP ratings—as the means for evaluation of design options for the luminous environment.

When VCP criteria are specified, the typical VCP objective is 70 percent, which means simply that 70 percent of the occupants of the space are expected to find glare conditions acceptable. This is an objective which can be attained under most circumstances by the use of moderately good lenses in recessed fluorescent fixtures. In view of how much money and energy is involved, this seems a singularly low objective: 95 percent satisfaction is not too difficult to achieve and seems a more appropriate standard of performance in this age of technical sophistication, yet such high standards are never set because most commercially available fixtures in conventional arrangements would fail to qualify.

It must be pointed out, in closing, that the VCP method only rates glare, which is just one aspect of the luminous environment, albeit an important aspect. There is nothing in the VCP rating system which guarantees that people will find environments with a good VCP rating either comfortable or pleasant. Similar criticism applies to the British discomfort glare rating system developed by Hopkinson.[1]

Recently, a new "qualitative" measure has been introduced into the conventional design process: *Equivalent Sphere Illumination*, or ESI. ESI measures the degree to which a particular lighting installation approaches the effectiveness of sphere lighting. When light comes from a uniformly illuminated sphere surrounding the task there is very little loss of contrast due to veiling reflections, because only a very small amount of the total incident light is delivered at the mirror angle. The ESI rating of a lighting installation indicates the footcandle level of illumination from a spherical source which would be required to produce an equivalent degree of accuracy in the performance of visual tasks as the lighting installation being evaluated. Although ESI represents an improvement over the use of raw footcandle measurements, because the ESI approach makes a gesture toward the quality of the luminous environment, the use of ESI footcandles in no way alters the invalidity of the premises on which the conventional design process is based. In fact, the use of ESI criteria raise a number of additional questions which have yet to be resolved:

- ESI relates to only one very limited aspect of the quality of the luminous environment,

[1] R. G. Hopkinson, "Daylight as a Source of Glare," Light and Lighting, vol. 56, pp. 318ff., 1963.

having to do with the legibility of written or printed matter of a certain size located flat on a desk directly in front of the reader. There is no guarantee, however, that this "most difficult task" will be either important or distributed throughout a space, nor is there any guarantee that, even if important and evenly distributed, the task will be performed in the manner specified: flat rather than inclined, directly in front of the reader rather than to one side, from a desk chair rather than a drafting stool or a lounge chair, etc. Since the geometry of the situation is critical to the determination of ESI, the stringency of the control conditions throws the validity and usefulness of the entire process into question.

- In all spaces ESI varies with the location and orientation of the task. Usually an average ESI value is calculated. This presumes that the visual tasks are distributed at random in the space. Yet there is no method available which the designer can use to make a meaningful comparative evaluation of two alternative designs with different distributions of ESI. For example, one cannot compare directly the "quality" of two spaces, one with a very low ESI in only 10 percent of the area (perhaps in an area where desks are unlikely to be placed) and a high ESI elsewhere, and another space in which the *minimum* ESI is higher but the minimum obtains throughout 75 percent of the space, including the most likely work positions. Without comparative techniques, the value of ESI as a meaningful working tool for the designer is greatly reduced.

- There are only a few instruments currently available for the measurement of ESI. This makes such measurements costly and difficult to obtain. ESI-based design therefore must rely heavily on meaningless patterns of fixtures which have been prerated by manufacturers, or on similar fixtures in comparable arrangements. This precludes the use of irregular fixture layouts which might respond better to the nature and distribution of tasks within a space, as well as effectively prohibiting the use of room surfaces as major sources of indirect light since these, being unique, have no listed ESI ratings. In short, ESI criteria restrict the *objectives* of design as well as the means available to the designer. This is exactly the same problem which is inherent in the use of VCP minima as design standards.

Although the use of ESI footcandle criteria as design objectives or code requirements is by no means a panacea, the underlying concept of ESI—that the quality of light is an important determinant of how well we see—is a valuable one. Since the relationship between task visibility and illumination levels is quite complex, however, illumination-level criteria of any sort should only be used as cross-checks on a design, not as the sole means of evaluation. There are several other interchangeable qualitative criteria related to ESI which can also be used as cross-checks: among these are the *Lighting Effectiveness Factor*, or LEF, which measures how effective the footcandles produced by a particular lighting installation are in relation to those produced by spherical illumination, and the *Contrast Rendition Factor*, or CRF, which measures the capability of a lighting installation to render contrast between detail and background of a task, as compared with that of a uniformly illuminated spherical source. LEF is calculated by dividing ESI by the level of illumination on a task, while CRF depends on a number of variables such as the location and size of light sources in relation to the task and the nature of the light distribution in the space, which also involves reflected light from room surfaces. The CRF can be greater than 1.00 because certain lighting configurations deliver even less illumination from the mirror angle than an evenly illuminated spherical source.

Variations on the conventional design process

In the design of flexible modular buildings such as speculative office structures, another variation of the lumen method may be employed. After required illumination levels have been determined by the usual procedure, fixture selection may be based on the worst possible condition: a small office with dark walls. Once a fixture and spacing have been found which can deliver the required amount of light under these worst possible conditions, the design is repeated throughout the entire building, from glass line to core, often producing more than twice the specified levels of illumination in the larger spaces. No consideration is given to the fact that most of the small offices will probably be on the perimeter, where daylight is quite sufficient for many tasks much of the time, and that the executives who usually inhabit small offices are likely to prefer to use a desk lamp. No allowance is made for the fact that the area around the core is usually devoted exclusively to circulation, which requires only minimal lighting for orientation and physical safety.

Because initial rather than operating costs tend to dominate decisions in the design of speculative structures, switching hardware and equipment such as multilevel fluorescent ballasts are generally omitted, despite the fact that such equipment would make it possible to adjust the luminous environment to suit specific activities in specific locations, conserving energy and lowering operating costs while improving the luminous environment in the process.

The objectives of, justifications for, and fallacies behind the conventional process of lighting design

When the conventional design process and the conventional design methodologies are considered in an objective light, it is hardly surprising that most conventional lighting designs fail to satisfy many of the needs of their users and do little to reinforce the specific character of an architectural design. How could they, when there was never any attempt to define the full range of needs; to ascertain the probable set of activities, their frequency, their probable locations, and priorities; to discover what furniture arrangements would be likely and what useful daylight contribution could be assumed? In the search for "quality," there is rarely an attempt to articulate the desirable, only an attempt to avoid or mitigate the intolerable.

The long-established conventional design method, which has become standard practice largely due to the influence of the Illuminating Engineering Society, is based on a number of false premises:

1. That the exact light levels listed in recommended standards have a clear-cut relationship to health and/or productivity.
2. That failure to provide the recommended levels of illumination everywhere would result in complaints if not in catastrophe.
3. That the "most difficult tasks," selected by IES committees as the standard on which quantitative recommendations are based, are in fact "common".
4. That, whether common or not, they are sufficiently critical to warrant their use as a basis for general criteria.
5. That these "most difficult tasks" may take place anywhere and/or everywhere in any space.
6. That "quality" of the luminous environment is something to mention, but not something for which quantity should be sacrificed.

An expert panel assembled in 1967 by the author at Saratoga totally rejected these assumptions, which have been used by the lighting and power industries to justify a design process with an inherent bias toward ever-increasing and wasteful light levels. The conference resulted in the following conclusions:[2]

1. Low levels of illumination cause no organic eye damage. According to available medical evidence, insufficient illumination no more causes organic harm to the eyes than indistinct sound damages the ears. Considerations of comfort and performance would therefore set the criteria for lighting.
2. A comfortable, pleasing, relevant environment is as important as visual performance in determining the conditions of good lighting.
3. In place of the footcandle—commonly used, but inadequate, since it is a measure of only the quantity of light—the development of a performance index which correlates with both quality and quantity was recommended.

[2]Reprinted with the permission of the New York State University Construction Fund, from their Performance Criteria for the Luminous Environment: An Abstract, State University Construction Fund, Albany, New York 1971.

4. Quality, rather than quantity, is the key to good lighting. A small improvement in the quality of the luminous environment produces better visual performance than a large increase in intensity. Increases in illumination operate under a law of diminishing returns.

5. Since visibility is satisfactory over a wide range of illumination, and since varied tasks, fluctuating daylight, and balance of quality and quantity of light all influence the determination of good lighting, rooms with uniform task distribution do not demand uniform lighting. If a major part of the area meets the intensity criteria during most frequent use, the lighting is likely to be satisfactory.

6. For rooms with nonuniform task distribution, the British practice of a moderate level of general lighting, combined with local supplementary light on work requiring performance of unusually difficult or specialized tasks, was endorsed in preference to systems of uniform lighting.

7. In addition, the current practice of specifying an all-time minimum lighting level for an entire room, based on the possibility that a critical visual task might be performed once in a while somewhere in that room, was rejected. Instead it was agreed that the probability of the occurrence of such a task and its duration should be realistically analyzed in advance and spaces should be lighted for critical visual tasks only if such tasks are unquestionably the predominant tasks to be performed in such a space.

But if many of the conventional premises are fallacious, what can be substituted for them as the grounds for more realistic, more productive design process and design objectives for the luminous environment? To answer this question, we must examine further the relationship between different qualities and quantities of light, the ability to see, productivity at work, and health.

Regardless of which specific criteria are utilized during the course of design, the basic objective must always be to provide optimal luminous conditions for as many as possible of the expected activities in a space and to satisfy biological information needs by using a moderate amount of light as effectively as possible. Unusually difficult or specialized visual tasks are best provided for by local lighting or by visual aids designed to suit the particular task in question. A generally high illumination level throughout a space makes sense only when the special tasks which demand those levels are also distributed throughout the space. The conventional justifications for the "more is better" approach to lighting design can no longer be defended—there is no evidence which suggests that indefinitely increasing illumination levels lead to corresponding increases in comfort, productivity, or health. But let us examine briefly the limited evidence which is available concerning the relation between light levels, comfort, productivity, and health.

Task visibility as a factor affecting productivity

Let us consider for a minute the simplistic argument which is often advanced, "The brighter things are, the better we will be able to see them." We know that this is not necessarily the case. While acknowledging the importance of adequate illumination levels as a factor affecting the quality of vision, the discussion in the preceding chapter brought out a number of other, equally important factors. How well we see is influenced by the experience and attention of the viewer, by the presence or absence of a positive focus or distraction, by the strength of competing visual noise, by the attributes of the background as they influence the ease of distinguishing figure from background, by constancies in our interpretation of visual stimuli, by the size and object characteristics of the subject of attention, by the directional qualities and color temperature of the light, by the pattern of sources, etc.

Is it true, then, that there is a clear link between increasing the quantity of illumination, higher task visibility, and improved productivity? There is little evidence which suggests that increased illumination levels alone lead to increased productivity, unless the initial levels were grossly and obviously inadequate. Increasing task visibility only affects productivity positively when task visibility is a limiting factor, which is rarely the case today.

We know that familiarity with the task is a factor—that unfamiliar tasks require more light and a better control of focus and distraction. A good activity environment creates a natural focus on the task, while providing alternative foci which may serve as visual rest centers during periods of inactivity or relaxation. All these factors play a role in determining productivity, yet they are very difficult to incorporate meaningfully into testing procedures which evaluate the effect on productivity of changing the luminous environment.

When increased light levels have been accompanied by increases in productivity, it seems that the productivity increase can be attributed just as easily to a perceptible improvement in the quality of the overall luminous environment as to the increased lighting levels.

I know of no experiments which have been performed which, in analyzing typical school and office activities, distinguish successfully between the influence of task visibility and the influence of other factors such as attitude, mood, mental speed, comfort, motor limitation, concentration, etc., as determinants of productivity. The exception may be in the task of viewing chalkboards, when low light levels combined with veiling reflections and fixed seat locations sometimes make it impossible to read the writing on the board. However, very large increases in light levels must be made if they are to be as effective as a minor change in other, related physical conditions, such as decreasing viewing distance, increasing the size of the writing, eliminating glare sources, or improving the directional qualities of the light.

As lighting levels across the country have been reduced in

response to the energy crisis, there has been substantial evidence of *increases* in comfort and productivity as a result of the *decrease* in light levels. People are finding out for themselves that if they turn off their lights (at least, some of their lights) they can see just as well—if not better—and more comfortably.

In industrial work, where productivity is obviously affected by visibility, especially in critical tasks such as electronics assembly, watchmaking, and product inspection, optical aids or specialized local lighting fixtures are usually used to increase the perceived size of the task or to highlight its essential characteristics by controlling the direction, color, polarization, focus, and contrast of the illumination. These demonstrate clearly the importance of factors other than simple quantity which affect the quality of task performance. It is far more effective to increase light levels in a small "task" area than to raise levels indiscriminately by the same amount throughout a space.

Motivation and productivity

While several instances of increased productivity due to increased task visibility have been reported, these findings are somewhat suspect in that the researchers usually fail to perform at the same time essential control experiments such as testing the effect of *reducing* light levels. The importance of such control experiments was demonstrated conclusively by the Hawthorne experiments performed by Professor Elton Mayo of the Harvard Graduate School of Business in the late 1920s.[3] In these experiments, Mayo measured the performance of workers under various conditions, and discovered that while productivity increased with increased lighting, it continued to increase when light levels were subsequently *reduced*. Mayo's studies do not prove that increased lighting cannot improve productivity, but they do demonstrate that productivity increases may be attributable to the feeling that management cares about working conditions in general, as evidenced by their alteration of the luminous environment. The Hawthorne studies and work by Adams[4] in Britain seem to suggest that *any* change indicating attention paid to workers by management may produce an attitude change in workers which may subsequently affect productivity in a positive way. I would hypothesize that task performance increases are more frequently brought about by improvements in the overall luminous environment which satisfy biological information needs, producing feelings of comfort and pleasure, than by improvements restricted to increasing task visibility. Thus, investment in better colors, carpeting, or a more pleasant environment by using modest levels of well-designed indirect or local lighting may well increase productivity more than an equal investment in increasing footcandle levels.

Comfort and productivity

In order to understand the relationship between visual comfort and productivity, we need to remember the discussion of "What Do We Look At?" Even in factory production work, the eyes are not glued continuously to the task at hand. They are constantly scanning the environment for the information which one consciously wants or unconsciously needs to know. Therefore, elements such as distracting foci, patterns of bright sources, and glare have a bearing on comfort and productivity. User surveys by Manning and Wells[5] and Langdon[6]

[3] *These experiments, conducted at the Hawthorne Plant of the Western Electric Company by Professor Mayo, are reported in detail in F. J. Roethlisberger and W. J. Dickson,* Management and the Worker, *Harvard, Cambridge, Mass., 1966.*

[4] *S. Adams, "The Effect of Lighting on Efficiency in Rough Work (Tile Pressing)," Joint Rep. Industrial Health Res. Board and Illum. Res. Comm. (D.S.I.R.), Stationery Office, London, 1935.*

[5] *Reported in P. Manning (ed.),* Office Design: A Study of Environment, *Liverpool, The Pilkington Research Unit, England, 1965.*

[6] *F. J. Langdon,* Modern Offices: A User Survey, *H. M. Stationery Office, London, 1966.*

in British office buildings show almost no complaints about the quantity of light (although the measured levels were generally below those recommended by the British Illuminating Engineering Society and a mere fraction of the levels required by current United States practice). On the contrary, the complaints which the researchers noted were mostly concerned with discomfort glare—typically a symptom of photometric glut rather than famine.

Discomfort glare

The volume of valuable work done by Hopkinson and others on discomfort glare suggests a stronger relationship between feelings of comfort and the overall design of an environment than between comfort and the absolute quantity of light in it.

Traditional lighting research has tried to evaluate the relative comfort and discomfort of various environments by attempting to define the borderline between comfort and discomfort in terms of abstract mathematical indices.[7] The basis of this rather negativistic approach is that if one could define the limits of discomfort, and then surpass them, one would have comfortable spaces. The conceptual poverty of the idea is rather disappointing; in effect, it says that the way to design good spaces is to avoid the positively objectionable. That seems a rather unambitious objective! Lighting technology has made it possible for us to go far beyond the borderline of discomfort, and lighting expenditures are sufficiently high that we ought to try for something a little better. In formulating new criteria for the luminous environment, we should concentrate on defining situations which give maximum comfort and pleasure, rather than looking for arbitrary borderlines which define the edge of pain. We should be able to design environments consistently which are so far from the threshold of discomfort that the tolerance of individuals should be unimportant. If we are still arguing over the threshold, we have not yet addressed the real problem.

After extensive study, Hopkinson concluded that:

> Discomfort due to glare is not only a subject of complaint, but it is reasonable to suppose that it affects the general efficiency of the worker as a result of a build-up of annoyance, frustration and irritation in people who are subject over a long time to what amounts to a minor emotional affront. It has been shown, however, that the effect on human "efficiency" is very difficult to measure, in much the same way as the effect of noise in a building is more important because of the distress which it causes than because of the actual reduction of the efficiency of working.[8]

Illumination levels and physical safety

If we cannot justify high footcandle requirements on the grounds that they contribute positively to environmental comfort, motivation, or productivity, can we still justify them on the grounds of physical safety? We know that lighting for orientation and physical security satisfies an important biological need, but *how much* light is actually required to satisfy this need?

In the normal course of lighting design, considerations of physical safety play a minor role, because *almost any lighting which suffices for other purposes will be adequate to assure physical safety.* In good design practice, spaces express their use clearly and consistently: materials,

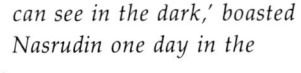

[7] *The variables generally evaluated as determinants of discomfort glare from direct sources are: the brightness of each source, the visual size of each source (as a solid angle from the eye), the number of sources, the direction of view in relation to the direction of the source, the brightness of the background, and the condition to which the eyes of the observer have grown accustomed.*

[8] *R. G. Hopkinson and J. D. Kay,* The Lighting of Buildings, *Praeger, New York, 1969, p. 58.*

[9] *Horizontal illumination means the amount of light (luminous flux) falling perpendicular to the surface of the earth.*

[10] *In 1974 Professor Gary Hack of M.I.T. and a group of graduate students surveyed users on their evaluation of street lighting in Norfolk, Virginia. Analysis of the survey data revealed definable and quite low levels of illumination which were regarded as satisfactory from the point of view of safety and security. Also further increases in illumination beyond these levels brought users no benefits in terms of increasing their feelings of safety and security. The researchers found that in the areas surveyed, 0.1 footcandle measured in any direction (not necessarily on the horizontal plane) was the critical value for residential streets (in Norfolk), while 0.4 footcandle was the critical value on arteries where the greater traffic volume induced higher expectations. This study has been published as* Improving City Streets for Use at Night: The Norfolk Experiment, *a report prepared for the Norfolk Redevelopment and Housing Authority and William Lam Associates.)*

[11] *D. G. Cogan, "Popular Misconceptions Pertaining to Ophthalmology,"* New England Journal of Medicine, *vol. 242, pp. 462–466, 1941. (Quoted from stenographic notes from the 1967 Saratoga Conference of the State University Construction Fund of New York. This opinion was confirmed at a symposium of experts sponsored in 1975 by the National Institute of Occupational Safety and Health. The report of this symposium, "The Occupational Safety and Health Effects Associated with Reduced Levels of Illumination," HEW Publication no. (NIOSH) 75-142, is excellent and recommended highly for those interested in pursuing the subject further.)*

[12] *William Lam Associates, "The Effects of Light On Health: A Review and Assessment," a report prepared for the Bureau of Human Ecology, Department of Health and Welfare, Ottawa, Ontario, March, 1976.*

forms, focal points, junctions, stairs, and other circulation elements are well-defined and comprehensible. Under such conditions, it is very unlikely that a safety hazard will exist except when misdirected or improperly shielded sources create disability glare conditions. Safety deserves particular consideration in interior situations where very low light levels are consciously sought, such as nightclubs, and at potentially dangerous exterior locations such as stairs, level changes, or on rough terrain. At night, a minimum of 1/10 footcandle from any direction is normally sufficient to prevent a person from stumbling or falling, unless the visual information is misleading or faulty—for instance, if there are confusing shadows—or if disability glare conditions exist. The average horizontal illumination level[9], which is the conventional method for specifying minimum exterior light levels for safety, is not as important as the minimum illumination level from any direction, especially at critical points. Levels as low as 1/10 footcandle have been measured by the author in a number of well-known buildings and streets, and the users of these spaces showed no signs that they found either orientation or movement to be a problem.[10]

One dangerous situation which should be avoided whenever possible involves disability glare from strong daylight sources such as a window at the end of a long corridor. This effect is aggravated if the corridor is finished with dark or specular materials, which increase the contrast between the corridor surfaces and the window. In such situations the brightness balance should be improved, either by increasing illumination of the corridor surfaces, increasing the reflectance of the corridor surfaces, or by controlling the source, direction, and distribution of daylight. The best solution consists of light-colored walls and ceiling, well illuminated. It should always be remembered that even outdoors, where the overall brightness balance of full daylight is fairly good, a dangerous situation will exist whenever one's line of sight must be toward the sun.

Illumination levels and health

Eye health is sometimes advanced as a justification for high levels of illumination, with the implication that low levels of illumination will damage the eyes themselves. Dr. David G. Cogan, director of Ophthalmology of the Massachusetts Eye and Ear Infirmary, states conclusively that "There is no generally acceptable evidence that poor illumination results in organic harm to the eyes, any more than indistinct sounds damage the ears or foul smells damage the nose."[11] Eyestrain may indeed result from the effort of trying to overcome a difficult seeing condition, but eyestrain is only a temporary discomfort and does no damage to the eye. The need for wearing glasses arises only from organic causes, not from inadequate illumination levels. Eyestrain can be caused by glare—too much light of the wrong kind— as well as by inadequate illumination, but eye *damage* can only be caused by overexposure to light.

In 1976 William Lam Associates was commissioned by the Canadian Federal Government to conduct an assessment of the effects of light on human health. During this project our staff reviewed the existing literature and interviewed many experts in the field, and were unable to find any scientific evidence *whatsoever* that low light levels had any negative effects on human health.[12]

Summary

Most of the conventional arguments advanced in support of continuously increasing levels of illumination seem untenable, once levels of 10 to 20 footcandles have been achieved. Improvements in task visibility will only call forth increases in productivity if task visibility is a major constraint on productivity at the outset. Under most circumstances comfort and motivation play equally if not more important roles in determining productivity. So far as we can tell, low levels of illumination have nothing to do with general health, as long as they are adequate for safety. The *arrangement* of the light sources is often more important for safety than the actual levels provided, since the arrangement can indicate movement patterns and highlight potential danger points, or it can be misleading, or it can create glare conditions, interfering with the perception of information required for orientation and safety.

There is little or no conclusive evidence which relates comfort to high levels of illumination. Most work on comfort has been concerned with the measurement and analysis of disability and discomfort glare conditions. Yet we all know from personal experience that feelings of comfort are affected by what we look at—by everything in the visual field—even in factory work. Therefore, the overall luminous environment must be regarded as the critical, and in many spaces the only, determinant of the sensation of visual comfort.

We are comfortable when the objects we see give us the information we consciously want or instinctively need to know. We are comfortable when the things we see please or interest or reassure us, and when the things we do not want to see are hidden from view. The key factor in assessing the qualities of a specific luminous environment is *relevance;* that is relevance of the available visual information to the activity and biological needs of the users.

Therefore, in setting new criteria for design, we need to eliminate negative elements such as sources of discomfort glare, distracting elements, and situations which by comparison (conscious or unconscious) will be perceived as gloomy. But in addition, we need to accentuate the positive aspects of the luminous environment, by providing lighting natural and relevant to activities and expectations, giving orientation clues, creating a focus on activities, and providing interesting visual rest centers, without simultaneously introducing glare or unwanted distractions.

Whenever a cheerful and bright space is expected during the day (lobbies, classroom, office, lab, library, etc.), large areas of walls or ceilings must be illuminated to balance daytime brightness (either visible simultaneously or remembered). Sufficient illumination of these surfaces to balance (but not necessarily equal) daylight levels will generally result in sufficient illumination for casual activities throughout most of the room. Such "environmental lighting" plus supplementary local illumination, controlled by the user for more demanding activities or in darker portions of the room (e.g., in study carrels shadowed by enclosure), is likely to produce the greatest comfort both for those using the local lighting and for others in the space—and at lowest cost. High levels of illumination for an entire space are justifiable only if critical tasks appear throughout the space and if the geometry of lighting, optimal for one occupant, is not detrimental to others in the form of glare.

A new process of design

Anyone who understands the perception process, acknowledges the existence of biological needs for environmental information, and recognizes the importance of optimum lighting geometries and qualities, will agree that the best, most relevant luminous environments are those which have been tailored to the unique requirements of the activities which they house, without compromising the general qualities required for the satisfaction of biological needs. The standard design process fostered by the IES which was described at the beginning of this chapter is obviously unsuited to produce such a high-quality fit between needs and luminous environment, nor was it ever intended to produce such a fit. A new, more integrated and comprehensive design process will be required if we are to make the creation of successful, relevant spaces the real objective of design. A closer cooperation will be required among all the members of the design team at all stages of the design process, with more emphasis on the formulation and achievement of perceptual rather than numerical objectives.

Hopefully, it is indicative of a new positive trend that in setting performance criteria for luminous environments, the advisory committee to the State University Construction Fund of New York agreed that the development and implementation of a new design process would be far more important than any numerical criteria, and recommended a design process which would bring designers and client agency together to go through the logical steps of problem definition and schematic design prior to the selection of any specific fixtures or the computation of illumination levels. The new design process recommended in the SUCF report[13] begins with the listing of activities, subactivities, biological needs, and their relative priorities, rather than with the selection of hardware or the blind listing of minimum levels of illumination to be achieved.

A lighting concept should be derived from the set of programmed activities and biological information needs, so that the definition of the luminous environment will complement and reinforce the general architectural concepts; then — and only then — should details and hardware be selected to execute the concept. This is the diametric opposite of the typical "engineered" approach, which starts with the selection of light fixtures and then, taking them as givens, places them in patterns to achieve predetermined illumination levels.

In theory, it might seem that detailed programming of activities and corresponding lighting needs for each space would logically lead to buildings consisting of sets of individually designed spaces, each perfect for its programmed set of activities. In practice, however, several factors make such an eclectic "tight-fit" solution unrealistic and undesirable in most buildings. Regardless of specific activity needs, people have important biological needs for orientation, order, and continuity, which demand that there should be common denominators and reference points in related spaces. Satisfaction of these important needs constrains the freedom of the designer to respond solely to the activity needs of each space. In addition, very few spaces are used for only a single purpose — one activity which would define one optimal lighting configuration. In most spaces, a number of activities take place, and an appropriate luminous environment must be either highly complex, with localized effects, or

[13]W. M. C. Lam and A. G. H. Dietz, "Performance Criteria for the Luminous Environment", draft of a report for the State University Construction Fund, Albany, N.Y., 1971. An abbreviated version of this document was issued by the SUCF as "An Approach to the Design of the Luminous Environment" in 1976.

flexible, with a range of possible effects controlled by combinations of switching and dimming.

Only when the illumination needs of a project are truly specialized and localized, as they are in a performing arts center, for instance, are the added time and expense required by a totally *ad hoc* approach justifiable. Very specialized, focused activities such as theater demand equally specialized luminous environments. Multiple activities which are not localized, on the other hand, call for flexible environments which are sufficiently neutral and adaptable so that the users can create foci on specific activities as they desire.

With the rare exception of certain special-use spaces, the illumination required to provide for most biological and activity needs can best be provided by the simple expedient of illuminating room surfaces and furnishings, which in turn illuminate the work surfaces. This is the condition one usually seeks when working out of doors: not the direct light of the sun, but rather the even illumination of the sky vault, supplemented by light reflected from the surrounding landscape.

In an interior space, the visible surfaces and the way in which they are illuminated *are* the design. They define space and its perceived meaning. They convey the intent of the designer or betray the lack thereof. Every element of a successful, relevant visual environment—activity areas, equipment, circulation, structure, mechanical services, etc.—should be carefully and clearly interrelated, articulated, and defined. Special activity areas may call for special lighting solutions. This approach produces easily comprehensible complexity and consistency without dullness, because elements which one expects to be consistent *are* in fact treated consistently, while those which are really different are expressed as such.

During the phase of concept development, the lighting designer should probe the possibilities with other members of the team to see whether alternative structural or mechanical systems are feasible which, in combination with a lighting proposal, would lead to a better luminous environment. Constraints of partitioning flexibility, acoustic separation, energy conservation, and cost must all be considered, as well as many other factors, but these should never be taken as *a priori* givens which cannot be altered in the search for a better overall solution.

Almost every localized design decision can be expected to have extensive repercussions on the rest of the design. For instance, the limited ceiling height which normally is inevitable with a disorganized two-way layout of air ducts dictates the use of recessed downlights which must be closely spaced to achieve an even distribution of light at the work plane. An increase in ceiling height, which may be possible either by coordinating the ductwork with structural elements or by consolidating bulky service elements into discrete service channels, can dramatically increase the lighting options. As another example, the selection of red brick walls and a dark wood ceiling for an office building practically guarantees inefficient lighting and uncomfortable, gloomy spaces unless light-colored furniture is introduced and the principal work lighting is localized to create positive foci. The advantages of having at least some of the walls in small rooms light-colored should always be considered—in such rooms, the walls rather than the ceiling tend to dominate the field of vision and it is the brightness of the walls which largely determines whether the space feels cheerful or gloomy. In large spaces with low ceilings, light walls make less of a contribution to the perception of a bright, cheerful space because they occupy less of the visual field. In such spaces, therefore, darker wall materials have a less negative effect than in smaller, higher spaces.

Every design element, from structure to finishes, affects the quality of the luminous environment, and it is the responsibility of every member of the design team to make decisions keeping this in mind. This requires a great deal of communication, and a common awareness of the principles of perception involved; of the effect of varying wall, ceiling, and floor reflectances upon the efficiency, light distribution, and perceived brightness of various lighting systems; and of the pros and cons of various light sources and light-control media — including the building itself. All design options must be evaluated in terms of the detailed objectives for the luminous environment.

The responses of the lighting designer to various design proposals should never be a simple "yes" or "no"; rather, recommendations and criticism should be phrased in terms of options and tradeoffs, seeking always to maximize the opportunities inherent in an architectural design. For such purposes, the author has found various simple graphic presentation techniques[14] helpful in communicating options and alternatives to those members of the design team who may be unable to visualize different luminous environments when described in numerical or verbal terms. Although a full discussion of such techniques is not possible within the scope of this book, readers may find useful the samples of presentation material and design tools presented in the context of the case studies which form the second half of this book.

Alternatives to the conventional design process

The case studies which follow illustrate the application of the principles of perception to the integration of architectural and lighting design. The various design processes employed by the author are explained, and examples of written programs, schematic diagrams, models, and mock-ups have been included so that the reader can see the actual working tools employed by the design team.

The kind of integrated design process required to produce good luminous environments is understandably more complex than one which aims only at the achievement of minimum footcandle levels, and since not all elements of the design process and not all process aids are used in every project, they will be discussed here. Ideally, all steps and aids would have been used in each project presented, but differences in timing, complexity, personnel, and design budget make that impossible. Design process aids serve to facilitate and deepen the communication between all parties involved. Here, despite the dicta of Mies, more is always more.

The chart printed inside the back cover of this book presents in summary form the design processes and process aids which were used in the case study projects, as well as indicating the formgiving effects of lighting considerations in each case.

Lectures and field trips

It has been my experience that most clients and members of design teams initially have a total misconception about lighting, in terms of

[14]Originally published as part of "Lighting for Architecture" in the Architectural Record, vol. 127, no. 7, pp. 219–229, June 1960; vol. 123, no. 1, pp. 170–181, July 1960; vol 128, no. 4, pp. 222–232, October 1960; and vol. 129, no. 1, pp. 149–160, January 1961.

both objectives and alternatives. Even while paying lip service to quality, they find it difficult to abandon traditional footcandle levels as the real objective of design. A lecture or field trip which brings home to all project personnel the principles of perception, the relevance of quality versus quantity, and what can be achieved, will always pay off in the end. If this is not done, the necessary reeducation must be done on an individual basis, in fits and spurts throughout the duration of the project.

A lecture on the principles of perception and lighting as formgivers for architecture can be supplemented with a field trip to illustrate specific principles and to show what is possible and what should be avoided. Any field trip will be much more effective if preceded by a formal lecture or discussion which teaches the participants what to look for and gives them a common terminology for further discussion of objectives and alternatives. Examples of the principles of perception can be found anywhere, once one knows how to look for them. Nevertheless, field trips are most productive when someone with considerable familiarity with perception is present to give guidance in what to observe and to explain the needs and processes involved.

Field trips can be particularly valuable when the design team is proposing or exploring unfamiliar types of luminous environments. Those without design training may be unable to visualize unfamiliar types of environments, and therefore may be afraid to accept and support them. A brief visit to an outstanding example of the type of environment under consideration will do more than any amount of persuasive argument in convincing all members of the design team of the importance of total synthesis and coordination in the visual environment. Once they have been shown what is in fact possible and more important, *desirable*, even the most recalcitrant people have been known to cooperate rather than resist in making the design tradeoffs required to achieve a good luminous environment. The principal objective of a field trip is to give everyone involved in the design process an opportunity to put himself in the place of the future users of the space, so that each specialist will apply his or her talents to the creation of an optimum environment rather than to a narrow-minded defense of his or her particular specialty, preconceptions, and habits of professional practice.

All persons who will play important decision-making roles should participate in the introductory lecture and field trip so that an early and irrevocable consensus is established as to the nature of the environment which will be the goal of the ensuing design process. Failure to include an important client or a key member of the professional team in these early phases of the design process has torpedoed a number of very promising projects on which the author has worked. A lack of understanding on the part of one important person who does not share the team's common frame of reference can throw an insurmountable roadblock into the path of design development. When this happens, a field trip to reestablish consensus should always be considered, since the cost of the field trip will certainly be insignificant compared with the price of delays, compromises, and backtracking in the design process.

Programming

Once the actual process of design begins, the programming stage is obviously critical. Rather than producing a list of footcandle levels to be achieved in the various types of rooms, the design team should list in the program the activities and biological needs, as well as their implications for the luminous environment, for each space or class of spaces weighted by importance, frequency, sequence, locality, etc. This type of listing can be used to generate performance criteria for each luminous environment, detailing its required characteristics and degree of flexibility. A suitable hardware system can then be selected on the basis of these criteria. Such a process can be extremely tedious and time consuming. However, the exercise of having gone through such a systematic, detailed process of conceptualization once is invaluable. An experienced designer goes through the process almost unconsciously in the design of every space, and is able to sum up the activities, the biological needs, and their respective environmental implications in simple summary statements of objectives and design concepts. A verbal summarization of a detailed activities program and its corresponding design objectives is much more valuable and productive than any amount of simplistic numerical criteria. There is a great difference between summarizing a complex program in words and the unfortunate general practice of singling out one aspect of one "most difficult" task as the basis for lighting criteria. The verbal program statement for the Washington subway system presented here is an excellent example of this kind of summary.

VERBAL PROGRAM STATEMENT FOR THE LUMINOUS ENVIRONMENT OF THE WASHINGTON SUBWAY SYSTEM

DESIGN OBJECTIVES

The lighting design of the Washington Metropolitan Area Rapid Transit System has been developed as an integral part of the total architectural concept with the purpose of creating an image consistent with the concepts of optimum comfort and pleasantness. Comfort implies freedom from visual noise such as disorderly, irrelevant patterns of overly bright lighting fixtures. The provision of a restful background maximizes the impact of positive experiences such as focusing on objects of interest: signs or light patterns which aid orientation and tell us facts which we want to know, consciously or unconsciously. A background free from visual noise also contributes to the pure pleasure of just looking around.

Orientation

Patterns of lights and illuminated signs should be designed to improve the clarity of circulation routes, structural elements, and sequences of architectural spaces. If the design is carried out well the passenger should unconsciously receive all the visual information needed to tell him where he is and how to reach his destination.

It is important to realize that passenger safety may be endangered less by excessively low lighting levels than by confusing circulation patterns, especially under crowded conditions. Special types of lighting will serve the dual purposes of enhancing the appearance of the spaces and improving safety and traffic flow.

Entrance Areas

The important functional elements marking the entrances to the system should, if possible, be standardized and be given a strong lighting expression. The combination of a distinctive symbol, ticket office kiosk, and stairway should be instantly recognizable, not only in the setting of an isolated park, but also against a brightly-lit commercial background. The image would be strengthened if all lighting in the immediate area were to come directly from these elements, without the daytime or nighttime clutter of other lighting standards and fixtures.

The *system symbol* should be distinctive wherever seen and should be the strongest design element in its immediate vicinity, thereby attracting traffic to the turnstiles. An illuminated station name, map and symbol will strengthen this image, as will a pattern of lamps which make the ticket office a chandelier, setting the office apart from the signs and advertising. The ceiling of the office should read as a bright plane of distinctive shape (i.e., round).

The *stair-escalator enclosure* if properly highlighted can also contribute to identifying the system.

From Entrance to Platform

After passing through the turnstiles, passengers should be able to find the desired platform without confusion. In the passageways leading to the platforms, therefore, maps and directional signs should be visually dominant. Highlighted advertising and art would reduce monotony along the way during the off-hours, but the reassuring directional signs should always remain predominant.

At the approaches to the platforms, blinking signs indicating the imminent arrival of a specific train might tell the passenger whether to rush or to saunter, while adding to the kinetic quality of the experience.

The Platform

At the selected platform one should find the atmosphere relaxing, free from glare and obtrusive patterns of lighting hardware. The architecture of the space should be revealed, but not so strongly that one cannot turn away. Murals and advertising posters should supplement the visual interest of the architectural details.

The *platform edges* should be clearly visible, perhaps emphasized by white edging. (To attempt to emphasize the edge with a glaring overhead light fixture would call more attention to the fixture than to the edge, defeating the purpose.) The approach of the train will be heralded audibly, of course, but the arrival would be dramatized and passengers would be alerted for rapid boarding if the platform edge and tracks were brilliantly highlighted momentarily as the train made its grand entrance and took over the stage.

The Train

Achieving a comfortable visual environment in the train itself requires the same approach as in the stations: bathing of light over the wall and ceiling surfaces, no glare, no annoying reflections from shiny ceiling surfaces, all contributing to a lighting quality equal to that of the best jet aircraft. There should be enough light to read by, but not so much as to destroy privacy. Remember the close quarters and the face-to-face seating.

The lighted maps should be dominant. One likes to be sure of the stops. The route one is on should be underscored, and the approaching station marked with a bright light. If feasible economically, perhaps the lighted spot could move along the route, which would be both fun and relaxing to watch, alleviating the need to peer out of the window at each station—often a difficult task in a crowded train.

Advertising, if required economically, should display lighted information against dark backgrounds if backlighted. Spaces between the advertisements should be masked with opaque panels. Otherwise, the car would become too bright and glaring, with the advertisments dominant rather than incidental background messages. An alternate means of advertising without dominance would be to use opaque advertising panels seen under light reflected from the car surfaces.

Illuminated destination-identification panels at the front of each car and over each door would be desirable for the boarding passengers.

UNDERGROUND STATIONS

To counteract the effect of subterranean gloom in the stations during daylight hours, the spaces must appear bright, cheerful, and airy. Such an atmosphere can be achieved by brightly illuminating walls and ceiling surfaces. (Although a high level of light directed to the floor or walls would produce adequate brightness on a white ceiling, the ceiling surfaces of the underground stations will be of unpainted concrete, and even high levels of light on the floor would not dispel the feeling of gloom which would strike the passenger entering a seemingly dark station interior from the bright sunshine outdoors.) The most efficient way to achieve bright walls and ceilings is to light them directly. Whenever it is appropriate therefore, an indirect lighting system shall be integrated with the structure and furnishings in such a way as to conceal the light sources themselves from view. Not only will such an indirect system be cheaper, in terms of both first cost and maintenance cost, than separate direct fixtures lighting the floor surfaces, but it will also minimize visual noise from discordant lighting patterns—a common problem in most subway stations. Wherever lighted graphics, kiosks, and direct light sources are used as aids for orientation or for special decorative effects, these effects will be enhanced by the general indirect system, rather than drowned out by it. At night, when the rider's frame of reference and adaptation level is to the dark night sky and to the relatively dim street lighting of the outdoor night environment, the brightness levels of the interior station surfaces can be reduced to a fraction of daytime levels without making the stations seem dark. While maximum brightness on walls and ceiling is no longer instinctively demanded at night, bright enclosing surfaces are still desirable in subterranean spaces to minimize feelings of claustrophobia. If the lighting is harsh or glaring, the fault will be much more apparent at night.

If these objectives of bright, cheerful spaces are achieved, there will automatically be enough light to see by.

SURFACE STATIONS

Consistent with the overall objectives stated above, the lighting for the surface stations shall be such that the shape and extent of the platform and canopies are defined without the light sources becoming either overbearing or inconsistent with the architectural elements. Because of the limited area of enveloping architectural surfaces around the platforms of the surface stations, direct sources shall be used wherever possible and the types of light sources used should provide the maximum feeling of ambient brightness together with a sense of activity and cheerfulness, by creating a chandelier-type sparkle. Where appropriate, the disposition of an array of fixtures should be such that it is an aid to orientation. Disturbance of the neighborhood through glare and unpleasant light spillage shall be avoided.

EXTERIOR SPACES

The lighting of exterior spaces shall be so organized that pedestrians and drivers alike are made aware of the organization of the area by providing for the maximum clarity and amount of visual information, and also for the safety and amenity of its users. The disposition of the lighting system for the supporting facilities such as the car parks, bus loading areas, etc., shall not cause annoyance to the neighborhood by glare and unpleasant light spillage, but rather should be so organized that it is a natural lead-in to the station mezzanine.

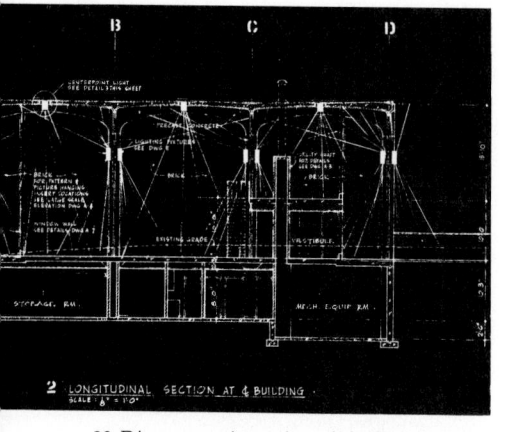

99 *Diagrammatic section of the Burndy Library, Norwalk, Connecticut (Sherwood, Mills & Smith/Architects; William Lam Associates/Lighting Consultants).*

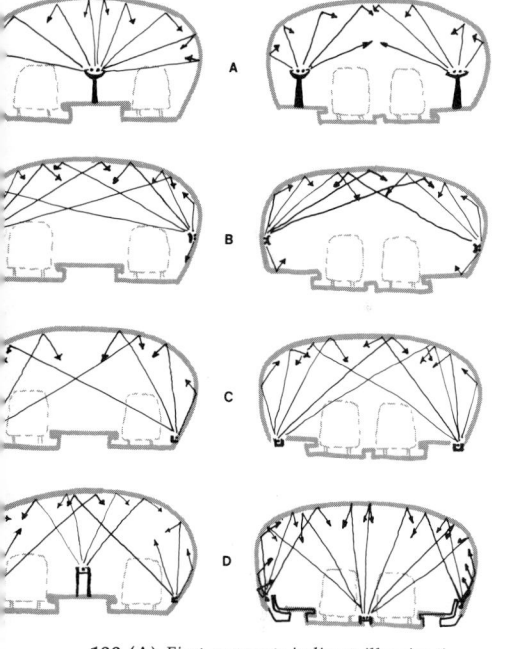

100 **(A)** *First concept: indirect illumination from "birdbath" fixtures. Problem: uneven vault illumination.*

(B) *Second concept: indirect illumination from continuous fluorescent valances. Good vault illumination but the dark band of fixture shields would have interrupted the continuity of the vault.*

(C) *Third concept: indirect illumination from continuous fluorescent fixtures recessed into the floor. Problems: high maintenance costs and unpleasant glare for those standing near or above the lights.*

(D) *Solution: use continuous fluorescent fixtures concealed behind benches in side-platform stations, supplemented from continuous fluorescent fixtures under the grille of the safety walk between the tracks. For center-platform stations use continuous fluorescent fixtures on both sides where the vault meets the trackbed, with supplementary lighting as required from fixtures concealed in the tops of pylons, telephone booths, and ticket kiosks.*

Schematic design: diagrams and models

Once the programming stage is well in hand and the actual physical form of a project begins to take shape, options can be explored through the use of schematic diagrams. We use freehand color-coded plans for this purpose and, wherever possible, building sections and details are always diagrammed to show the location of light sources and the incidence of the light which they produce. **Fig. 99** is an example of this sort of conceptual diagramming. Such diagrams are particularly useful for communicating why the reflectances of certain surfaces—particularly those which will serve as sources of indirect light or which form major elements in the visual field—are more critical than others. As the design develops, the freehand color-coded diagrams can be transferred to standardized tape-and-symbol codes on sepias of the architectural drawings, which can be more easily reproduced for distribution to the various members of the design team. Samples of this sort of symbolic lighting plan are presented in **Figs. A3–2** and **A3–3.** To represent individual fixtures of different types we use precut adhesive press-on symbols (developed for use in the design of printed circuits).

As an example of the sort of freehand schematic diagrams which are used for concept exploration and design development, a series of the diagrammatic sections which were used to develop the lighting for the underground stations of the Washington subway system is presented in **Fig. 100.** Since the plan of the tubular stations was so simple and consistent, and could be described in words, only section diagrams were required for this particular project. Objectives of the conceptual program for the WMATA stations included illumination of the ceiling vault to minimize feelings of claustrophobia, the minimization of visual noise, and the provision of maximum guidance for orientation and circulation. The use of schematic diagrams enabled the design team to explore the implications of a number of alternative designs and to converge on the best combination in a very short period of time.

Schematic tools can be developed as the need arises. Unlike the design of the underground stations, the design for the surface stations of the Washington transit system obviously had to be developed both in section and plan. Having developed concepts which worked for the first few sites, the designers were still faced with the problem of applying those concepts to 33 sites which vary substantially in terms of terrain, site size and shape, the amount of parking provided, the layout and configuration of access roads, etc. A hierarchy of standard luminaires and pole heights had been worked out to provide maximum orientation information: paired globes at entrances, low single clear globes for pedestrian pathways, multiple sources in simple rectangular hoods on higher poles oriented away from surrounding residential areas to illuminate the parking lots, etc. The team used various types of map pins stuck in the site plans to represent the different types of luminaire as a means of exploring the legibility of the resulting patterns in terms of the optical guidance which they would provide for the users, and to ensure that the various designs for the different stations were mutually consistent. For each type of luminaire, the light distribution at ground level was calculated using a computer program and the resulting distributions were transferred as shaded patterns onto transparent film. These reproducible film templates were overlaid on the site plans by the designers to explore options for the design of each station and to determine fixture spacing, eliminating much tedious calculation. Examples of the template and map-pin techniques are presented in **Figs. H6–6, 20, 21, and 22.**

Illuminated models and mock-ups

Illuminated models and mock-ups are extremely valuable for exploring design concepts, communicating them to clients, and making measurements of light levels and distributions. Unfortunately, many designers use models only for presentation of the finished design to the client. Such models are usually too expensive and are executed too late in the design process to make them of any value in actually *refining* the design or exploring alternatives. Inexpensive study models are one of the most economical means of generating productive discussion within the design team itself, especially when some team members may be trained to think only in terms of numbers and not in terms of visual relationships.

There are various types of useful lighting models. Room models **(Figs. G2–5, 6)** enable one to visualize and measure the luminous environment in a room which is to be illuminated by daylight, by artificial sources, or by a combination of both. The materials of which the model is built should have the same reflectances as the materials to be used in the actual design. The scale of the model should be whatever is convenient to build and to look at.

Finding light sources of the proper scale for a model may be difficult, but this is rarely a critical problem since it is always possible to make allowances for scale inaccuracies when viewing the model or making quantitative measurements. For example, when viewing the illuminated models of the Washington subway stations **(Figs. 101–103;** see also **Case Study H6),** we assumed that in the real stations the brightness gradients in the immediate vicinity of the sources would not include the hot spot which could not be avoided in the model because of the exaggerated scale size of the neon tubes used and the impossibility of achieving in a model the same quality of control over light distribution which can be expected from a full-size fixture. The scale error was minimized in this instance by taping out part of the oversize lamp, but it was still noticeable.

In making quantitative measurements, the following assumption should be made: in the model, the ratios of generated light (expressed in lumens per real square foot of model floor area) to measured illumination (in footcandles) and to brightness (in footlamberts) will be the same as the corresponding ratios in the full-size space. For instance, if 500 lumens in a 2-square-foot model (250 lumens per square foot) produce an average horizontal illumination of 100 footcandles on the floor and an average wall brightness of 75 footlamberts, then a 200-square-foot room with the same proportions and surface reflectances would require $500 \times 100 = 50{,}000$ lumens (250 lumens per square foot) introduced in an identical manner to produce identical average measurements.

If a model is placed outdoors under the real sky, assuming that correct reflectances have been used for all visible surfaces and correct transmission properties have been used for all windows and skylights, no scale corrections need to be made in the evaluation of

Harry Weese & Associates

101 *WMATA presentation model*

Harry Weese & Associates

102 *WMATA surface station model: as in the models of the subsurface stations, lighting effects were simulated with inexpensive custom-made lengths of neon tube.*

a daylighting design, because in a scale model the reduction in the area illuminated is offset by the simultaneous and proportional reduction of the size of the daylight sources (the openings in the model).

Room models may be evaluated most conveniently and realistically via the medium of projected color slides, which minimizes visual noise from surrounding, out-of-scale elements in the visual environment, thereby maximizing the perceptual credibility of the model scene.

Even though a model may have been built only to evaluate a lighting effect or to make measurements, it is essential that it be furnished as realistically as possible if it will be shown to observers or clients who are not designers. Because visual perception is a gestalt process, a poorly executed or furnished model can destroy the credibility of both the model and the design team in the eyes of the client.

Component models

When a design involves repetitive elements such as ceiling coffers which are to be used as indirect light fixtures, a component model may be useful in demonstrating the appearance of a single module and can be used to generate quantitative data concerning light distribution characteristics and efficiencies which can be extrapolated for various larger spaces. Such models can be executed in very little time, and the subsequent extrapolations are not difficult. To simulate the appearance of larger areas, the component model can be placed between mirrors.

Engineers frequently oppose design proposals involving integrated lighting systems, in which the "luminaire" is a system of ceiling coffers and room surfaces (so that the room itself acts as a light fixture) because they are unable to calculate the illumination levels which such a system will produce. There are indeed no cookbook formulas and tables which can be consulted to determine the performance of such a system, but illuminated models can be built and measured to find the required data. One must remember, though, that the *exact* quantity of illumination is relatively unimportant, compared with the appearance and relevance of the final luminous environment.

When lighting is to be integrated into architectural elements such as walls, handrails, kiosks, bollards, or furnishings, component models make it easy to test and evaluate the concept and to refine the details. Illuminated models of hardware can also be built to evaluate the appearance, efficiency, and light distribution characteristics of novel fixture designs. These models can be built from such simple materials as reflective mylar, cardboard, and tracing paper, combined with commercially available fixtures and lamps (for an example, see **Fig. C5–12**).

Renderings

The rendering has always been an important graphic tool of the designer, but most contemporary renderings do not accurately convey what the luminous environment will actually look like. With some care and thought about where the light will come from and how it will affect the relative brightness of the various visible surfaces, a realistic

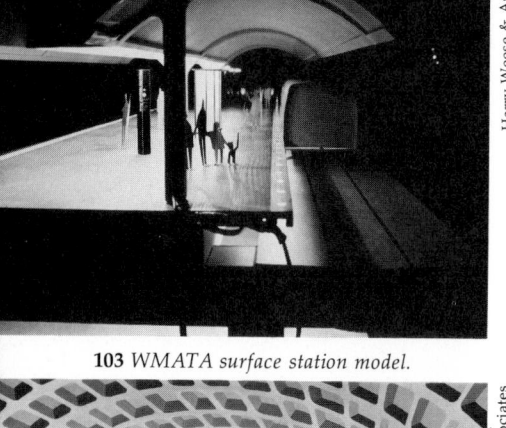

103 *WMATA surface station model.*

104 *Rendering, Metro Center Station.*

rendering is not too difficult to produce and can be almost as effective as model photographs in forecasting the actual appearance of a project as built. Compare **Figs. 104** and **101,** a rendering and a model photograph of one of the stations in the Washington subway system.

Renderings have the additional advantage that proposed furnishings can usually be more easily and convincingly sketched than modeled. Since renderings are produced for other purposes, they ought to be used to illustrate the planned lighting scheme as well.

Mock-ups

When no similar design exists, or when no comparable examples are available within a convenient distance for all involved in final decisions, a room mock-up can be invaluable, even though it may be necessary to substitute plywood for concrete, etc. On a major project where hundreds of thousands of dollars may have been invested in developing a design, the price tag of a well-detailed mock-up or of a field trip clear across the country will be insignificant compared to the costs of a major redesign or of having to start over again from scratch.

Because all perceptions are holistic, mock-ups even more than models must be realistically furnished as well as technically accurate in lighting details. They must be visually isolated from adjacent areas, particularly if these areas are unrelated to the design under study; otherwise, those who visit and evaluate the mock-up will be unable to ignore these unrelated and distracting elements in the visual field. When unfurnished and empty, a mock-up just like an actual building usually appears dull and gloomy, because the viewer subconsciously expects an interior environment to be complete and furnished, and frustration of this unconscious expectancy generates a negative response. Two identical spaces with identical lighting, one empty and one fully furnished, will elicit quite different responses from the same observers. Furnishings provide natural foci, obviously intentional points of interest, without which the eye roams about, seeking something else to look at that is worthwhile. Without normal furnishings and decorative elements, the attention of the viewer is drawn to features which in a furnished room would go unnoticed, such as uneven illumination of a wall, air grilles, minor defects in workmanship, etc. Omission of furnishings from a mock-up can easily lead to a totally erroneous and misleading negative evaluation.

Though the cost of a mock-up can often be justified for lighting purposes alone, they are valuable for many other purposes as well: the testing of unconventional air-distribution systems, the evaluation of the visual qualities of structural forms and surface finishes, detailing, etc. There are always many unexpected benefits from building full-scale room lighting mock-ups.

Evaluation of mock-ups must be done with great care so that any variances from reality are made explicit to all concerned. For instance, measurements of illumination levels made in a small, enclosed room mock-up, in which reflected light from the walls is an important component of the measured levels, will not give an accurate prediction of light levels in a space of different proportions or with different reflectances even though the lighting scheme may be identical. Though this should be obvious to anyone who understands the principles of perception and interreflection involved, far too often mock-ups are

Harry Weese & Associates/WMATA

105 *Partial full-scale mock-up of a typical subsurface WMATA station.*

Lam

106

viewed, measured, and evaluated without proper explanation of the differences between mock-up and reality.

The author has experienced all too many occasions when improper use of a mock-up led to serious misjudgment: library stack lighting evaluated with only a 4-foot length illuminated; rooms evaluated for pleasantness of lighting when unfinished, unfurnished, windowless, and with the temperature at 100° F; an on-site mock-up evaluated with the room temperature at 10° F and the lamps operating at about 5 percent of their normal output (since the fixtures had not been equipped with low temperature ballasts), mock-ups with the wrong room and furniture reflectances, etc.

When the construction of a realistic mock-up is impossible for cost or other reasons, the mock-up design should be modified as far as possible to compensate for the unavoidable distortions. It would have been prohibitively expensive, for instance, to build a full-scale 500-foot-long mock-up of an entire subway station, so we built only a 16-foot length of the station using the actual materials **(Fig. 105)**. The mock-up was furnished with the end of a real train, graphics pylons, and other equipment. In a long tubular space such as one of these subway stations which is illuminated from strip fixtures running along the long axis (between the tracks and concealed along the outside edges of the platforms), however, much of the light which falls on any point of the walls and ceiling comes from secondary reflections from other surfaces, not from the sources themselves. In a 16-foot length of a 50-foot-diameter tube, the proportions of the space are significantly different from those of a 500-foot-long section of the same tube from the point of view of how they interreflect light. In a short tube much of the light is lost out the open ends, which in a longer section would fall on other surfaces of the tube and contribute to its illumination. To correct for this relative inefficiency in the mock-up, we increased the number of fixtures per running foot of station over the number called for in the actual design until the ceiling vault reached the correct luminance. The use of mirrors on both end walls of the mock-up would have increased both the realism of the mock-up and the efficiency of the fixture utilization, but this expensive refinement was deemed unnecessary since the clients were able to evaluate the overall effect from the very realistic scale model **(Fig. 101)**.

There are, however, times when building a mock-up can cause more harm than good. It is unwise to build a mock-up where it can be seen by the client before the design team is satisfied with every detail, especially if the design is unconventional. If the client's first experience with a space is of a mock-up full of errors, omissions, and outdated details in incongruous combinations, the initial impression is likely to be very negative, and this kind of impression can be almost impossible to erase. The design of at least one major project was seriously compromised because this general rule was violated. The mock-up **(Fig. 106)** was built in the project field office, and was used regularly for meetings during a lengthy period of experimentation and refinement of the design. Obsolete details were left in place next to their successors, so that the viewer was left with an indelible impression of visual chaos and overall lack of coordination. Still worse, neither the enclosing walls nor the proper furnishings were ever installed. It is virtually impossible to convey to a client the image of a building system free from visual noise when visual noise in the spaces surrounding the mock-up is not screened off.

While it was possible for the designers to use this mock-up to measure light levels and distribution from which they could calculate the anticipated illumination levels in the finished building, it was almost impossible for inexperienced observers to imagine what the finished space would be like. In the space they saw before their eyes, much of the light was lost to the dark, unrelated surroundings, rather than being reflected back by light-colored walls—a key part of the design which was never installed in the mock-up.

Properly executed mock-ups were built for the Hyatt Regency Houston Hotel, the MacMillan-Bloedel Building in Vancouver, and the Santa Clara County Civic Building (respectively **Case Studies C9, E8,** and **E5**). These mock-ups—properly furnished, consistent in detailing, and realistic in materials and finishes—were eminently suitable as communication devices which could be shown to people outside the design team without fear of producing misconceptions.

When making mock-ups of perimeter rooms in which daylight will play an important role in the overall lighting scheme, the mock-up should always be built to produce a similar daylight effect, whether real or as accurately simulated as possible. If for some reason this is impossible, then the room should be evaluated only for nighttime conditions, and only at night. Because an observer adapted to daylight conditions expects daytime levels of brightness and a view through windows during daylight hours, he or she cannot realistically evaluate a mock-up which should include a daylight component and view, but does not. For the same reason, one cannot evaluate a nighttime effect during daylight hours.

Mock-ups of modular elements comprising less than a full room are used primarily for the gathering of data about illumination levels. For this purpose they are no more accurate than models, unless the type of lamps to be used are not available in a scaled-down version.

Fixture mock-ups

The construction of fixture mock-ups is unnecessary as long as standard catalog models are to be used. However, any special fixture designs should be tested for appearance and light distribution before being manufactured in quantity. Unless a special design incorporates critical optics or reflectors, cardboard construction which can be done in the designer's office will usually be adequate for the purpose. Like room models, fixture mock-ups are most valuable when used to refine the design.

Job site mock-ups

Full-scale room mock-ups can often be built at the job site for little if any extra cost. All that is required is for the contract documents to call for the completion of a small part of the building in advance. The minimal extra costs involved usually disappear in the competitive bidding process. If no models or mock-ups have been built during the design process, it is always worthwhile to test out the final design in all its details in time to make changes and improvements before the start of the full-blown construction process. Even if models and mock-ups have already been built, the design can always be refined further. Contractor errors can be discovered before they have been repeated thousands of times; usually, the contractor as well as the design team will benefit, since unanticipated problems and cost-saving alternatives

107 *Fixture mock-up (from* **Case Study E3**).

108 *Room mock-up (from* **Case Study E3**).

may also be brought to light by this simple expedient. Furthermore, final decisions on detailing, colors, and finishes can best be made using actual samples of the real materials, juxtaposed in the correct relationship to each other under the real illumination in which they will actually be seen and used.

Cost-benefit studies

Of the various measures of performance commonly used, there is none more familiar than costs. Traditionally, cost criteria have often been set as the primary—and sometimes the *only*—explicit constraint to be met by a design. Because it is relatively easy to state cost controls in precise terms, there has been a tendency to overemphasize cost per delivered footcandle as a measure of performance.

There are two principal ways of looking at costs in relation to design decisions. First, costs can be used as an absolute constraint: "For *x* amount of expenditure, what is the best possible environment which we can create?" Second, costs can be used as a measure of *relative* performance: to evaluate the relative merits of different design solutions *if all solutions meet the design criteria equally well.* Whenever possible, we prefer to use costs as a measure of relative performance, not as an absolute constraint to which the design must conform.

Cost-benefit studies should conform to the following common-sense but often ignored principles:

- *It is not valid to compare the costs of apples and oranges.* Costs being compared must always be carefully evaluated according to the relative "benefits" to be derived from alternative luminous environments. These must be put on some sort of comparable footing.

- *It is not valid to compare the costs of only certain individual components such as lamps or light fixtures.* Comparisons of both initial and operating costs must incorporate cost changes for *all* elements of the building which will be affected by the lighting decision in question. These may include costs of structure, mechanical components, operating costs of heating and air conditioning, painting, maintenance, moving of partitions, etc. A large percentage cost difference between two lamps may be an absolutely insignificant part of the total project budget, and therefore should not be taken as a basis for judgments which affect the user value of the entire project.

- *It is totally worthless to compare only costs per footcandle, since the footcandle per se is not a valid index of benefits.* The reader should understand by now that footcandle levels are only one dimension of a total luminous

environment, and a relatively unimportant
dimension at that, once quite low levels
have been achieved.

With all the perceptual subtleties inherent in the evaluation of
alternative luminous environments, the most realistic way to judge
their relative merits is to present the client not with numbers but with
full-scale mock-ups of the alternatives, with their corresponding price
tags. This was done during the design of the MacMillan-Bloedel
Building; the mock-ups are shown in **Figs. E8–10** and **E8–11.** The
type of judgment involved in the ranking of alternative luminous
environments is in principle no different than choosing between cars
or chairs of varying qualities and prices. Weighing the benefits of
various alternatives can be facilitated by a checklist tabulation against
the programmed objectives and their relative priorities. A weighted
judgment based on an evaluation of all factors is much more likely to
be sound than a judgment based solely on an exact measurement of
only one of the many factors involved, such as horizontal
footcandles—the touchstone of the conventional design process.

Summary: new objectives and design implications

In terms of both methodology and objectives, the conventional
contemporary process of lighting design is highly unsatisfactory. The
tools at the disposal of the designer are often conceptually deficient,
the design process is poorly structured to maximize communication
between members of the design team, and the objectives themselves
are frequently irrelevant and sometimes even counterproductive. There
is little attention to energy conservation in terms of both operating
procedures and hardware development. There is little recognition of
the complexities and subtleties of human perception and of the
desirability of using light and lighting equipment to do more than just
deliver footcandles—to provide orientation and guidance information,
to minimize visual noise, to satisfy biological information needs, etc.

There is a great need for new design processes and tools, more
communication between the members of the design team, more
relevant objectives, and simpler and more visual working tools. The
creation of successful, relevant, comfortable, well-integrated, and
consistent luminous environments must once again be reinstated as
the overriding objective of lighting design. We need to *do* more with
less, to fight against wasteful and counterproductive levels of
illumination promoted by the power and lighting industry. We need
to add positive objectives such as the creation of positive focus,
sparkle, orientation, and guidance, and lighting for biological needs, to
the conventional objectives of eliminating glare, providing adequate
task lighting, etc. To this end, a number of design recommendations
based on the principles of perception outlined in the previous
chapters are summarized in the following rules of thumb.

Some rules of thumb for good design

1. A clear design intent should be evident in all elements of the visual field. Visual perception is a gestalt experience: clear synthesis of related elements and architectural systems facilitates their comprehension, and establishes a consistent background of visual relationships which can be modulated in a meaningful way to provide subtle but extremely valuable orientation and guidance information.

2. When structure is to be illuminated directly, the resulting gradients of light should emphasize its salient characteristics—the module, the shape, and the material—in a consistent and complementary fashion. When structural elements cannot be positively and consistently illuminated, the designer should not light them directly at all, but should rather rely on reflected light from other directly illuminated surfaces to light the structure.

3. In general, one should illuminate continuous planar elements such as walls evenly, or with even gradients, so that they *appear* continuous. When an expression of the continuity of a flat surface is not regarded as an important design feature, the surface *can* be illuminated unevenly without appearing unnatural or distorted—for instance, when a decorative element such as a painting or plant hung on the wall is to be highlighted, or when the wall receives spill light from lamps which clearly relate to furnishings or which are used as wall brackets to define entrances, or when a definite rhythm of light gradients is clearly related to rhythms of panel joints, structural beams or coffers, etc.

4. To conform with expectations, use light sources of relatively low color temperature at low levels of illumination, and sources of higher color temperature at higher levels of illumination. For interior lighting, warm colored sources such as incandescent and warm white fluorescent are preferable.

5. Because of adaptation and time orientation, a given amount of artificial lighting in interior spaces will appear much brighter at night than during the day. To conserve energy, provide switching and dimming controls so that illumination may be reduced at night to the relatively low levels which are expected and required for nighttime activities.

6. Whenever possible, design glazing to satisfy the basic biological needs for a view of outdoor conditions and contact with sunlight. In general, the principal function of windows should be to satisfy these important biological needs, rather than to provide task lighting for activity needs which can usually be more easily and economically provided by artificial lighting. Fenestration should be planned in conjunction with artificial lighting, so that the two complement each other. In most buildings, artificial lighting at the perimeter should be placed on separate circuits *with easily accessible switches* so that it can be turned off when daylight provides adequate illumination.

7. The shape and placement of exterior windows should be derived primarily from the nature of the view. Avoid clerestories through which nothing can be seen, unless they are used to bring sunlight into interior portions of a building which would otherwise have no contact with exterior conditions. In high buildings the portion of windows above eye height is of little use from the point of satisfying biological needs, and usually introduces substantial sky glare. Since the response to unpleasant sky glare is typically to draw the draperies, which cuts off the desirable portions of the view at the same time as the offending portions, it is advisable to restrict window height to less than, say, 7 feet. Alternatively, if full height windows are to be used, provide a means by which the upper portion of the window can be screened selectively—blinds, for instance, rather than or in addition to draperies.

8. To eliminate sources of visual noise, it is better to use large-scale elements such as deep window reveals for sunshading so that the resulting areas of uninterrupted view are sufficiently large to be comprehensible. If this is not possible, go to the other extreme, using very fine mesh screen, draperies, or blinds which overlay an even texture on the view rather than

adding a competing pattern, creating a figure-background conflict.

9. There is no unique and perceptually "correct" method for the illumination of three-dimensional objects. As long as the nature and location of the sources of light are evident, almost any approach which reveals the desired information characteristics of the objects can be used without causing confusion.

10. Because of simultaneous contrast and adaptation, objects with identical luminance levels appear brighter when seen against a darker background. This fundamental principle is particularly useful in the design of relevant foci for the luminous environment. When, for reasons of preservation, illumination levels on a painting must be kept low, for instance, the painting alone should be illuminated against a relatively dark background, and both direct sunlight and views of objects illuminated by direct sunlight should be excluded from the space, so that the eye will adapt successfully to the low illumination levels in the display space. Remember that for the eye to detect a noticeable difference in brightness, the luminance of the focal object should be *at least* twice that of its immediate surroundings. To create a real sense of focus, a brightness ratio of at least 10 to 1 is usually necessary.

11. Judgments of an environment as orderly or chaotic are always made with reference to background and context. Irregular arrangements of architectural elements such as lighting equipment, partitions, and furnishings seem more orderly and less distracting when seen against plain backgrounds. Partitions which are higher than eye level will be perceived against the context of the ceiling structure, and should therefore be carefully related to the visual organization of the ceiling structure. Irregular or directionless office landscape partitioning should be kept at or below eye level, unless the ceiling is directionless and visually neutral.

12. Emphasize potentially dangerous edges in circulation paths by changes in material, the use of color, or definitive shadows, particularly when illumination levels must be low for some reason.

13. To maximize the signal-to-noise ratio of backlighted graphics, use signs in which the letters are brighter than the background. Avoid backlighted signs in which opaque lettering is superimposed on an illuminated translucent background.

14. The various elements of the visual environment have an inherent hierarchy of attractiveness to the focus selector, which is influenced in part by their relative (not their absolute) brightness. Where directional graphics are important, avoid placing competing, distracting patterns of informationless light fixtures near the graphic elements.

15. To avoid the "black hole" effect in windows at night from interior spaces, cover them with drapery or, better still, illuminate elements of the exterior environment which you would like to see—landscape, sculpture, etc. The latter solution increases feelings of security by reducing the unknown and therefore potentially threatening aspects of the exterior environment.

16. Do not try to backlight draperies in an attempt to simulate the effect of daylight. The human mind is too keen to be taken in by such tricks. For similar reasons, a backlighted Kodachrome mural of a landscape cannot create a successful illusion of an exterior view in an interior or an underground space.

17. Grazing light always highlights any irregularities in the surface upon which it falls. It can be used to bring out the texture of a wall, as a positive design element, or, if used incautiously, it can emphasize every defect in workmanship. When a wall is to be illuminated with grazing light, therefore, be sure that it has a desirable and appropriate texture—use raked joints for brickwork **(Fig. 109),** or lay the units up with deliberate irregularity. Use rough textured concrete forms, or accentuate joint lines and tie holes when using plywood formwork. If a wall which will be illuminated by grazing light is intended to be perfectly smooth and regular, on the other hand, specify that it should be constructed under illumination conditions similar to the final design. When designing smooth walls which are likely to be imperfect for reasons of workmanship, try to plan the arrangement of likely trouble spots such as joints in

drywall construction so that their visibility will be minimized—orient them parallel to the direction of the incident illumination rather than perpendicular to it, or hide them with elements such as tack strips, bumper rails, picture-hanging slots, etc.

18. Avoid creating a focus in the luminous environment on unpleasant, undesirable or distracting elements. It is just as important to decide what *not* to light as it is to decide what to light. Obviously, a design methodology which aims only at providing more than some specified minimum level of illumination throughout a space has a built-in bias against this sort of selective illumination.

19. Wherever possible, avoid creating figure-background conflicts, such as those caused by striped or "checkerboard" lighting configurations where illuminated areas of ceilings are approximately equal in size and shape to adjacent unlighted areas.

20. Avoid the use of very low (i.e., 10 percent or less) transmission glass when the glazed area will be regularly compared with clear or unglazed openings such as open windows or doors. Under these conditions, low-transmission glass will always make the exterior seem gloomy by comparison.

21. Avoid materials such as translucent walls and glass blocks, unless they serve a definite decorative purpose—stained glass, for instance. Avoid translucent skylights which take on the informationless character of featureless fluorescent diffusers, destroying potential contact with biologically desirable sunlight and exterior conditions. Use clear skylights of relatively small area for desirable architectural definition and to introduce elements of direct sunlight into interior spaces. If the skylights themselves would appear too small in proportion to the room, use pyramidal skylight wells to increase their apparent size without increasing the solar heat load or the projected area in which the direct sunlight may interfere with activities.

22. In the interests of minimizing visual noise, avoid using light-control devices such as louvers in skylights and artificial lighting details if such devices are not really necessary. Such elements, in and of themselves, are of little visual interest, and

they should be used only when the same purpose cannot be accomplished through careful integration of the lighting hardware with other architectural elements. Light sources may be effectively baffled using elements such as the edges of ceilings, beams, valences, cabinets, etc. Fixtures can be concealed in bollards, handrails, recessed slots, and in the flanges of major structural elements. Under most circumstances, the use of simple, understandable, unobtrusive control devices such as the low brightness "black cone" in direct lighting fixtures is preferable to the use of louvers of more complex shape, unless the light fixture in its designed context is intended to serve as a true positive focal element, a piece of sculpture in its own right. Since baffles and louvers used to control light distribution are typically very close to the sources themselves, they can very easily become the brightest elements in the visual field, achieving an entirely unwarranted and inappropriate prominence.

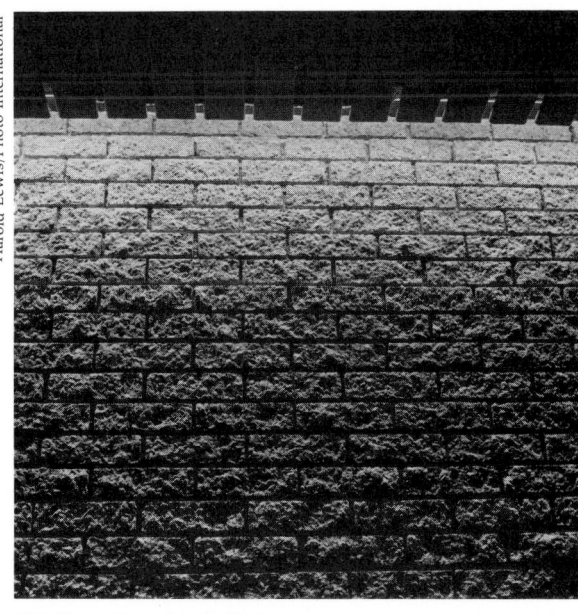

Harold Lewis/Photo International

109 (*From* **Case Study H5**).

CASE STUDIES

PRINCIPLES APPLIED IN PRACTICE

All case studies presented here are from the consulting practice of William Lam Associates, Inc.

Introduction

In any given project, the real design process is always influenced by many factors: among them are timing, design budget, the attitude toward teamwork of the various persons involved, and the complexity of the problem. The quality of the design process is always reflected in the quality of the finished product. A lighting designer may be involved in the overall design process at a number of levels. He or she may be reduced to making the best of a series of prior decisions over which he or she had no control or influence. Better, lighting input may lead to modification of structure, mechanical systems, and other elements of the finished building to achieve a more successful, appropriate, comprehensible luminous environment. Ideally, lighting considerations and perception principles become principal formgivers in an integrated team design process.

In the following case studies, examples of each level of involvement are presented. The case studies demonstrate how the perceptual requirements of different activities may affect all aspects of design, and how similar activity needs may imply different design forms under different circumstances. The use of various tools in the design process is discussed at some length, as are a number of design failures and their causes.

The case studies have been grouped into various categories to simplify discussion and to demonstrate that the application of perception principles is never simple, but is affected by every nuance of other decisions. There are many ways in which the case studies might have been grouped. The cross-fertilization of concepts and their gradual refinement would have been most easily traced in a chronological presentation. Arrangement by building types was considered, but was rejected on the grounds that it would not necessarily bring out the most important common organizational features of related projects. To clarify these features, therefore, projects have been grouped by complexity of program and of the corresponding design process, starting with single interior spaces and buildings dominated by a single space, graduating in complexity to growth systems, clusters of spaces, and finally to entire complexes of buildings.

The first category of projects includes spaces in which the lighting design primarily responds to the activities housed. This category is further subdivided into two groups: BUILDINGS DOMINATED BY A SINGLE MAJOR SPACE and SINGLE SPACES DEFINED BY MODULAR ELEMENTS.

The third group, SEQUENCES OF MAJOR SPACES IN A SINGLE STRUCTURE, demonstrates how the design of individual spaces may be affected by the design of other spaces in the same structure, even though they may have quite different uses.

In the fourth group, SEQUENCES OF SPACES ORGANIZED ALONG FIXED CORRIDORS, projects are presented in which the existence of a system of fixed corridors was used as a strong organizing principle for the entire design, reinforced and expanded through lighting.

The fifth major group, SEQUENCES OF SPACES WITHOUT FIXED CORRIDORS: ARTICULATED SYSTEMS FITTED TO PREDETERMINED EXTERIOR FORMS, contains projects for which the design team developed integrated building systems—systems which include lighting, mechanical, and structural components—which would allow a wide range of spatial subdivision. The structural, mechanical, and lighting systems of projects in this group were given a strong exposed expression.

In the sixth group, SEQUENCES OF SPACES WITHOUT FIXED CORRIDORS: FLAT-CEILING SYSTEMS FITTED TO PREDETERMINED EXTERIOR FORMS, programmatically similar projects are presented in which structural and mechanical systems were hidden above a "homogenized"[1] uniform suspended ceiling plane with a regular pattern of recessed light fixtures.

The seventh group, GROWTH SYSTEMS, is one of the most interesting. It includes projects varying in size from single buildings to entire building complexes, each of which was largely the result of the development of a flexible, articulated, integrated module incorporating structure, mechanical channels, and lighting systems.

[1]By a "homogenized solution" I mean an approach which conceals all structure and mechanical appurtenances above a suspended ceiling, usually flat and unarticulated, and in which there is little or no evident intent to integrate structural and mechanical systems in such a way as (1) to maximize perceptible room volumes within a given floor-to-floor dimension, (2) to create natural service channels in the structure, and (3) to use the actual surfaces of the structure as sources of illumination for the spaces which they enclose, through the use of indirect lighting (sometimes supplemented by unobtrusive direct lighting).

With these basic three-dimensional building blocks, expansion of projects in any direction, in small or large increments, is always possible as desired—hence the title "growth systems." The special characteristics of these structures make them particularly suitable for infill projects.

Combinations of spaces and groups of spaces, which taken as individual buildings would fall into one or more of the preceding groups, have been consolidated into the eighth group, BUILDING COMPLEXES. Special attention is paid to the problem of providing adequate orientation in complexes which are linked below grade.

All the case studies have been selected from projects in which the author was personally involved, so that the design process and initial intent could be presented as well as the final results. For most projects, the statement of programmatic objectives given in the case study is verbal, as it was during the actual design process. The reader can judge whether or not the stated conceptual objectives were realized in the projects as built. In many instances, comments and criticism have been included to point out where mistakes and compromises eroded the initial design concepts.

As an index for the reader who is particularly interested in one specific building type, combination of integrated building systems, lighting strategy, etc., the chart printed inside the back cover summarizes the salient characteristics of all the case studies, listed chronologically.

CASE STUDIES GROUPS

A   BUILDINGS DOMINATED BY A SINGLE MAJOR SPACE

B   SINGLE SPACES DEFINED BY MODULAR ELEMENTS

C   SEQUENCES OF MAJOR SPACES IN A SINGLE STRUCTURE

D   SEQUENCES OF SPACES ORGANIZED ALONG FIXED CORRIDORS

E   SEQUENCES OF SPACES WITHOUT FIXED CORRIDORS: ARTICULATED SYSTEMS FITTED TO PREDETERMINED EXTERIOR FORMS

F   SEQUENCES OF SPACES WITHOUT FIXED CORRIDORS: FLAT-CEILING SYSTEMS FITTED TO PREDETERMINED EXTERIOR FORMS

G   GROWTH SYSTEMS

H   BUILDING COMPLEXES: SEQUENCES OF MAJOR MASSES

CASE STUDIES GROUP A

BUILDINGS DOMINATED BY A SINGLE MAJOR SPACE

The design of the luminous environment for the buildings in this first group of case studies responded primarily to the needs for visual information inherent in the principal space or space type around which each is organized. We know that the luminous environment for any space must relate to the activity and biological needs of its users, and that a good visual environment is one in which all visual information is relevant—visual noise is at a minimum. This happens when the illumination for each activity comes from an environment that simultaneously serves other needs, either activity or biological—an environment which appears relevant, in which constancies are not upset and everything appears "natural" for each specific activity at each specific time. If a space houses only a single activity, then design is easy: provide optimum illumination for that activity. A theater during the performance, for instance, is almost totally focused, the information needs of the audience being entirely related to the stage activities. In fact, however, a pure single need for visual information almost never exists. Even in the theater, for instance, the audience needs to know how to escape in case of fire — hence, the competing EXIT sign, the aisle lights, etc.

Then comes intermission, and the needs of the audience shift to relaxation, social stimulation, perhaps the sense of "event," orientation within the space and to others in the building, reading of programs, notices of future attractions, etc. When activities with very different needs take place sequentially, as in the theater or a classroom, then the luminous environment must be adaptable to those changing needs. A theater must appear very different during the performance than during the intermission.

If, on the other hand, many activities with very different needs take place simultaneously but in different rooms or areas of a room, it may be necessary for the user to move within the space that is provided for the various specific activities in order to find optimal luminous conditions for each activity. Where simultaneity of varied activities prohibits the responsive adjustment of the entire luminous environment to meet local needs, provision of a variety of different lighting conditions in different areas of the space may be the only feasible solution.

Only if all activities must take place simultaneously and in fixed locations — so that the luminous environment cannot be readjusted and the occupants cannot move to a new place for each new activity — is it appropriate to provide a luminous environment with a high *overall* level of neutral general illumination, giving a satisfactory condition at all locations for all activities with a minimum of visual noise and maximizing the occupants' ability to focus at will. Where local lighting of critical tasks is feasible, however, it is generally more economical to combine local lighting on demanding tasks with a much lower level of general illumination appropriate to and adequate for less critical activities elsewhere in the space.

Effective illumination of spaces defined by the shape of the room is simple, effective, and economical when it can be easily accomplished from totally concealed sources, or when the room definition can be combined with the creation of a desired local focus. A study illuminated by a single desk lamp which simultaneously illuminates the ceiling and walls is a good example of this type of lighting.

REMODELLING OF THE INSTITUTION FOR SAVINGS
Newburyport, Massachusetts

Stahl/Bennett, Inc. (architect); Lawrence F. Roeder (project architect); William Lam Associates, Inc. (lighting consultants); Herosy Associates (electrical engineers); Barstow Engineering (mechanical engineers); LeMessurier Associates (structural engineers). Construction completed 1969. Lighting load: 1.9 watts per square foot.

1

The Newburyport Institution for Savings **(1)** was built in 1870 and is considered an important part of the town's architectural heritage. Before calling on a lighting consultant, the owners had rejected proposals for "improving" the illumination via the usual engineered array of pendent direct/indirect fluorescent fixtures, unrelated to either existing forms or materials, which would have satisfied only a few of the many needs. The visual noise inherent in such a system would have destroyed the character of the space.

In a bank, the general lighting design should create a pleasant, cheerful environment which fosters communication between staff and customers, provides well for clerical activities, and conveys an image of a progressive institution with a sense of human values.

Design

The location of counters and screen walls in relation to the walls and ceiling made illumination of the latter surfaces from the former the obvious solution. Details **(2,3)** were developed to minimize the presence of the sources and the amount of necessary construction. The indirect lighting was supplemented by neutral, recessed incandescent downlights. While downlights alone could have supplied all of the required desk-top illumination, the darker walls and ceiling would have rendered the space more gloomy on overcast days and more glaring at night.

Photos by
Harold Lewis/Photo
International

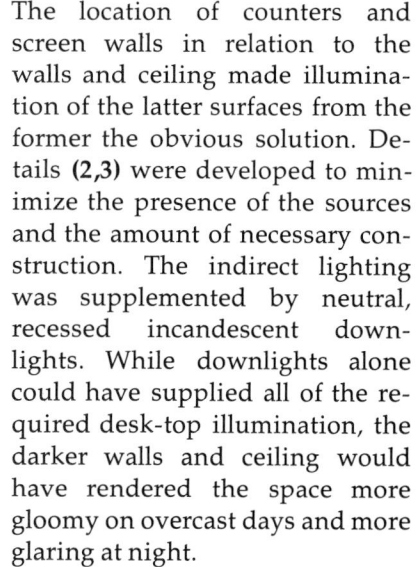

2

3 *Indirect mercury fixtures concealed in the screen wall.*

4

1

AUDITORIUM, OSCAR G. MAYER HALL
BELOIT COLLEGE
Beloit, Wisconsin

Harry Weese & Associates (architect); Benjamin Weese and Stanley Allan (project managers); William Lam Associates, Inc. (lighting consultants); Michael J. Kodaris (acoustical consultant); McKee-Berger-Mansueto, Inc. (cost consultants); Dolores Miller & Associates (interior design consultants); S. R. Lewis Associates (mechanical and electrical engineers); The Engineers Collaborative (structural engineers); Cunningham Brothers, Inc. (general contractor). Schematic design started May 1965. Construction completed September 1967.

When lighting design began, this room within a science building **(1)** was characterized by its rounded brick walls that flowed out into the adjacent lobby. While the auditorium floor rakes downward, its ceiling plane was extended throughout the adjacent spaces at a constant height with no change of materials, to express the continuity of the spaces.

Design

The wood-screen ceiling **(3)** seemed an appropriate means to express the continuity of the lobby and the auditorium, while allowing the necessary variations in acoustic treatment, air conditioning, and lighting. Its detailing began with the placement of downlighting fixtures so that they would articulate junctions in the ceiling rather than penetrate it arbitrarily. Bands of slats containing the fixed lighting were fastened permanently in position, while panels of slats between were left removable for access.

Two separate sets of baffled downlights were arranged: the first to illuminate the perimeter walls defining the space and the second to illuminate the seating area without spilling onto the walls **(4)**. During projection, only the latter are used, dimmed **(5)**.

Critique

At the stage end, the ceiling was to have been held back from the front wall so that chalkboard light-

ing would be totally concealed (above and behind the front edge of the ceiling). Unfortunately, this detail was omitted and the resulting visible recessed lights **(7)** are an unnecessary distracting blemish.

Had the illuminated walls been contained entirely within the auditorium rather than allowed to flow continuously into the lobby, the edge-slot technique would have been used rather than the recessed wall-washer units within the ceiling screen.

Note that the lobby **(8)** is intentionally illuminated unevenly, with walls and entrance points highlighted to provide desirable orientation and a pleasantly focused environment.

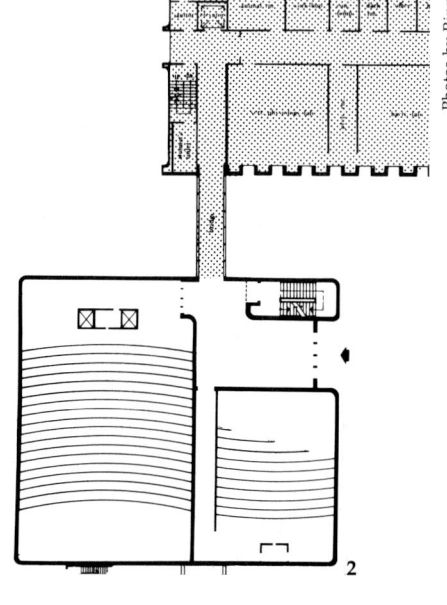

2

3 *Ceiling structure (which would normally be invisible) is revealed by the photographer's strobe.*

Photos by Ripman

7

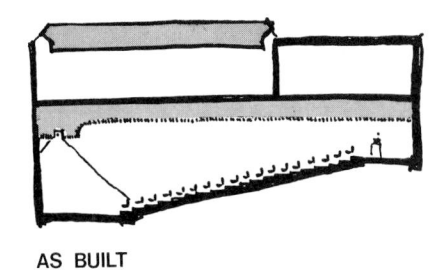

AS BUILT

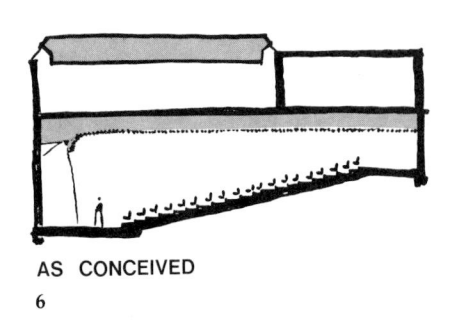

AS CONCEIVED

6

8

FIRST BAPTIST CHURCH OF COLUMBUS
Columbus, Indiana

A3

Harry Weese & Associates (architect); Dan Kiley (landscape architect); William Lam Associates, Inc. (lighting consultants); Dolores Miller & Associates (interior design consultant); Samuel R. Lewis & Associates (mechanical engineers); The Engineers Collaborative (structural engineers); Repp & Mundt Construction Service (general contractor). Schematic design started 1963.

1

The primary needs for illumination in a church are biological. Architect Harry Weese's concept was to create a warm, restful, lofty space with a focus on the side-lighted area at the front.

From the exterior, this complex of buildings appears as two powerful roof shapes sitting on a base of brick walls. The major interior spaces are also dominated by the roof shape. Thus, the obvious illumination scheme for the space was to balance the brightly daylighted chancel by highlighting the lofty wood surfaces of the roof—not uniformly, but in a manner that would emphasize the shape of the space and the "seating" of the roof structure of the brick base.

The brick ledge around the nave offered a natural place for locating fluorescent lamps with which to crosslight the vault **(7a)**, and the decking was raised some-

what to increase the lamp-to-decking distance, to minimize any "hot spots" above the fixtures **(4)**. Note that wide spaces such as this are primarily crosslighted. Only the ceiling near the lamps receives more light perpendicular to its surface from the adjacent lamps than from those on the opposite side. The lighting at the ledge is continued wherever the ledge-roof relationship remains constant. But at the chancel, the brick screen and altar are emphasized via skylights during the day and in several possible ways at night **(5,8)**.

Architecturally neutral incandescent "cans" at the apex **(7b)** can be used to supplement the indirect lighting system. More important, they can be used *instead* of the glowing ceiling—at night, when there is no need to balance the brightness of the day-lighted chancel, or when a more

dramatic, dark space is desired, e.g., for a candlelight service.

Note that with these room proportions, only one row of cans at the apex is required to illuminate the floor area uniformly. If, however, the architectural decision had been made to place the fixtures lower, more fixtures on a tighter spacing would have been required **(7c)**. Fixture spacing to achieve a uniform *distribution* of light is a function of the mounting height and beam spread characteristics of the fixtures chosen; size of lamp can be subsequently selected to provide the desired illumination levels.

Equal consideration was given to supporting spaces such as classrooms, social hall, offices, etc. These are illuminated in a manner similar to the main church and chapel, varied according to their own geometry and activity needs **(6)**.

2   3

Photos: Harold Lewis/Photo International

4 . 5

6

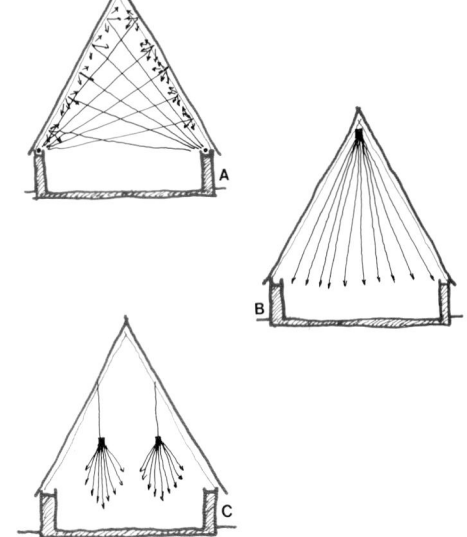

7 *Schematic lighting sections:*

   (a) *Continuous indirect fixtures on top of the perimeter walls crosslight the vault surfaces evenly.*

   (b) *By locating the downlights high in the space the team was able to achieve very even illumination with good glare control. If the fixtures had been located lower in the space, as in* **(c)**, *more fixtures would have been required to achieve the same uniformity of lighting and a great deal of unpleasant visual noise would have been introduced into the space by the pendent hardware.*

8 →

1

THE JAMES MADISON BARKER ENGINEERING LIBRARY
Massachusetts Institute of Technology
Cambridge, Massachusetts

A4

Skidmore, Owings & Merrill (architect); Walter Netsch (partner in charge); William Lam Associates, Inc. (lighting consultants); Bolt, Beranek and Newman (acoustical consultants); Fuller Construction Company (general contractor). Schematic design started 1965.

The central dome has always been an important part of the exterior image of MIT. The interior space immediately under the dome was originally the library, an important space (although never a visual focus or an important traffic junction because of its third-floor location). In the 1940s, the grand space was remodeled for "better" and more efficient lighting. In the process the space was completely obscured with a visually noisy, dingy, luminous plastic ceiling and its arbitrary supporting structure (6). When the library was converted into the James Madison Barker Engineering Library, the architects and consultants had the opportunity to retrieve the original assets, a grand space with fine details of the period still intact (2).

Design

To provide unobtrusive, complementary general lighting, the shape of the dome was emphasized by cross lighting from within (made possible by the presence of a surrounding attic). Walls and columns were painted white in order to minimize the dominance of the dome and to maximize utilization of reflected light. Additional illumination for specific activities was provided by local carrel lighting, with angled louvers (5,7) to minimize reflected glare, and by local highlighting of the publication racks. These illuminated racks were also conceived as an important source of diffused general lighting. Supplementary local lighting was provided for the reading chairs.

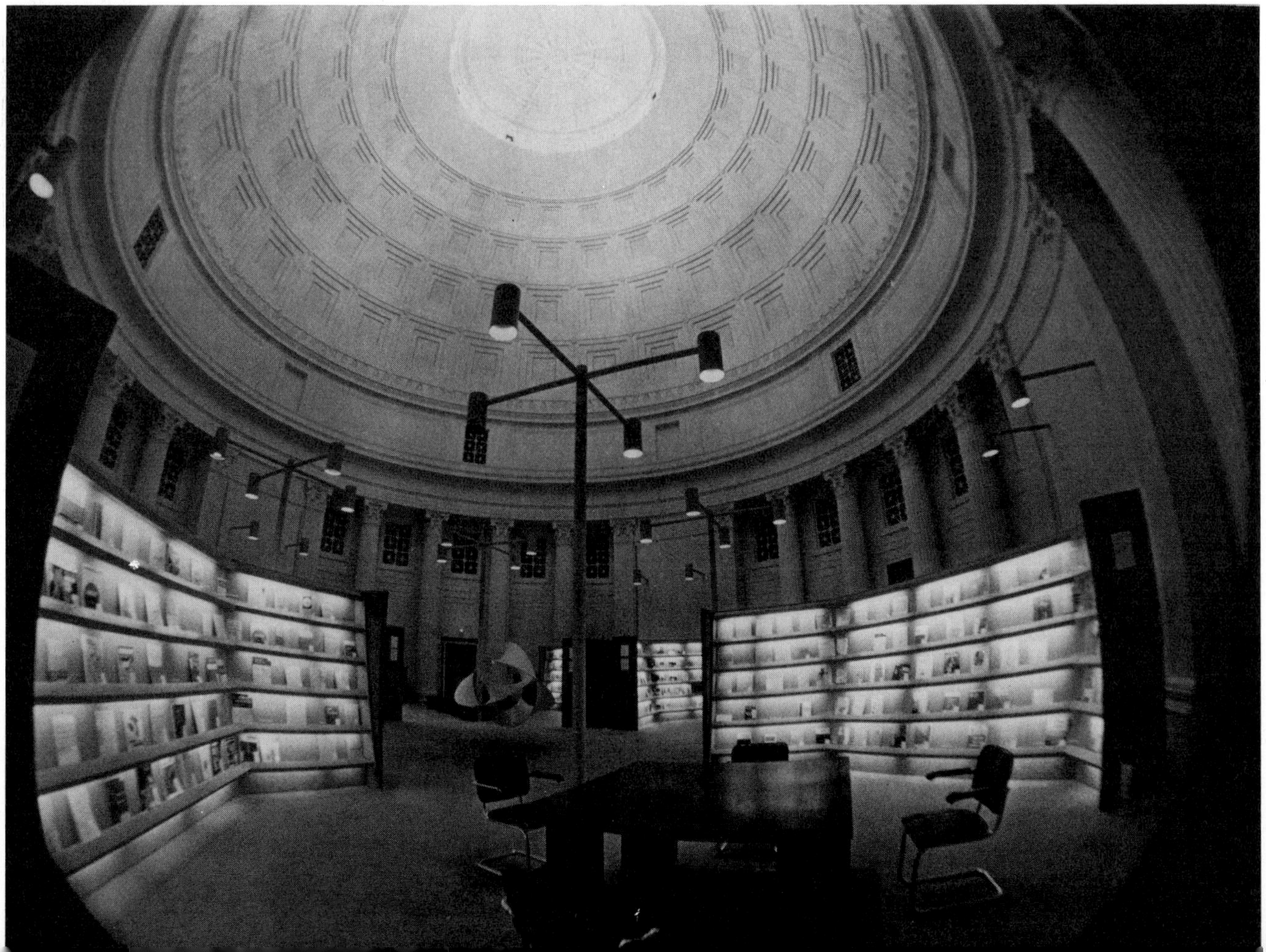

2

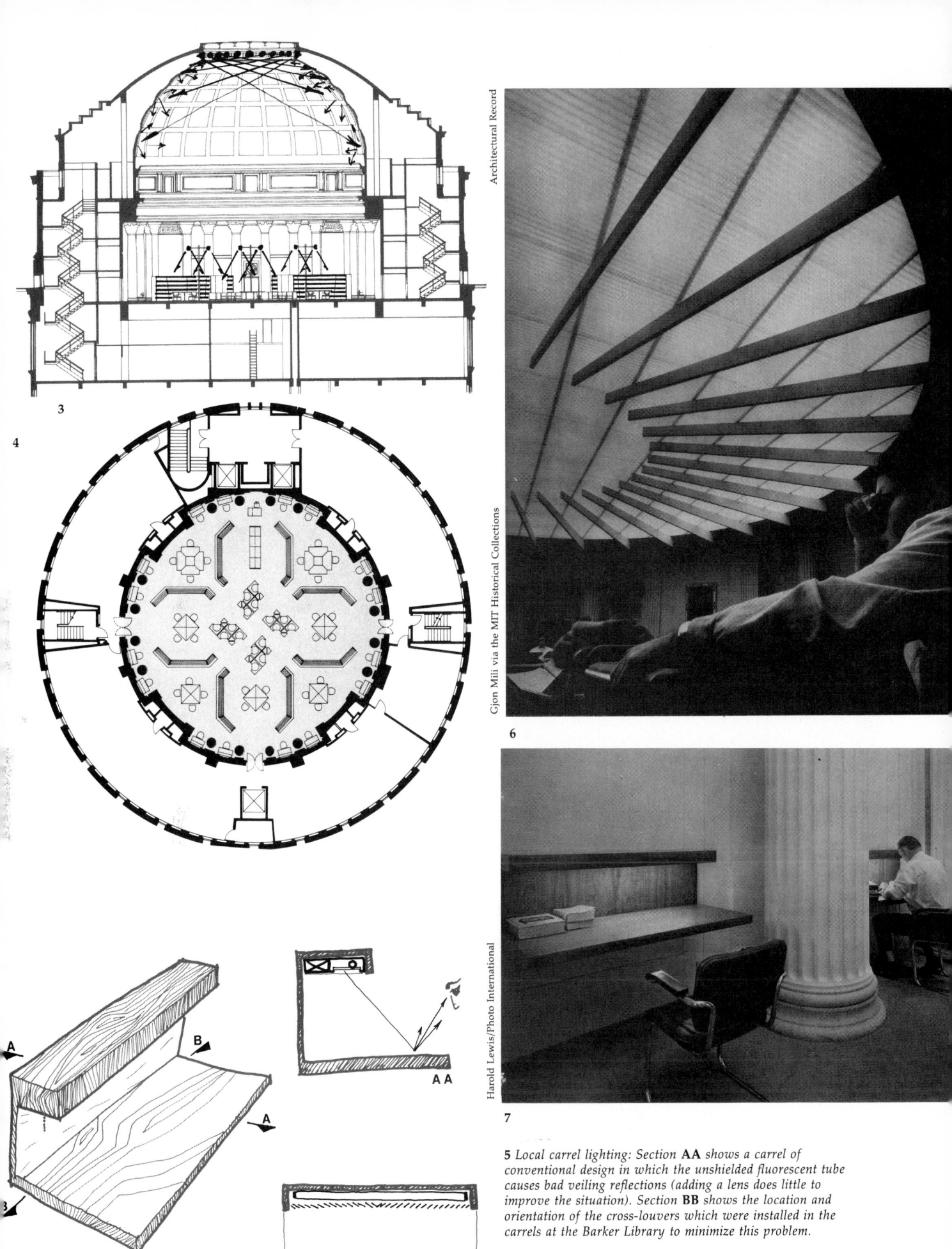

5 *Local carrel lighting: Section* **AA** *shows a carrel of conventional design in which the unshielded fluorescent tube causes bad veiling reflections (adding a lens does little to improve the situation). Section* **BB** *shows the location and orientation of the cross-louvers which were installed in the carrels at the Barker Library to minimize this problem.*

DRAKE UNIVERSITY DINING HALL ADDITION
Des Moines, Iowa

1

A5

Harry Weese & Associates (architect); Ben Weese (project architect); William Lam Associates, Inc. (lighting consultants); Dolores Miller & Associates (interior design consultants); S. R. Lewis & Associates (mechanical and electrical engineers); Paul Gordon (structural engineers); Weitz Company (general contractor). Cost: $700,000. Square footage: 27,882. Schematic design started 1964.

Harry Weese's extension **(1)** to the original Saarinen building maintained the cornice line and materials of the older building. The interior space, however, is of a totally different character, though similar materials and overall dimensions were used.

Design

Instead of giving interest to the large expanse of ceiling by the "attractions" of arbitrary circular lighting indentations **(4)**, as Saarinen had done, the shape of the total space in the Weese addition was emphasized by "floating" the ceiling free from the surrounding structure and highlighting the walls. The space was further articulated by raising and illuminating the central area of ceiling adjacent to the featured mural wall **(5)**, which was emphasized by means of a skylight supplemented by integral incandescent fixtures. The core, containing serving lines, meeting rooms, coatrooms, etc., was outlined by edge-slot lighting **(2)**. Note that no louvers are visible—the wall disappears into the slot, with the lamps out of sight from normal viewing positions.

Feiler Photo

2

3

Photos: Harr/Hedrich-Blessing

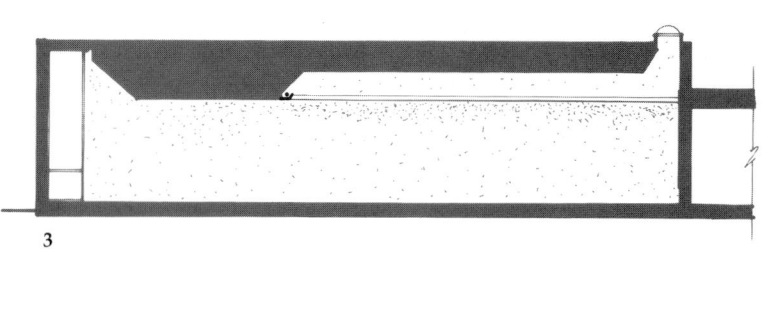

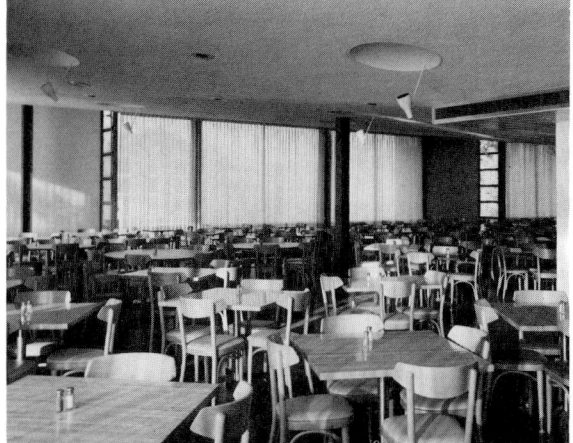

5

4

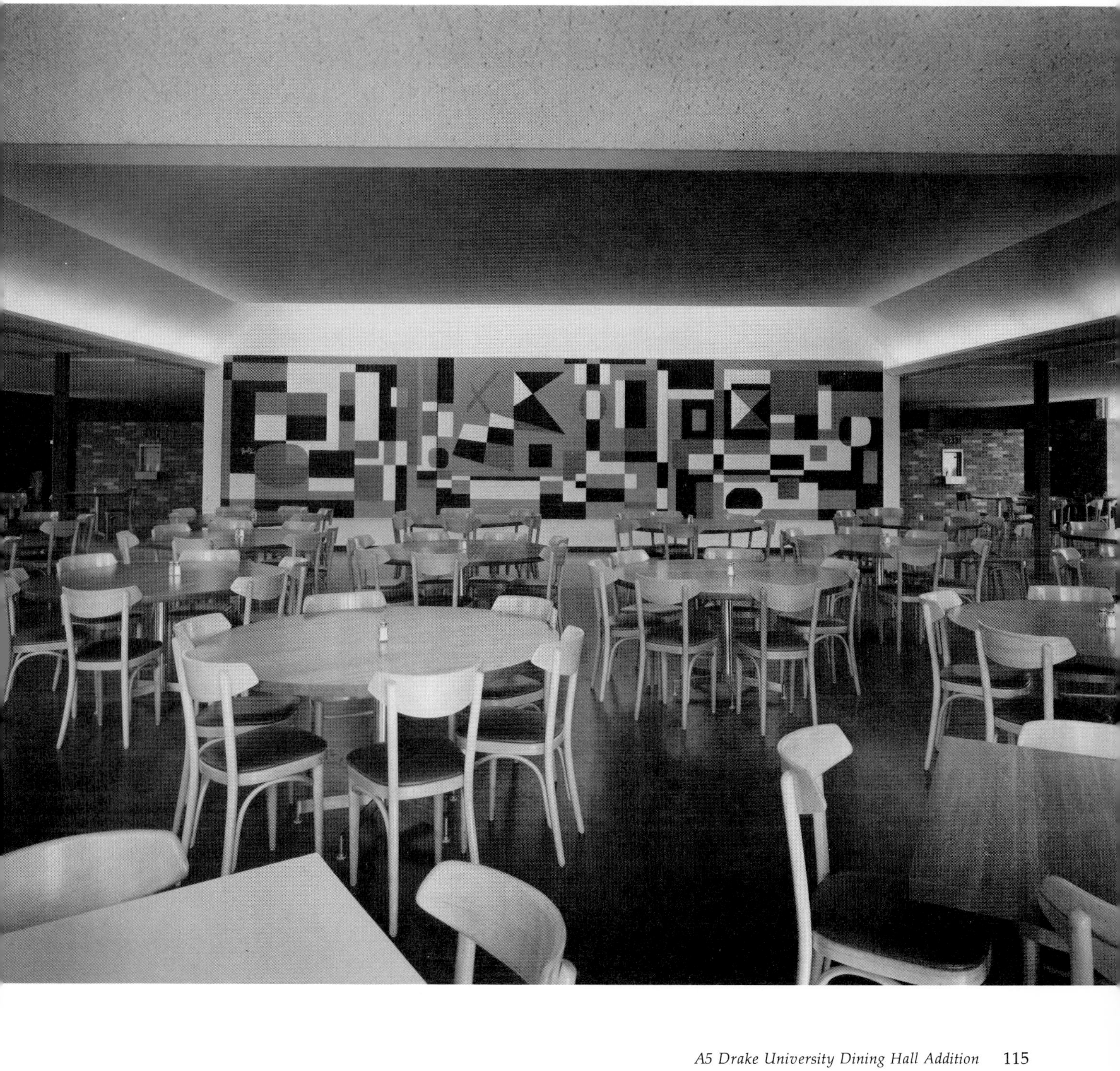

CALVARY CHURCH
Milwaukee, Wisconsin

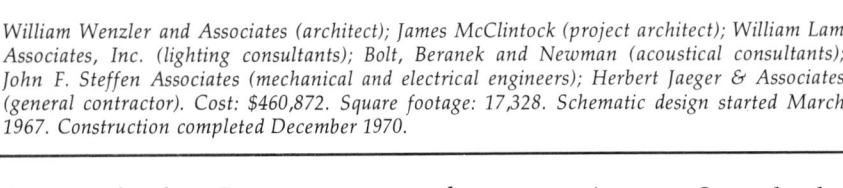

A6

William Wenzler and Associates (architect); James McClintock (project architect); William Lam Associates, Inc. (lighting consultants); Bolt, Beranek and Newman (acoustical consultants); John F. Steffen Associates (mechanical and electrical engineers); Herbert Jaeger & Associates (general contractor). Cost: $460,872. Square footage: 17,328. Schematic design started March 1967. Construction completed December 1970.

1

As at Columbus Baptist, it was desired that the auxiliary spaces of Calvary Church, such as classrooms, should be related in character to the main church. In this project, the lighting design of the main church could not be separated from that of the auxiliary spaces, since all lie under one continuous, unifying spiral of walls and roof.

Design

The most obvious way to illuminate such spaces was with fluorescent lamps from the tops of perimeter walls in a manner similar to Columbus Baptist **(Case Study A3).** However, this method was not used for several reasons. First, there was no way to conceal the fixtures on top of the wall, which slopes as it changes height. Dark louvers could have controlled the glare but would themselves have

been conspicuous. Second, the distance between the top of the wall and the decking was too close to permit even illumination without hot spots. Third, the beams were spaced irregularly and close together, so that lamps of varying lengths would have been required to produce light gradients in a consistent relationship with the irregular structure.

Therefore, bowl fixtures, using quartz rather than fluorescent lamps, were placed low on each wall facet to get good light distribution over the ceiling **(4).** The quartz-lamp fixtures were selected because of the precise optical control possible. Only minimum light is spilled on the wall adjacent to the fixtures. A tradeoff between low initial cost and relatively high operating cost is acceptable in a church with limited operating hours.

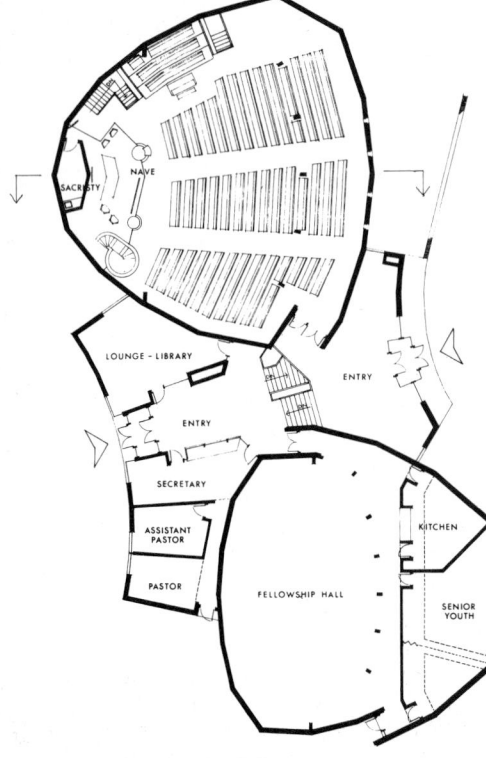

MIDDLE AND UPPER LEVELS

2

3

INDIANA UNIVERSITY
MUSICAL ARTS CENTER
Bloomington, Indiana

A7

Woollen Associates (architect); Evans Woollen (principal); Lynn H. Molzan (project architect); Frits Loonsten (landscape architect); William Lam Associates, Inc. (lighting consultants); Bolt, Beranek and Newman (acoustical consultants); Ben Schlanger, Olaf Soot, Jean Rosenthal (other technical consultants); J. M. Rotz Engineering Co., Inc. (mechanical and electrical engineers); Fink, Roberts & Petrie (structural engineers); F. A. Wilhelm Construction Co., Inc. (general contractor). Schematic design started 1965.

1

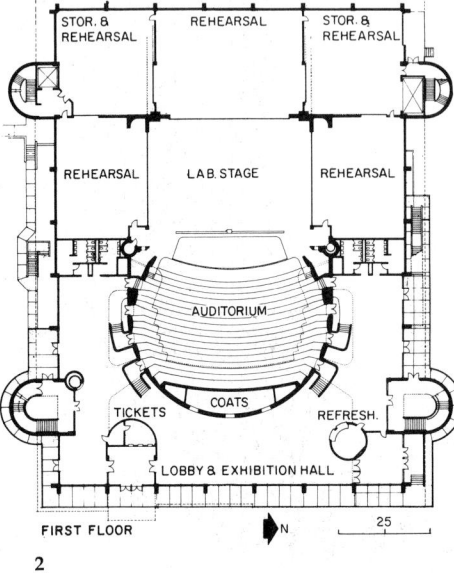

THIRD FLOOR

FIRST FLOOR   N   25

2

The Indiana University Opera Hall **(1)** is one of the few single-purpose opera houses in the United States, and home of the country's only opera school. Evans Woollen's design manages to accommodate most of the extensive supporting school facilities above grade, without obscuring the drum of the hall itself, achieving both good working conditions and a clear public image for the hall.

Design

Definition of the shape of the round drum both from within and without was the starting point of the lighting design. Within the main hall **(3)**, ceiling slots were created to accomplish this end. The slots were interrupted to accommodate structure; the resulting lighting appears natural rather than uneven in this context. The wall-washing effect was given maximum impact by painting the walls in rich colors **(6)**. Most of the supplementary downlighting required to cover the areas out of reach from the wall slots could be done in an inconspicuous, glare-free manner from a concentrated area located in the rear of the main ceiling, out of sight for most of the audience **(5)**. The great height of the hall made this possible.

On the lobby side, illumination of the drum was to have been from slots created by floating the

ceiling. However, the pattern of structure made this detail too expensive; instead, recessed wall-washers were used **(9)**.

Architect Woollen was against extensive "acoustic clouds"—surfaces to reflect sound—that would have obscured the upper space of the hall and appeared mechanistic. Therefore, the necessary sound reflectors above the audience were developed as structurally uncluttered disk chandeliers **(5)**, and the chandelier pattern was developed according to the acoustic density requirements.

The chandeliers consist of clear incandescent lamps which project through convex clear Plexiglas disks (sprayed gold on the upper surface). These act as sound reflectors. To aid relamping and to allow adjustment of the vertical composition of the disks for acoustic or visual reasons, the reflectors were suspended on retractable lamp cords.

To avoid visual noise from window framing of the projection booths in the rear wall of the hall, the glazing was deeply recessed and the holes shaped to have sculptural significance **(7)**. This sculptural treatment was repeated at the check room **(8)**, air outlets, etc., when possible.

On the exterior, floodlamps to illuminate the Calder stabile **(10)** were housed in tubes chamfered to get maximum distribution of light on the sculpture with a minimum of glare.

4

3

5

7

8

9

10

1

ST. THOMAS AQUINAS CHURCH
Indianapolis, Indiana

A8

Woollen Associates (architect); Lynn Molzan (project architect); William Lam Associates, Inc. (lighting consultants); Dr. James Hyde (acoustical consultant); Fr. Aiden Kavanaugh, O.S.B. (liturgical consultant); J. M. Rotz Engineering Co., Inc. (mechanical engineers); Fink, Roberts and Petrie, Inc. (structural engineers). Schematic design started 1967.

St. Thomas Aquinas Church **(1)** differs from Columbus Baptist in that the identity of the church comes at least as much from the forms of the stepped wall as from the roof. On the interior, daylight is better balanced throughout the church. Therefore, artificial illumination is used only for nighttime illumination and to supplement the natural lighting on dark days.

Design

Consistent with the vertical windows, incandescent lamps were arranged vertically within the window recesses. Though hidden from view during the service, they are seen as decorative patterns of clear lamps by people leaving the church or viewing it from the exterior. Highlighting of the altar at night **(3)**, from reflector lamps concealed behind a beam, is consistent with the normal direction of daylight **(4)**.

Photos by Ripman

3

Architectural Record

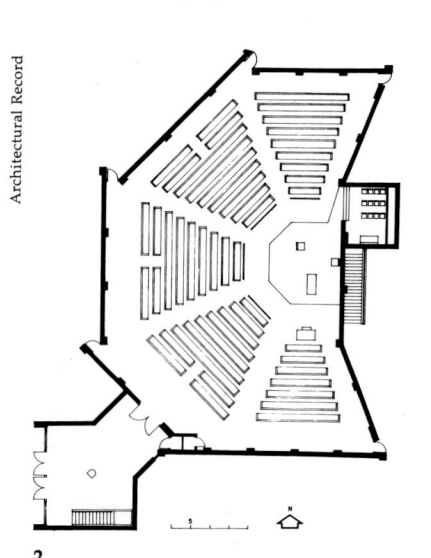

2

4

CASE STUDIES GROUP B

SINGLE SPACES
DEFINED BY
MODULAR ELEMENTS

REMODELLING OF ORCHESTRA HALL
Chicago, Illinois

B1

Harry Weese & Associates (architect); Howard Hershberger (project architect); William Lam Associates, Inc. (lighting consultants); Bolt, Beranek and Newman (acoustical consultants); Kerekes & Kerekes (electrical engineers); S. R. Lewis & Associates (mechanical engineers); The Engineers Collaborative (structural engineers); Sumner Solitt Company (general contractor). Cost of restoration: $2,000,000. Schematic design started 1965. Construction completed 1966.

Orchestra Hall is the dominant single space buried within the shell of a multistoried building on Michigan Avenue **(2)**. Proposals had been made for bringing the Burnham-designed hall (1904) up to date, with air conditioning, more comfortable seats, modern elevators, modified acoustics, etc., that would have created a totally new "movie theater" space. A change in management led to a new look at the problem.

The new team saw the problem not as that of creating a new space but instead as one of restoring and enhancing what they believed was a superb original concept which had been eroded over the years through poor decorating and maintenance **(4)**.

Design

Walls and ceilings of the hall were painted in a solid beige (replacing a tricolor scheme), and new red seats and carpeting were installed. Acoustically, the volume of the hall was increased without changing the visual volume by replacing a number of solid panels with visually solid but acoustically transparent, perforated material.

For the new scheme **(1)**, the major portion of the original lighting system seemed excellent and was restored. This system had defined the shape of the hall with exposed carbon filament lamps projecting in bands through gilded plaster friezes and clustered on balcony fronts. Substitution of inside-frosted and bottom-sil-

vered lamps had been unfortunate. These were replaced by clear filament lamps (which appear similar to the original carbon filament lamps when dimmed). The sculptured plaster background

was regilded. Additional bands of clear lamps with contemporary detailing were placed above the upper balconies to continue the theme, and new chandeliers were added to the upper lobbies.

3

Ripman

The negative aspects of the original scheme, however, were eliminated during the restoration. Where they interfered with the view of the audience behind, white glass "drums" under balconies were replaced by neutral low-brightness recessed fixtures. Drums which formed a positive pattern over the row of boxes and presented no glare problems were replaced by fixtures with a positive sparkle (clear lamps in prismatic glass enclosures).

Like the main hall, the reception room seemed like a once-elegant room that had become dull because of poor redecoration and maintenance. The chandeliers and wall brackets needed merely to be fitted with clear lamps, cleaned, and regilded. The sparkle was then amplified and the space unified by replacing the small scattered mirrors with extensive, panel-size mirrors **(5)**.

Spaces, such as the entrance lobby and upper foyer, that had no positive character were made neutral by recessed downlighting **(6, 7)**. For occasions when the hall surfaces should appear neutral and unlit, low-brightness downlights were placed in the ceiling over the orchestra seats. Similarly, the stage lighting was supplemented from sources concealed behind the proscenium and in the rear wall **(3)**. Small quartz lamps in specially designed fixtures were concealed in valances between the organ pipe balconies, to minimize glare and to eliminate hot spots on the rear wall of the stage.

Note on Details

The 70-year-old original scheme for relamping ceiling, hall, and stage lighting was ingenious. The fixtures were not permanently attached to the structure, so that the lampholders could be retracted, relamped from above, and dropped back into place through holes in the ceiling.

4
5

6
7

Photos by Harold Lewis/Photo International

1

Engineering Building
CUMMINS RESEARCH AND
ENGINEERING CENTER
Columbus, Indiana

B2

Harry Weese & Associates (architect); J. Herschel Fisher, Pat Y. Spillman (associated architects); William Lam Associates, Inc. (lighting consultants); Bolt, Beranek and Newman (acoustical consultants); Dolores Miller & Associates (interior design consultants); Eitingon & Schlossberg (electrical engineers); Cosentini Associates (mechanical engineers); The Engineers Collaborative (structural engineers); Messer Inc. (general contractor). Cost: $24,000,000. Square footage: 360,000. Schematic design started 1964. Construction completed 1968.

This factory building was to be similar to others previously built at Cummins by Weese and Saarinen. The initial design called for the same combination of steel trusses, skylights, and a "spaghetti" of ductwork radiating from a central mechanical room **(5).**

In a factory of this kind, most of the floor space is occupied by materials in temporary storage between production operations. Lighting needs are primarily biological. Factory environments are usually more chaotic and gloomy than necessary **(2,3).** An uplight component from typical industrial lighting fixtures can help, as will skylights above (illuminating the structure and ductwork which in turn reflect light to the ceiling); however, if the ceiling is chaotic and cluttered, the net effect can be negative.

For several reasons, indirect lighting of wall and ceiling surfaces was a very efficient method of getting the kind of bright, cheerful space that would provide the needed illumination for storage and movement of materials and for most manufacturing operations. The considerable depth of structure (10 feet) permitted a generous fixture-to-ceiling distance, reducing the hot-spot effect

2

3

Photos without credits by Lam

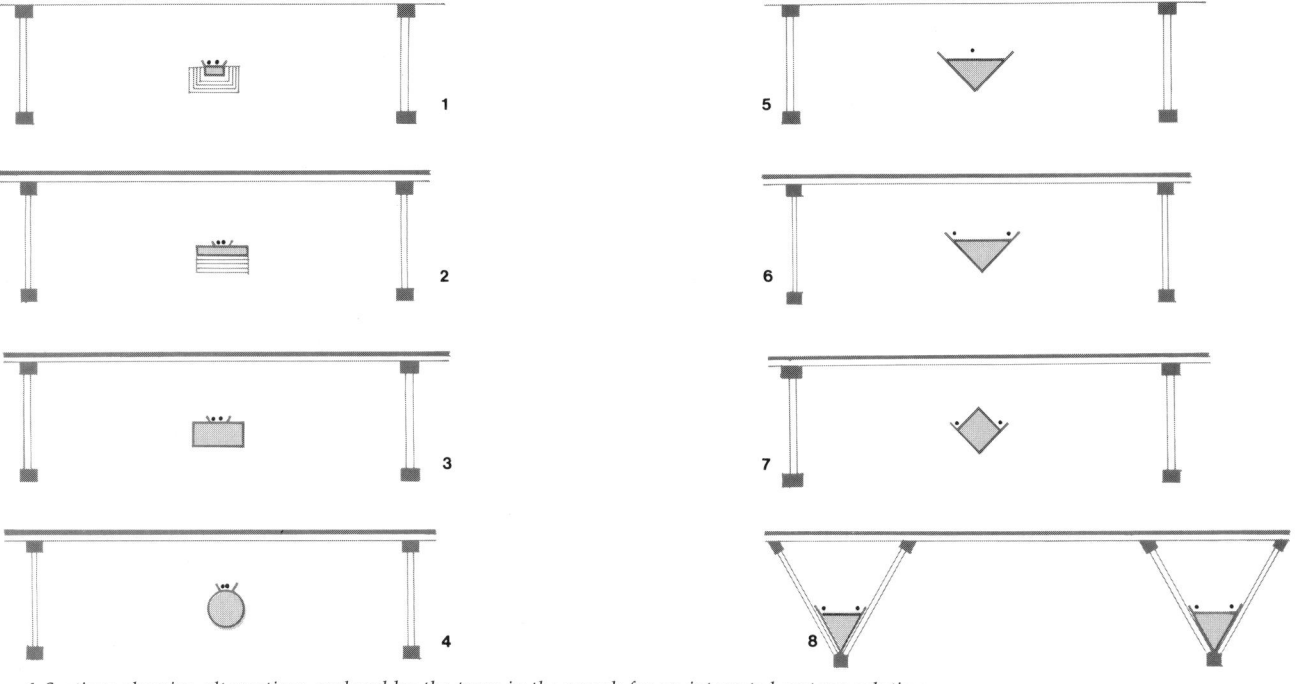

4 *Sections showing alternatives explored by the team in the search for an integrated systems solution.*

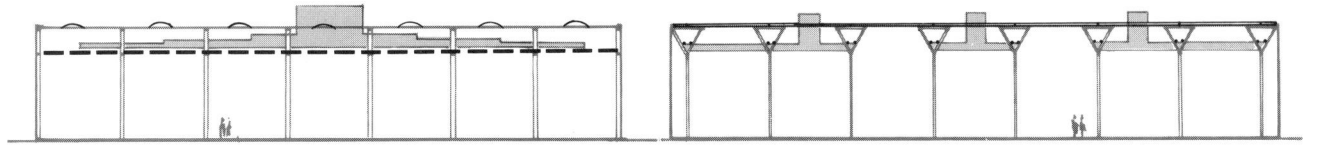

5 *Initial design—no integration of systems*

6 *Final integrated systems design.*

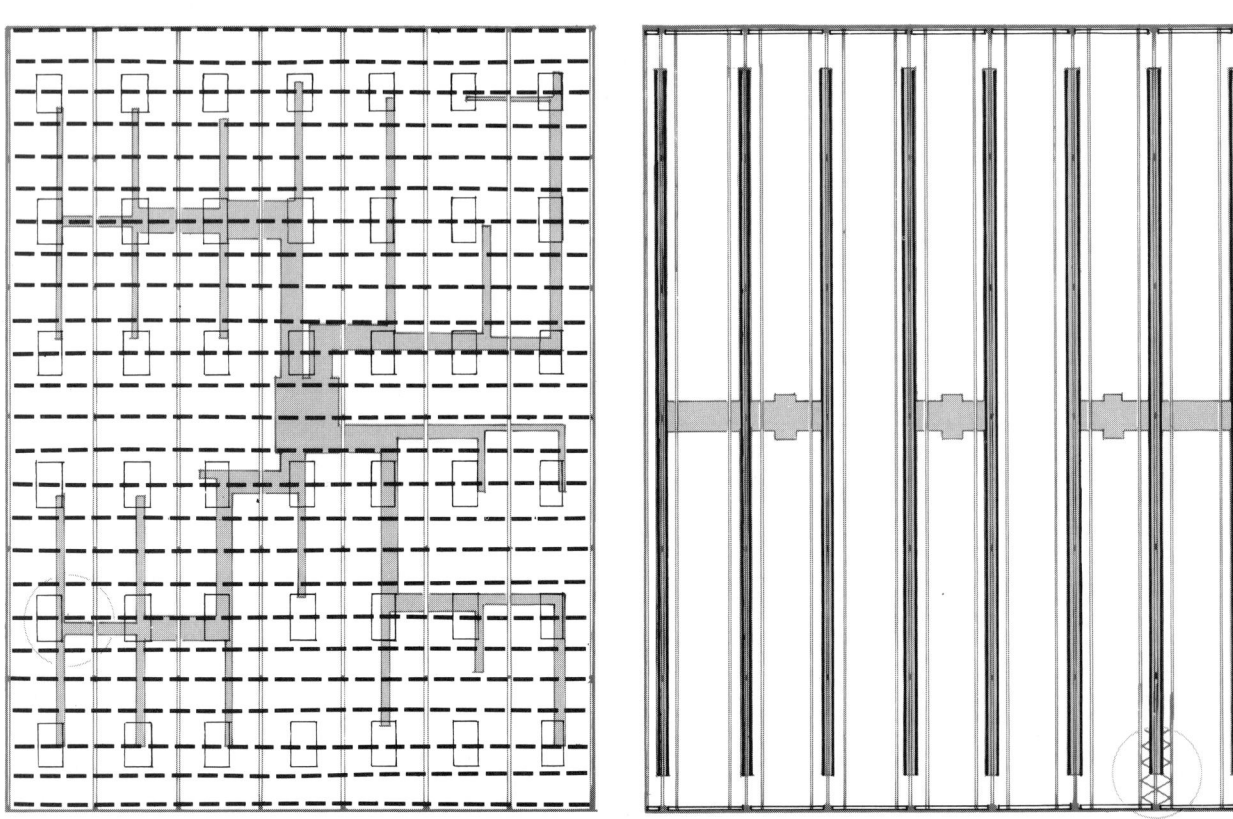

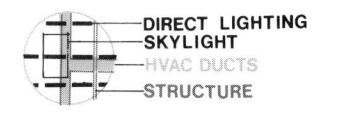

DIRECT LIGHTING
SKYLIGHT
HVAC DUCTS
STRUCTURE

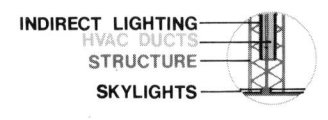

INDIRECT LIGHTING
HVAC DUCTS
STRUCTURE

SKYLIGHTS

7

generated by fixtures mounted too close to the surfaces which they illuminate. The indirect system was supplemented with downlighting in local areas as required. Indirect lighting is excellent for storage areas because rows of storage need not be located in relationship to light fixtures, and shelving shadows are minimized. Recent experience in designing the IBM building **(Case Study E2)** gave the team added incentive to see if an integrated system could be developed.

Design

The greatest contributor to potential "visual noise" from the ceiling was the layout of the air-conditioning ductwork. The opportunity and challenge were rearranging ductwork to relate to the structure and to baffle the indirect light sources. A "fishbone" layout with several smaller fan units (rather than a single fan system) proved to be an economical, satisfactory approach, and the shape of the ducts was refined to provide a uniform mounting and shielding

condition for the indirect fluorescent lighting. The ducts were supported within triangular delta trusses **(4)**. The additional cost of the trusses was offset by savings in duct and fixture support, and by their doubling as catwalks.

Thus, the ceiling **(7)** is not perceived as an endless plane penetrated at random by arbitrarily placed lighting fixtures, but rather is articulated by the integrated structural/mechanical/lighting system whose clarity satisfies the biological needs for the under-

8

9

standing of structure, orientation (definable ''bays''), etc. Work illumination and orientation were also improved by highlighting of the perimeter walls with skylights using integral fluorescent fixtures for night use, and by downlight accents in local areas that benefit from increased illumination, shadows, and reflections. The changing daylight of the skylights and a narrow horizontal band of view windows provide desirable contact with the exterior.

When closed cubicles within the space were necessary to keep out dust, noise, etc., they were related to the larger space by the sloping skylight and low-brightness downlighting (9) which not only reduces glare for the cubicle occupants but also keeps views of the cubicle fixtures from dominating and contributing visual noise to the surrounding major space.

The engine test-cell building contiguous to the large loft type structure contains test cells along a series of fixed spines containing the observation-control stations (12). These were illuminated in a nonindustrial manner: indirect lighting of the ceiling plus local lighting of the instrument panels (11). The space is properly focused; unlike earlier test cells at Cummins, none of the light sources in the test cells are visible to observers (10). A similar relation between viewer and activity to be illuminated led to a similar solution at the handball courts designed for Johns Hopkins University in conjunction with Meyer, Ayers, and Saint (13-15).

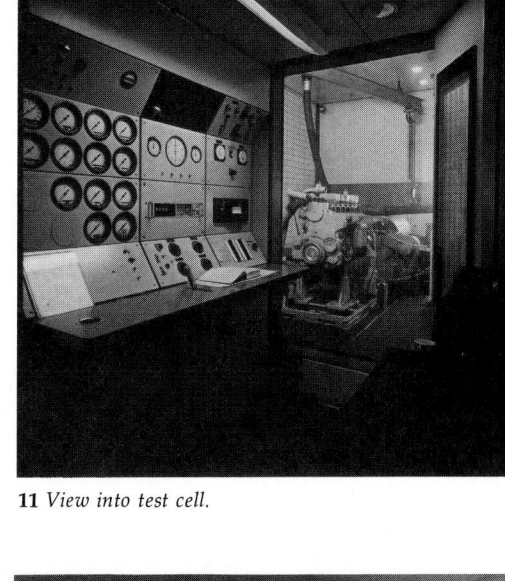

10 *View from test cell toward control booth showing lights positioned to be invisible to the observer in the booth (the spotlights in each corner are used as work lights).*

11 *View into test cell.*

12

13

14 *Spectators' gallery at the Johns Hopkins Athletic Center, Baltimore, Maryland (Meyer, Ayers and Saint/ Architects; William Lam Associates/ Lighting Consultants).*

15 *Handball court at the Johns Hopkins Athletic Center.*

I. MILLER SHOWROOM
New York, New York

B3

Victor A. Lundy (architect and interior designer); William Lam Associates, Inc. (lighting consultants); Fred S. Dubin Associates (mechanical engineers); Harold L. Mindell (partner in charge); Severud–Elstad–Krueger Associates (structural engineers); Fred Fischer, Jr. (partner in charge); John Gallin & Son, Inc. (general contractor). Cost: $554,160. Square footage: 14,600. Construction completed 1967.

In creating a totally new interior space within an existing structure, architect Lundy decided to define the space by an obviously non-structural lining of wood screening. Elegant organic forms were created by the pattern of wood strips radiating from columns and pilasters.

The lighting objective was the provision of an elegant environment in keeping with the prestigious location and product line. The display of a limited number of products could easily be accomplished in discrete self-illuminated displays. For the customer, flattering lighting at the full-length mirrors was essential.

Design

Direct lighting onto the dark wood-slat screening was avoided as much as possible in order not to illuminate the messy hardware and spaces between and beyond. Downlighting through holes or around the edges of the screens was considered desirable (2,3). The tour de force came with the elimination of the usual clutter of uncoordinated mirrors (in typical shoe stores). By making the mirrors radiate in plan from the semicircular pilasters and follow their curving profile in elevation, the pilasters were made to appear as full-round "columns," thus expanding the space and making the mirrors positive contributors to the spatial organization (5). Floating the mirrors free from the walls then allowed concealment of light sources that illuminate the infill walls and provide reflected light onto persons standing in front of the mirror.

Critique

The lamps were centered between wall and mirror, rather than placed as designed for maximum glare shielding and uniformity in illumination of the wall (4).

Photos by George Cserna

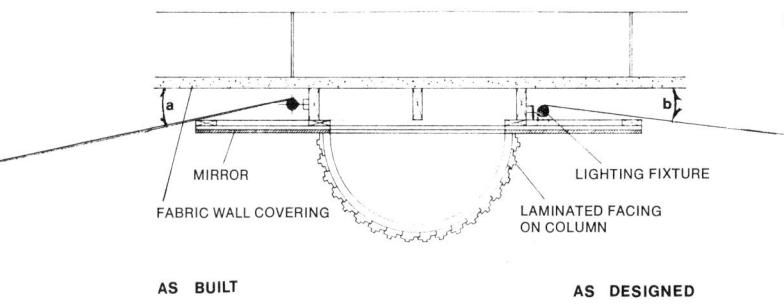

MIRROR

FABRIC WALL COVERING

LIGHTING FIXTURE

LAMINATED FACING
ON COLUMN

AS BUILT

AS DESIGNED

4 *As built, the lamps are not so well concealed as they would have been if located at the front of the pocket as intended.*

3

TOWN OF MOUNT ROYAL LIBRARY
Mount Royal, Quebec

B4

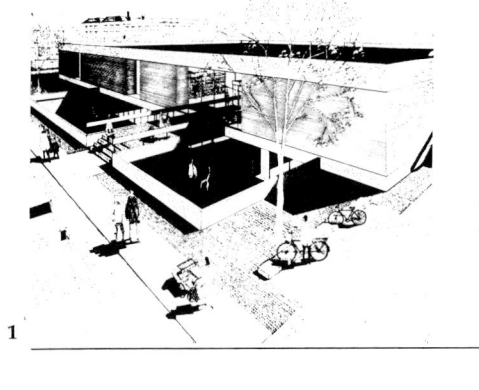

Donaldson Drummond Sankey Architects (architect); Michael G. Werleman (project architect); Harold Spence – Saves (landscape architect); William Lam Associates, Inc. (lighting consultants); T. A. I. C. Taylor (electrical engineers); Brais Frigon Hanley (mechanical engineers); F. M. Kraus & Associates (structural engineers); Leon M. Adler Construction Ltd. (general contractor). Cost: $500,000. Square footage: 20,000. Schematic design started June 1965. Construction completed June 1967.

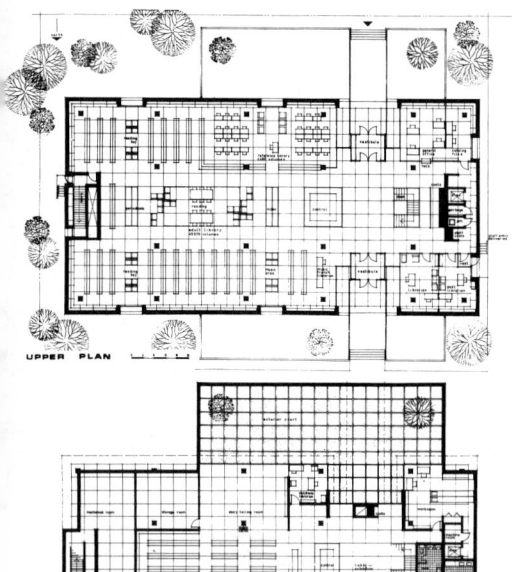

UPPER PLAN

LOWER PLAN

2

The general scheme of this pavilion library for a Montreal suburb was the winner of a competition. Lighting design capitalized on the planned ceiling structure. Perimeter skylights (3) were used instead of clerestory windows, reducing glare and giving the ceiling structure the appearance of floating free from the walls of the library. Thus sunlight is brought into the space in a way which improves the environment without interfering with the activities of the readers.

Design

Since the size and layout of the room made it possible to handle all air-conditioning requirements from the perimeter walls, the exposed waffle ceiling could be uninterrupted. Low-brightness direct/indirect louvered fixtures[1] utilizing the twelve-inch-square panel lamp were used within each

6 × 6 foot cell to provide direct lighting with a minimum of direct glare, while the glowing ceiling coffers reduce shadows and define the ceiling plane.

The original design, which called for the use of clerestory windows, was changed to use clear edge skylights in order to get the desirable dynamic quality of daylight without the attendant problems of glare control from clerestory windows (4). At night and on dark days, incandescent lamps substitute for daylight. The main desk area is given prominence by skylights with decorative Plexiglas baffles.

On the lower level, as a compromise to initial cost, exposed incandescent lamps were centered in each coffer (5). Comfort and operating cost, while clearly not as good, were still judged acceptable.

[1]*Previously developed for the office segment of the Cummins Engine plant,* **Case Study E3.**

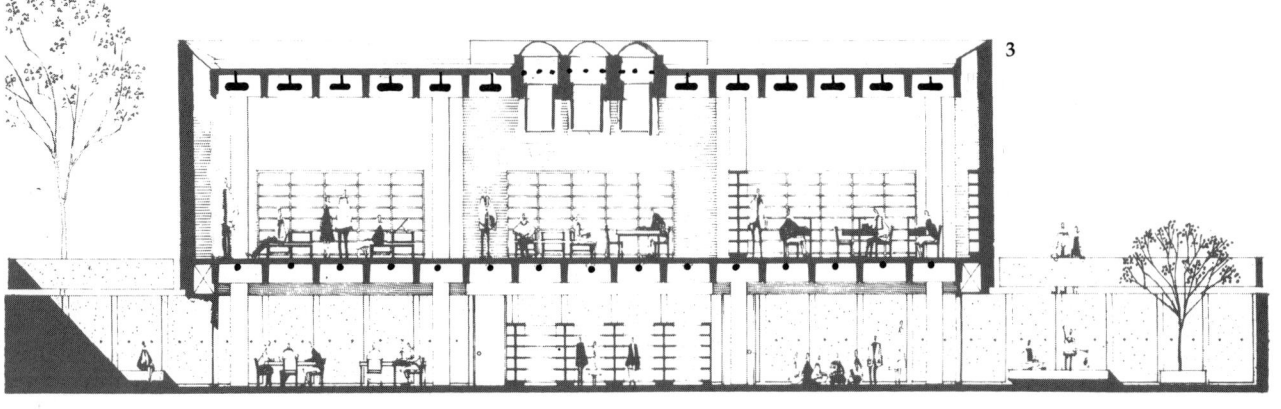

3

Michael Drummond/Montreal

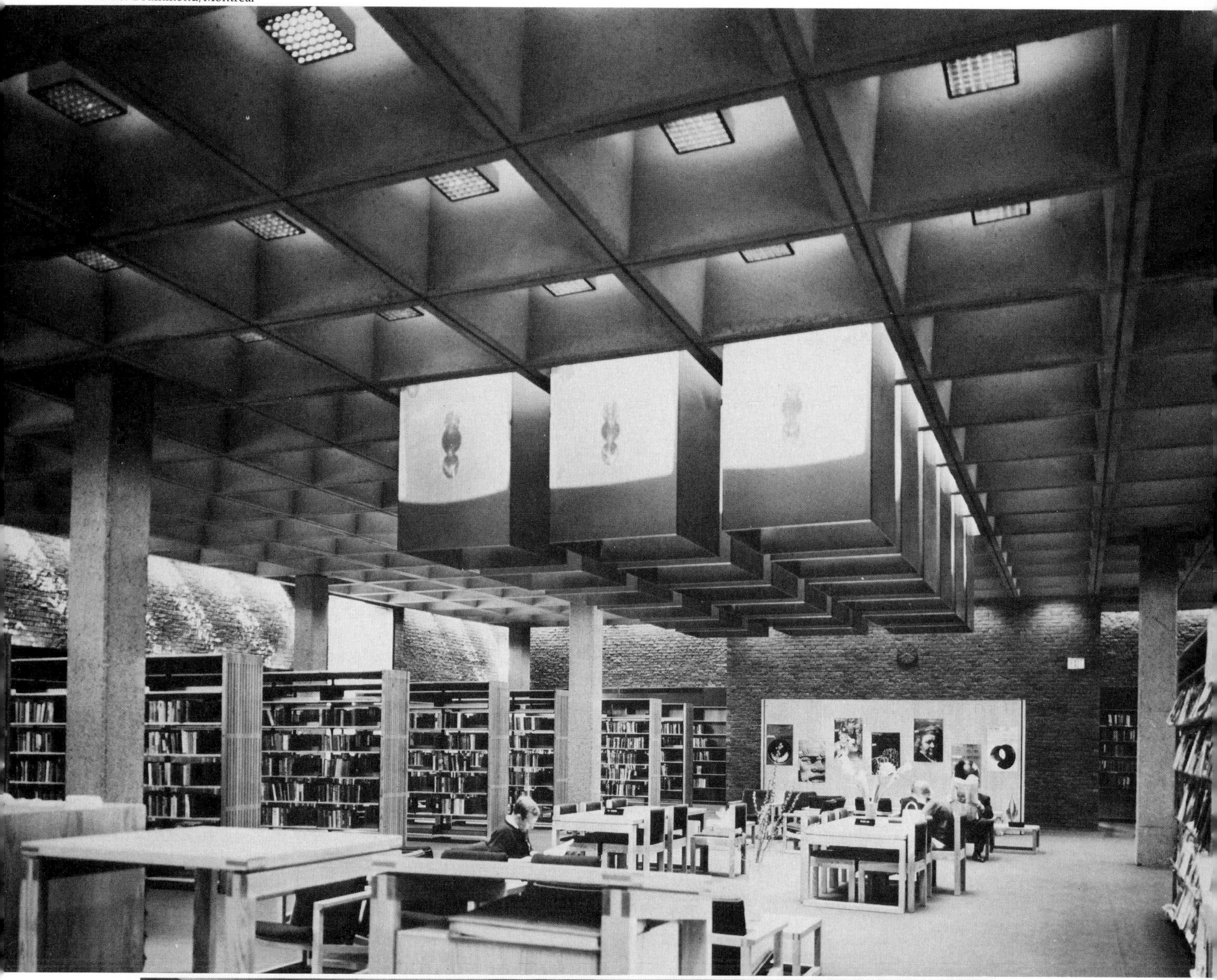

4 5

Harold Lewis/Photo International

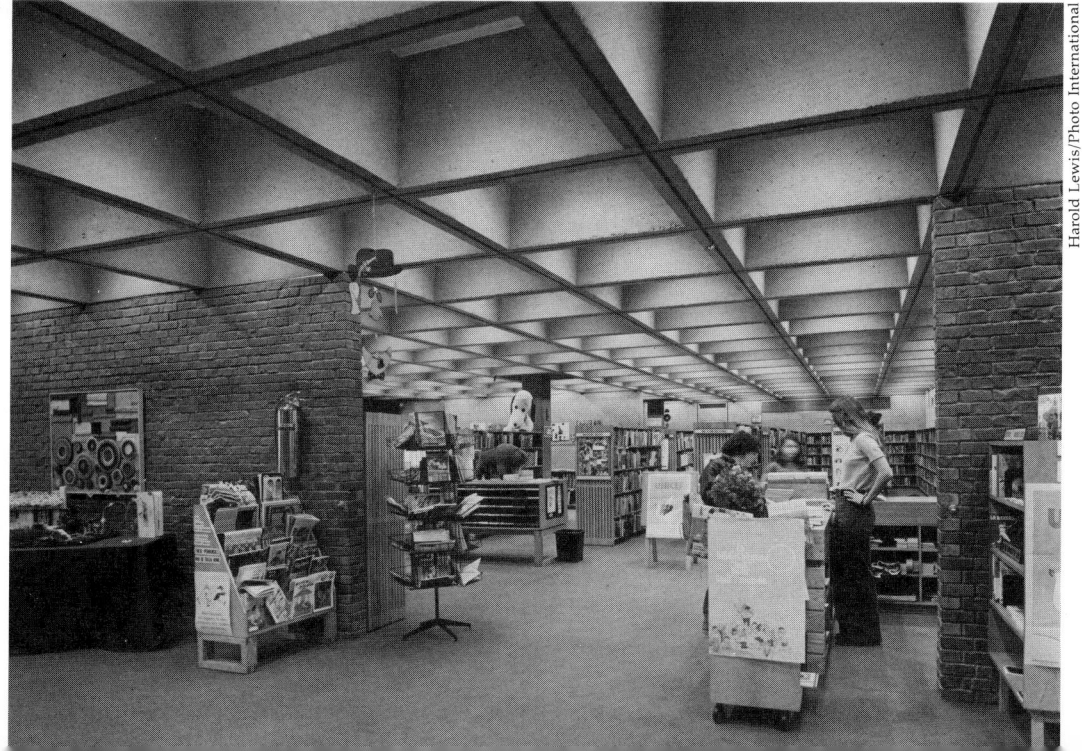

EDEN THEOLOGICAL SEMINARY LIBRARY

St. Louis, Missouri

B5

1

William Wenzler and Associates (architect); James McClintock (project architect); William Lam Associates, Inc. (lighting consultants); Bolt, Beranek and Newman (acoustical consultants); Talisman House (interior design consultants); Lunde, Gordon, Parker & Steffen (mechanical and electrical engineers); Gamble Construction Company (general contractor). Cost: $996,458.83. Square footage: 37,356. Schematic design started October 1964. Construction completed June 1968.

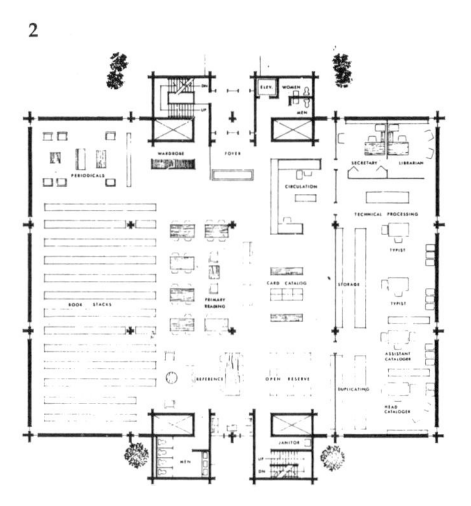

2

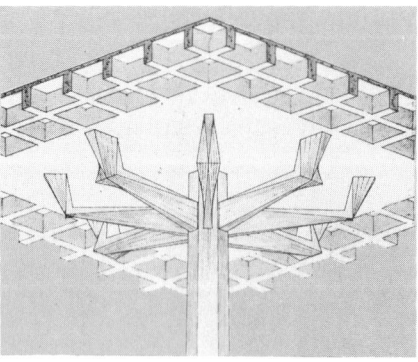

3 *Structural tree with indirect fixtures concealed in the "branches" (wood grid ceiling not shown).*

Coordination of lighting and structure for the Eden Library began before the first diagrammatic sketch. The problem: how to serve the activity needs within an environment that would be warm and Gothic, in harmony with the existing campus. The architect, William Wenzler, hoped to achieve this character with maximum use of brick (the predominant campus material) and wood.

Objectives were to provide adequate but comfortable illumination for stacks and reading-work areas. Stacks were to run in either direction and reading-work areas were to be distributed freely and interchangeably. The goal: a cheerful yet low-key luminous environment.

Design

In order to avoid gloom and to minimize glare, a starting premise was that a wood ceiling, if used, would have to be either illuminated indirectly or used as louvers, since freely distributed stacks meant that frequent white walls were not available to use as sources of indirect illumination. The desire for a Gothic expression suggested a Gothic structure. The total concept, developed on the back of the classic napkin, was that of concrete "trees" (sculptured concrete structures being a specialty of the architect) with an infill of wood louvers that would conceal the services and provide

pleasant overall illumination from a warm, glowing plane **(5)**. This was a modification of the scheme used in Place Bonaventure **(Case Study C5)**.

Since such dark louvers are relatively inefficient, the large-scale louver ceiling module was developed around the then highly promoted new 12-inch-square fluorescent lamp and low-brightness louver designed to fit the lamp precisely (thereby yielding maximum efficiency with low brightness). The lamp and louver provide local downlighting, and the upward component, reflected by the white painted slab and ductwork above, illuminates the surrounding unoccupied cells of the wood grid. Supplied from flexible cables, these units can be moved in minutes without tools to accommodate changes in the placement of stacks, work tables, etc. Interchangeable panels with recessed incandescent wall washers were placed to illuminate perimeter brick walls. The structural "trees" **(4)** contain concealed light sources within the branches which illuminate the trees themselves and the surrounding slab.

Critique

The final result is highly satisfying: the space is defined by glowing wood louvers, with local highlighting related to use and furniture layout. This was a good "rustic" solution for the program.

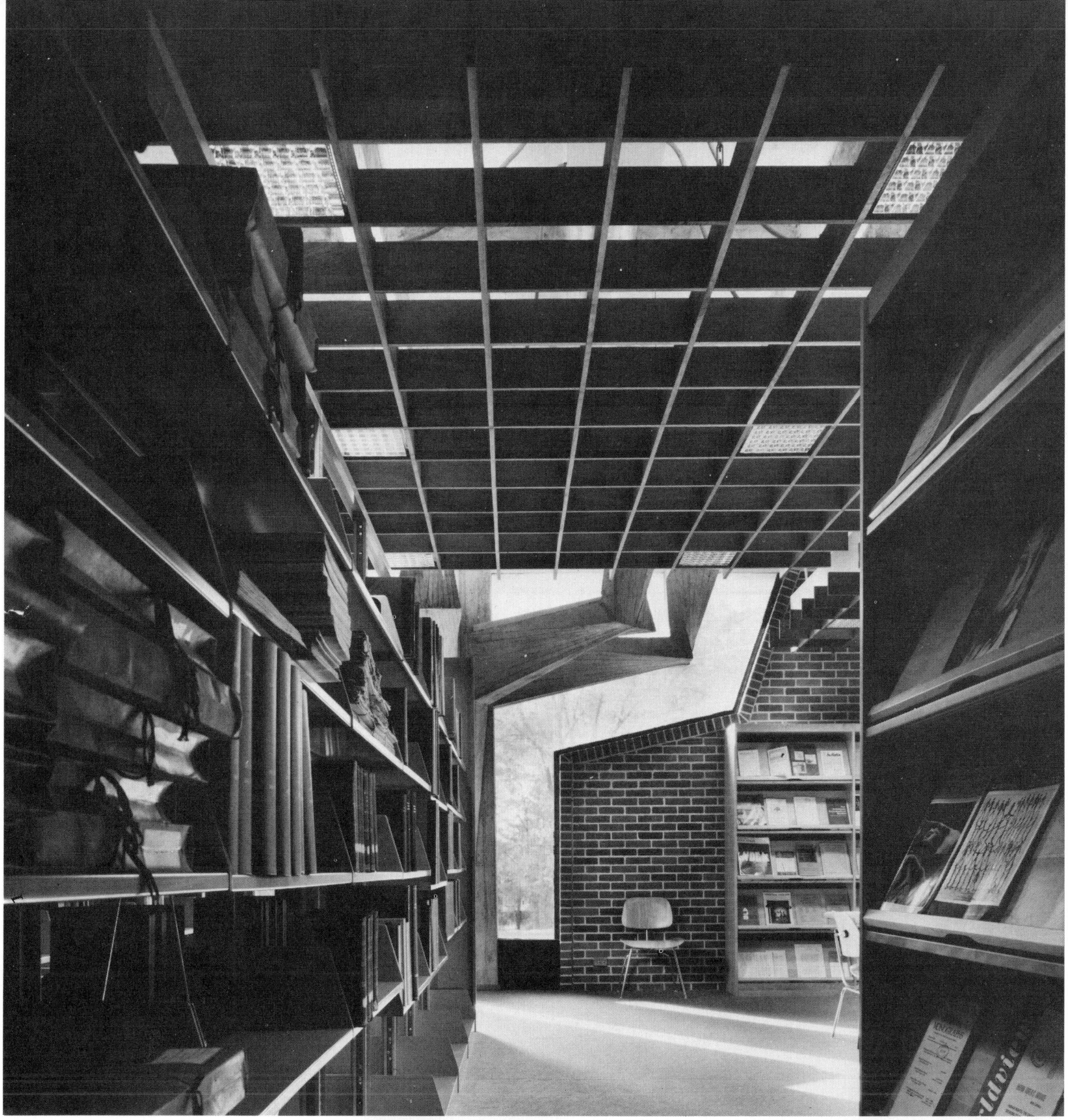

Photos by The Picture Place

4

5

Robert A. Dorn

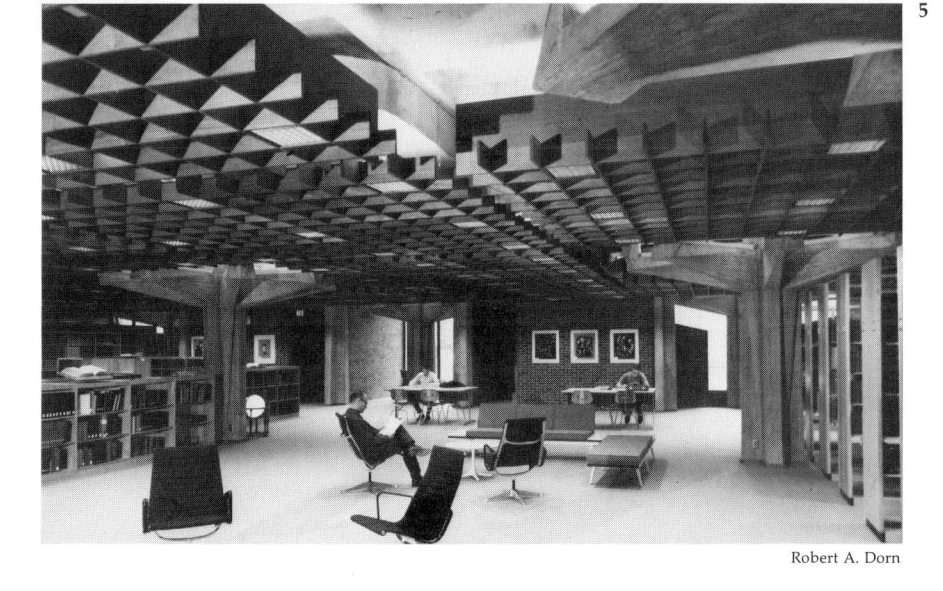

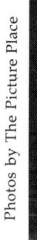

However, edging the louvered service zones with deeper members to screen the mechanical services from view could have produced a more definitive, more refined appearance for a negligible increase in cost.

Unfortunately, because of unanticipated manufacturing difficulties the price of the fluorescent panel lamps went up sharply, rather than following the usual downward trend that goes with increasing production and amortization of development and tooling costs.

CASE STUDIES GROUP C

SEQUENCES OF MAJOR SPACES IN A SINGLE STRUCTURE

When a number of major spaces occur within a building, the design of each should be influenced by the design of the others. Even if common denominators are not advantageous for practical reasons, such as ease of construction, reduced cost of common details, materials, etc., there are good biological reasons for maximizing the design consistency, *unless* differences are dictated by real needs and are substantial rather than arbitrary, merely for the sake of "variety" (design without underlying concept). One may ask "Why bother with consistency if the related spaces cannot be seen at the same time?" It must be remembered, however, that "seeing" involves the brain and not only the eye. Seeing is inseparable from association with remembered mental images.

There are many possible solutions for the design of any individual space. With a sequence of spaces, only tentative conclusions should be reached for any one space until the solution for all begins to emerge. Ideally a design which may seem arbitrary in any single space will exhibit an appropriate relevance to all associated spaces when seen as part of a sequence.

1

LOYOLA-NOTRE DAME LIBRARY
Baltimore, Maryland

C1

Meyer Ayers Saint Stewart Inc. (architect); Richard W. Ayers (partner in charge); William Lam Associates, Inc. (lighting consultants); Lloyd J. Williams (acoustical consultant); Stephen Matthias (graphics consultant); Westburg-Klaus Associates (interior design consultant); Egli and Gompf, Inc. (mechanical and electrical engineers); Van Rensselaer P. Saxe (structural engineers); Henry A. Knott Co. (general contractor). Schematic design started 1969.

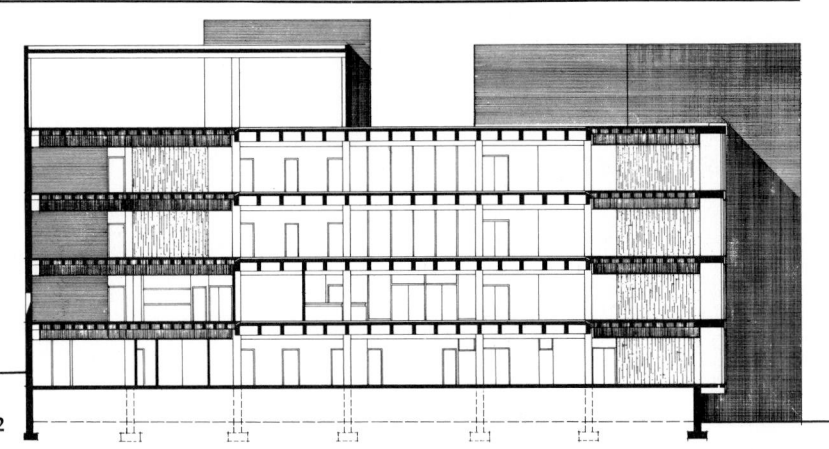

2

The building committee for the Loyola-Notre Dame Library expressed a strong desire for "an arrangement that is direct, logical and easily understood and an environment that is friendly, intimate, warm and pleasant." In response to this and other programmatic objectives, the design team came up with a simple, comprehensible concept for this roughly square building: four rectangular perimeter spaces arranged in a pinwheel around a major central space **(4)**. Both central and perimeter spaces were programmed to accommodate a mix of stacks and reading areas which could be changed at will, though the majority of stacks were to be concentrated in the central zone while most offices and reading areas were to be located in the perimeter spaces.

Architectural development and lighting design reinforced the clarity of this organizing concept. Although the roughly square plan form might have suggested the use of a uniform field of square ceiling coffers and light fixtures throughout the entire floor, the pinwheel arrangement and the expressed desire for maximum orientation led to the clear differentiation of the central and perimeter zones through the use of different lighting and ceiling systems **(5)**. Since service and circulation cores were located in two of the perimeter areas, the logical approach to mechanical distribution was to run the major mechanical services above a suspended

ceiling in the perimeter zone. This concentration of service elements opened up the possibility of a full-height ceiling in the center zone with only local mechanical distribution elements concealed in the ceiling depth **(2)**.

The stack arrangement in the perimeter zone—consistently perpendicular to the exterior walls—suggested the use of a directional metal-slat ceiling oriented parallel to the lines of the stacks, with integral recessed single-lamp low-brightness fluorescent fixtures. Because of the pinwheel plan, the design team was able to treat each of the four perimeter spaces as a separate entity, thus avoiding the most common problem inherent in the nature of a directional ceiling texture: that of turning the corner. The 8-inch-wide luminaires, which replace two of the metal slats, were selected because of their high efficiency and very low brightness. The design team judged these to be more valuable characteristics than the attributes of narrower fixtures,

which blend into the ceiling only when switched off (compare with **Fig. 23, Case Study C5**). Even when switched on, the larger low-brightness fixtures are relatively unobtrusive in the context of the linear ceiling texture, producing far less visual noise than the brighter single-slat-width fixtures **(3)**.

Light-bronze-colored slats were chosen to produce an ambience of intimacy and warmth. In general, dark-colored ceilings which extend over large areas appear depressing and gloomy during the day, even though desks, furniture, and bookcases may be adequately illuminated. However, at Loyola this effect is minimized because the areas of dark ceiling are fairly small, and each is surrounded by windows, illuminated walls at corners **(6)** and cores, and the bright central space in which square fixtures are located in each coffer of a large-scale waffle ceiling. Table tops are light-colored. Most of the visual field is therefore quite bright,

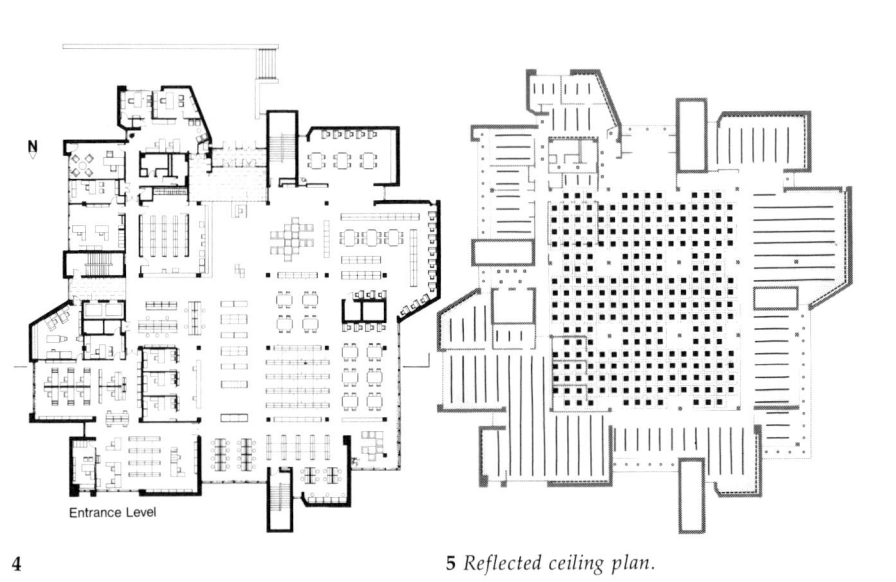

3 *Typical perimeter space.*

which compensates for the relatively dark ceiling overhead. Windows were designed primarily for the view rather than for the daylight, although reading areas near windows were planned to utilize the available daylight illumination; the incandescent lighting provided in these areas is intended for nighttime use only.

In the central area **(8)**, every coffer is illuminated to avoid producing a visually noisy checkerboard pattern of alternating light and dark coffers (compare with **Fig. 49**). Wrap-around plastic diffusers were used in the 2 × 2 foot fluorescent fixtures, rather than diffusers with opaque sides, to eliminate shadow lines which would otherwise interrupt the light gradients which define the shape of the coffers **(7).** Air supply and return were handled through slots concealed in the light fixtures. Two 40-watt U-shaped lamps in each fixture illuminate the diffusers uniformly but generate more light than required except in isolated reading areas. The

Entrance Level

4

5 *Reflected ceiling plan.*

6 *Typical corner reading area.*

use of two-level ballasts was recommended, so that each fixture could be operated at either full output or half output. Hardware such as the two-level ballast makes it possible to tailor the luminous environment at will to the specific requirements and locations of the activities in a space, conserving energy while maintaining the designated patterns and order of the visual field. However, the project proved too small to make the manufacture of special ballasts a financially attractive proposition; therefore, light levels were adjusted by using two different types of ballasts, installed in an arrangement dictated by the furniture layout. This compromise makes it more difficult to adapt the luminous environment to changing use patterns, since the ballast must be replaced to change the output of any fixture. However, our request for multilevel ballasts on this and several subsequent projects has led the ballast industry to offer several types of multilevel ballast as standard catalog items.

7 *Section through typical ceiling coffer in the central space.*

8

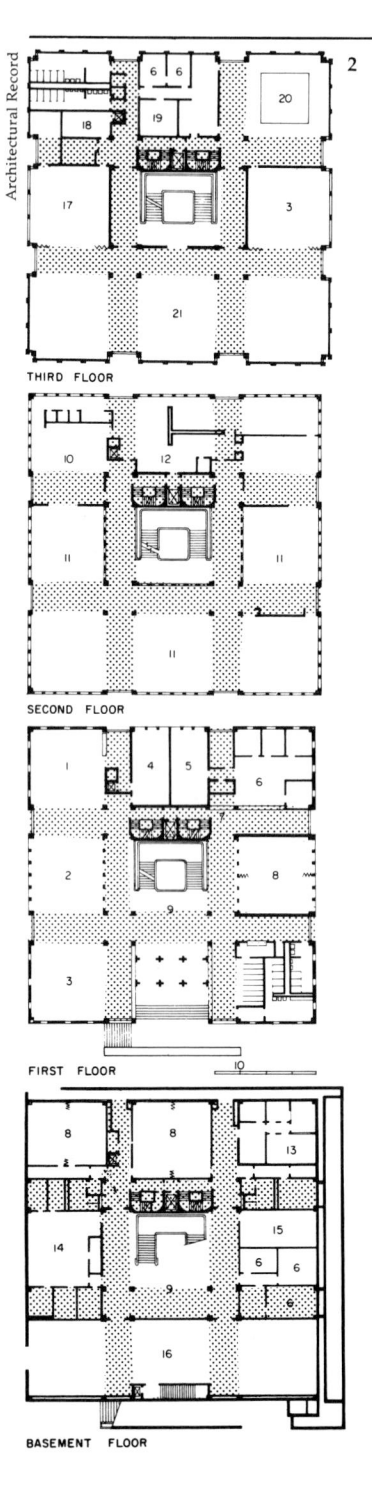

1

McGILL UNIVERSITY CENTER
Montreal, Quebec

Affleck Desbarats Dimakopoulos Lebensold & Sise (architect); Guy Desbarats (partner in charge); Thomas E. Blood (project manager); I. Reichman (job captain); William Lam Associates, Inc. (lighting consultants); T. G. Anglin Engineering Co. (mechanical and electrical engineers); McMillan & Martynowicz (structural engineers); Douglas Bremner Contractors & Builders Ltd. (general contractor). Schematic design started 1964.

2

THIRD FLOOR

SECOND FLOOR

FIRST FLOOR

BASEMENT FLOOR

UNIVERSITY CENTER
1. Coffee lounge
2. Exhibit lounge
3. Lounge
4. Reading and dining
5. Council room
6. Offices
7. Tickets
8. Meeting rooms
9. Lobby
10. Cafeteria
11. Dining
12. Kitchen
13. Studio
14. McGill Daily
15. Post graduates lounge
16. Bookstore
17. Music room
18. Servery
19. Make-up room
20. Rehearsal theater
21. Ballroom

The architectural concept of this student center was very formal: in plan **(2)**, nine squares separated by corridor/service bands; in section, layers of major rooms surrounding a skylighted well **(5)** with ceremonial stairs.

The environmental needs in a student center are primarily biological. Objectives are therefore the creation of pleasant, cheerful spaces suitable for circulation, lounging, conversation, eating, drinking, etc. Activity needs such as serious reading, studying, and office work take place in a few selected locations in the public spaces and in designated student offices which should be given special treatment.

Design

The strong plan organization (eight squares surrounding the central square skylight well and separated from it by service bands) suggested strongly that this organization be reinforced by the lighting design. Consequently, the eight squares were illuminated indirectly from their perimeter

beams (from integrally cast recessed coves). The wash of light on the exposed concrete-grid ceiling effectively balances the brightness of windows. Downlight "can" fixtures provide supplementary light during the day and when used alone can provide a subdued alternative at night. While this lighting is suitable for the dining rooms, in the lounges **(4)** additional local lighting for reading was provided by portable lamps, creating a more intimate scale. In the bookstore, lighting tracks were provided to supplement the general indirect lighting system.

In the ballroom **(6)**, where the major walls are solid, perimeter walls could be illuminated from behind benches as well as from coves and downlights overhead. The desired combinations are selected by dimming. It was decided not to create any additional decorative "chandelier" effects since the adjacent skylight/chandelier/stair system in the central well would be visible from all floors.

Critique

The lamps in the skylight/chandelier **(3)** are hard to reach, and were to have been operated at reduced voltage and at night only for a very long life, so that relamping would have been required only at intervals of several years. Unfortunately, a false economy was achieved by elimination of the dimmer, thereby reducing lamp life and increasing relamping costs considerably.

4
3

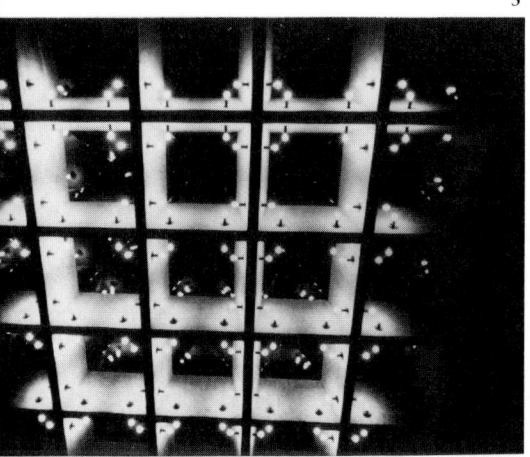

5

6

ADDITION, WALTERS ART GALLERY
Baltimore, Maryland
C3

Shepley Bullfinch Richardson & Abbot (architect); Hugh Shepley (project architect); Meyer Ayers Saint Stewart (associated architect); William Lam Associates, Inc. (lighting consultants); Bolt, Beranek and Newman (acoustical consultant); Egli & Gompf, Inc. (mechanical and electrical engineers); Ewell, Bomhart and Associates (structural engineers); Piracci Construction Co. (general contractor). Cost: $460,872. Square footage: 99,600. Schematic design started January 1968. Construction completed September 1974.

Principal characteristics of the Walters Gallery addition are the diagonal shapes of the main spaces and the daylighted enclosing screen walls on the street side.

With the diagonal spaces, large-scale expressive horizontal structure would have conflicted more than usual with the works displayed on the walls. Therefore, a "homogenized" neutral ceiling was sought. Starting with the need for an accessible ceiling, the design team was faced immediately with the problem of finding a ceiling material whose inherent visual geometries would not conflict with the diagonal plan forms of the perimeter galleries. The use of a conventional rectangular material such as acoustic ceiling tile would have made it impossible to avoid the usual nasty little irregular triangular bits of cut tile whenever the ceiling intersected a diagonal wall. In addition, the ceiling had to accommodate runs of lighting track parallel to every major wall;

with a rectangular tile ceiling, a number of runs would have had to cross the tiles on the diagonal.

The problem was solved with a continuous plane of bronze-colored metal ceiling slats that appear as a continuous texture meeting both principal walls at the same angle. The lighting tracks, which needed to be parallel to the walls, were placed above the ceiling slats. Stems of the movable light fixtures penetrate between the slats (easily removable for rearrangement of lighting and servicing of air conditioning). Thus hidden lighting tracks could be placed anywhere needed for display without introducing any additional, conflicting, strongly directional linear elements into the room **(3, 4, 5)**.

On the office and library level, the slatted ceiling is white rather than bronze, with lighting introduced through the slats as in the galleries and from fluorescent wall washers around the "floating" edges of the ceiling.

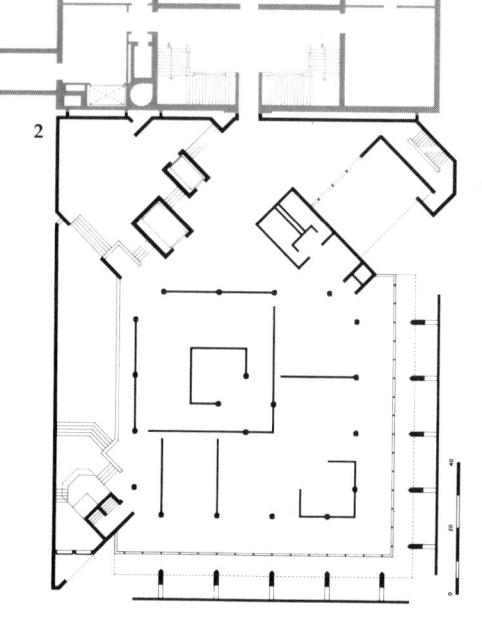

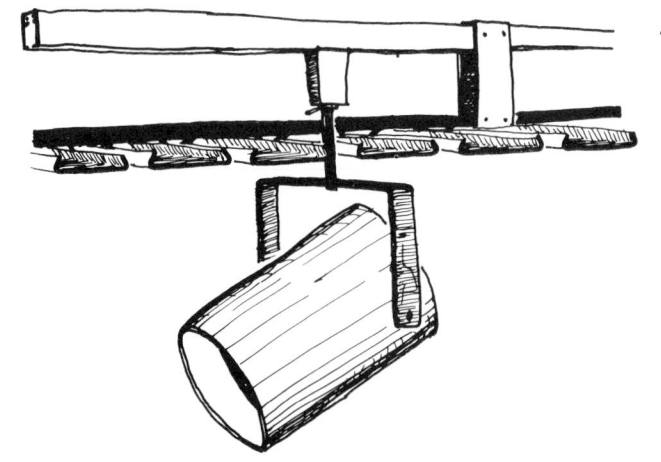

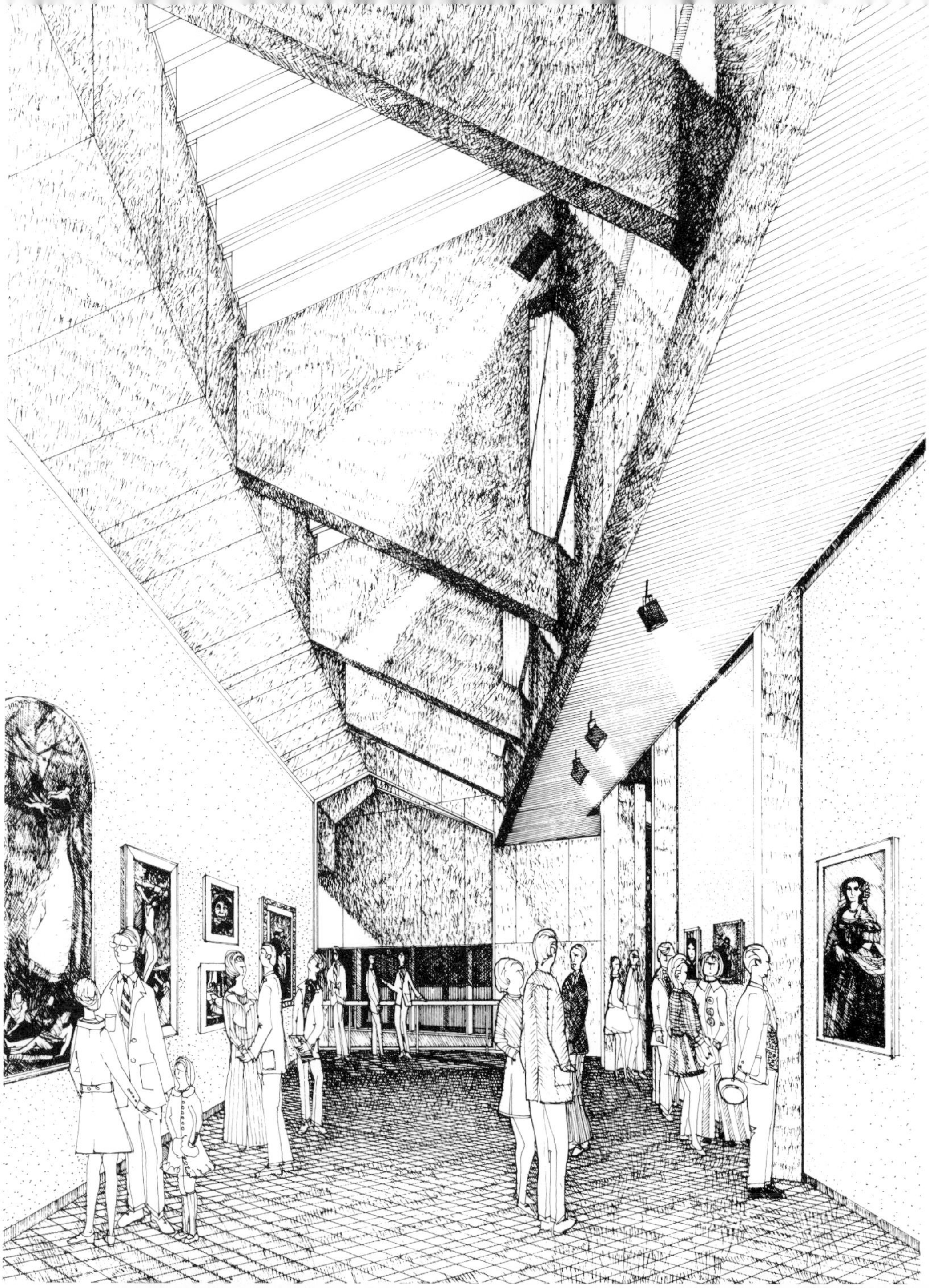

Shepley Bullfinch Richardson & Abbot

5

6

7

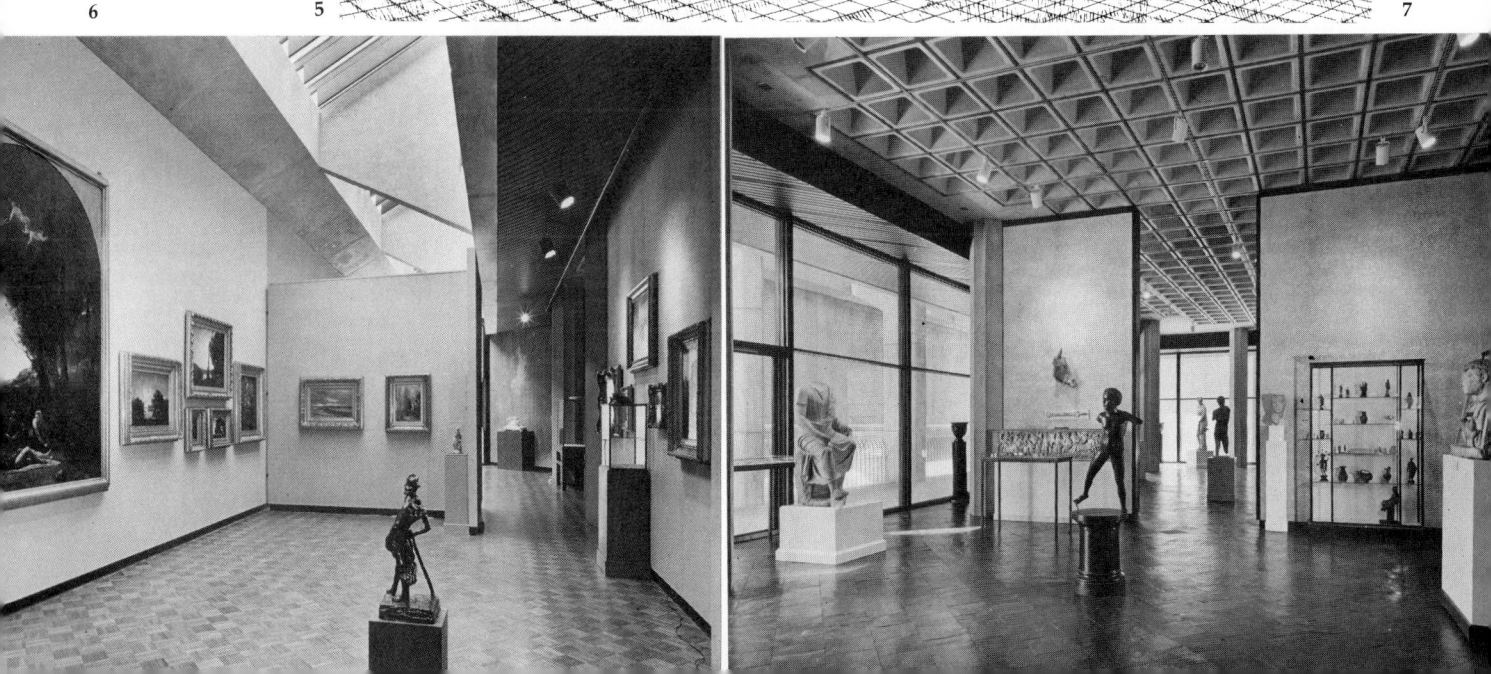

ADDITION
HUNTINGTON MUSEUM
Huntington, West Virginia

C4

The Architects Collaborative (architect); Walter Gropius (principal); Malcolm Ticknor (associate in charge); Walter S. Donat (associated architects); William Lam Associates, Inc. (lighting consultants); Architectural Concrete Consultants (concrete consultants); Bevers, Urban, Klug & Pittenger (mechanical and electrical engineers); Souza & True (structural engineers); Persun Construction Co. (general contractor). Schematic design started 1967.

Photos by Louis Reens

1

Buildings consisting of a few major spaces on a single floor are generally less affected by mechanical distribution requirements than are more complex structures. Since the required ductwork can be placed in the basement and run up vertically within the walls, uninterrupted ceilings are possible in galleries and corridors. In such cases, a continuous waffle-slab ceiling can work well as natural centering or louvering for lighting.

At Huntington, lighting design began with the assumption that the principal focus should be on the exhibits hung on the walls and on pole-supported panels inserted between the floor and the concrete ribs above. In order to minimize the visual competition from the ceiling, the waffles were used as a subtle organizing texture and centering for the fixtures rather than as lighting baffles. Point outlets for track-type fixtures were located in cells adjacent to the permanent walls and expected panel positions. They were circuited so that each wall and panel area could be switched or dimmed independently. Outlets in every cell throughout would have been both more costly *and* more flexible than required, unless the cell size were much larger.

In a few carefully selected areas, the waffles were used as louvers. For instance, in two axial areas which would be natural places for sculpture, the possibility of diffused light from "artificial skylights" was created by having outlets in every cell, fitted with clear or bottom-silvered lamps. Sculpture is highlighted from spot lamps in adjacent cells **(3)**.

The design uses controlled daylight to give vitality to the spaces. The scoop-type clerestories **(4)** introduce a constantly varying mix of daylight and in-

candescent light. During the day it is very apparent that some walls are bathed in daylight, others by incandescent. The color mismatch might seem unnatural in a photograph, but goes unnoticed in the understandable context of the gallery itself. The frequent visitor probably welcomes the opportunity to "live with" the works under the range of conditions he would have at home. The view window to the lovely surrounding countryside (the focal point in a major gallery space) is welcomed by most as a pleasant diversion

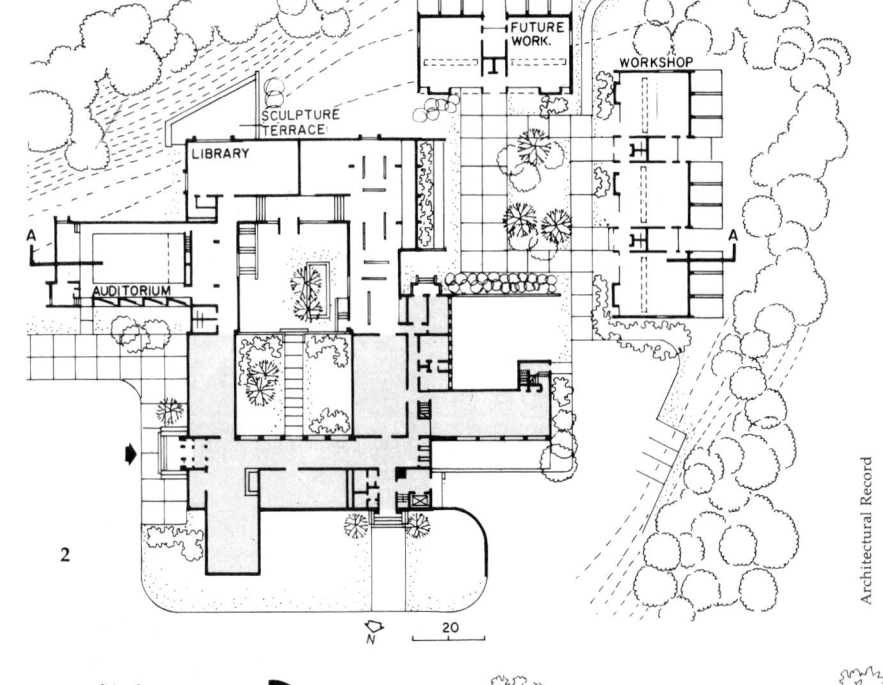

2

20
N

Architectural Record

SECTION A-A
10

| LOBBY | AUDITORIUM | GALLERY | LOWER COURTYARD | GALLERY | OUTER COURTYARD | WORKSHOP |

4

rather than competition to the art on display. The opportunity to shift attention to a distant focus is restful for the eyes.

The auditorium **(5)** was treated very differently, reflecting its different construction and purpose. The steps in the side walls were emphasized by recessed lights; the stage rear, by lighting concealed behind the front edge of a "floating" ceiling.

Having programmed probable positions for sculpture in the garden and terrace, outlet points and fixtures were placed at suitable positions on walls and in the ground to provide adaptable outdoor lighting **(6).**

At the time when the photographs were taken, baffles in the fixtures for control of spill light had not yet been installed, and some undesirable spills can be seen on the edges of the coffers.

5

6

Photos by Louis Reens

Michael Drummond/Montreal

1

PLACE BONAVENTURE
Montreal, Quebec

Affleck Desbarats Dimakopoulos Lebensold & Sise (architect); R. T. Affleck (partner in charge); J. E. LaRiviere (project manager); Eva Vecsei (project designer); D. Lazosky, H. K. Stenman (project architects); N. Holloway (project administrator); Herman Pallas (specifications); T. O'Brien, Antoine N. Haddad (design coordinators); R. Khosla (tenant architect); I. Reichmann (lighting and graphics coordinator); H. de Koning (interior design); Sasaki Dawson Demay Associates (landscape architect); Masao Kinoshita (principal in charge); William Lam Associates, Inc. (lighting consultants); N. J. Pappas & Associates (acoustical consultant); Paul Arthur & Associates Girard, Bruce, Garabenian & Associates (graphics consultants); Roland William Jutras Associates, Inc. (hotel interior design consultant); Vincent Ponte (town planning consultant); DeLeuw Cather & Partners (traffic and parking consultant); Jas. P. Keith & Associates (mechanical and electrical engineers); R. R. Nicolet & Associates Lalonde, Valois, Lamarre, Valois & Associates (structural engineers); Concordia Estates Development Co. (developer); Concordia Construction Co. (general contractor); Cost: $75,000,000. Square footage: 3,100,000. Schematic design started 1964. Construction completed 1967.

Place Bonaventure, as most people who have been to Expo now know, is not what its name suggests—neither a public square with a monument in the center, nor a great plaza, serving as a platform for a typical arrangement of office towers, high-rise apartment buildings or great halls for the celebration of the arts. Place Bonaventure has no real plaza at all. One of the largest buildings in the world and relatively low in comparison to surrounding office and hotel towers, it is a dense monolith which almost completely covers its 6-acre site. As a building type it has no counterpart anywhere.

Designed by Montreal architects Affleck Desbarats Dimakopoulos Lebensold & Sise, this $80-million complex has been constructed primarily to provide space at many scales for the exhibition and sale of products, and supplementary space to shelter and feed those involved in viewing and buying. Its great showrooms serve the international businessman, and the shopping

concourse accommodates the local worker on his way to the subway. Built on air rights above the Canadian National railroad tracks, the massive building is shaped by a complicated circulation network which accommodates underground truck routes, parking, a subway station, and sheltered pedestrian passageways, all of which link with corresponding systems which are being developed as an integral part of Montreal's 200-acre urban core. The complexity of these interrelated functions constituted a major architectural challenge. As a prototype for the dense, multi-use urban complex of the future, Place Bonaventure's brilliant and unusual *parti* deserves careful study.

Place Bonaventure's lack of an actual *place*, and its dense monolithic shape can be explained by an analysis of the program requirements. The owner's essential demand was for the type of space which should be artificially lit. Merchandise displayed in exhibition and shopping areas is shown to best

advantage under carefully controlled lighting conditions and daylight can be a positive handicap. The provision of vast interior spaces became a practical answer. Only the hotel, auxiliary office spaces for the display areas, and principal public elevator lobbies required perimeter locations to provide daylight and views. This meant horizontal circulation had precedence over vertical circulation for eminently functional reasons. The vertical distance to be travelled by elevators was minimized as was the area of perimeter wall and windows. These fundamental considerations made the conventional tower plaza

solution infeasible.

Public enjoyment of the little outdoor open space which the Place Bonaventure complex affords is limited to users of the restaurants which are centered in the roof-top hotel garden shown in the hotel level plan or to future patrons of the small terrace cafe which is planned for the southern end of the west plaza shown in the shopping-level plan. This plaza's principal purpose is to serve as an appropriately imposing drive-in entrance to the lower hotel lobby which is connected by express elevators to the main hotel lobby on the roof. The plaza also conceals parking facilities for about 1,000 cars.[1]

The design process

The project size, its complexity, and particularly the short time cycle between schematic design and occupancy (3 years) might have led to the all-too-frequent design approach which requires little design coordination—a ho-

[1]*"Place Bonaventure, A Unique Urban Complex,"* The Architectural Record, *December 1967, pp. 139–140.*

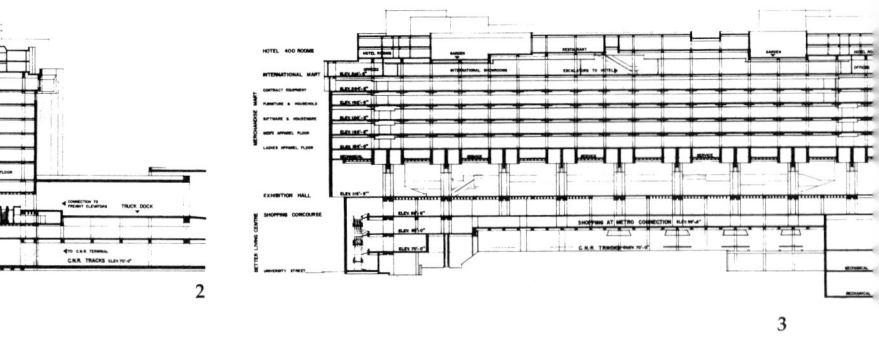

2

3

mogenized approach of quickly erected steel loft spaces covered by a suspended ceiling that can conceal any arrangement of services.

Instead, Place Bonaventure represents a commitment to excellence through articulation and integration, despite the time limitations, by means of an unprecedented *team* effort. All relevant design disciplines worked closely together from concept to execution along with the builder (who, fortunately, was also the owner). Only the quality of the decision-making process and project management could have made possible the consistency of concept in the design and execution of the many integrated, articulated systems and the hundreds of details throughout the building.

The Place Bonaventure character comes from the consistent expression of concepts so clear that they can be expressed in words. The close designer/builder collaboration also meant that all forms were greatly influenced by the actual construction process used. It was not uncommon for structural details to be modified a day before the concrete was poured because of some problem in forming, etc. Since the lighting vocabulary was in concept rather than hardware, on such occasions the lighting was easily redesigned on the spot. The themes were few,

the variations many.

Even in single buildings—a shopping center, an exhibition hall, a merchandise mart, an office building, a hotel, etc.—the integration of structural, mechanical, and lighting systems is not easy. When such diverse structures were brought together within a single building envelope with a desire for consistency of details, the difficulties were considerably multiplied. Clarity of design concepts was essential to the achievement of a successful, sophisticated building, especially in view of the extremely tight schedule.

Architectural and lighting concepts

In a typical urban place, buildings of widely varying functions are given a common identity by their relationship to the connecting outdoor space. Since such a relationship is not possible in a series of "buildings" within a common shell, the common denominators must necessarily be limited to those which can only be perceived sequentially.

The concepts which unified Place Bonaventure were as follows: The building was to be masculine, of urban rather than building scale. Public spaces and paths were to be treated as "streets and plazas" rather than as "corridors and lobbies." Positively defined cores at the corners would contain

common facilities such as elevators, washrooms, emergency stairs, etc. The decision to wash the exterior of these cores with light required that they be treated architecturally as "tubes" with punched openings. The common material was to be concrete in a range of textures. On all levels, the concrete itself was to be formed to conceal light sources, creating glowing lanterns—large lanterns, such as the structural concrete "trees" of Concordia Hall, the floating stairs, the hotel skylights, the hotel entrance canopy, and smaller-scale elements, such as telephone booths (5), step lights, lanterns, bollards, and posts. For sparkle, a vocabulary was built around a common element of clear incandescent lamps baffled with sheets of bronze glass, used for wall brackets (21), room-scale chandeliers, and artificial "skylights." Globes were considered too "feminine." Because of the great size of each level, the provision of clear information for orientation was particularly important. Sign requirements were taken as form determinants (sign chandeliers (6,8,10,20), wide transoms and door frames).

On the concourse level, the principal focus and source of the interior "street" lighting was to come from shop windows and signs. However, when shops are unlit or have no display windows,

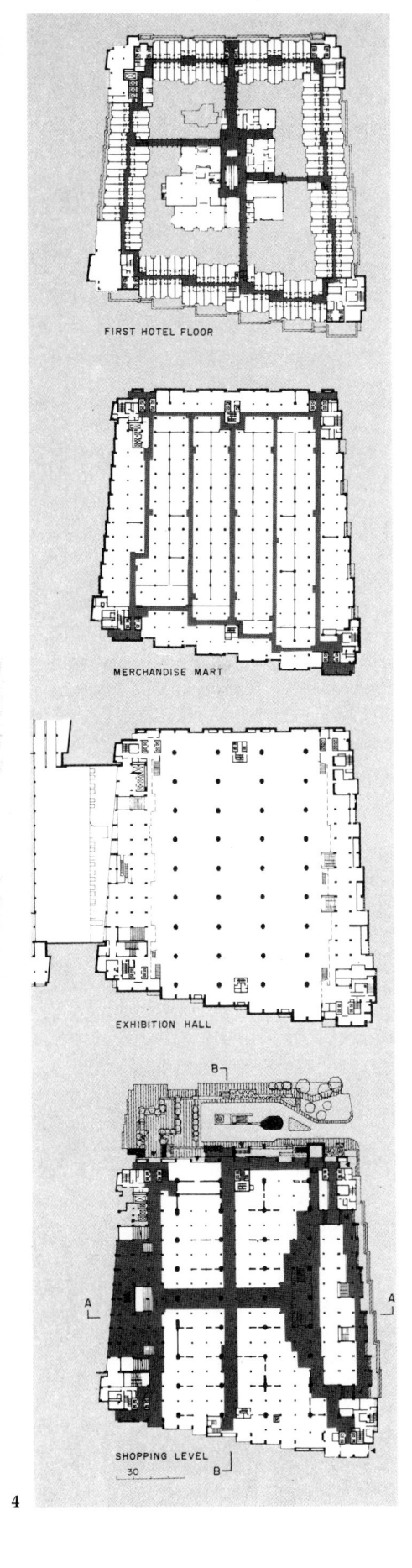

FIRST HOTEL FLOOR

MERCHANDISE MART

EXHIBITION HALL

SHOPPING LEVEL

30

Roger Jowett

6

Harold Lewis/Photo International

Chris Payne

7 *Half-inch-scale study model of artificial "skylight" shown in* **Fig. 8** *below.*

8

Michael Drummond/Montreal

4

9

10

column-mounted lanterns fill in and give continuity. As the most consistently available element, columns were kept sacrosanct for this purpose.

Orientation clues are important in such a large enclosed area without normally available orientation information such as exterior building forms, direction of sunlight, etc. Graphic chandeliers of positive rather than apologetic scale were created to display the needed information. The well leading to the Metro station (7,8) was emphasized as a sharply outlined "skylight." Similar concrete ceiling areas elsewhere on this level were intentionally left unlit, except insofar as they received a soft glow from the windows, column brackets, and "chandeliers" that define the "eddies" in the main corridor. As on other floors, exterior walls of the cores were washed with light. Entry points, etc., were highlighted from neutral downlights. A model was used to test the effect of lighting and signing. It verified the effect of the single, main "skylight" above the metro well but led to a change from a uniform band of standardized signs to a more lively, random, bazaar-like scheme.

Objectives and assumptions regarding Concordia Hall, the major space in the complex, were as follows: for the staging of

shows the space should appear *neutral* (i.e., the pattern of lighting should not compete with displays). The ceiling should provide an integral catwalk system from which any amount of totally adjustable lighting could be directed to any display that is not self-illuminated. Neutral "house" lighting should be kept to a minimum. As a place for assembly and receptions, a *positive*, distinctive Place Bonaventure character was required for the space. A positive space might also be desired for some shows. Lighting (and overhead mechanical and electrical services) should be flexible, without sacrificing the permanent character of the building.

Design development

Since lighting coordination started from the beginning of design development, it was possible to develop an integrated structural/mechanical/lighting/display system within a few days.

The original schematic post-and-beam structure would have implied a wasteful structural depth with a hung ceiling to cover the usual disarray of service elements. Extensive perforation of the structure itself to accommodate mechanical runs would have been necessary. A tree-type structure (13,16,17,18) was evolved in order to create clean architectural surfaces which might be positive-

ly illuminated to express the maximum volume and to transfer the loads of 25 × 25 foot bays overhead to the 50 × 75 foot bays of the Hall, while still providing the necessary two-way distribution of mechanical services from the corner cores. The trees were braced with a permanent ceiling catwalk system of concrete waffles pierced with an extensive distribution of portholes for lighting, drop cords, hanging displays, and air distribution.

The lighting system incorporated incandescent can fixtures in portholes as neutral house lights. The perimeter walls and trees which create the character of the space were defined by decorative patterns of exposed incandescent point sources. More efficient linear sources (such as fluorescent) were avoided because they would have interrupted the structural continuity of the trees for those persons looking up. Continuous high-capacity lighting track was provided along rows of portholes in the ceiling for flexibility.

In circulation spaces within the merchandise mart, cores were given typical treatment (wall washers). Display windows were to dominate corridors with minimum competition, to create the proper focus on the merchandise. Light spill from the displays is quite sufficient to illuminate corridors (9). Supplementary per-

14

11

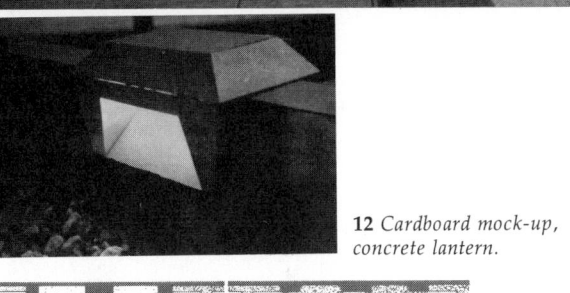

12 *Cardboard mock-up, concrete lantern.*

15

16 *Study model of Concordia Hall.*

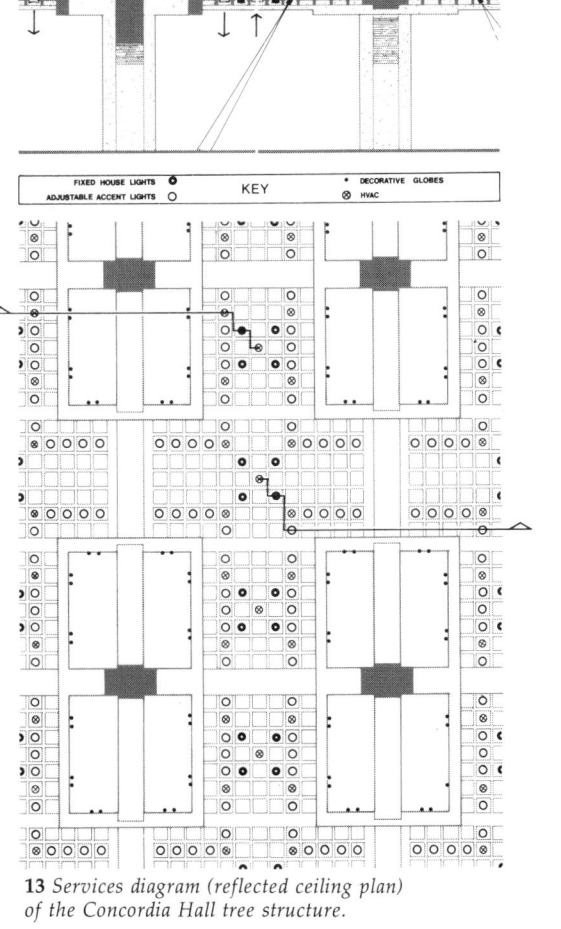

		KEY		
FIXED HOUSE LIGHTS ●			● DECORATIVE GLOBES	
ADJUSTABLE ACCENT LIGHTS ○			⊗ HVAC	

13 *Services diagram (reflected ceiling plan)
of the Concordia Hall tree structure.*

17

Photo overleaf/Michael Drummond

C5 Place Bonaventure   151

manent corridor lighting was provided from each door header, and graphic chandeliers were located to define and give orientation at each circulation junction **(10)**.

Walking through other merchandise marts revealed visual chaos as characteristic. Dominant ceilings, varied arbitrarily in materials and lighting over the course of several tenant changes, produce confusion and disorder. A consultant on merchandise marts advised "have an inviolate ceiling."

The design team did propose a unifying concrete-grid system with flexible service space above and provisions for an unlimited amount of lighting flexibility. This ceiling would have been "inviolate" in that very few tenants would have bothered to apply a second ceiling over an existing attractive, exposed structural ceiling. Unfortunately, this scheme had to be abandoned because of the method of financing. It would have been economical if the owner were to have completed all construction, leasing totally finished spaces. However, to reduce the initial capital investment required, the decision was made to lease unfinished spaces that would be air conditioned and finished entirely by tenants at their expense.

The metal-slat ceiling selected as the building standard **(23,24)**

does help unify the commercial areas, creating a quality that can be maintained over the years and through tenant changes. Unfortunately, the lighting effects are not controlled by management, but the system does encourage some standardization in the form of lighting track and slat-width fixtures.

The hotel variation on the general theme began with an entrance canopy with clear lamps set in concrete coffers and decorative sign chandeliers. Column-mounted brackets at concourse level were repeated closely spaced around the elevator core at hotel level (which is not one of the corner cores). In the lobby, bays of concrete-baffled clear skylights were edged with chandeliers. Long hotel corridors were interrupted by skylit wells **(27)**. The decorative lamp theme was extended to the mirror lighting in each suite **(22)**. Bridges **(25)** linking the central activity pavilion to the perimeter bedroom zone were illuminated from handrails in such a way as to avoid reflections that would interfere with viewing the garden at night. Unfortunately, heat- (and light-) reducing glass was used in windows looking out onto the garden, which, though they reduce solar heat gain, also reduce the visibility of the garden at night.

To create a ballroom which

could be both neutral for meetings and elegant for special functions, a design incorporating neutral downlights, adjustable accent lights, and reflecting chandeliers was developed. Fully collapsible, easily removed chandeliers were conceived to meet the programmed requirement that the full ceiling height be available for projection. However, in the final version **(19)** the adjustable features[2] had to be abandoned and the chandeliers reduced considerably in scale.

The hotel garden features ponds, fountains, and trees. Several forms of concrete lanterns **(11,14,15)** were designed to provide low-level pavement illumination. Where possible, the sparkling incandescent lamps of these lanterns were placed to reflect in the ponds.

Comment

By 1973 the owner (operator of a supermarket chain) had replaced the original vocabulary on the concourse level with uniformly distributed and domineering patterns of fluorescent fixtures, much to the detriment of the space.

[2]*Later accomplished at the Hyatt Regency at O'Hare Airport, Chicago* **(Case Study C7)**.

Clear incandescent lamps set the theme at Place Bonaventure

Photos without credits by Harold Lewis/Photo International

20

21

22

23

Courtesy of Luxalon® Ceilings   Courtesy of Luxalon® Ceilings

24

HYATT REGENCY SAN FRANCISCO HOTEL
San Francisco, California

C6

John Portman & Associates (architects); John Portman, Jr. (architect in charge); William Lam Associates, Inc. (lighting consultants); Morris E. Harrison & Associates (electrical engineers); Elster's (interiors); Britt Alderman & Associates (mechanical engineers); Harding, Miller, Lawson & Associates (soils consultants). Jones-Allen-Dillingham (general contractor). Cost: $758,677. Square footage: 17,328. Construction completed 1973.

The atrium of the San Francisco Hyatt demonstrates dramatically the effectiveness of a minimal area of clear skylighting in creating the ambience of a pleasant, outdoor public plaza when used with plantings of the proper scale and outdoor materials such as tile pavers and concrete. The highlighted metal sculpture gives a strong focus to the space, while the concrete trellises above the sunken lounges create pockets of space with a more intimate atmosphere at the floor of the cavernous lobby. The lighting scheme for the lobby consists only of the lighted sculpture, trellises, and trees, complemented and set off by a single band of decorative clear lamps around the perimeter which draws the line between the surrounding commercial space and the lobby proper. The upper surfaces of the atrium are washed with a soft glow of indirect illumination from the handrail-lit balconies.

At the stand-up bar (6) the design team indulged in a bit of perceptual trickery, using the polished metal sides of the hood over the bar to mirror the glittering ceiling around them, so that the ceiling appears to extend in an unbroken plane over the bar.

5

4

6

HYATT REGENCY O'HARE HOTEL
Chicago, Illinois

John Portman & Associates (architect); John Street (project architect); Sasaki Dawson Demay Associates (landscape architect); William Lam Associates, Inc. (lighting consultants); Thomas P. Hughes, AID (interior design and public space planning consultant); Morris Harrison & Associates (electrical engineers); Britt Alderman, Jr. (mechanical engineer); J. A. Jones Construction Co. (general contractor). Cost: $30,000,000. Schematic design started 1969.

1

2

3

Architectural Record

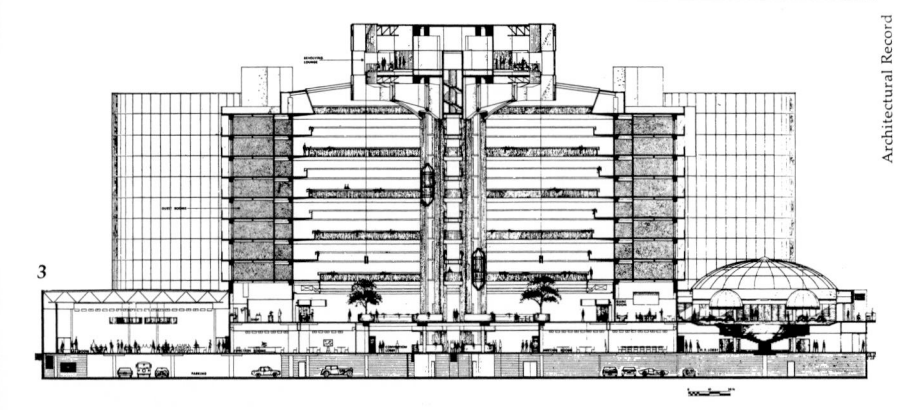

4

Alexandre Georges

The distinction of this hotel comes from its lobby **(6)**—extraordinarily vital both spatially and socially.

On the basis of biological needs, it was predicted that this vast interior space would be greatly enhanced by the introduction of sunlight to emphasize the spatial volume in a continuously varying manner (with much more variation than would be possible with only a single oculus). During the day, a ring of skylights high above the lobby creates the desired, striking effect. On overcast days, the space is not quite as appealing, just like any outdoor space, but the sparkle of moving elevators, the illuminated trees, the myriad of highlights, and the minimum of visible overcast sky all combine to reduce the effect of inclement weather.

The skylighting is valuable not because of the *amount* of light introduced but because of the specific *characteristics* which the daylight brings to the space. The directional light defines surfaces

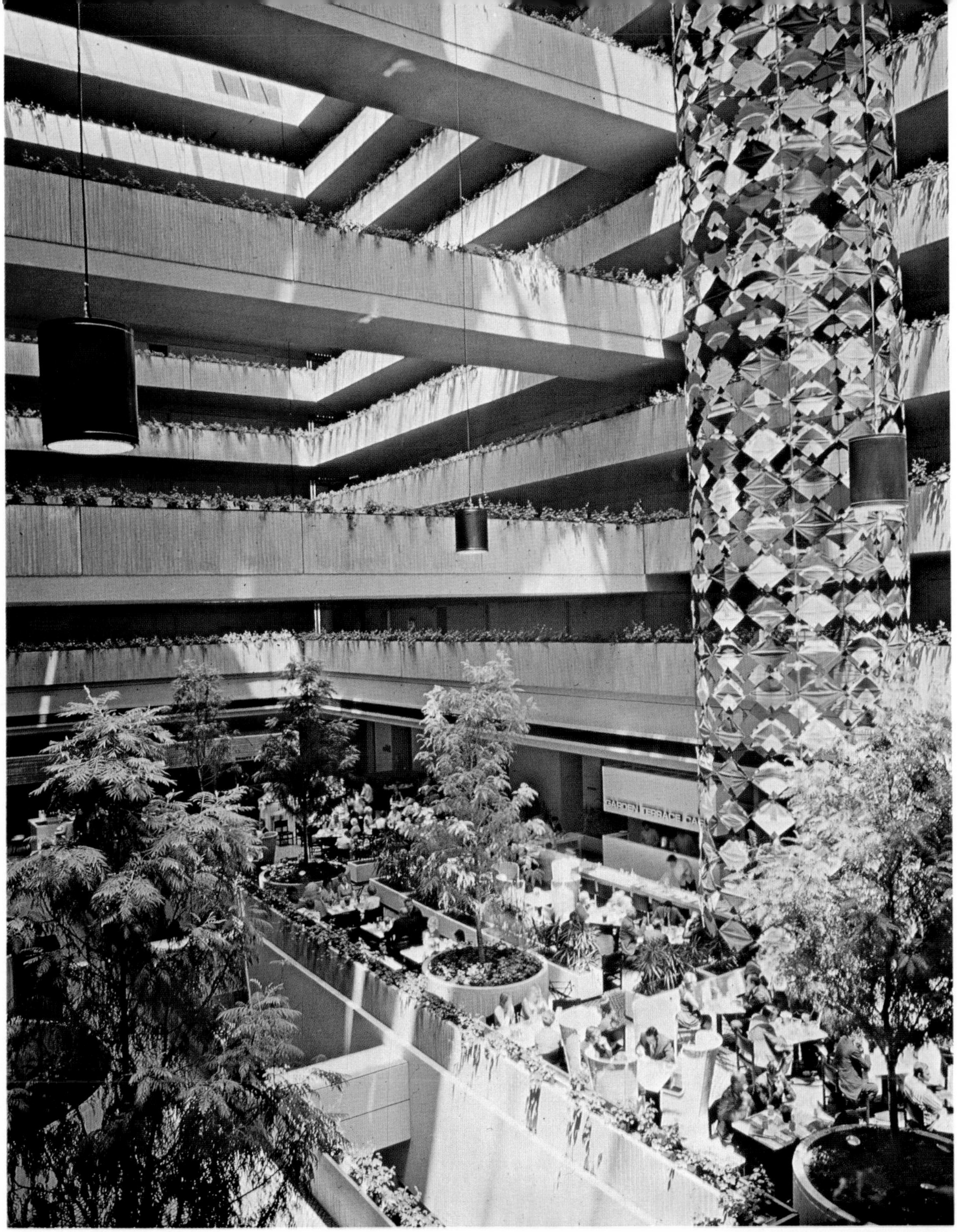

6

Photos without credits by Harold Lewis/Photo International

5

Courtesy Hyatt Regency

7

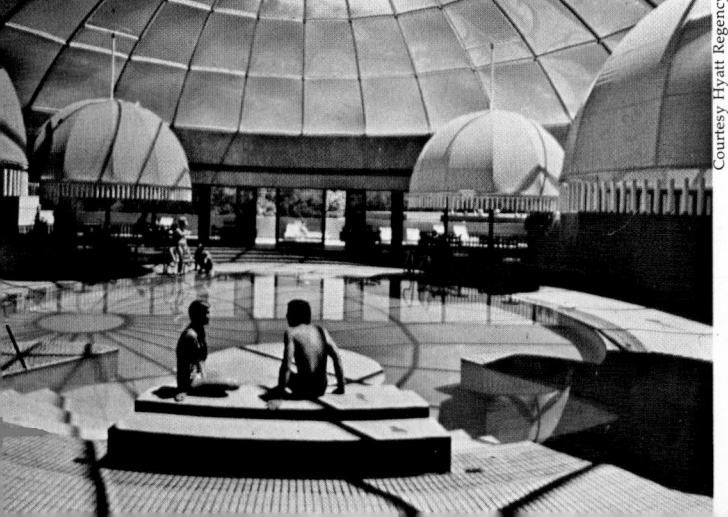

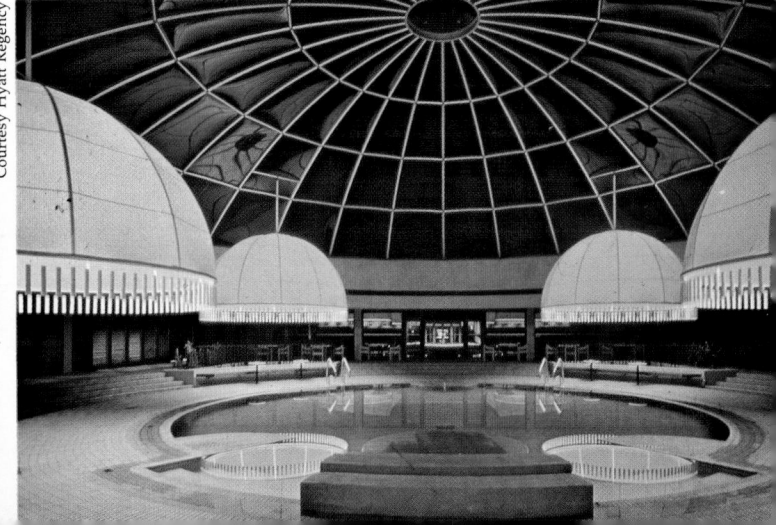

Photos by Alexandre Georges   **8**

9

11

10

and volumes dramatically, which become secondary sources illuminating the rest of the lobby. The decision to expose the Polaris Lounge structure to view from the lobby and to use clear glazing for connecting it to the perimeter mass (2) was a late design change. The original scheme called for a luminous plastic ceiling over the entire court with the Polaris Lounge totally separated from interior view. Had the original scheme been executed, a feeling of "permanent overcast" and of interior rather than outdoor space would have resulted, because of the diffuse quality of the light and the glaring nature of the translucent material. On the contrary, the daylight design along with the use of exterior materials and generous planting gives this vast interior space the feel and vitality of an exterior space. The presence of real rather than "artificial" sunlight is biologically important and gives subconscious pleasure to the users of the space. Openings were created in the lobby floor to serve as skylights for the reception level below (17), to establish some contact with outside conditions for this otherwise subterranean space.

At night, too, the space was treated as an exterior. As the sky darkens, so do the skylights, with no attempt to replace the daylight artificially. The lobby lighting becomes totally different as the daylight fades and lighting becomes more intimate, with concealed lighting from handrails, uplighted trees, the glitter of exposed clear lamps, some low floor lamps, and candlelight (4).

While any of the other major spaces might have been no different if located in another building, the common denominators that they share in concept and details give them a natural, perceptible relationship, subtly increasing the impact of each and all.

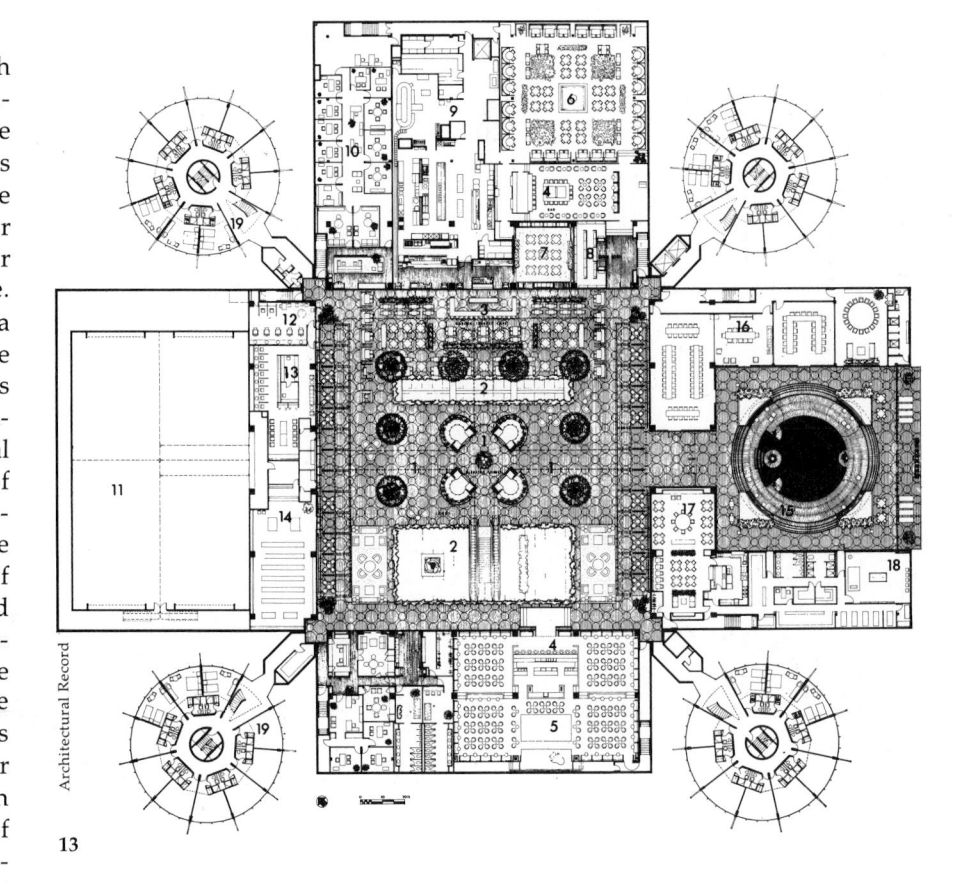

Architectural Record

13

Positive emphasis of the daytime-nighttime reversal is exemplified by the swimming-pool design, which shifts at dusk from sky dominance (5) to low focus (7). At night, the effect is created by umbrella-chandeliers (with clear lamps visible from close up) and underwater lighting.

In gourmet dining areas, daytime focus is on a daylighted pool. By night, the focus is on illuminated fountain/chandeliers (with clear lamps). The captivating effect of the pool itself is reinforced by application of the perception principle that biological instincts are aroused by water about to spill (18). The attraction is much greater than if the water level were

6 inches below the edge.

Hotel ballrooms are a challenging design problem. They must be suitable for a range of activities (from business meetings and banquets to fashion shows, balls, weddings, etc.) and usable as full rooms or subdivisible into a variety of spaces. Lighting therefore must provide totally different environments for all these possibilities. Any single design arrangement sufficiently flexible to provide for *all* these activities and conditions cannot be anything but a compromise. Any design effect can be varied by dimming, but the variability of effect is maximized when the relative *focus* (or the pattern of foci) is variable as well as

14

the intensity.

It was necessary to develop for the ballroom a ceiling system with integral lighting which could be used to create a number of different ambiences. The first and most basic function was to provide neutral downlighting throughout the entire space, with ceiling and light fixtures as inconspicuous as possible **(19).** Wall lighting which can be modified as required is essential to the creation of a really flexible space — while some walls were to be treated with a decorative chandelier effect, others would have to serve at times as neutral, highlighted backgrounds for displays, etc. In addition, the basic lighting

system had to provide focal lighting at potential "head table" locations, and at all potential locations of staged activities. Beyond these more functional requirements, the lighting had to provide a rich decorative effect, preferably with a distinctive character which would identify each individual ballroom. Any chandeliers had to look balanced and appropriate with either the subdivided or the whole room. A successful system would permit the easy creation of appropriate combinations of decorative and unobtrusive functional lighting to suit all possible events.

The ballroom ceiling is made up of Plexiglas cubes, some of which enclose fixed downlights

for neutral house lighting, while others house adjustable fixtures which can be used to accent head tables and impromptu stages. Perimeter cubes were left open on the outer face to house wall washers. A similar ceiling system was developed for the function rooms **(23).** A pool and fountain **(24)** provide a dramatic entry to the complex of function rooms and the lower lobby.

The decorative chandelier effect was accomplished by a large, room-scaled sculpture of reflecting plastic balls **(22)** that can be lowered and illuminated from neutral sources, and raised to disappear above the ceiling plane when a business-like environ-

C7 Hyatt Regency O'Hare Hotel 165

19

20

21

ment is desired or when a room is subdivided. Various degrees of intimacy can be attained depending on the height of the chandelier and the relative brightness of chandelier and other areas.

Screens of reflecting plastic balls and mirrors also line some of the walls and can broaden the decorative effect when desired. Unlike traditional internally illuminated chandeliers and wall brackets, these reflecting sculptures and curtains do not look unnatural when not illuminated.

The reflecting chandeliers, mirrored walls of the ballrooms, and patterns of clear lamps of the lobby and pool were repeated with variation in the bar (20), the executive health club game room (10), and the nightclub. The glowing red fabric of the nightclub ceiling was intentionally illuminated unevenly from the perimeter with hot spots related to the spacing of louvers. A ceiling with similar variation of luminance in an accidental, unplanned pattern would appear unevenly lighted, rather than giving evidence of a coordinating design intent.

The problem of lighting rooftop restaurants such as the Polaris Lounge is to enliven the atmosphere during dull days while interfering as little as possible with the view at night. The mirrored inside walls of the Polaris Lounge add to the view both day and night. The glowing ceiling, dimmed at night (21), reflects high in the windows but does not impede the downward view to the Chicago skyline. The guest tower roofs were outlined to give a close exterior view and reference point to those in the lounge, as well as to add to the exterior image of the entire hotel. The dramatic impact of the Polaris lobby was maximized by the use of a single light source (and focus) day or night — the skylight/chandelier (11).

22

Alexandre Georges

23

Ripman

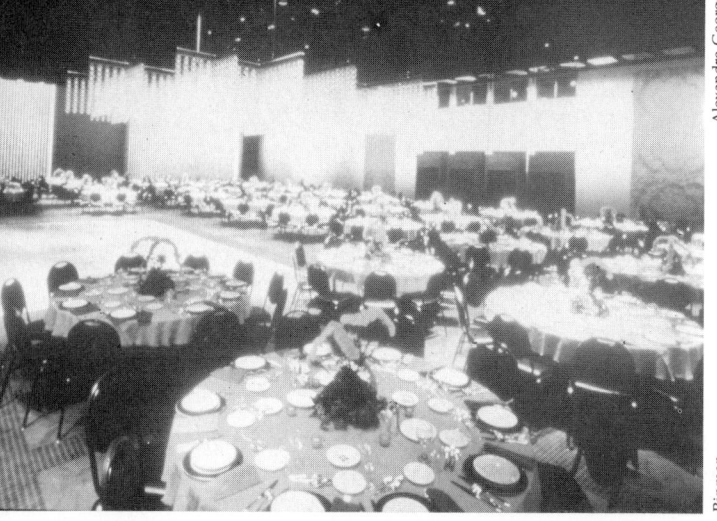

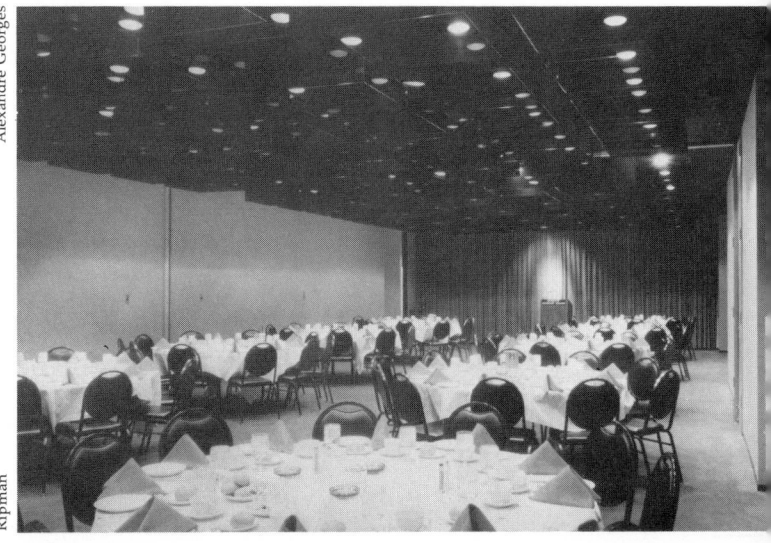

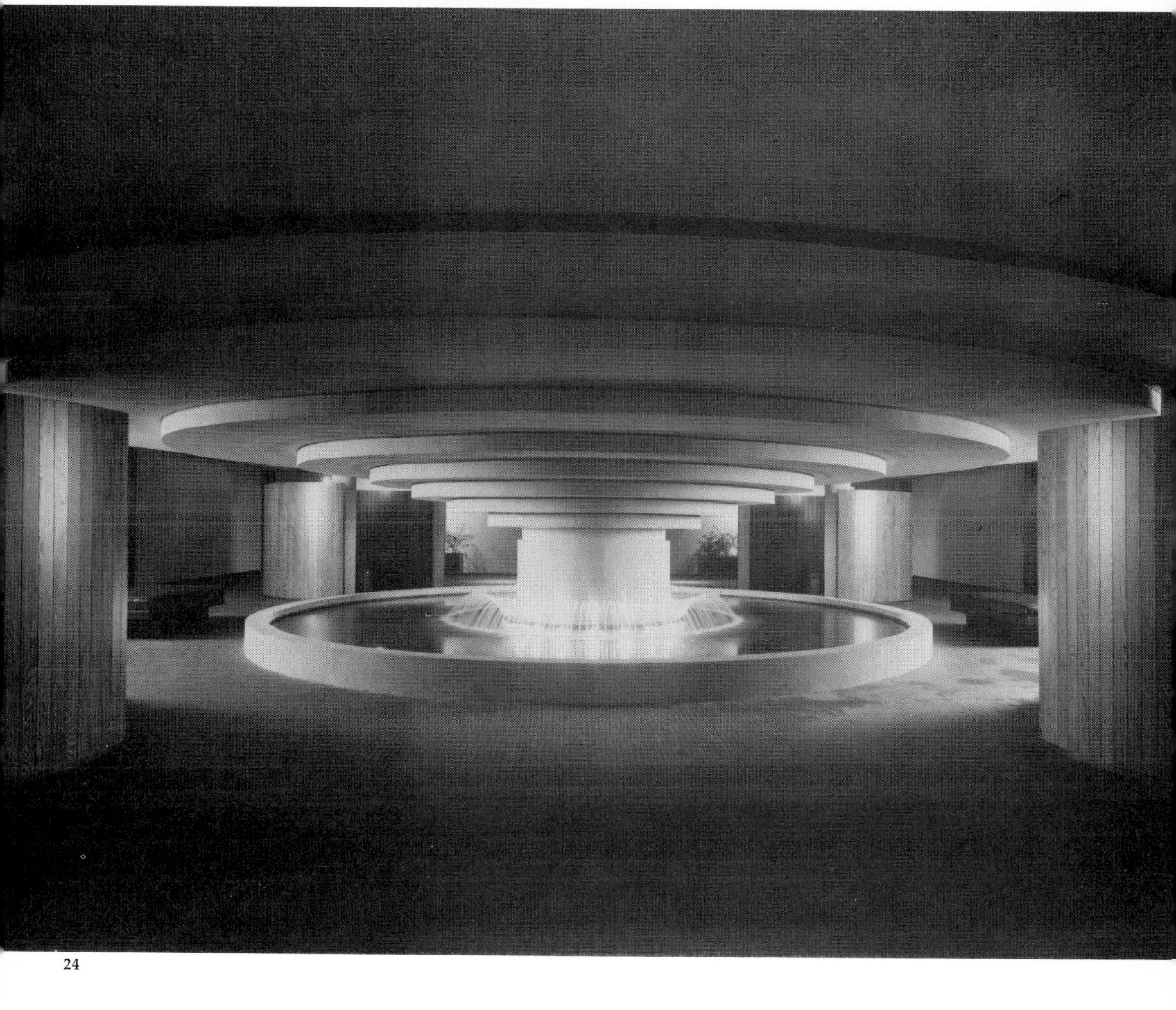

24

BELOIT COLLEGE ARTS CENTER
SOUTH CAMPUS COMPLEX
Beloit, Wisconsin

1

William Wenzler and Associates (architect); William Lam Associates, Inc. (lighting consultants); Bolt, Beranek and Newman (acoustical consultants); McKee-Berger-Mansueto (cost consultants); Jean Rosenthal and Associates (theater consultants); John F. Steffen Associates (mechanical engineers); Strass-Maguire and Associates (structural engineers). Schematic design started 1970.

The typical college arts center is usually built as a cluster of separate masses, each with its own structural system, connected by corridors for services and public circulation.

At Beloit (1), the integrated design process began with a field trip conducted for the design team to instill in the individual members an appreciation of what could be accomplished with an articulated approach which would integrate structural, mechanical, and lighting elements into an expressive architectural solution—as opposed to the homogenized solutions which might otherwise have been proposed. The investment of time and expense seemed to have been extremely worthwhile, to judge from the interdisciplinary cooperation which followed throughout the course of the project.

The initial schematic plans led to a tentative exploration of a tree-type structural approach,[1] but this line of exploration was abandoned for several reasons. Primary among these reasons was a shift in the architect's concept from formal, rectangular spaces toward informal, irregular polygonal spaces as the most appropriate to accommodate the variety of spaces in the program.

Therefore, the approach shifted from a highly articulated structure to a *totally* neutral one. The very tight budget suggested that all spaces be created within concrete lofts hung on a regular col-

umn grid. The desire for partitioning flexibility *with* good acoustic separation between the subdivided spaces led to the selection of a flat slab, lightened with tubular inserts. Against this hard, flat ceiling, partitions can easily be placed and sealed in any configuration desired without sacrifice of acoustic isolation, an objective which would have much more difficult to achieve with a waffle slab, a steel frame structure, or a rib slab—any of which might easily have been selected during the early phases of a conventional sequential design process.

Design

With the flat slab thus predetermined, lighting design commenced by addressing the most limiting factor: the distribution of air conditioning and other services. With two levels of public spaces, ductwork could not be channeled entirely within the walls or run directly up from the basement, which might have been possible in a smaller and simpler building. Under these circumstances the most common approach is to use lowered ceilings in corridors to conceal the necessary services so that the major spaces can be kept free of ductwork.

However, because of the desire to use the connecting spaces as important galleries and public spaces, an alternate design was developed in which the perimeter of the major spaces is used for the

distribution of services to those spaces themselves and to adjacent public areas (2). For this purpose a valance system (3) was developed to conceal ducts while supporting and baffling light fixtures. The dual purpose led to a universal rack for services and an unusually deep valance, with light sources fairly far out from the walls. The maximum display height on the walls is reduced somewhat with this system, but the design team felt that this was a worthwhile tradeoff in exchange for full-height circulation spaces.

The valance system was used wherever appropriate throughout the center, supplemented as required by other systems. During intermissions, the theater (5) is illuminated by wall lighting plus inconspicuous downlighting from the ceiling of the hall. During lectures with projection, the downlights alone are used. For the display of art and other material (4), wall lighting plus track-mounted adjustable downlighting was provided; art studios received a similar treatment. In music practice areas, wall lighting is quite sufficient for illumination of the back rows; supplementary downlighting was provided for front rows.

---

[1]*Tree-type structures, based on two-way cantilevered platforms with integral perimeter service distribution channels, are discussed in* **Case Study B1-f** *(Place Bonaventure) and in* **Section E,** *below.*

Renderings by Ralph Winter of William Wenzler Associates

ARED CLASSROOM

ANTHROPOLOGY EXHIBITION HALL

2

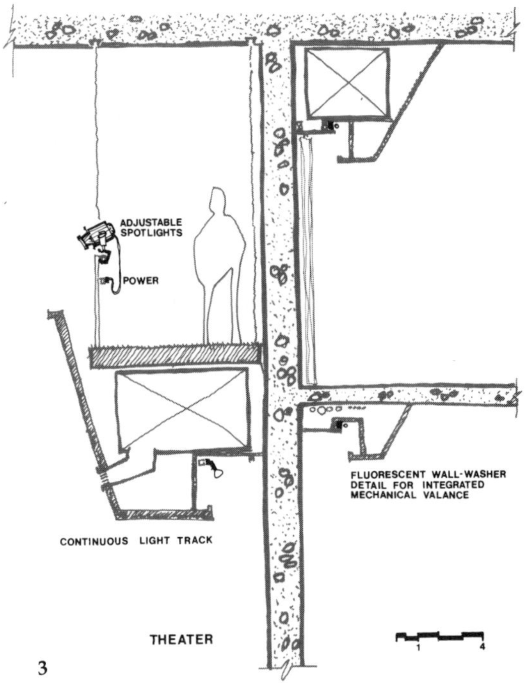

ADJUSTABLE
SPOTLIGHTS

POWER

FLUORESCENT WALL-WASHER
DETAIL FOR INTEGRATED
MECHANICAL VALANCE

CONTINUOUS LIGHT TRACK

THEATER

3

VIEW OF THE COMMONS

4

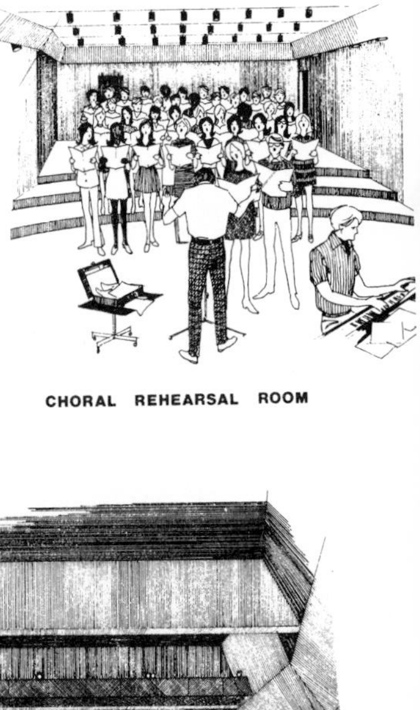

CHORAL REHEARSAL ROOM

RECITAL HALL

5

HYATT REGENCY HOUSTON HOTEL
Houston, Texas

(C9)

(JV III), Koetter Tharp & Cowell, Caudill Rowlett Scott, Neuhaus & Taylor (joint venture architects); William Lam Associates, Inc. (lighting consultants); DuBose Gallery (art consultant); Chenault & Brady (mechanical engineers); Walter P. Moore & Associates (structural engineers); W. S. Bellows Construction Corporation (general contractor); Elster's (interiors contractor). Schematic design started 1970. Construction completed 1972.

1 *Early scheme.*

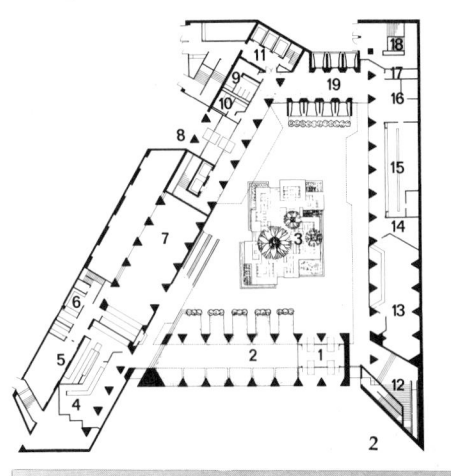

Lobby Level Plan

1 main hotel entrance
2 Whistler's Walk (sidewalk cafe)
3 Park in the Lobby (sunken seating garden)
4 Coffee Shop
5 service kitchen
6 service bar
7 Keeping Room (restaurant)
8 auto entry
9 women
10 men
11 service elevators
12 access to tunnels
13 Back Room (music bar)
14 news and tobacco shop
15 front desk
16 administration
17 baggage
18 fire stair
19 elevators

2

For the Hyatt Regency Houston Hotel, the design team attempted to attain some of the successful qualities of the O'Hare Regency lobby while working under the handicaps inherent in greatly different room proportions—narrow and high rather than wide and low. Fortunately, lighting coordination took place early enough so that modifications were still possible in the plan as well as in fenestration and other details.

The success of the O'Hare lobby came from the deep penetration of sunlight, which reflects from large areas low in the space throughout the day and creates a pleasant, outdoor environment. The intimate people-watching contact was equally important but less easily obtainable in a tall building such as the Houston Regency. It was observed that the Atlanta Regency lobby seemed comparatively "dead" because the small, clear oculus allows only small patches of sunlight to be seen. A luminous ceiling was to be avoided. The pendent fixtures used at O'Hare to help the growth of trees were to be avoided if possible.

Design

While desirable, a transparent roof over the entire space was not within budget. Consequently, clear skylights were placed along two edges of the space **(5).** Sunlight penetrates deeply into the space for much of the day. These bands of skylights were then con-

3 *Final scheme.*

Walt Bell (Joint Venture III)

tinued as windows down to the ground (3) to further increase the sunlight penetration low in the space and to add an element not present at Atlanta: some visual contact with the surrounding city. Concentration of planting in this area of high natural daylighting should make it relatively easy and inexpensive to maintain.

The decorative clear-lamp scheme of Chicago was expanded at Houston to define the elevator shafts (7) as well as the moving cars and to screen their shafts (the lines of bright sources making it more difficult to discern the details of the darker shafts behind). Lines of clear lamps above the elevator doors signal the arrival of cars (11). Doors to guestrooms were recessed, and it was natural to express their rhythm with strips of the same clear lamps. Handrail

lighting could thus be restricted to the public levels, since the lamps over the guestroom doors provide ample corridor illumination. At the Houston Regency the handrail lighting was not considered a major architectural theme to be used consistently throughout the building, and a more neutral detail was developed (compared with O'Hare) based on the standard handrail designed for the Houston Regency.

It is relatively difficult to grow trees in most large interior spaces. While the trees in the Houston Regency lobby receive some daylight from the skylights, a steady additional 250 footcandles was estimated as desirable. Seven very-narrow-beam spotlights could have been used to provide the required illumination from an oculus in the ceiling. This

Alexandre Georges

6

Section

1 motor entry
2 Keeping Room (restaurant)
3 garages
4 exhibition hall
5 kitchen
6 offices
7 laundry
8 Imperial Ballroom
9 ballroom foyer
10 mechanical
11 Back Room (music bar)
12 meeting rooms
13 Window Box (gourmet restaurant)
14 elevators
15 Spindletop (revolving restaurant-lounge)

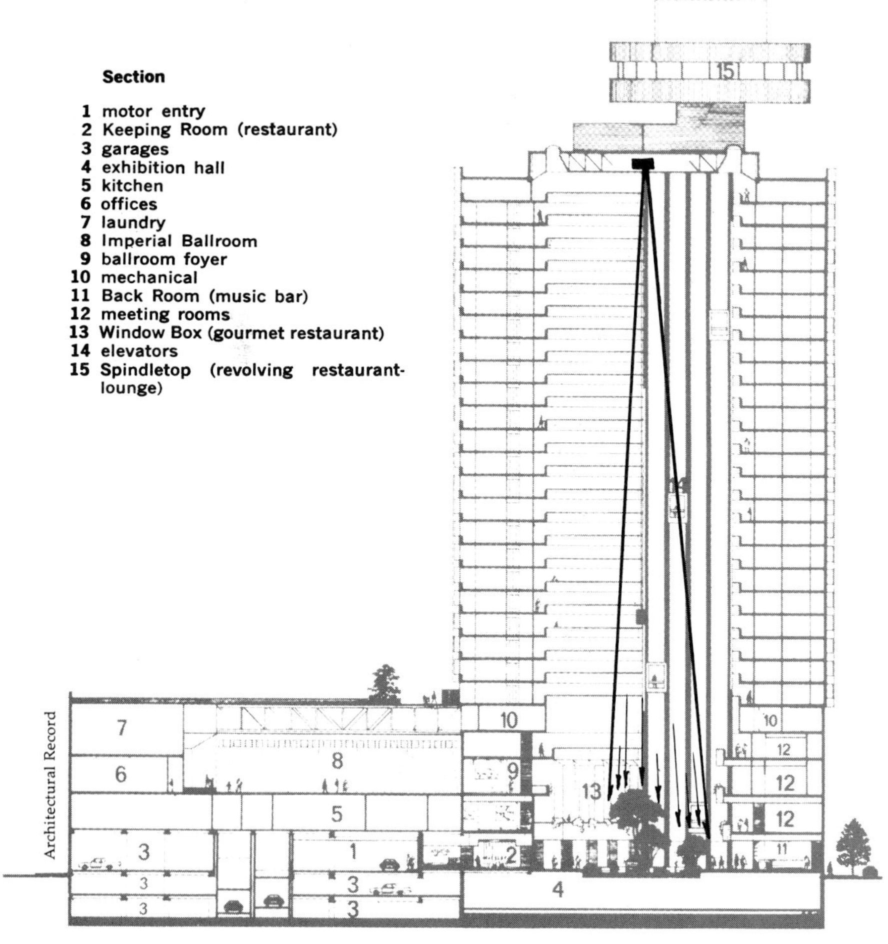

4 Tree lighting from a single oculus.

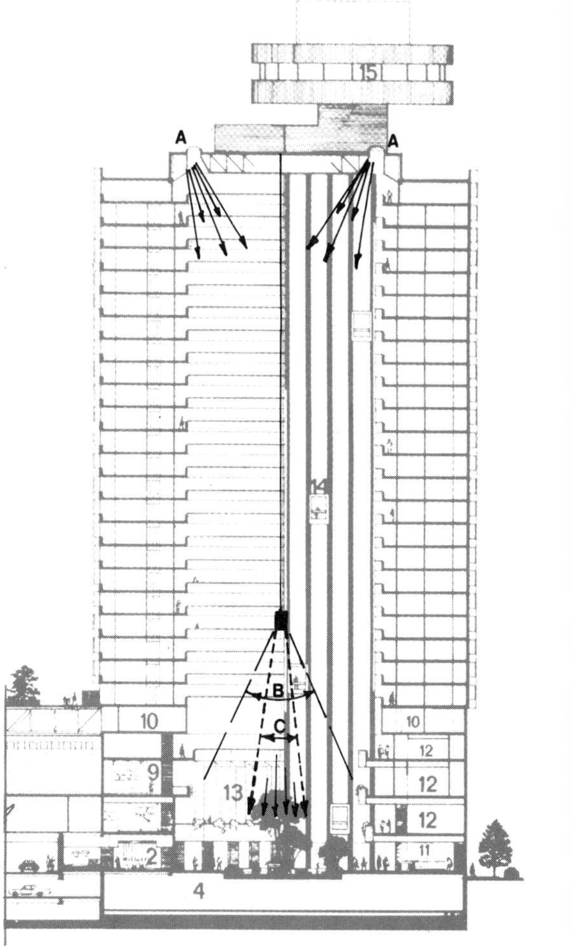

5 Tree lighting from a pendent chandelier. **(A)** *Skylights.* **(B)** *Beam spread from tree chandelier as built.* **(C)** *Beam spread as designed*

7

scheme would have required an expensive fireproof room around the oculus. Therefore, an alternative was developed—a large chandelier 200 feet above the trees—which would be less expensive both to install and to operate **(4,5).**

The clear-lamp theme is continued in the nightclub and terrace restaurant **(8),** while reflecting metallic sculpture provides the chandelier effect in the ballroom **(10)** and gourmet dining areas **(9)**. Reflecting sculptured forms were spread out throughout the ballroom space and shaped so that any segment of the sculpture seems complete and natural when the space is subdivided. Original plans for lowering and raising

chandeliers were dropped in favor of keeping the forms close to the ceiling where they would interfere as little as possible with any activities in the space.

In the design of any major hotel ballroom, a number of problems are almost always encountered. How to conceal tracks for partitions used to subdivide the space? How to provide flexible stage lighting? How to create a space which can be used as a single unit or as several separate units, yet present a finished appearance in any state? At O'Hare, the rectangular geometry of the ballroom suggested a ceiling of rectangular Plexiglas boxes which screen partition tracks, mechanical equipment, light track, and

downlights. At Houston, a similar inexpensive ceiling was created out of short lengths of Sonotube sprayed with flock and hung below the ceiling hardware. The choice of circular forms grew out of the hexagonal room shape. Because the budget did not permit the design team to illuminate every tube, the downlights were designed so that they spill no light on the tubes themselves—a totally neutral solution which can be supplemented at will with sparkle from the glittering chandeliers and rich color from the walls.

The copper coffer/chandelier theme designed for the health club at O'Hare was reinterpreted for a new stand-up bar at Hous-

Alexandre Georges

8 *Whistler's Walk.*

9 *The Crystal Forest.*

10

Alexandre Georges

11

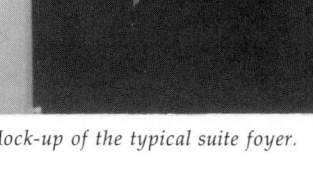

12 *Mock-up of the typical suite foyer.*

ton. In the Crystal Forest **(9),** the intent was to create a sense of glittering trees of metal and light. The ceiling was too low to create full-height artificial trees, so half trees were hung from circles of mirror which complete the illusion.

The Houston design team was able to maintain control of the guestrooms **(12,13,14,15),** which was not the case at O'Hare. Early commitments to lighting concepts made a new type of room foyer possible **(12).** The space was kept full height and its apparent width extended by the lighted transom and low closet doors. In the bathrooms **(15),** the quality environment was maintained by edging mirror tops with clear lamps. The usual unsightly access panels were neatly integrated into the bathtub niche.

The wall return enclosing the bed ends helps to give the bedside lighting a built-in look, even though the fixtures are traditionally "lamp-like" in form. Cost of the decorative ceramic lamps was kept down by detailing the fixtures so that the Mexican-made ceramic shades could be bought directly (separated from the electrical contract) and installed or replaced without an electrician.

The general design themes and qualities were extended to the automobile entrance, to the adjoining parking facilities, and also to an office building **(Case Study F3),** by the same developers and design team, connected to the hotel by a pedestrian walkway.

Critique

Late in the development stage, the lighting consultants lost control over the "tree-growing" chandelier. The substitute chandelier designed by the manufacturer failed to produce the very sharply defined narrow beam required to minimize glare directed toward the rest of the lobby.

Photos by Lam

13 *Mock-up of the typical suite.*

14 *Mock-up of the typical suite with downlight only.*

15 *Mock-up of the typical bathroom.*

CASE STUDIES GROUP D

SEQUENCES OF SPACES ORGANIZED ALONG FIXED CORRIDORS

As the design of any sequence of major spaces should relate each to the others, so a series of spaces along a fixed corridor should be interrelated in even more specific and definable ways. Such relationships, expected if the design is to seem natural, offer a challenge and an aid to the creation of a clear, ordered, forceful, and comprehensible design, rather than one which is homogeneous and characterless (the uniform, suspended ceiling with a regular pattern of light fixtures) or even disordered.

Assuming that the luminous environment of each space provides for its specific activity needs, what are the expectations which must be met to satisfy biological needs of orientation?

If one were to look out of several windows on the same wall, one would expect to see the same horizon, weather condition, time cues, etc. One would also expect the frame of reference, the window wall, to have some consistency in terms of structure, materials, etc., unless there was an apparent reason for variations. Because seeing is a mental rather than a merely photographic process, these expectations hold even if the windows are viewed sequentially rather than simultaneously.

Similarly, in walking down a corridor one expects similar consistencies in the corridor "view." The ceiling, walls, etc., should be treated consistently and any variations should seem to be naturally derived from perceptibly different influences to which the design responds.

From a design viewpoint, the fixed corridor is a great help. Like the fixed window wall, it can be an anchor, giving a fixed condition to which other elements can be related. The fixed corridor position can be useful in the placement of skylights, lighting equipment, ductwork, mechanical rooms, load-bearing walls, columns, changes of ceiling height and materials, etc. Care must be taken, however, to assure that projected space subdivisions will not be unduly handicapped by the fixed corridor position.

Whether or not the opportunity is given strong expression, fixing of the corridor position almost always offers potential economy over more flexible designs. Building types in which fixed corridors are likely to be the selected tradeoff include hospitals, dormitories, hotels, and some types of laboratories, schools, and office buildings.

1

REMODELLING OF THE OLD U.S. CIVIL SERVICE COMMISSION BUILDING FOR THE
NATIONAL COLLECTION OF FINE ARTS
SMITHSONIAN INSTITUTION
Washington, D.C.

D1

Faulkner, Kingsbury & Stenhouse (architect); Bayard Underwood (associated architect); William Lam Associates, Inc. (lighting consultants); Architectural Graphics Inc. (graphics consultants); Walsh Construction Co. (general contractor). Cost: $6,000,000. Square footage: 320,000. Schematic design started 1965. Construction completed 1968.

The original design for this fine old building (dating from 1836) was based on a fixed-corridor scheme. Major architectural assets of the original design were the different types of vaulted brick ceilings which graced the various spaces. These positive assets as well as other important features were ignored when the other half of the building was remodeled to house the National Portrait Gallery **(2)**.

The subsequent remodeling for the National Collection of Fine Arts might have been handled with similar insensitivity had not director David Scott engaged consulting architect Bayard Underwood. Despite the fact that remodeling plans had been underway for years, the new design team was able to halt the process, and redesigned most elements—particularly the lighting. There was to have been much unnecessary new construction, with air-conditioning grilles, fire-hose cabinets, and other elements placed in locations which would have interfered with the best display positions. These false starts were rectified wherever possible. Plans had called for the installation of very large, cumbersome fluorescent/incandescent valance fixtures, which might have been appropriate under other circumstances; however, when applied indiscriminately

2 *Obtrusive lighting forms in the National Portrait Gallery.*

3

4

Ripman

5

across windows and in no consistent relationship to the several types of ceiling vaults, such valances were totally misused and out of place. To preserve and accentuate the old construction, new lighting was designed to complement rather than nullify the existing forms.

Design

Rooms with groin vaults and fixed walls (3) suggested the placement of a single pendent fixture (4,5) in the center of the space to illuminate the vault (when desired) and to house adjustable reflectorized lamps that could be directed anywhere on the four walls to accent the displayed works. The fixture forms evolved from the function: to provide louvering and a clean profile to reduce the dominance of the fixtures without excessive restriction of the aiming flexibility.

In the Lincoln Ballroom (in which President Lincoln held his Inaugural Ball), larger-scaled versions of the pendent "flower" fixtures were to have supplemented existing indirect fixtures located in the column caps (6). Their omission at the last moment was unfortunate and resulted in exten-

sive use of local lighting mounted on display panels and overhead track (11). These add counterproductive visual noise when used in such a large open space.

Barrel-vaulted spaces (7; compare with 8) were illuminated from lighting track arranged parallel to the axis of the vault. Here the valance design could have been used with less conflict with the structural forms.

In corridors (9), small brick vaults run perpendicular to the main corridor axis. This suggested the use of discrete sources rather than the use of either continuous light sources or continuous power distribution track crossing the vaults. While a line of exposed adjustable fixtures aimed at both walls would have been satisfactory, the predictability of the fixture locations and the desire to keep the ceiling plane as unblemished as possible led to development of fixtures that could be aimed at both sides of the corridor, while presenting a clean profile when viewed down the corridor. These were related in concept and detailing to the pendent flower fixtures.

Galleries with new suspended ceilings were illuminated from recessed downlights (10).

6 *Sketch of design proposal for the Lincoln Gallery.*

Bayard Underwood

8 *Treatment of a similar space in the*
7 *National Portrait Gallery.*

9 10

11

Courtesy Smithsonian Institute

D1 National Collection of Fine Arts, Smithsonian Institution   179

Photos by Bill Rothschild

1

STAMFORD HOSPITAL
Stamford, Connecticut

D2

Perkins & Will (architect); David L. Ginsberg (project architect); Sherwood, Mills and Smith (associated architect); William Lam Associates, Inc. (lighting consultants); I. S. D., Inc. (interior design consultant); Segner & Dalton (mechanical and electrical engineers); Sol Marenberg Associates (structural engineers); F. D. Rich (general contractor). Cost: $4,940,000, including site. Square footage: 147,160. Schematic design started December 1963. Construction completed June 1968.

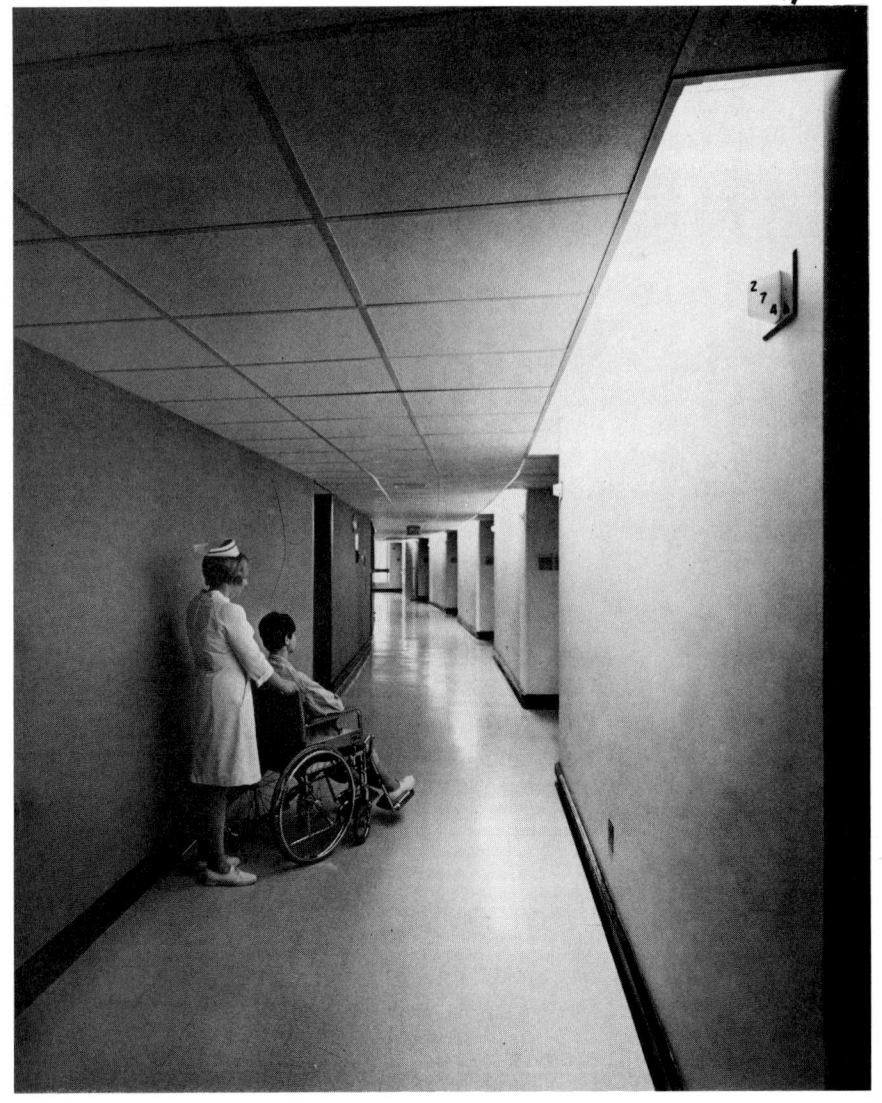

2

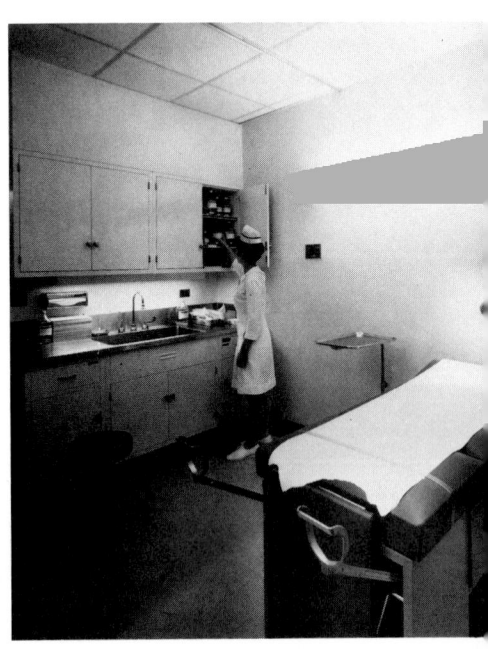

3   4

Buildings with air conditioning and heavy service requirements frequently devote even more of their volume than necessary to mechanical services. Such waste is easily avoided in a typical hospital plan, with narrow zones of patient rooms at the perimeter separated by fixed corridors from interior work spaces. Since all spaces can be easily serviced from the corridors, the upper portion of the corridors themselves can be used as the main service distribution channel, and the surrounding spaces can be made correspondingly higher with only minimum enclosed ceiling depth.

Starting points of the design at Stamford were a desire to express the curving corridor shape and to take advantage of the change of ceiling heights. Inter-mittent light slots were made to accentuate the curving walls and the openings which penetrate them **(3).** These slots also house incandescent nightlighting. Patients are not exposed to the usual glaring fluorescent lenses when looking into the corridors. The subdued corridor patterns made emphasis of the nurses' station simple. Patient rooms **(5)** are orga-nized against the service wall which contains the intercom, oxy-gen, etc. Therefore, it was natural to organize the lighting around this headwall and the stipulated bed positions.

From this wall, it was simple to provide indirect illumination for a substantial part of the ceiling and wall surfaces, in order to over-come the sensation of gloom that results from dark room surfaces when contrasted with bright win-dows. This indirect illumination is also sufficient for most room activities. Additional direct light-ing from 4-foot-long fluorescent sources in the same fixtures was supplied for reading. This di-rect/indirect combination makes most examinations possible with-out limiting posture or necessitat-ing constant adjustment of the exam light (as would be the case with more concentrated incandes-cent sources). Indirect nightlight-ing, using 7-watt incandescent lamps, distributes a small amount of light throughout the room rath-er than at one spot on the floor. A night-light in this position can easily be used by a nurse to read a thermometer, etc., making it un-necessary to turn on other room lights which might disturb the patient.

The scheme established for the repetitive patient floors is con-tinued to the extent possible on the main floor **(6),** which is subdi-vided irregularly for offices, etc. Supplementary local lighting **(4)** is provided as necessary.

Photos by Bill Rothscild

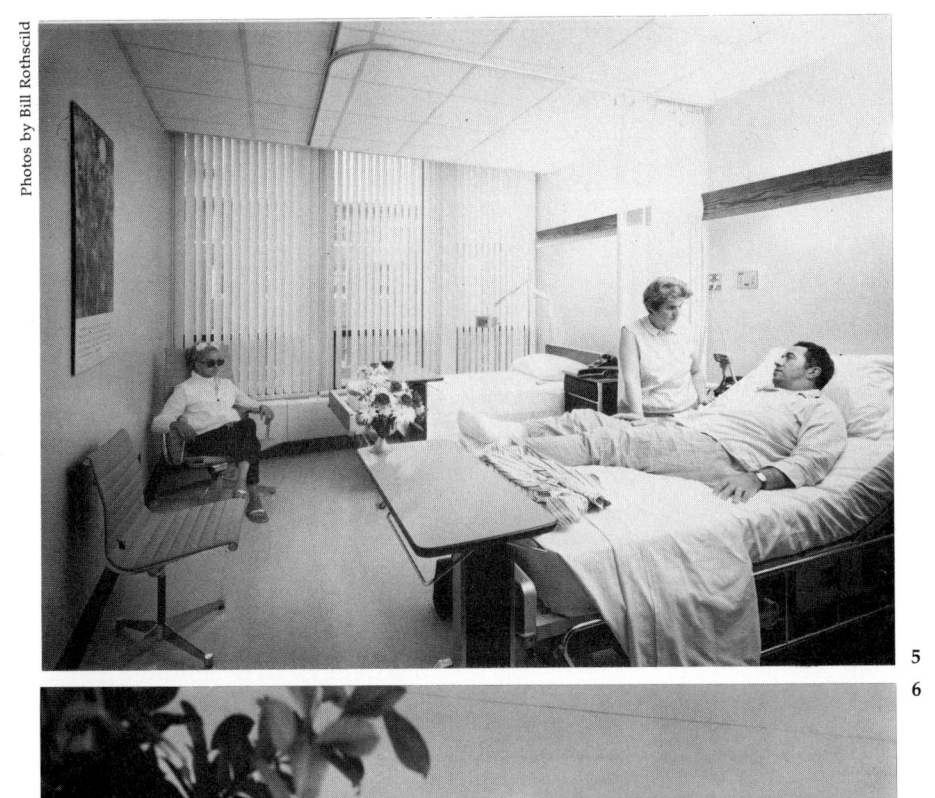

5

6

1

SUTTON ELEMENTARY SCHOOL
Sutton, Massachusetts

D3

Johnson · Hotvedt and Associates (architect); E. Verner Johnson (principal in charge); Norman M. Saunders (project architect); William Lam Associates, Inc. (lighting consultants); Lottero & Mason Associates (electrical engineers); Progressive Consulting Engineers (mechanical engineers); Souza and True (structural engineers); Charles Construction Co. (general contractor). Cost: $2,900,000. Square footage: 67,500. Schematic design started October 1970. Construction completed September 1973. Lighting load: 2.2 watts per square foot.

Designed by the same team which was responsible for the Plymouth Schools **(Case Study D9),** the Sutton School takes on its distinctive character from the deep plaster-enclosed steel structure which spans between the main corridor and the perimeter walls of the building, creating a series of 20-foot-wide bays. This visually strong framing system offered the means for a consistent indirect lighting approach which could be applied throughout the school. Continuous, extruded aluminum cove fixtures were mounted on the bottom edges of the main beams which define each bay. Because of the considerable distance between the central corridor and the exterior wall, several lines of monitored clerestory windows were introduced. These define the main corridors **(4)** and the edges of class-

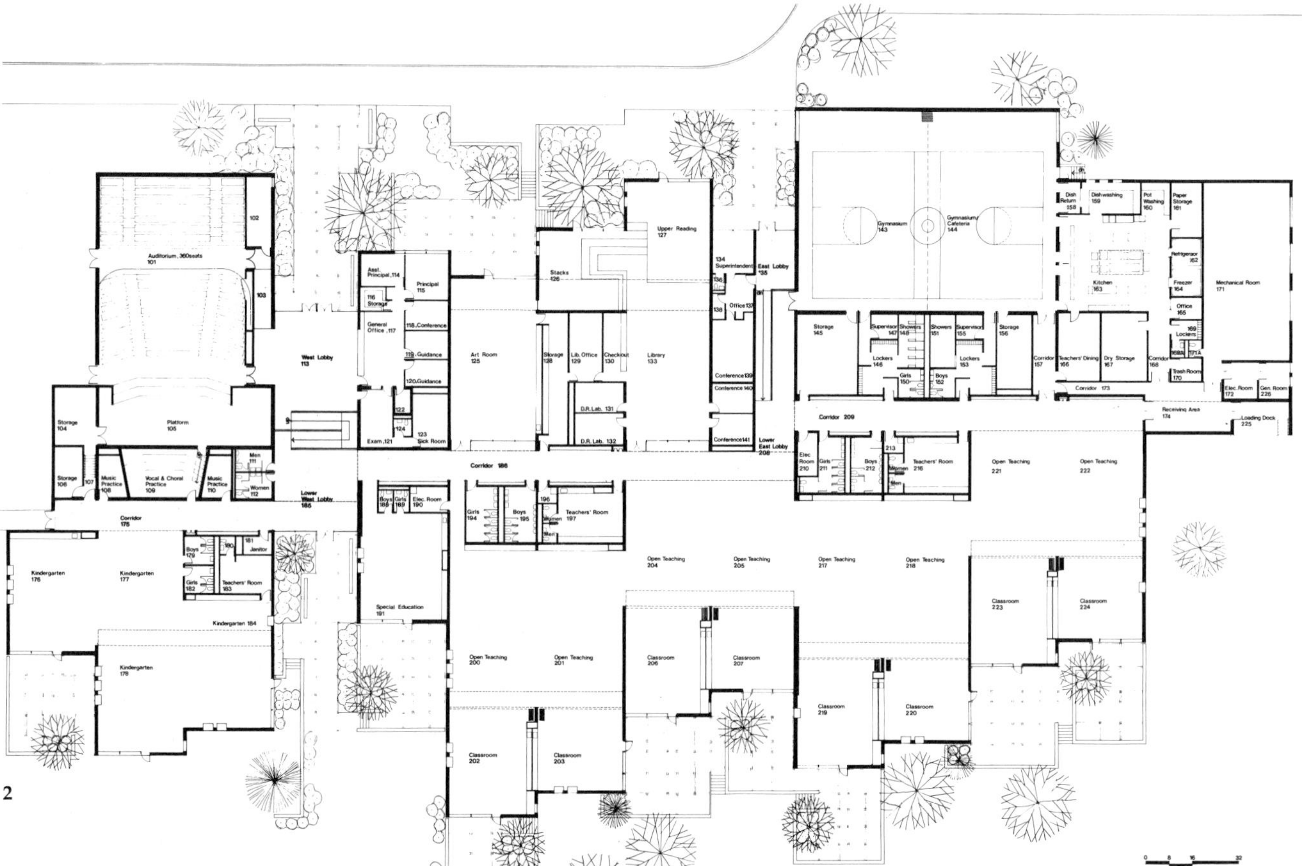

2

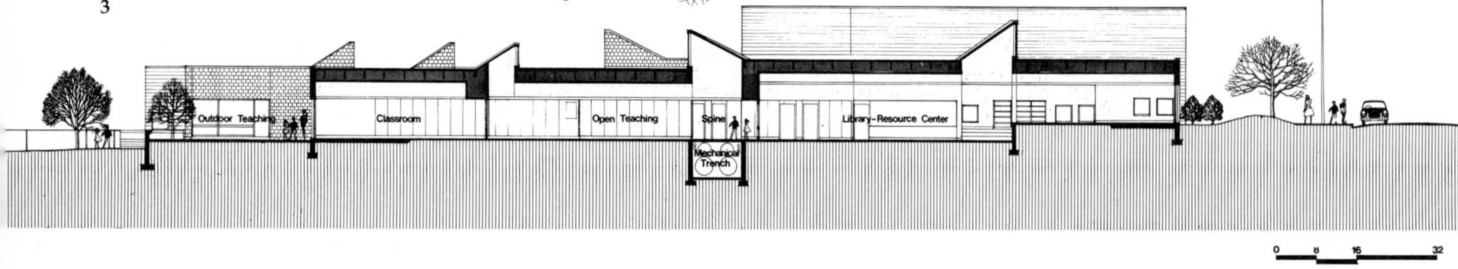

3

Lateral Section

5 *Library.*

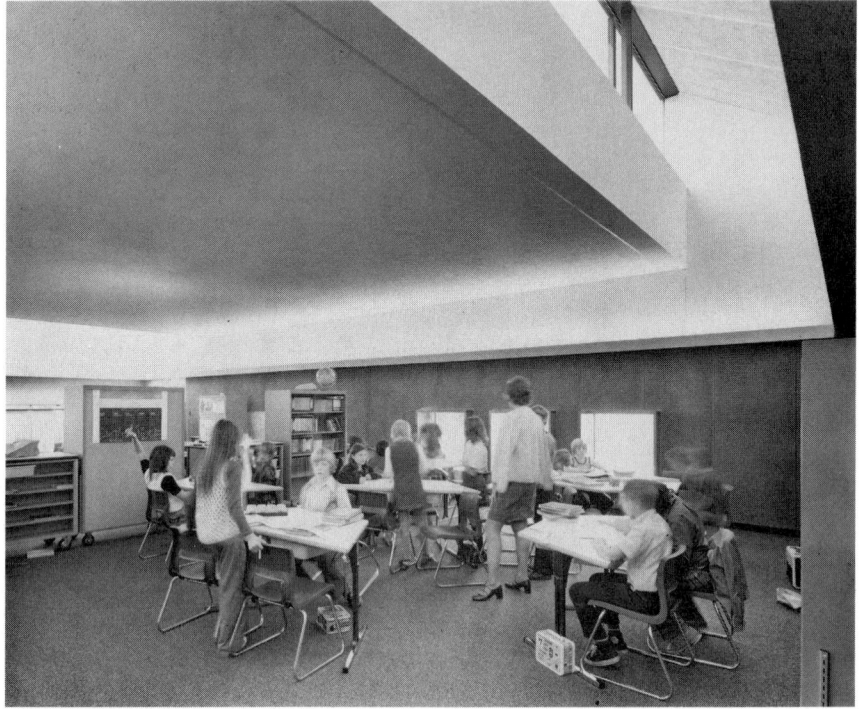

6 *above, typical interior classroom.*   7, *below, typical perimeter classroom.*

room spaces. Classrooms can be divided by folding partitions; the monitors were coordinated with both the movable partition lines and the permanent walls of the classrooms **(6,7).** The corridor monitors admit sunlight, which helps to meet the biological information needs for sunlight, weather, and time orientation without interfering with other activities.

Because of the different nature of the biological and activity needs to which it must respond, the luminous environment of the windowless auditorium **(8)** is quite different from that of the typical classroom. Walls are illuminated from slots at the top, which has the effect of floating the suspended ceiling free from the walls. The glowing walls, which respond to expectations for bright surroundings during the day, provide a pleasant, cheerful environment for most activities. The slot lighting is supplemented by architecturally neutral recessed downlights in the ceiling, which can be used for note-taking during projection, when the room surfaces need to be dark. The downlight system can be dimmed.

In the gymnasium **(9),** on the other hand, a completely different system was called for due to the requirements for a cheerful, bright space free from glare when viewed from any position or angle. This was accomplished by indirect lighting, with continuous fixtures attached to the bottom chords of alternate roof trusses—a variation on the theme established in the classroom zone. Where it might be needed, supplementary track-mounted flexible downlighting was designed for special occasions. Unlike a college gymnasium, with its special spectator and TV lighting requirements, there was no need at the Sutton School gym for high-intensity downlights.

8 →
9 →

1

ENDERS PEDIATRIC RESEARCH LABS
CHILDREN'S HOSPITAL
Boston, Massachusetts

D4

The Architects Collaborative (architect); John C. Harkness, Jean Fletcher, Roland Kluver (principals in charge); Joseph Hoskins (senior associate in charge); Edmund K. Summersby (associate in charge); Lawrence Zuelke (landscape architect); William Lam Associates, Inc. (lighting consultants); Engineer Incorporated (electrical engineers); Metcalf & Eddy (mechanical engineers); Souza & True (structural engineers); Turner Construction Co. (general contractor); Square footage: 142,000. Schematic design started 1967. Building lighting load: 3.5 watts per square foot.

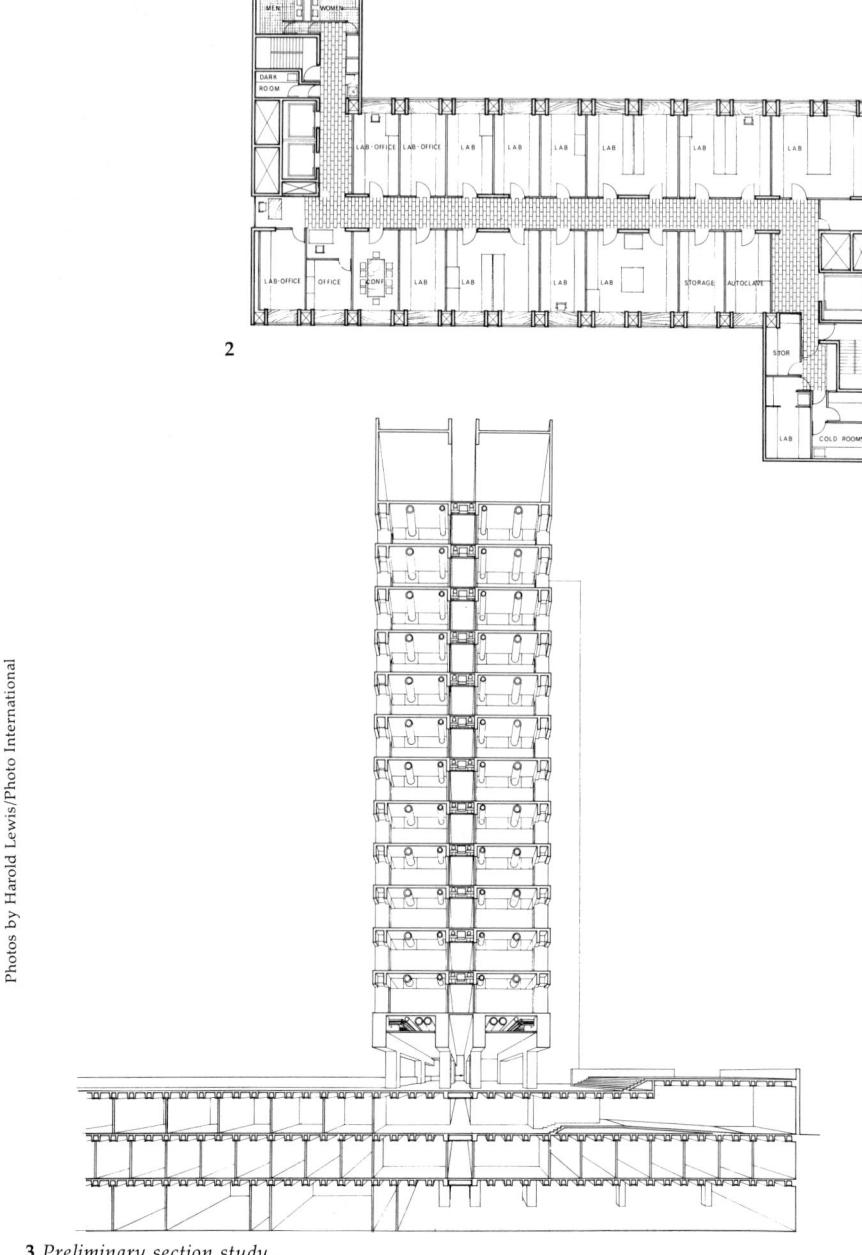

2

3 *Preliminary section study.*

This design capitalized fully on a fixed-corridor scheme, which is given strong expression both in the facade and the open first-floor lobby **(4).**

Design

Lighting takes advantage of and reinforces the lines of the paired corridor edge beams and paired perimeter edge beams that were created to enclose service runs.

On typical floors, indirect cove fixtures along the edges of these concrete service channels illuminate the exposed concrete slabs in between. Since the large exposed duct would have blocked off some of the indirect light from below, the duct itself was used to shield additional indirect fluorescent strips, and its shape was changed from round to oval to improve its performance as a glare baffle **(7).** The indirect lighting could have been located on the other axis (perpendicular to the corridor), but this scheme was rejected since it would have created a hot spot on the bottom of the duct directly above each fixture. The selection of fixture lengths was determined by the partitioning module. The natural gaps between fixtures in the cove fall on the module, so that partitions can be added or removed without requiring any modification to the lighting system **(6).**

Regardless of the level of general illumination, local lighting is

Lam

5

4

often desirable in laboratories, particularly those with overhanging cabinets. Local lighting is also an appropriate response for infrequently used counters by windows which are normally well lit during the daytime, rather than

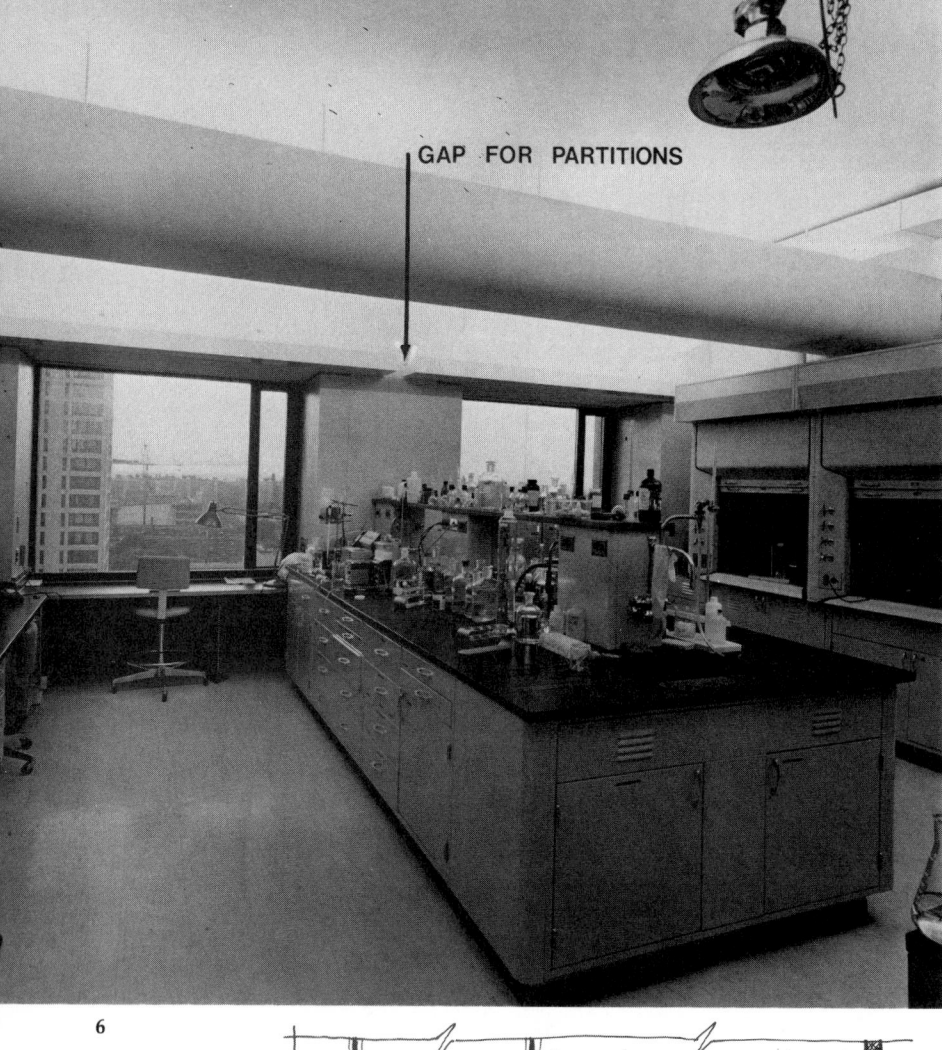

Harold Lewis/Photo International

GAP FOR PARTITIONS

6

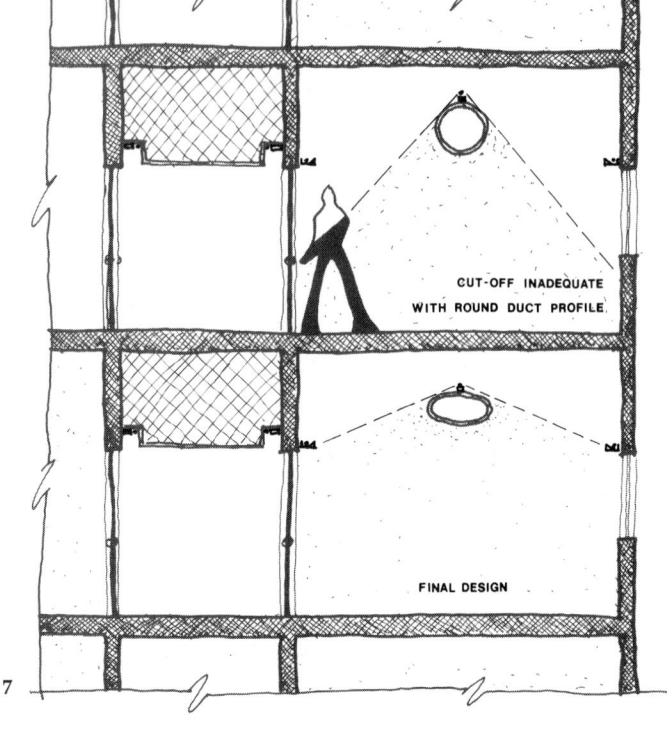

CUT-OFF INADEQUATE
WITH ROUND DUCT PROFILE

FINAL DESIGN

7

trying to increase the level of general illumination so that these areas are always lit at night as well. Power and budget were allocated for this purpose. Individual room switching is also desirable because of the varying activity needs. The cost of individual switching in each room can be quickly offset by the great economy gained by keeping the artificial lighting off when daylight is sufficient or when rooms are unoccupied.

In operating rooms (9), the adjustable operating light is supplemented by the illuminated walls.

When fluorescent lighting was not feasible because the magnetic and other fields produced by both lamps and ballasts would interfere with sensitive instruments, the same scheme was executed with incandescent sources.

The high quality of the luminous environment achieved with this system is immediately obvious when comparison is made with basement rooms (8) and other spaces in which the general lighting scheme was compromised.

Critique

The corridors (5) would have been more spacious and interesting if treated asymmetrically (light slot on one side only) reflecting the asymmetric position of the elevator lobbies rather than the symmetry of the corridor-lab structure. An asymmetric arrangement of indirect corridor (10) and office lighting (11) was used, however, at ground level under the podium. On that level the structural coffers themselves were not used as light baffles for bare lamps except in a limited area to define an elevator lobby (12). Where the intent was not to create a focus, more neutral downlights were placed in the coffers.

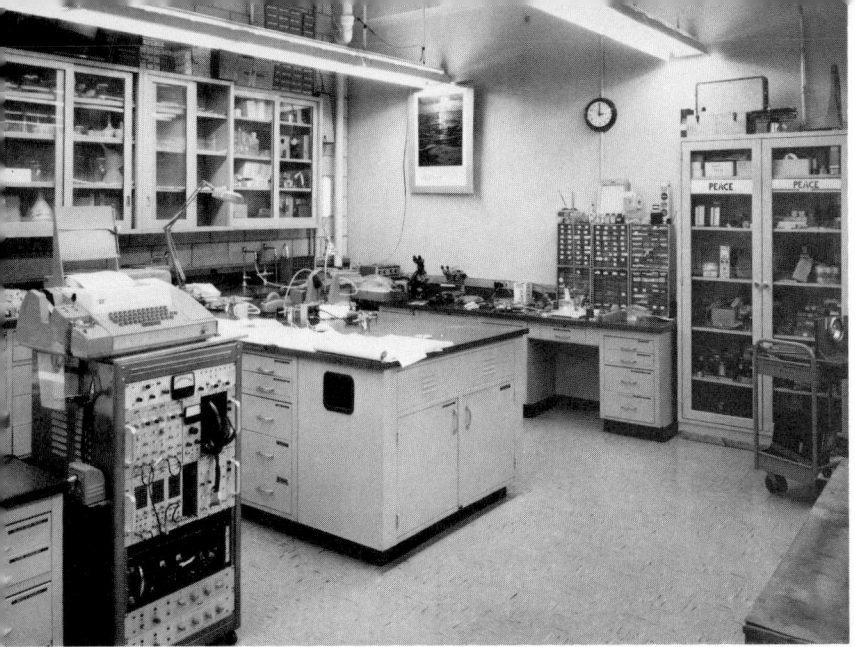

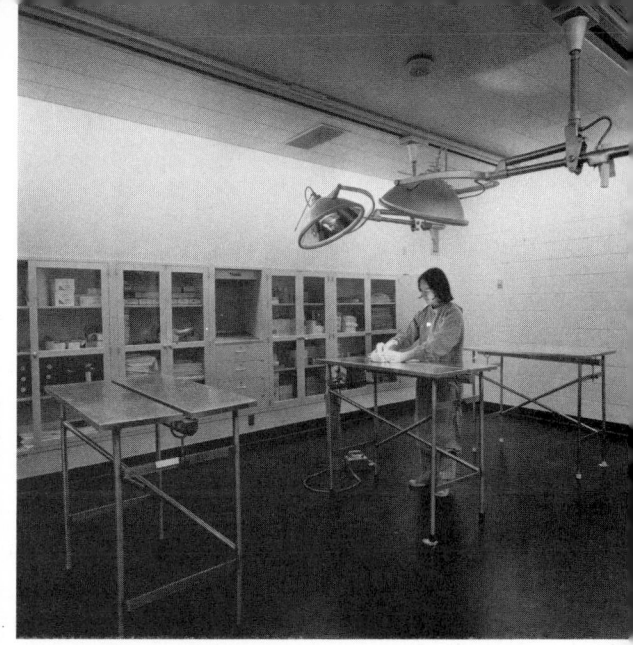

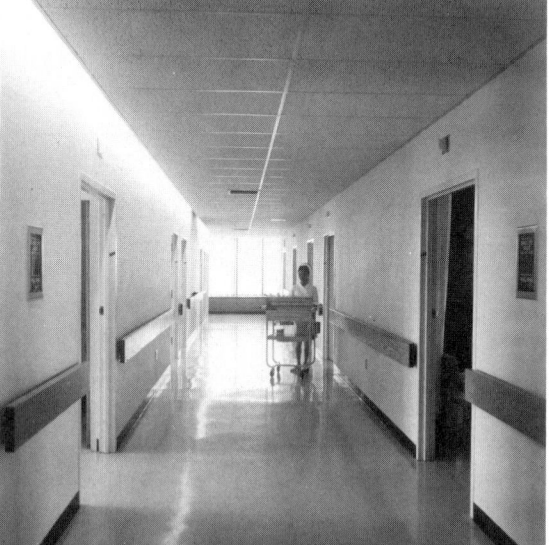

GRIFFIN HOSPITAL
Derby, Connecticut

Isadore and Zachary Rosenfield (architect); Herbert Bienstock (project associate); William Lam Associates, Inc. (lighting consultants); Starr, Miller Inc. (mechanical and electrical engineers); Lev Zetlin Associates, Inc. (structural engineers). Schematic design started 1964.

When the plan organization, section, and materials in two hospitals are similar, one would expect to find similar lighting solutions; in this respect, the Griffin Hospital closely resembles the Stamford. However, one should not take these as universally applicable details. A glance at the Easton Hospital **(Case Study E6)** shows that where the nature of the building is radically different, entirely different lighting solutions are both possible and desirable.

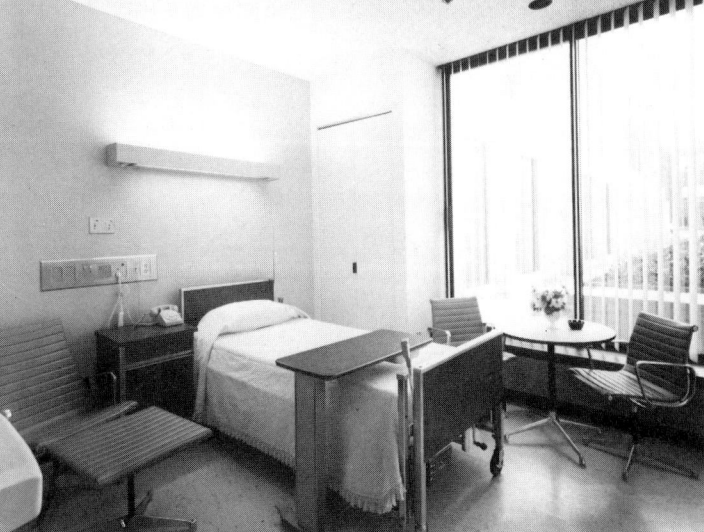

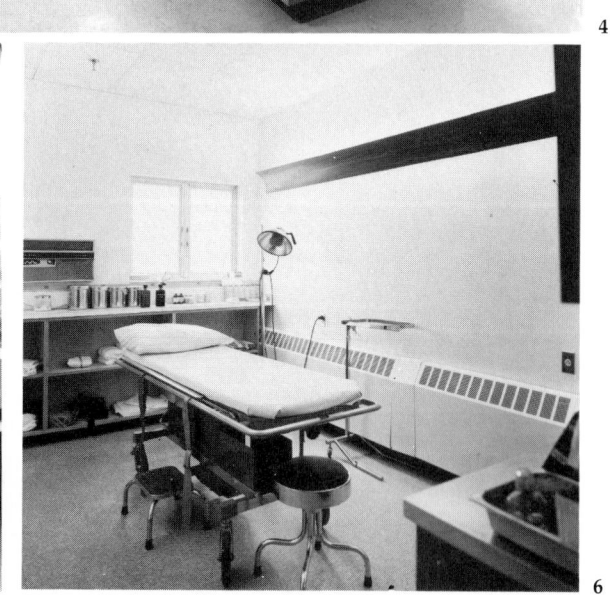

Courtesy Isadore & Zachary Rosenfield

Photos by Gil Amiaga

Courtesy Isadore & Zachary Rosenfield

NORTH PARK COLLEGE SCIENCE BUILDING
Chicago, Illinois

D6

Daniel Bryant and Associates (architect); William Lam Associates, Inc. (lighting consultants); Lyle Yerges (acoustical consultant); Maglet Myhrum (interior design consultant); Beling Engineering Consultants (mechanical and electrical engineers); Jack Scanlan (structural engineers); Mercury Builders (general contractor). Schematic design started September 1963. Construction completed March 1966.

1

2

3

In a science and classroom building, one expects the spaces to appear bright and shadowless rather than dramatic. Diffuse rather than strongly directional light is usually best, minimizing direct and reflected glare at desk tops. Design for comfort in viewing the chalkboard, teacher, and fellow students is at least as important as providing optimum conditions for note-taking and reading pencil handwriting—the task often taken as the simplistic basis for minimum footcandle criteria.

For accommodation of lighting and mechanical services, a small-cell waffle structure is no better than a flat slab. The structure provides no integral, easily accessible channels for services. It is only useful for baffling light if a lamp in each cell can be afforded or if a busy checkered pattern is acceptable. However, when downlighting from point sources is called for, small waffles can be a sympathetic background for mounting incandescent cans. While no better than small-scale waffles from the point of view of running ductwork, larger waffle structures allow more possibilities for lighting (compare with the Mount Royal Library, **Case Study B4,** and the lower levels of Quebec Government Center, Complex "G," **Case Study H5**).

Design

The waffle structure of the North Park College Science Building was treated as a flat slab. In corridors, dropped ceilings enclose ductwork, with the corridor and elevator recesses defined by edge lighting. This concentration of services allowed the classrooms the full height of exposed structure.

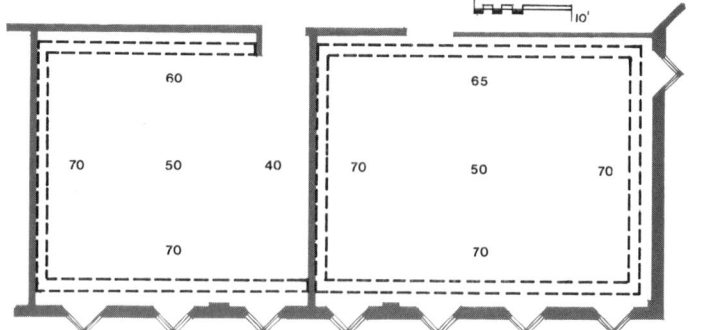

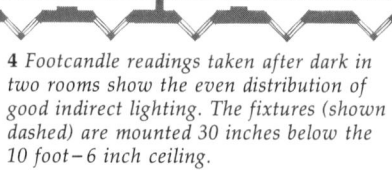

4 Footcandle readings taken after dark in two rooms show the even distribution of good indirect lighting. The fixtures (shown dashed) are mounted 30 inches below the 10 foot–6 inch ceiling.

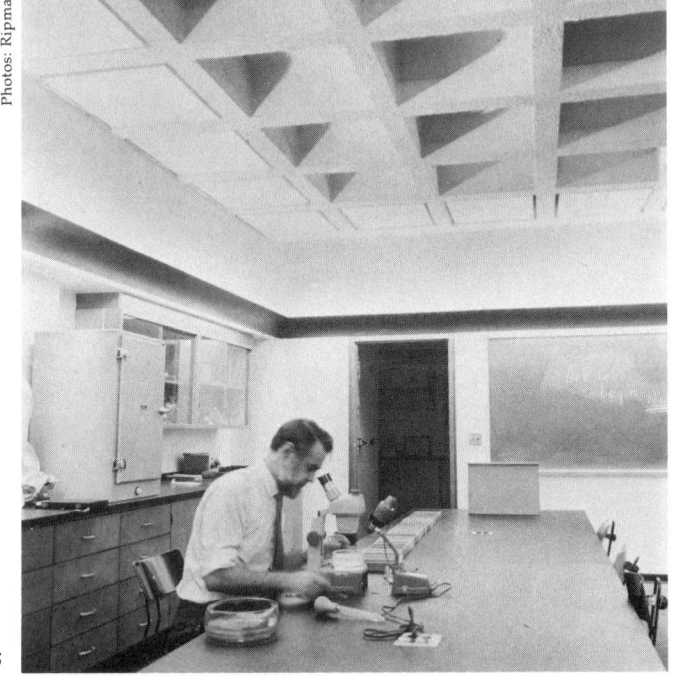

Photos: Ripman

5

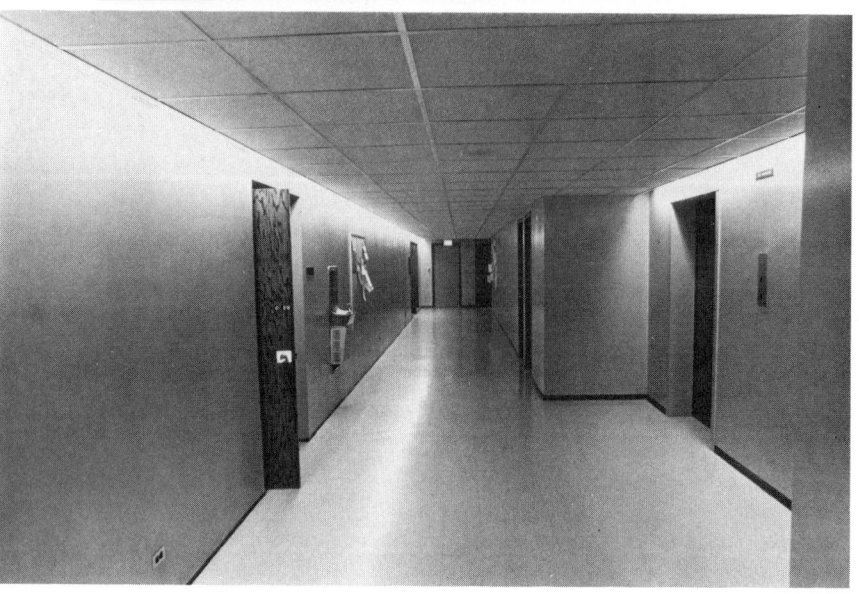

6

The corridor-to-window depth of these rooms was sufficiently narrow (20 feet) to make illumination from only two sides both feasible and practical (4). In recognition of the irregular room lengths, all indirect valance lighting was placed on corridor and window walls (3). Although the lamps were centered on each wall, valances were run from wall to wall in order to appear natural rather than stuck on.

The indirect lighting was made more effective by keeping the window height level with the door headers to allow maximum space above valances for light distribution (3). Panels required for acoustic purposes were placed level with the bottom of the perimeter cells to reduce trapping of the light by those cells (5).

Unlike the fixtures in buildings with a well-defined transverse module, such as Children's Hospital, the lighting fixtures at North Park Science must be rearranged if room lengths are changed in the future. Such changes, however, were expected to be very infrequent, and the cost of rearranging the lighting was estimated to be an insignificant percentage of the total cost of moving a wall.

The adjacent first-floor auditorium (7) was expressed as a totally different structure, both within and without. The connecting lobby has a waffle structure, but was illuminated very differently from the classrooms (with decorative incandescent globes) to reflect the difference in use and to show its relation to the auditorium.

Exaggerated programmatic maintenance demands for the biology labs, requiring sealed fixtures to prevent the accumulation of dust, dictated a large compromise in the visual environment (8). In some laboratories indirect lighting was possible, and the resulting environment was far more cheerful and comfortable (9).

7   Photos: Lam

8   9   Harold Lewis/Photo International

1

AMAX HEADQUARTERS
Greenwich, Connecticut

D7

LCP Associates, Inc. (interior planning); Eugene Reugamer (partner in charge); William Lam Associates, Inc. (lighting consultants). Schematic design started January 1974. Construction completed May 1975. Building lighting load: 2.3 watts per square foot.

Blocked from erecting its own headquarters building by zoning restrictions, the AMAX Company negotiated a long-term lease on a conventional Emery Roth lofttype speculative office building under construction in downtown Greenwich, and hired the LCP team to create interior spaces appropriate for the headquarters of a multinational corporation.

Design

The consistent placement of private offices at the perimeter with supporting staff functions, conference rooms, and reception areas clustered in and around the core suggested that the conventional field of glaring-lensed fluorescent fixtures in a flat acoustic tile ceiling could be replaced by an integrated ceiling and lighting design which would respond far better to the distribution of space uses. It was anticipated that the corridors would not be realigned during the lease period. The design recognized that the perimeter offices could be comfortably and effectively illuminated during the day with daylight from the windows balanced by indirect illumination from the corridor wall.

To increase the distribution and effectiveness of the indirect illumination, it was desirable that the ceiling should be as high as possible in this area within the constraints established by structure and mechanical runs. By keeping the major ductwork within the core zone, it became feasible to increase the ceiling height in the corridors as well as in the perimeter offices. The transition is made with a sloping plaster band which further defines the core zone **(2)**. By glazing the upper portion of the corridor wall, both corridor and perimeter offices could be illuminated indirectly from a fluorescent strip located in a continuous shallow cove which caps doors, closets, and filing and counter recesses on the office side **(3)**. Orientation in the interior zones is provided by the continuous clerestories, by windows at the ends of the major corridors, and by the consistent illumination from slots of all walls on the core side of interior work stations. Nondirectional low-brightness 2 × 2 foot fluorescent fixtures were used to provide supplementary lighting for the perimeter offices at night **(4)** and were coordinated with the interior work stations in the core zone **(2)**. Incandescent lighting was provided for wall washing, and to highlight planting, works of art, and reception desks. The design team concluded that any resulting deficiencies in task lighting could be corrected through the use of local lighting under shelves or desk lamps.

Criticism

Several decisions which were made without our knowledge or approval somewhat undermined the effectiveness and economy of the original lighting scheme. The owner of the building doubled and in many instances quadrupled the number of recessed fluorescent fixtures called for in our layouts. Problems of glare were further aggravated when both dark furniture and dark carpet were installed. The team had originally called for light-colored carpet and furniture to improve the light distribution and brightness balance of interior spaces, and had capitulated to a request for dark carpet provided that the specified light furniture would be installed. This was not done. Bronze glass panels were installed between triple secretarial alcoves in the core zone **(5),** rather than solid partitions, which further reduced the reflectance of these spaces, worsened the brightness balance in them, and added unpleasant multiple reflections of the fluorescent fixtures, as well as making the spaces somewhat gloomy. The slot lighting at the rear of these alcoves was converted to under-shelf lighting throughout the project when shelving was called for in several areas, which reduced the effective contribution of the slot lighting to the general room illumination.

Despite these deleterious compromises, enough of the original concepts were implemented to create a distinctive environment, more comfortable and pleasurable than most.

2

3

4

5

WEST WING
BOSTON MUSEUM OF SCIENCE
Boston, Massachusetts

Johnson·Hotvedt and Associates (architect); E. Verner Johnson (principal in charge); William Lam Associates, Inc. (lighting consultants); Bolt, Beranek and Newman (acoustical consultant); C. E. Maguire (structural, mechanical, and electrical engineers); Aberthaw Construction Co. (general contractor). Cost: $6,000,000. Square footage: 120,000. Schematic design started January 1966. Construction completed May 1972.

1

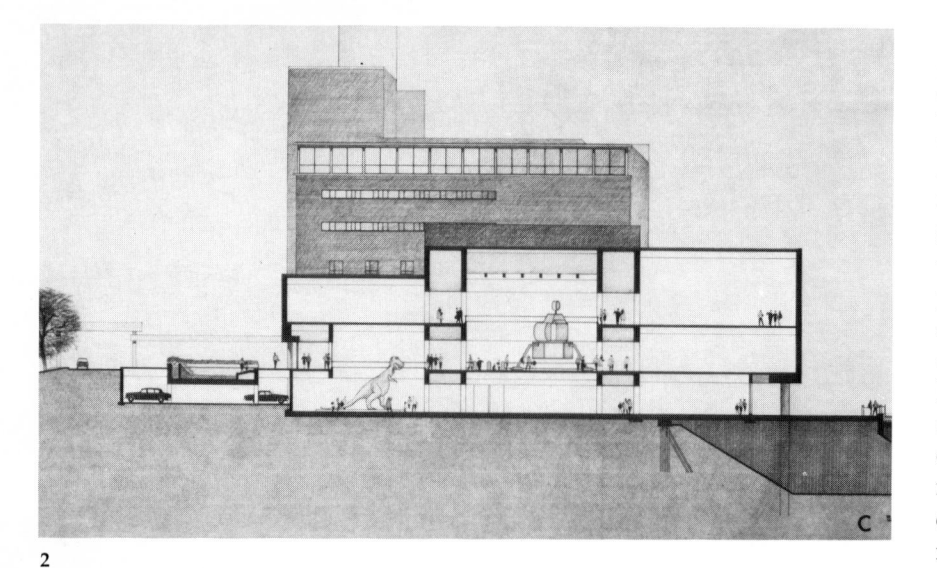

2

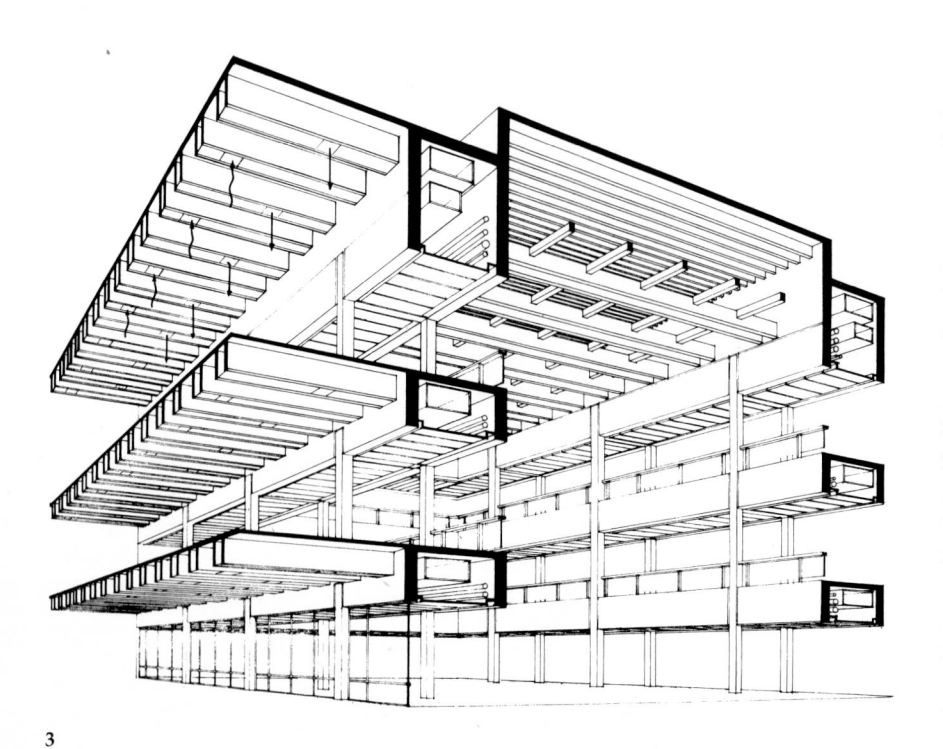

3

For introverted buildings such as museums, fixed corridors are likely to serve not only as the main channels for mechanical services and traffic but also as a replacement for windows as points of reference (orientation) and as visual rest centers (change of pace). In this second role, corridors are often supplemented by courtyards. In the west wing of the Boston Museum of Science, fixed corridors serving display spaces encircle an artificially illuminated multistory interior court, which contains large objects such as submarines and space vehicles. Controllable artificial lighting is usually best for the display of such diverse objects, since it can be used to create a variety of moods and effects suggestive of their natural settings.

Architects have traditionally felt that the display of *paintings* in a museum should not be much different than in the home or building for which they were originally created. "Rooms" should be provided to which the paintings will have a normal-scale relationship. However, the "natural habitats" of many objects in a science museum bear no relationship to "rooms" (consider an artificial wave or a locomotive), and such objects are probably best exhibited in settings quite divorced from conventional rooms.

Unlike hospitals or schools in which partitioning is likely to be

4   Photos by Harold Lewis/Photo International

5 *Integrated lighting and support catwalk above the central exhibit well.*

PIPE RAIL

EXHIBIT
SPOTLIGHT

POWER

PRECAST
JOIST

PRECAST
CHANNEL BEAM

INCANDESCENT
DOWNLIGHT

SUSPENSION CABLE
FOR EXHIBITS

7

6

Ripman

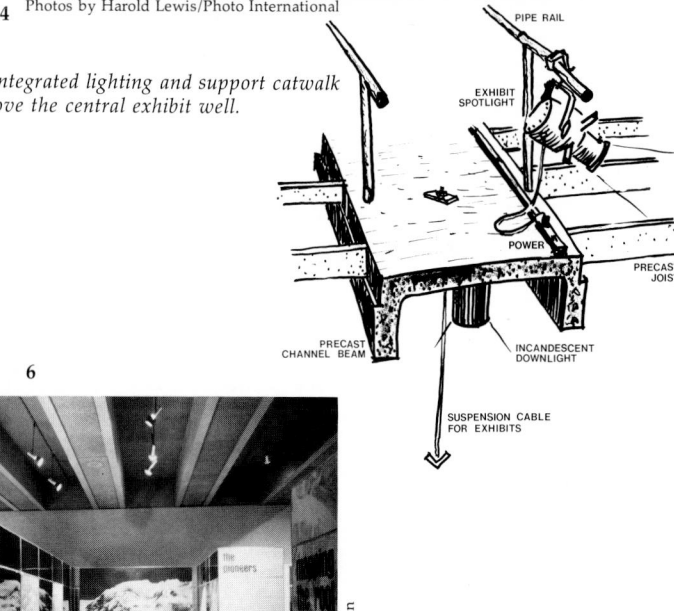

8 9

10 11

198   *D8 West Wing, Boston Museum of Science*

permanently fixed, the series of spaces in this museum undergoes constant change. Therefore, a major design objective was to accommodate those expected changes with reasonable ease and flexibility.

Design

Although anticipating that the ceilings would be dark in color (to minimize competition with the exhibits), the design team nevertheless wanted to give a strong visual order to whatever structure was visible. A system of alternating mechanical service and lighting channels fed from the corridors **(3)** was designed to accommodate any service requirement (both above and below) with maximum convenience and without the appearance of "scarring" which occurs when a flat ceiling is interrupted by fixtures and by the inevitable random splashes of light accidently spilled from displays **(6).** The robustly expressed structural/mechanical/-lighting system camouflages such irregularities and provides sufficient solid surfaces for anchoring partitions, etc. More "refined" types of structures, such as waffle slabs, would have had almost no flexible service capability, while continuous suspended louvers would have given much more flexibility than necessary.

Over the courtyard the ceiling/roof structure was somewhat modified. The service channels **(5)** were conceived as catwalks for suspension of displays and support of irregularly placed special lighting equipment. A regular pattern of house lighting was placed within the channels for ease of access for relamping and aiming.

In contrast to the exhibition spaces with their irregular accent and integral display lighting, the connecting corridors were illumi-

12

13

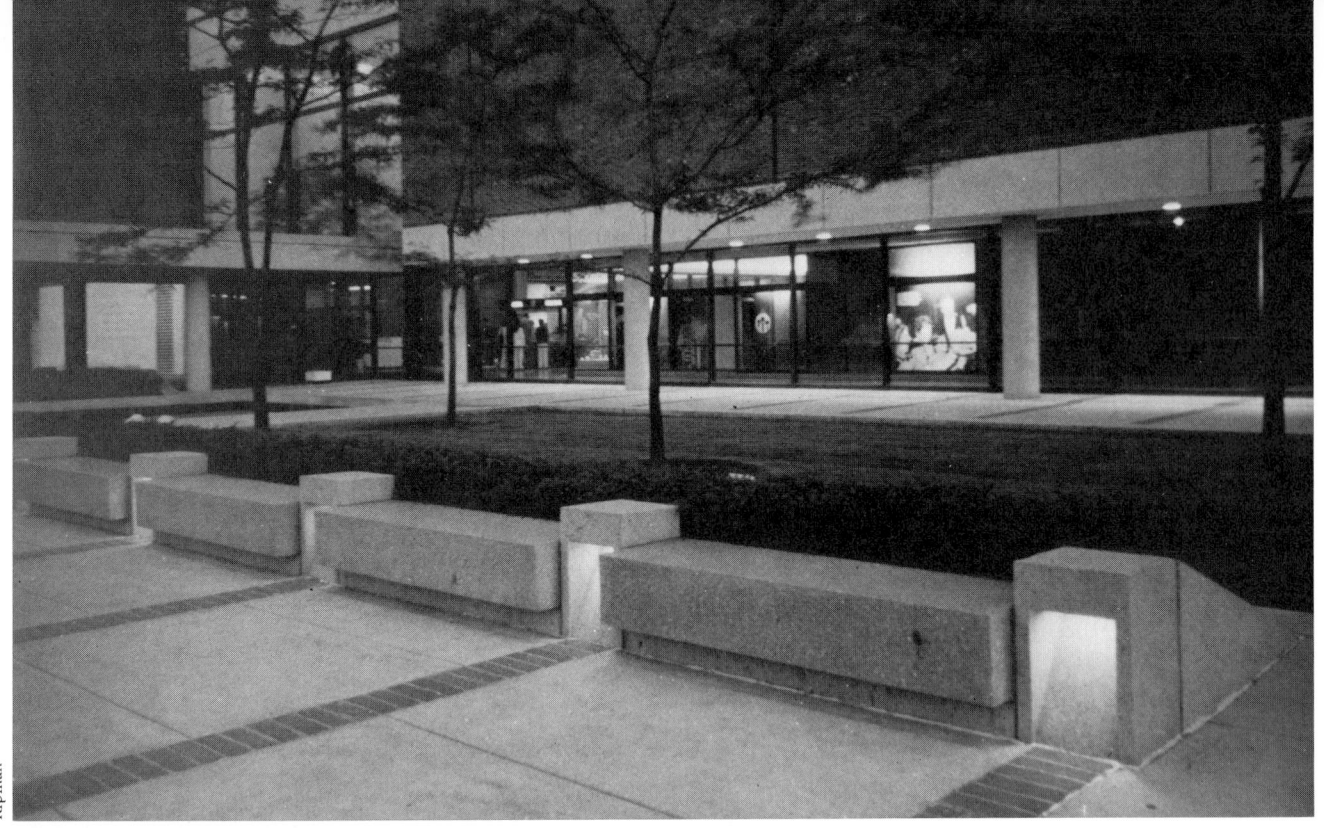

Ripman

14

Courtesy of Johnson-Hotvedt

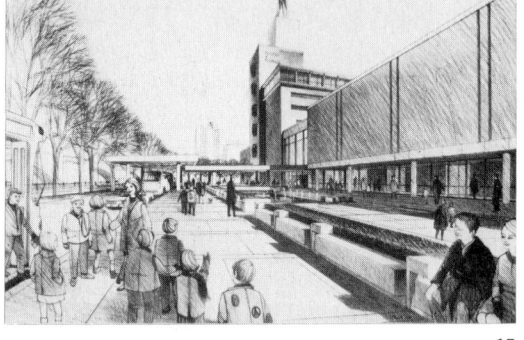

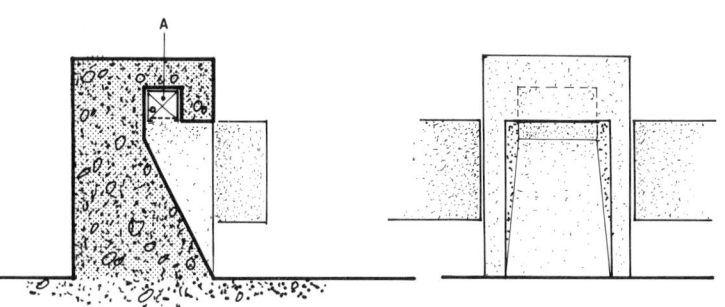

15

16 *Conventional steplight* **(A)** *with glass lens cast into concrete bollard.*

17 *Entry canopy.*

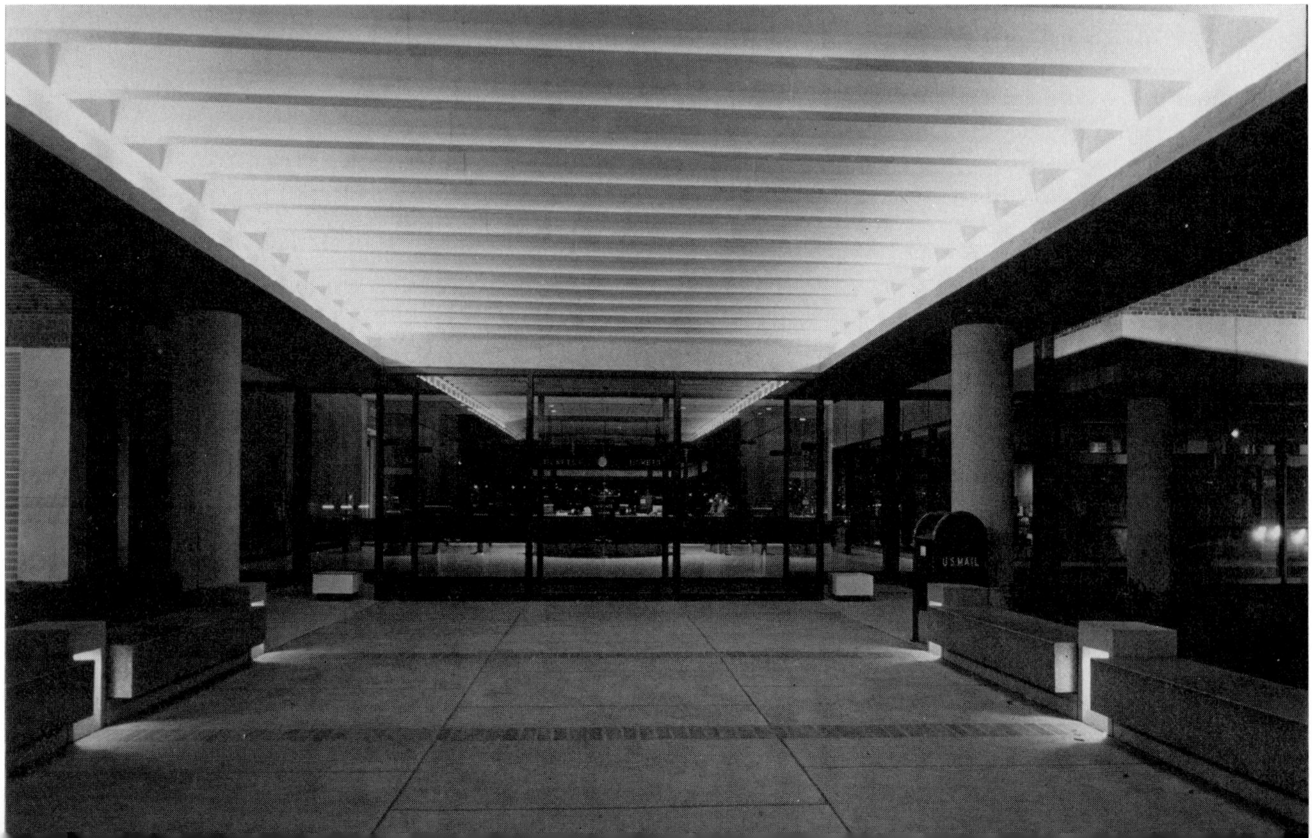

nated to be visually simple organizing spines. Concealed, louvered slots were placed at the edge of a totally accessible ceiling of tectum planks (4,20). A similar approach was used in the stairs (11) and in the new main lobby (18,19) connecting the new wing to the original Museum.

In this lobby, clear edge skylights reduce the usual problems of joining to existing buildings with different materials, detailing, etc. (In this case, the old wall was resurfaced.) Note that supplementary lighting in the lobby is intentionally nonuniform, accenting the turnstiles and the landing to clarify circulation destinations (7).

In the auditorium, infill panels were placed between the service channels for acoustic control. Light sources were either concealed behind beams and panels or made architecturally neutral in appearance. The overall system was designed to permit a variety of effects by switching and dimming (8,9,12,13).

The book store was given a conceptually similar treatment—architecturally neutral sources, glowing wood, and highlighted displays (10).

Concepts of light sources concealed by structure were extended to the site; fixtures were integrated into bollards (14,16), benches, and the ramps of the adjacent parking garage. In contrast, decorative exposed lamps were used to create a positive focus at the entrance canopy (17) to aid orientation.

To minimize skyline clutter, the garage roof level is illuminated by one fixture of neutral shape and full cutoff, which eliminates spill light beyond the building. This fixture will be simple to move as the garage expands upward. Because service trucks would have some difficulty reaching the roof deck, the steel pole was provided with removable climbing rungs.

18 *Study model of the main lobby.*

19

20 *Emphasis on circulation (corridor edge slot illuminated).*

ELEMENTARY SCHOOL AND AREA HIGH SCHOOL
Plymouth, New Hampshire

D9

Johnson · Hotvedt and Associates (architect); Kenneth F. DiNisco (principal in charge); William Lam Associates, Inc. (lighting consultants); Bolt, Beranek and Newman (acoustical consultant); Lottero & Mason Associates (electrical engineer); Progressive Consulting Engineers (mechanical engineers); Simpson Gumpertz & Heger (structural engineer); Curran-Cossette Construction Company (general contractor). Cost: $2,905,000. Square footage: 115,797. Schematic design started Fall 1967. Construction completed September 1970. Lighting load: 1.7 watts per square foot.

Photos without credits by Gorchev & Gorchev

The Plymouth Schools represent a building type in which all spaces are massed along fixed corridors in major clusters joined by lobbies. In this essentially linear scheme, corridor ceilings were lowered to provide channels which accommodate all major services.

Design

Since the distance between corridor wall and the exterior was not excessive, it was possible to emphasize the organizing function of the fixed corridors in the lighting design. All major lighting comes from these fixed elements **(4)**. For the most part, lighting was kept away from the transverse walls, because they vary in their spacing. In special-purpose rooms, such as the art studio, the indirect lighting system was supplemented with incandescent fixtures mounted on tracks.

A large central open teaching area and the gym vary in execution but not in concept. The exterior and corridor walls of the central room **(8)** were defined by skylights. The gym **(6)** is indirectly illuminated from fixtures mounted on the bottom chords of the roof trusses. Shape and position of ducts were selected to relate to the lighting.

In the lower library level, where low ceiling height and furniture arrangement did not offer possibilities for indirect lighting, low-brightness 1×4 foot fluorescent downlights were used. In the two-story area, light from the large north-facing window was supplemented by illumination of the upper walls from slots and by incandescent downlighting.

The connecting lobbies **(5)** were treated as "weather enclosures" for the intervening spaces, which are crossed by bridges and ramps. The walls spanning between the major masses are totally glazed. Daylight is supplemented by illumination of the end walls of the masses from fixtures on tracks and concealed in the edges of the floating ramps. Floating of the ramps accentuates the perception of the lobbies as bridges between the major masses. The free-floating lobby roofs make this relationship even more clear. A similar concept was applied in the design for the lobby of the Boston Museum of Science **(D8),** and at the University of Wisconsin at Stevens Point **(H4).**

2

3

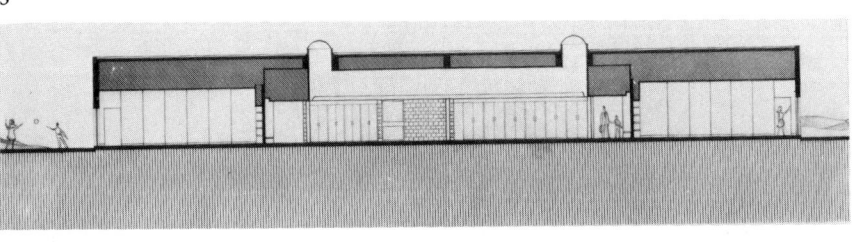

4

5

6

Two photos: Harold Lewis/Photo International

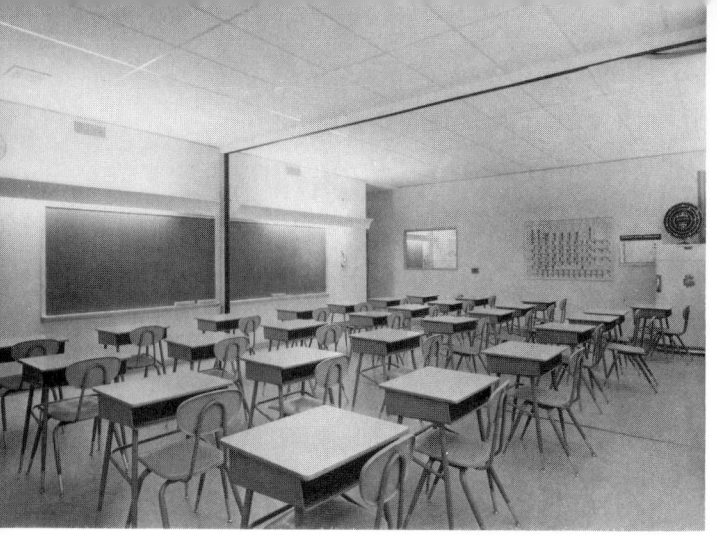

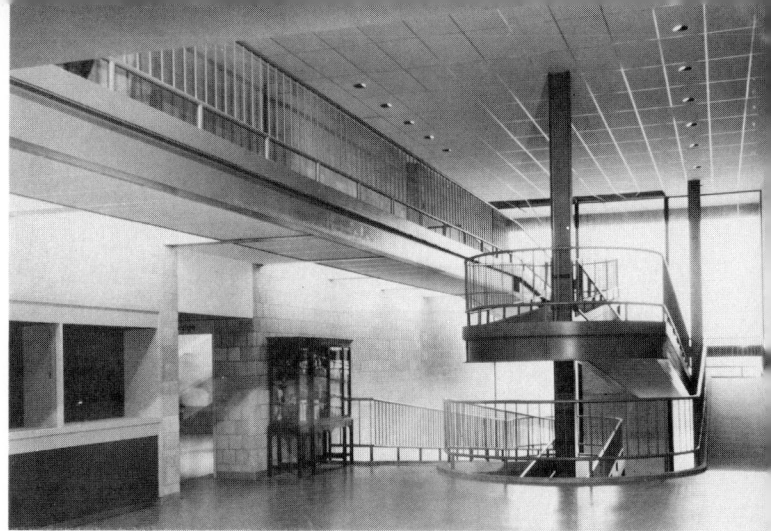

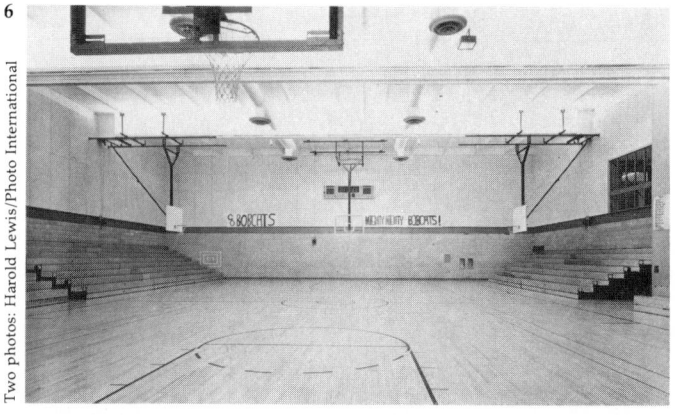

7

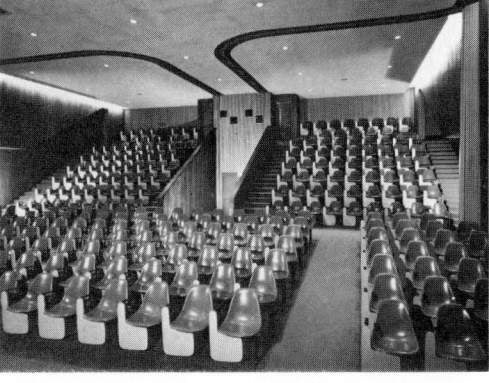

8

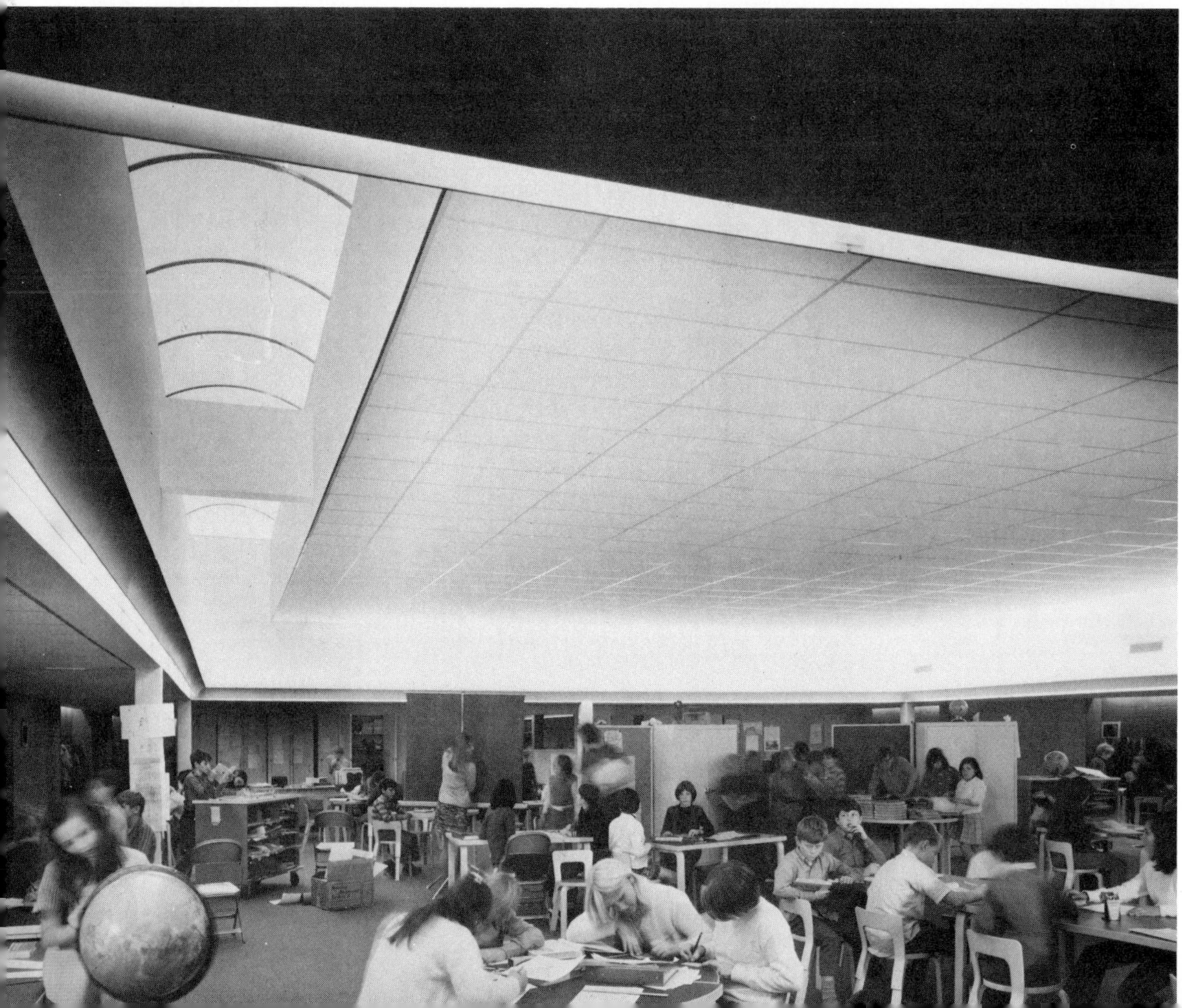

1

REMODELLING OF THE McGILL UNIVERSITY OLD ARTS BUILDING
Montreal, Quebec

D10

Affleck Dimakopoulos Lebensold Sise (architect); Thomas Blood (project architect); William Lam Associates, Inc. (lighting consultants); George Izenour (theatrical design consultant); James T. Keith & Associates (mechanical and electrical engineers); Eskenazi & Baracs (structural engineers); J. G. Fitzpatrick (general contractor). Schematic design started 1964. Construction completed 1965.

Most older academic buildings were built with fixed corridors and with walls that were rarely if ever moved. When the Old Arts Building at McGill University (1) was remodeled for better lighting, acoustics, and air conditioning, the design team attempted to retain as much of the original character as possible, for aesthetic as well as economic reasons.

The classrooms offered lighting opportunities usually unavailable in new structures: high ceilings which could be used to efficiently distribute indirect lighting. With all walls permanent, the natural solution was to apply valance lighting as low as possible (2). A continuous band just above the chalkboards might have appeared to bisect other walls where no chalkboard was present. At McGill, however, the valances could be coordinated with acoustic wall panels provided between the valance line and the ceiling to give needed acoustic absorption. Valance lighting from three sides

was used to balance off the daylight distribution from the fourth wall.

When it was necessary to divide a classroom-sized space into smaller offices, the new "horizon line" created by the valances was maintained as an unlighted cap to the partition walls; the spatial and lighting character was maintained with clear glass transoms. Since the indirect lighting was made less efficient by the reduced area of reflecting "sky" available to the smaller rooms, the lighting there was supplemented by incandescent downlights. In the art department, a balcony was introduced, but the lighting organization was maintained (3) with some special detailing to accommodate the different room geometry.

With the corridors fixed, there was good reason for them to be finished and lighted quite differently from the classrooms. The existing pendent fixtures appeared somewhat dreary and were given sparkle by substituting clear

lamps and glassware. In the form of a contemporary chandelier, sympathetic but different treatment was given the stairwells (along with new plaster ceilings and walls).

Similarly, in remodeling the auditorium, the character was maintained with lighting improvements. The windows were blocked off, and chandeliers refinished and supplemented by neutral downlighting (5). When used alone, the dimmed downlighting system provides an alternate luminous environment with unlighted walls and ceiling (6) to allow note taking during lectures.

To achieve a space of better proportions for the display of paintings and to hide the busy original skylighting details, narrow corridors in the art department were reduced in height (7). Lighting track and fluorescent strips concealed behind the new large-scale wood louvers provide unlimited display possibilities very simply and economically.

2

3

4

5

6

7

CASE STUDIES GROUP E

SEQUENCES OF SPACES WITHOUT FIXED CORRIDORS: ARTICULATED SYSTEMS FITTED TO PREDETERMINED EXTERIOR FORMS

When the exterior forms of a project have been determined prior to the inception of lighting design, it is still possible to develop an articulated "system-of-systems" integrating structural, mechanical, and lighting elements which fits into the predetermined forms and provides required flexibility for moveable corridors and other subdivision, while achieving outstanding, successful, appropriate visual environments.

The case studies presented in this section illustrate three different design approaches: In the first two case studies, a predetermined structural system was maintained, while the proposed mechanical system was modified to accomplish lighting objectives. In the fourth, the MacMillan-Bloedel Building **(E8),** the intial structural system was modified to conform with new mechanical and lighting concepts. In other cases (the Cummins Building **[E3],** the University of Lethbridge **[E7],** and the Easton Hospital **[E6]**), entirely new structural systems were developed. In these buildings, both the interior environment and the exterior expression show clearly the influence of lighting as a formgiver.

While good results have been achieved in fitting integrated systems to predetermined exterior forms, the design possibilities of these systems are inevitably restricted by the constraints inherent in the foreordained designs. Better results have been achieved in projects where the starting point was the development of an integrated system-of-systems to meet the broadly outlined objectives at the stage of schematic planning. These latter cases, in which both exterior form and plan evolved through the application and refinement of a system-of-systems, are described in **Case Studies Group G.**

AMERICAN REPUBLIC INSURANCE COMPANY NATIONAL HEADQUARTERS BUILDING
Des Moines, Iowa

E1

Skidmore, Owings & Merrill (architect); William S. Brown (partner in charge); Gordon Bunshaft (partner in charge of design); Roger N. Radford (project designer); Walter A. Rutes (job captain); William Lam Associates, Inc. (lighting consultants); Syska & Hennessy, Inc. (mechanical and electrical engineers); Paul Weidlinger (structural engineer); Arthur H. Neumann & Brothers, Inc. (general contractor). Cost: $4,274,000. Square footage: 150,000. Construction completed 1965. Building lighting load: 3.7 watts per square foot.

Lighting consultation for the American Republic Building began after the architects and engineers had developed a 4-foot-6-inch deep structure utilizing precast T beams spanning between the hollow walls of the building (which double as duct shafts). In the initial design, lighting louvers were to be placed flush with the underside of the beams to hide fluorescent lamps and the usual irregular array of stepped ductwork **(5)**.

Design

In order to gain the spaciousness of the full structural depth, and so that spaces would receive illumination from perceptually meaningful surfaces, the louvers were eliminated and regularly spaced ducts of uniform cross section were suggested as shielding for super high-output Power Groove fluorescent lamps oriented with the grooves sideways (to distribute maximum light to the side of

beams rather than to the slab above) **(6).** Excellent teamwork with the Syska and Hennessey engineering staff made possible the development of a detailed solution in 1 hour. Round, square, diamond, and triangular ducts were considered. The 14-inch-diameter round duct was selected as the cleanest, most economical shape to shield the lamps without creating a heavy silhouette that would compete unnecessarily with the structure. Alternate ducts supply and return air throughout the building. The need for acoustical absorption led to the selection of a perforated exterior casing **(7)** — a very effective sound trap when located within a coffer.

Within a few days, testing of a full-scale mock-up verified the calculations which had shown the feasibility of the air distribution details and the efficiency of the indirect lighting system. Some modification of the original structure was required. To break up the continuous lengths of duct and to

give them support, cross-ribs were provided in the ceiling coffers. These served yet another purpose: most partitions oriented perpendicular to the main structure could be butted up against the undersides of the ribs to achieve good acoustic separation between adjacent spaces. Infrequent partitions not located on the rib module were handled by running the ducts through sealed glass transoms.

The new design proved to be economical, yielding substantial savings over the original louver-enclosed ductwork design. The environment created has been enthusiastically received by the users **(8).** While examination of a photograph of a single room might give the impression that the large-scale ducts overpower the space, one does not get that feeling in the actual building because of the consistency of the entire "sky" and the clear legibility of its parts as concrete structural elements and lightweight tubes.

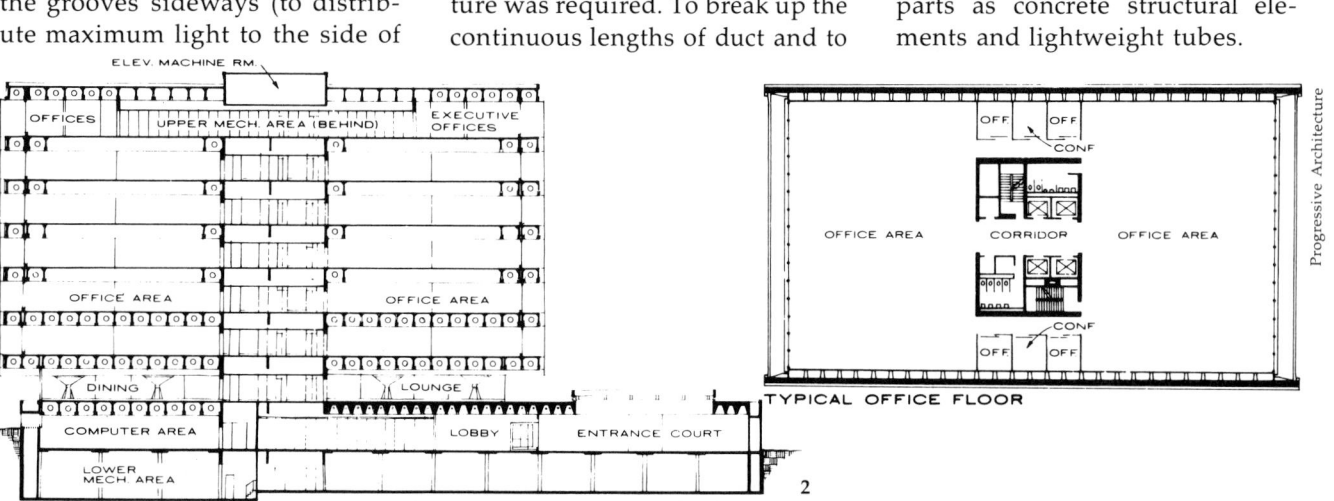

ELEV. MACHINE RM.

OFFICES | UPPER MECH. AREA (BEHIND) | EXECUTIVE OFFICES

OFFICE AREA | OFFICE AREA

DINING | LOUNGE

COMPUTER AREA | LOBBY | ENTRANCE COURT

LOWER MECH. AREA

LONGITUDINAL SECTION

OFF | OFF | CONF

OFFICE AREA | CORRIDOR | OFFICE AREA

CONF | OFF | OFF

TYPICAL OFFICE FLOOR

Progressive Architecture

2

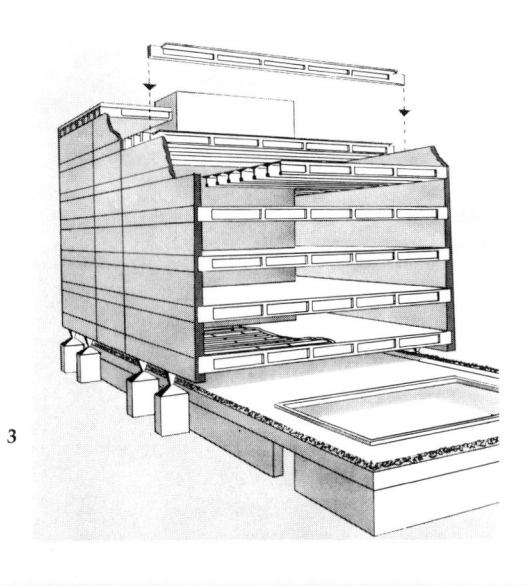

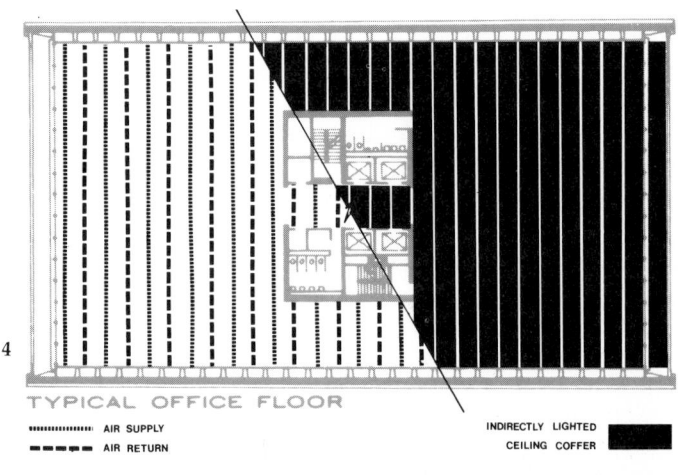

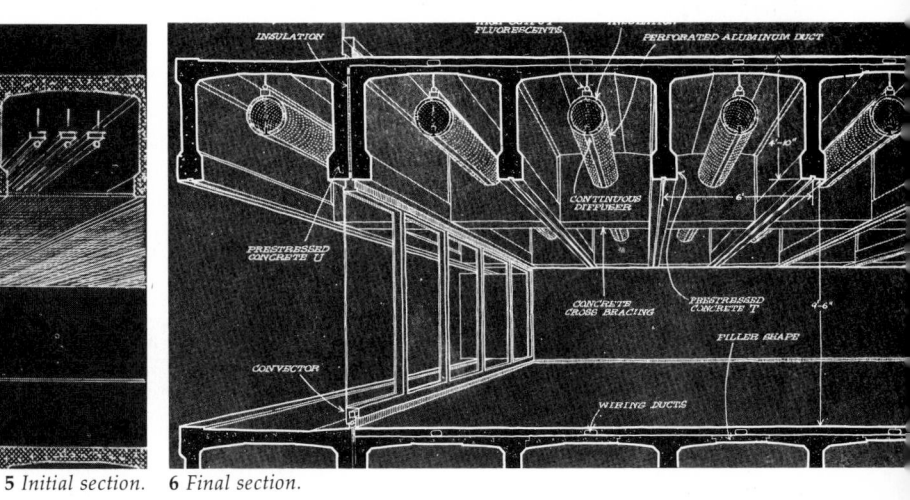

5 Initial section.   6 Final section.

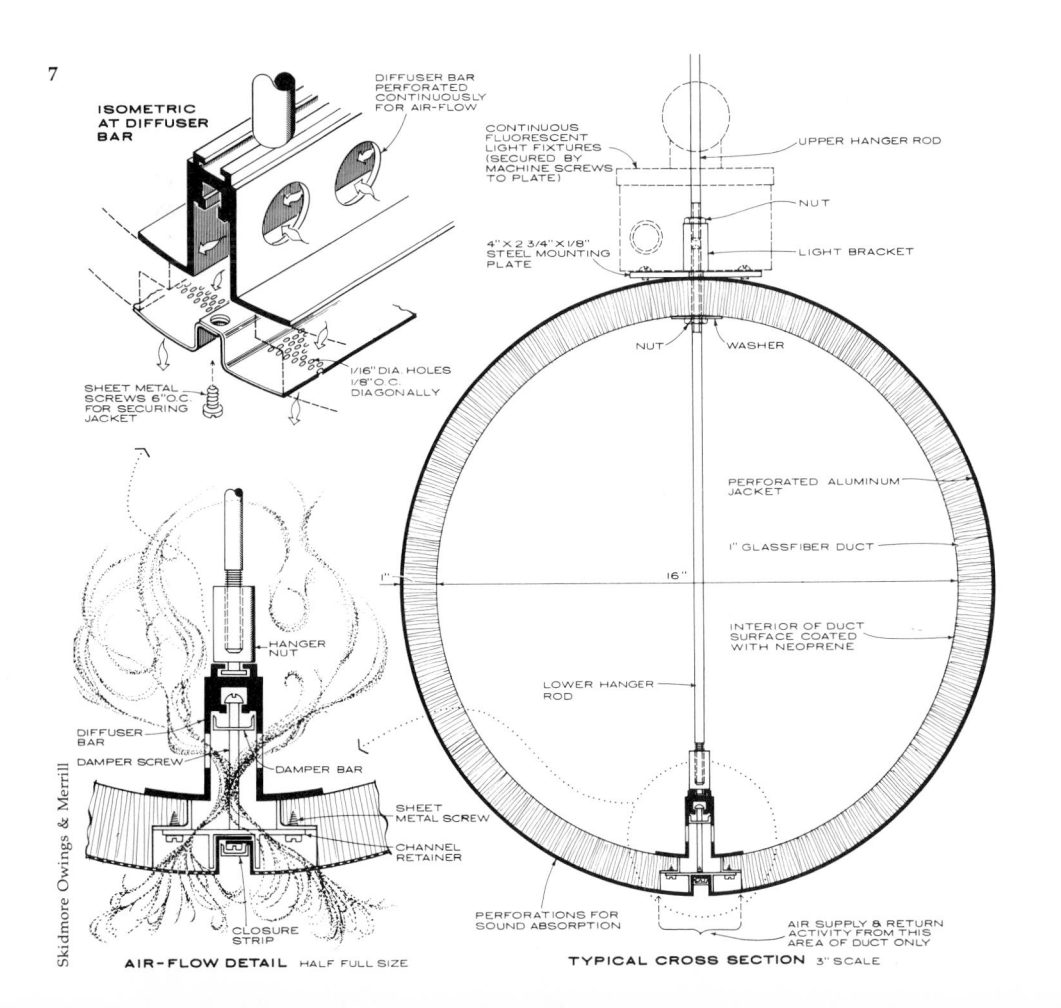

Critique

The American Republic system is suitable for large blocks of single-use space which require no variation in mechanical services or lighting (i.e., for offices, not for a *mixture* of offices, classrooms, labs, etc.). Although comfortable, comprehensible, and pleasant, the spaces are not as good as those which can be generated with systems based on a larger module which permit the creation of visually simpler, more spacious, and restful environments (see, for instance, the MacMillan-Bloedel Building **[E8]** on its uncompromised floors, and the projects in **Case Studies Group G).**

It seems to be typical practice in contemporary office building design that executive and cafeteria levels are made vastly different from typical office floors. This is due to the fact that biological needs, calling for a pleasant, comfortable environment, are usually given full recognition on cafeteria and executive levels only, while a less satisfying environment designed only around criteria for desk lighting is seen as acceptable for the typical floors. When the initial concept is to design a system which will produce an excellent environment for *all* spaces, however, there is no need to design new systems for executive or cafeteria levels. Slight variations in finishes, furnishings, floor-to-floor height, intensity of illumination, and additional decorative lighting for sparkle are all that will be needed to adapt the basic system to all spaces.

Unlike most office ceiling systems, the American Republic lighting/ceiling system **(9)** was eminently suitable for use in other spaces such as the cafeteria **(8)**, and even the executive floor was designed with the same system, with a greater ceiling height and accent lighting for artwork **(10)**.

Related integrated building systems have subsequently been used by Skidmore Owings and Merrill in the Great Southern Life Insurance Company Building in Houston, Texas; the headquarters of the American Can Company in Greenwich, Connecticut **(11,12)**; and by the author with architect James Goldstein at the Wayne TSPS Building for New Jersey Bell Telephone.

8

9

10

11 *Headquarters of the American Can Company, Greenwich, Connecticut* (Skidmore Owings & Merrill / Architects).

12 *Typical interior of the American Can Company headquarters.*

IBM BUILDING
Milwaukee, Wisconsin

E2

Harry Weese & Associates (architect); The Office of Dan Kiley (landscape architect); William Lam Associates, Inc. (lighting consultants); S. R. Lewis & Associates (mechanical and electrical engineers); The Engineers Collaborative (structural engineers); Selzer-Ornst Co. (general contractor). Cost: $3,117,596. Square footage: 199,013. Construction completed March 1965. Building lighting load: 3.9 watts per square foot.

1

2 *Mock-up of direct lighting scheme.*

3 *Mock-up of indirect lighting scheme.*

IBM-Milwaukee was built using a precast load-bearing exterior wall with slip-formed concrete core. The differences between the integrated system-of-systems solution at IBM-Milwaukee and that of American Republic reflect the differences in plan **(5).** At IBM, the span between core and exterior walls is only 30 feet; consequently, much shallower precast beams could be used, and air supply could be handled from induction units at the perimeter and nozzles at the core.

Design

Lighting design began near the end of the working drawings. By that time, a mock-up had been built to test the air distribution and to demonstrate the pattern of pendent direct/indirect fluorescent fixtures **(2).** Though most of the building floors were expected to remain as open spaces occupied by IBM, rental floors had been designed with a band of suspended ceiling surrounding the core to enclose ductwork crossing the corridors.

Full indirect lighting was proposed instead of the glaring, busy, discontinuous pattern of pendent fixtures and their entrails of stems and outlet box covers. The superiority of the new concept was readily demonstrated to the clients, with the mock-up **(3),** and then refined. A V-shaped fixture profile was selected to avoid any confusion between lighting elements and the edges of the

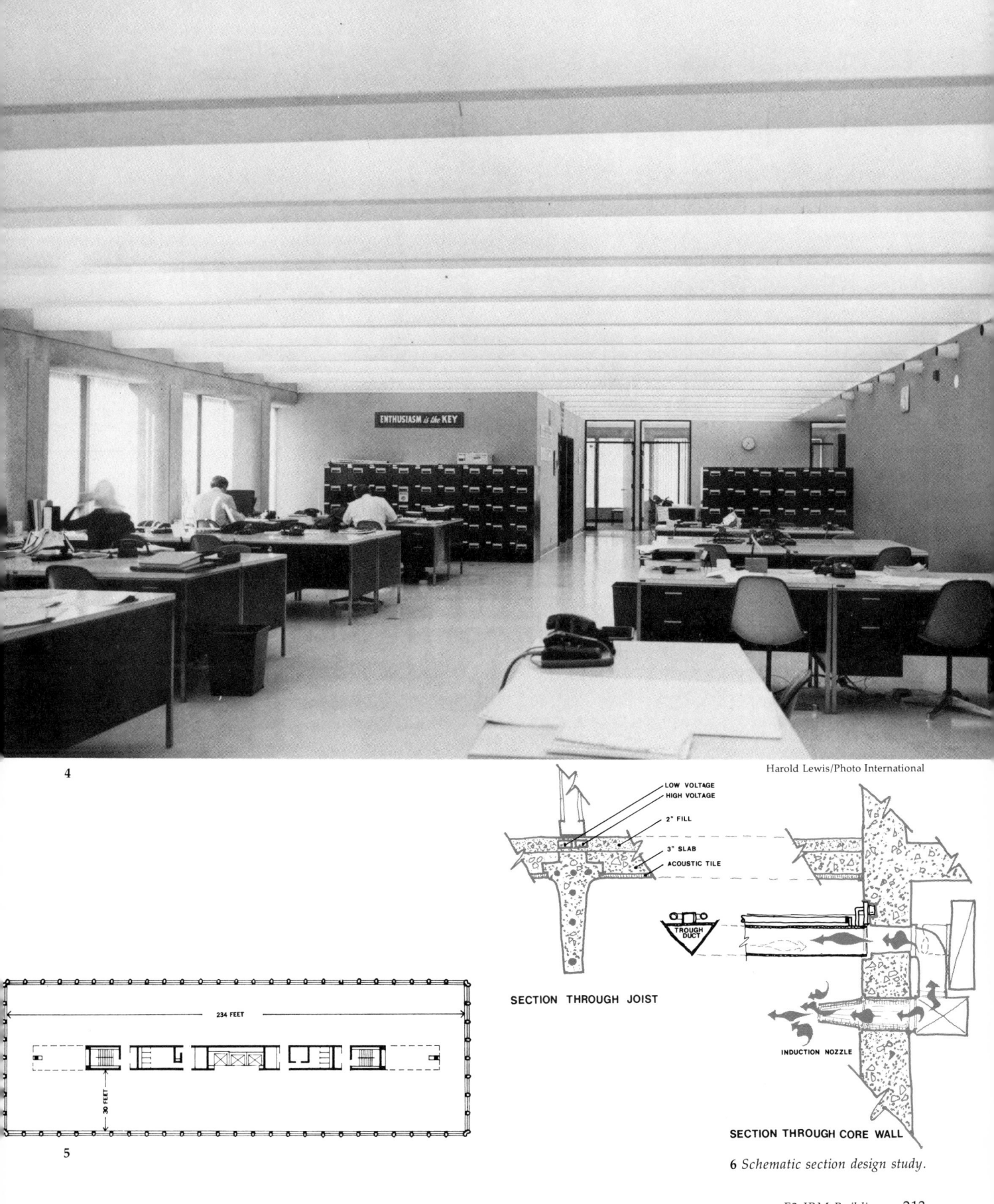

Harold Lewis/Photo International

4

234 FEET

30 FEET

5

LOW VOLTAGE
HIGH VOLTAGE

2" FILL

3" SLAB

ACOUSTIC TILE

SECTION THROUGH JOIST

TROUGH DUCT

INDUCTION NOZZLE

SECTION THROUGH CORE WALL

6 *Schematic section design study.*

7

8

structural beams. Modular lamp lengths were selected so that future partitioning would fall in the gaps between lamps.

Running the fixtures from wall to wall gave them a more integrated appearance, allowed them to be wired from the core, eliminated stems and cover plates (1/4-inch rod supports were used instead), and eliminated any need for suspended ceilings on tenant floors. Enlargement of the fixture cross section and separation of the wiring allowed use of the fixtures as air ducts to feed transition boxes and grilles at the partitions **(7).** Transparent gasketing was designed for acoustic seal between glass and fixture and to provide channels for running low-voltage switch wiring between glass joints; unfortunately, the gasketing was omitted in the actual construction in favor of field-applied silicone sealer.

On the ground floor, the core walls were illuminated from the edge of the suspended ceiling. The band of incandescent lamps was purposely left unshielded to act as a chandelier **(9).** In the corners, more neutral post-mounted chandeliers were combined with benches.

9

BUILDING RESEARCH 64
CUMMINS ENGINE COMPANY, INC.
Columbus, Indiana

Harry Weese & Associates (architect); J. Herschel Fisher, Pat Y. Spillman (associated architects); William Lam Associates, Inc. (lighting consultants); Bolt, Beranek and Newman (acoustical consultants); Delores Miller & Associates (interior design consultants); Eitingon & Schlossberg (electrical engineers); Cosentini Associates (mechanical engineers); The Engineers Collaborative (structural engineers); Messer Inc. (general contractor). Cost: $24,000,000. Square footage: 360,000. Schematic design started 1964. Construction completed 1968.

As in the factory building for the same owners, described earlier **(Case Study B2),** the structure of this office building was derived from its function as one component of an integrated structural/mechanical/lighting system. The plan **(2)** was originally developed on the basis of columnless spaces with a steel frame structure. At this early stage, the tentative lighting/ceiling design was to suspend 6-foot-square pyramidal precast plaster coffers with recessed fluorescent fixtures mounted at the top.

When, for cost and other reasons, the requirement that the space be column-free was dropped, a poured concrete solution became feasible. Having just positively evaluated the mock-up of IBM-Milwaukee, project architect Hans Neumann hoped to use similar full indirect lighting at Cummins. Two limitations forced the design in a different direction.

First, the square plan shape with mechanical core at one corner meant a two-way network of service channels, hence, a symmetrical module. Second, the program requirement for a 6-foot partitioning module meant that the symmetrical modules would be quite small. Perceptually logical, continuous channels were created for the elements requiring continuity (air distribution), and the elements with static shapes (lighting) were placed in between. Chaotic, nervous spaces are created when this relationship is reversed (as at the Boston City Hall **[5],** or the Blue Cross–Blue Shield Building, Boston.

A 2'–4'–2'–4'–2' grid system was developed **(3),** which provided more than the programmed partitioning flexibility, but the resulting 4-foot-square cell limited the lighting hardware choices. Consideration of the biological needs for symmetry and for maximum comprehensibility of the structure suggested that lighting elements should be centered in each cell and baffled by it. Of the possibilities for indirect lighting sources, incandescent was too inefficient, mercury too expensive (in small sizes), and the economical 4-foot fluorescent lamp of the wrong shape. The choice was narrowed down to direct lighting from relatively uneconomical 2-foot fluorescent lamps in 2 × 2 foot fixtures, or direct/indirect lighting from the then-new 12-inch-square panel fluorescent lamp, which proved to be very efficient in the

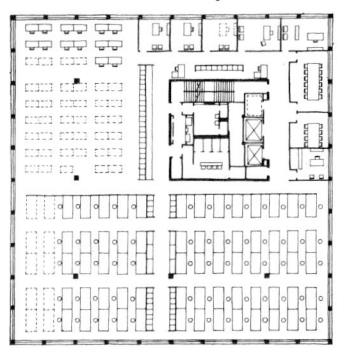

2

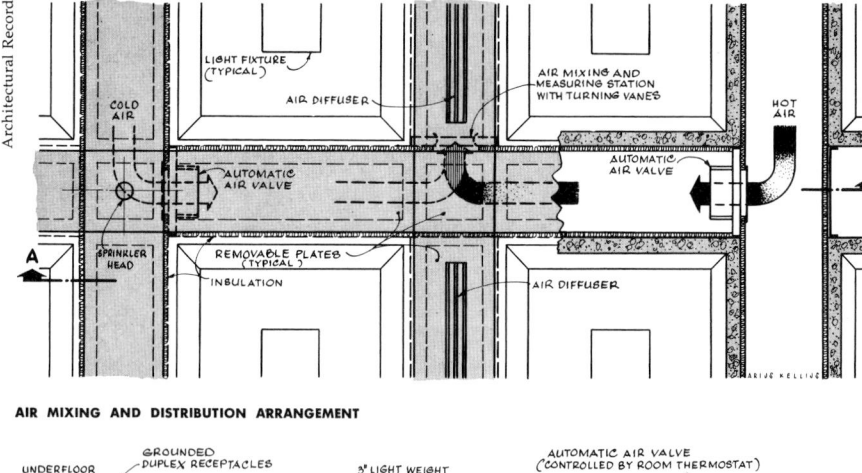

AIR MIXING AND DISTRIBUTION ARRANGEMENT

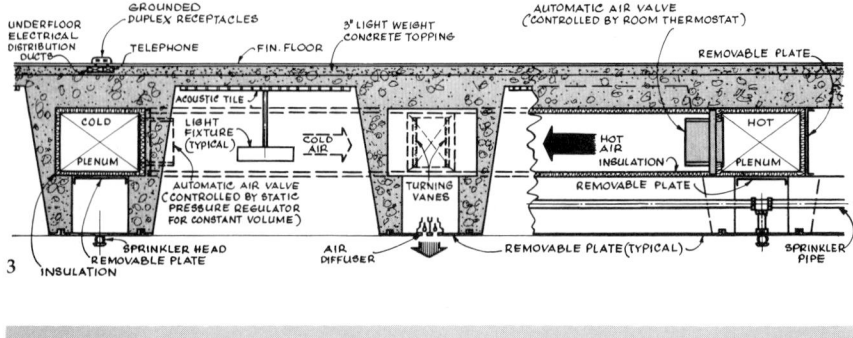

manner used. An 87 percent efficiency from the front face of the lamp was attained using specially molded low-brightness louvers, and light generated from the rear face (usually trapped ineffectively in a recessed fixture) was utilized to illuminate the coffer indirectly.

A mock-up was built to demonstrate the effect and to corroborate the quantitative forecasts. Because of the time and expenditure which would have been necessary to build an exact facsimile, it was necessary to approximate the fixtures to yield the desired information. For measurement of illumination level at desk top, white louvers of equal efficiency were substituted in the mock-up (Fig. 108) for the parabolic wedges. To give the clients the impression of how a single cell would appear, one fixture was fitted with an available parawedge louver with smaller baffles than called for, which while less efficient, demonstrated accurately the expected low surface brightness of the fixture (Fig. 107).

Illumination levels estimated from a mock-up of a single coffer were confirmed by the full room test, and subsequently in the completed building.

Critique

The environment produced appears very satisfactory for its purpose (6,7). However, I do have some second thoughts. Concrete surfaces were given a very smooth finish, and the semigloss paint applied to the entire ceiling disguises the difference between the lightweight metal infill panels and the concrete. Repainting the concrete in a matte white to contrast with the semigloss eggshell panels would help to differentiate the two elements.

Cost studies of using the then highly promoted new panel fluorescent lamp were predicated on

5 *Boston City Hall* (Kallman & McKinnell/ Architects).

the normal price reductions anticipated with time and increased production. Instead, the lamp was practically discontinued and prices were raised before the building was even complete. Responsibility on the part of lamp manufacturers cannot always be depended on.

It is open to question whether a larger module—for instance, $3'-7'-3'-7'-3'$—would not have been sufficiently flexible. The larger module would have been both more spacious and less expensive. Compare the spaces created with the Cummins module to those of MacMillan-Bloedel **(E8),** which are based on a larger module.

Harold Lewis/Photo International

6

7 Balthazar Korab

TOZZER LIBRARY
HARVARD UNIVERSITY
Cambridge, Massachusetts

Johnson·Hotvedt and Associates, Inc. (architect); Robert N. Hotvedt/Verner Johnson (partner in charge); William Lam Associates, Inc. (lighting consultants); Bolt; Beranek and Newman, Inc. (acoustical consultants); Moriece & Gary, Inc. (landscape); Galson & Galson (mechanical and electrical engineers); Harvard University Construction Management Division (project administration); Conmatan, Inc. (specifications); Souza & True, Inc. (structural engineers). Schematic design started 1972. Construction completed 1975. Approximate building lighting load: 2.6 watts per square foot.

The ceiling, lighting, structural, and mechanical systems of this library were manipulated by the design team to create spaces quite similar to those in the other case study projects in this section, although the execution was in plaster rather than exposed concrete due to the relatively small scale of the project.

Design

By concentrating mechanical runs at the perimeter of the spaces, it became possible to create large, indirectly illuminated coffers with integral lighting coves on their long sides. Solid exterior walls were illuminated from slots. The book stacks were oriented perpendicular to the long axis of the coffers so that the books would "see" the brightest portion of the ceiling **(3)**. At the ends of the building, the lowered ceiling band was widened beyond the depth required for mechanical runs so that the small rooms in these zones would have single rather than double-height ceilings. In these areas low-brightness 2×2 foot recessed fluorescent fixtures were provided for nighttime illumination, and switched separately so that they can be turned off when daylighting provides adequate task illumination **(4)**. To make possible the highlighting of works of art and planting, lighting track was installed at appropriate locations throughout the building. Track lighting is also used to provide supplementary task illumination when the larger coffers are subdivided to form small offices **(6)**. Local lighting is built into each carrel **(8)**.

Comments

The Rochester Institute of Technology Library in Rochester, New York (for which we acted as consultants to Harry Weese and Associates) is very similar in concept and execution **(Fig. 26)**.

Although the large coffers created in these projects were illuminated indirectly to provide excellent and well-balanced task and environmental illumination, this is not the only treatment possible for this sort of ceiling articulation. At the Cornell Commons, Cornell College, Mt. Vernon, Iowa **(9)**, the same team used large-scale coffering to define spaces within the rather open plan of the Commons, but in this case the coffers were treated as room-scale chandeliers with continuous strings of decorative incandescent lights, since the use of the spaces called for a more sparkling treatment than would have been possible with full indirect lighting.

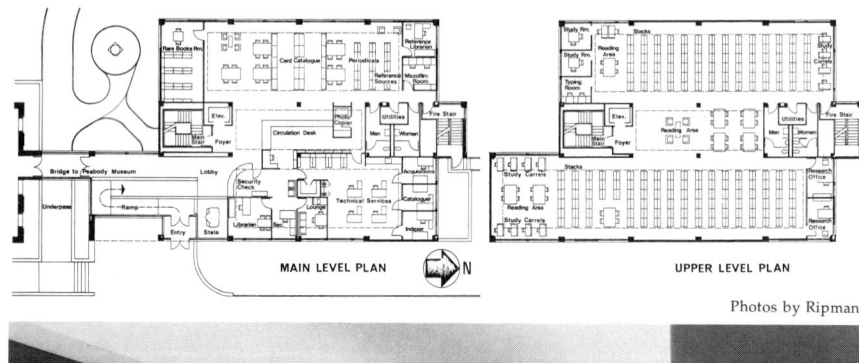

MAIN LEVEL PLAN   N   UPPER LEVEL PLAN

Photos by Ripman

4

5

6

7

8

9

Caudill Rowlett Scott, Los Angeles (design architect); Paul Kennon (project designer); Albert A. Hoover and Associates (principal architect); James Foug and Associates, William W. Hedley Associates (consulting architects); William Lam Associates, Inc. (lighting consultant); L. S. Good-friend & Associates (acoustical consultant); Mark Thomas & Company (civil consultant); Edwin H. Hesselberg (elevator consultant); Flambert & Flambert (food consultant); Arutunian/Kinney Associates (landscape consultant); Rodgers Associates (office landscaping consultant); Earth Sciences (soils consultant); Ackerman Engineers (electrical engineer); George A. Greene Company (mechanical engineer); Pregnoff/Matheu/Kellam/Beebe (structural engineer). Schematic design started 1971. Construction completed 1976.

After seeing the design drawings and mock-up for Governors State University **(Case Study G5),** at the Houston office of CRS, architect Paul Kennon conceived of a similar luminous environment for the Santa Clara County Civic Building **(1):** large coffers indirectly illuminated from architecturally integrated coves. The finished interior spaces bear a clear resemblance to those at Governors State, though there are important differences stemming from differences in plan and from the unusual structural requirements at Santa Clara.

The governing consideration which dictated a steel frame rather than a concrete structure was that the center of civil defense in an area prone to earthquakes should have maximum resistance to earthquake damage. The recommendation of the structural engineer was to frame *every* floor with two independent layers—one above the other—of one-way longspan steel beams 28 feet on center, spanning between the exterior walls without intermediate columns. The beams in the upper layer always run perpendicular to those in the lower layer at each floor. The steel frame is fireproofed with a concrete cover which will crack during an earthquake, damping out shocks and putting the structure out of resonance.

Since none of the previously developed concrete-based integrated systems could be adapted directly to suit these stringent conditions, the design challenge became how to create the same spacious interior environments and unified, consistent appearance, using the unusual column-free, double-depth steel-and-concrete structure.

The cavities in the upper layer of beams were assigned to primary mechanical distribution (fed from the perimeter cores). To provide local mechanical distribution, drywall service channels were created between each pair of beams in the lower layer. Concentration of services into a system of discrete, regular, minimal channels left the remainder of the volume in the lower structural layer available for use as indirect lighting coffers. Both beams and service channels were edged with integral light coves. Air is distributed to the rooms via slots at the lower edge of the coves which border the service channels. An acoustic ceiling was hung at the top of these coffers, level with the top flanges of the lower steel beams.

Since a one-way coffer system like that of the IBM-Milwaukee Building **(Case Study E2)** would have been inconsistent with the symmetrical exterior designed for Santa Clara, cross baffles were introduced on 28-foot centers to break up the linearity of the coffers. Although the symmetrical exterior suggested the use of square coffers, a rectangular coffer was selected, after a model study of various coffer proportions. Even with square coffers, the disparity between the logical dimensions for structure and service channels running in one direction and the lightweight cross baffles running in the other would have destroyed any perception of a symmetric two-way system. The rectangular coffers reduce the directional characteristics of the ceiling, without confusing the delineation of structure, service bands, and cross baffles as distinct but related components of an integrated system.

Generally speaking, the complex relationships between all the systems of a building can best be explored and most easily communicated through detailed model studies such as those made during the design of the Civic Building. Similar studies should be a regular part of the design process for any kind of integrated structure.

The final design proposal was tested and refined in a full-scale mock-up. Fully furnished and accurate in detailing, finishes, and furnishing, this mock-up could be shown to clients, unlike the incomplete mock-up for Governors State University which was only used by the design staff for photometric measurements. Clients are

Richard Karl Koch

generally confused and alarmed, rather than reassured, when shown an incomplete mock-up. The presence of adjacent, unrelated rooms, incorrect or sloppy details, and inaccurate materials and finishes is hard to ignore, and those untrained in design and unfamiliar with the true intent of the designer find it hard to fill in the missing elements of the finished environment in their imagination. The Santa Clara mock-up was important both as a visible demonstration of the quality of environment which could be anticipated and as proof to the usual skeptics that the predicted levels of illumination could in fact be achieved, despite handbook data which suggested otherwise.

On the typical floor, the fluorescent cove lighting was to have been supplemented with incandescent fixtures recessed into the service channels. Although these fixtures would be required for task lighting in only a few furniture and partitioning arrangements, the supplementary incandescent units provide interest and orientation while highlighting objects low in the space.

For variety, and to respond to the different nature of activities in the ground-floor cafeteria and meeting rooms, the coffer system was maintained in these areas with decorative arrangements of clear lamps substituted for the indirect coves.

Comment

While this building is not as efficient (in terms of the ratio of habitable to total built volume) as any of the concrete tree or channel systems presented here, it does come close to the objective of maximum visible volume within the constraints imposed by this particular approach to earthquake-resistant construction. The standard approach—a hung ceiling below the lowest layer of structure—would

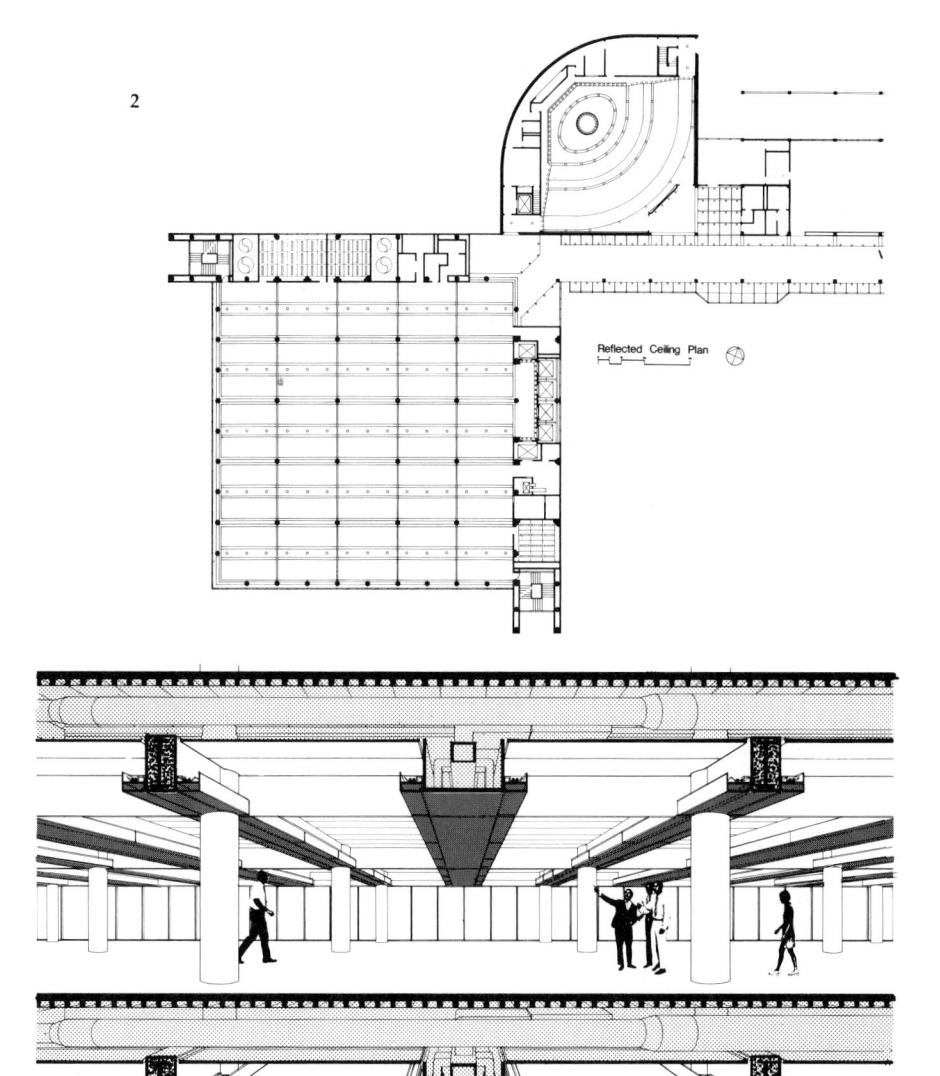

2

Reflected Ceiling Plan

3

Systems Section

have been a terrible waste of the potential for a truly spacious environment inherent in such an unusually deep structural system.

Because of an unfounded concern for measured uniformity of lighting, low-brightness fluorescent fixtures were substituted for the proposed supplementary incandescent fixtures without our knowledge. The change was unnecessary. A mock-up had demonstrated that the proposed task lighting would have been entirely adequate and that the drop in light levels under the unlit service bands would have been almost unnoticeable. The resulting environment is neither as pleasant nor as interesting as the original design, in which supplementary

fixtures were to have been used only for specific purposes such as accent highlighting. The change was also a false economy, consuming more energy than a selective layout of incandescent fixtures as proposed. Although fluorescent lamps are inherently more efficient than incandescent lamps in terms of converting electrical energy into light, the overall energy consumption in a space may be higher if unnecessary fluorescent fixtures are used indiscriminately merely to make a regular pattern or to achieve some misconceived objective such as perfect uniformity of lighting, rather than using a smaller number of less efficient fixtures only where they are needed.

1

ADDITION, EASTON HOSPITAL
Easton, Pennsylvania

Isadore & Zachary Rosenfield (architect); William Lam Associates, Inc. (lighting consultants); Ranger Farrell (acoustical consultant); Economides & Goldberg (mechanical engineers); Conti & Saunders (structural engineers); R. S. Noonan (general contractor). Cost: $4,500,000. Square footage: 59,000 (new) and 9,000 (alteration). Schematic design started June 1970. Construction completed September 1973.

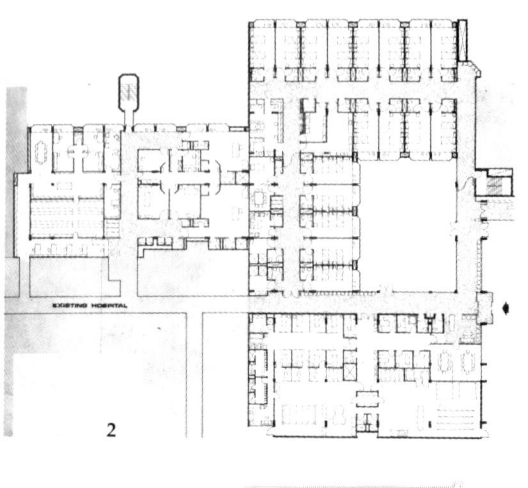

2

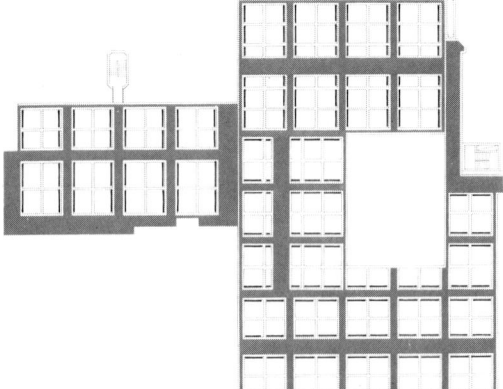

3 *Reflected ceiling plan showing location of indirect fixtures.*

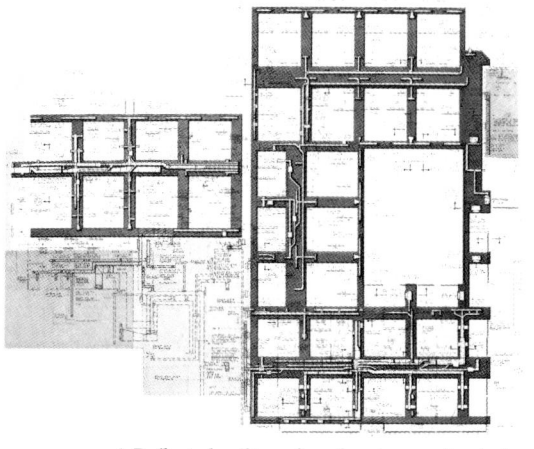

4 *Reflected ceiling plan showing mechanical service channels.*

Unusual problems are often encountered in the design of an infill addition to a hospital, which would not be encountered in the design of a new hospital or a freestanding addition. For the Easton Hospital infill addition, the design team developed a special configuration of the "tree structure"[1] to meet lighting and mechanical requirements within the constraints imposed by the preexisting plan.

Design

Each half of the six-cell directional concrete trees defines two single rooms and a bathroom. Since all services are easily accommodated in the continuous gaps between

[1]*These two-way cantilever structures are discussed in considerable detail in* **Case Studies Group G.**

the edge beams of the trees **(4,5),** no suspended ceiling is necessary within the trees, not even in the bathrooms. Room services are even more accessible than they would be with a complete suspended ceiling system.

Room lighting **(3)** and nightlights are indirect, reflected from the coffers formed by the beams of the tree structure, and supplementary reading light is provided from locally switched fluorescent strips concealed behind the edge beams **(7, 8).**

Similar trees, which vary in size because of the asymmetric layout of this building, house services and more powerful indirect lighting for labs and other areas. Gaps between the new tree structure and the existing buildings were defined by clear skylights **(13).**

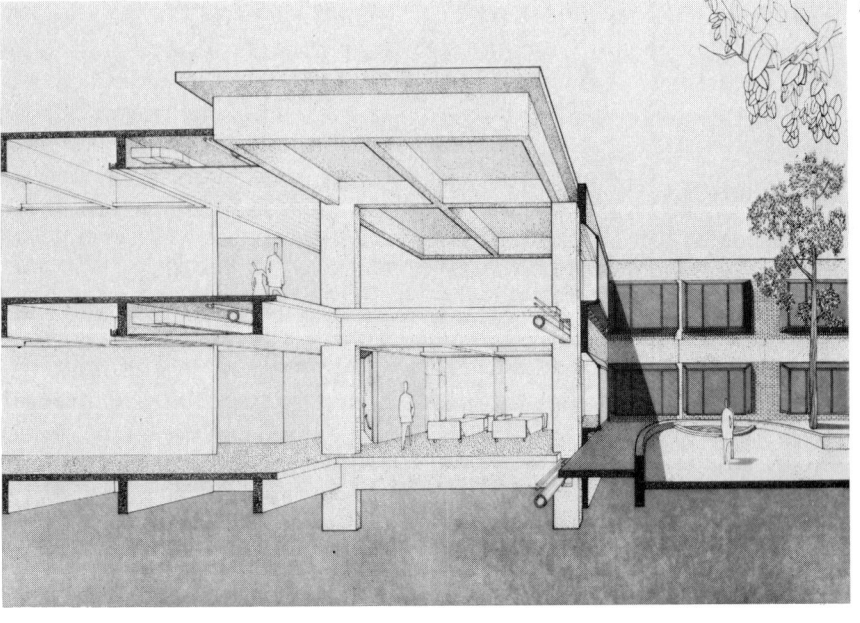

5

Photos by John T. Hill

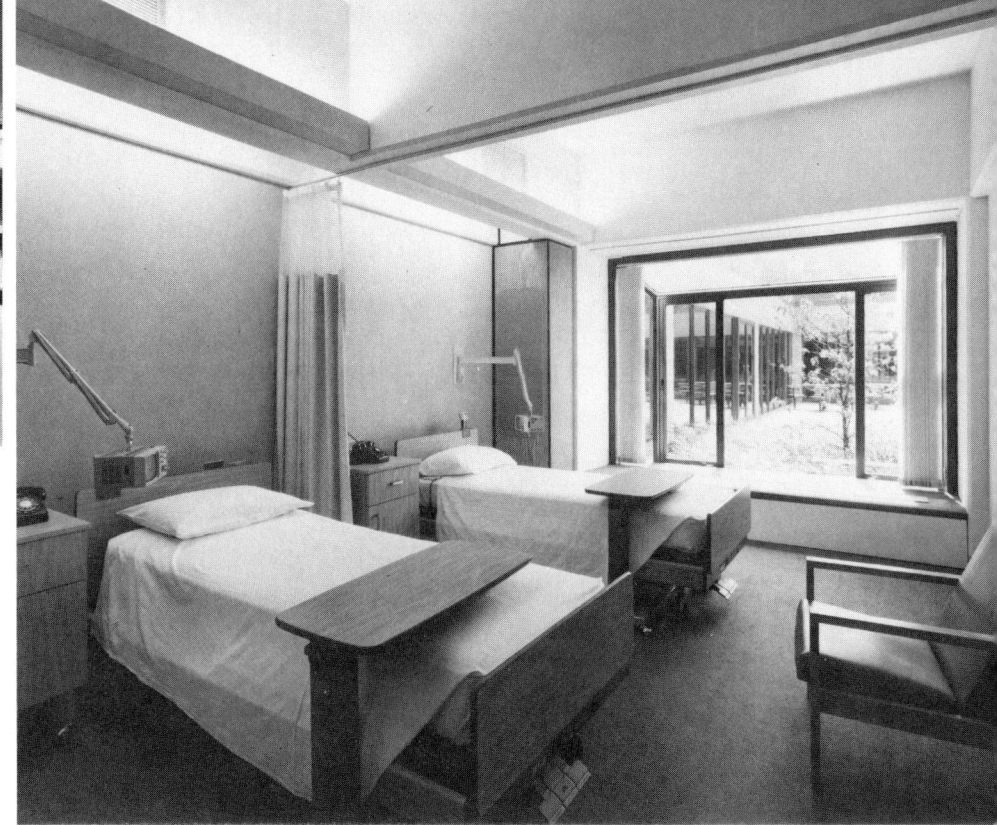

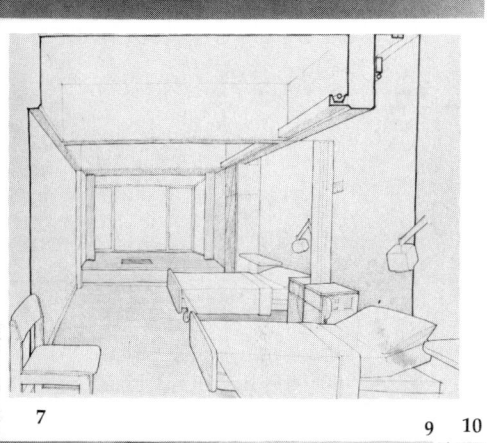

7

Courtesy of Isadore & Zachary Rosenfield

9   10

8

11

UNIVERSITY OF LETHBRIDGE
Lethbridge, Alberta

Erickson/Massey Architects (architect); Arthur Erickson (designer); Ron Bain (associate in charge); Gary Hanson (project architect); Robins Mitchell Watson (associated architect); William Lam Associates, Inc. (lighting consultants); Barron & Strachan (acoustical consultant); F. S. Dubin (mechanical consultant); Ripley Klohn & Leonoff International Ltd. (foundation engineers); Reid, Crowther & Partners Ltd. (mechanical and electrical engineers); Bogue Babicki & Associates (structural engineers); Poole Construction Ltd. (general contractor). Schematic design started March 1968. Construction completed 1969.

Architectural Record

In order to achieve an articulated building system that would create optimal environments for the wide variety of functions of this new residential university, a close collaboration of the complete design team was initiated from the beginning of schematic design.

One decision, however, limited the possibilities of developing a simple, integrated module that could be multiplied into an entire academic complex (as at Governors State University **[Case Study G5]** or at Pierrefonds Comprehensive High School **(E9)**). The

architecturally exciting decision to bridge the 500-foot-wide coulees (with broad layers devoted to academic, administrative, and social activities above and narrower layers of housing below) meant that further growth would have to take place in large increments (other bridges). The bridging, upward-expanding form limited the range of structural possibilities.

Design

With these limitations, a scheme similar to the Pierrefonds system was developed but proved to be too costly. However, a good alternative system with somewhat less service flexibility but even more visual spaciousness was developed and used throughout most of the building. For the academic/social office levels (6 and 7) the system consists of building-length bands of indirectly illuminated decking interrupted only by partitions and framed by natural-finish precast concrete girders that span between columns 36 feet on center **(3)**. These girders contain integral coves for indirect light-

ing. Decking is white-painted precast concrete double-T's, the undersides of which form the lighting reflectors. The T's provide natural shielding for direct lighting of the cross walls (which run parallel to the T's). The 20-foot-wide indirectly illuminated band of double-T's generally occurs on both sides of a central band connecting vertical cores 130 feet apart. In the core zone **(5)** a suspended ceiling encloses major mechanical services and low-brightness recessed fluorescent or incandescent lighting.

On level 5, which has small offices **(6)** and seminar rooms all along the perimeter, a schematic reversal of the lighting system was indicated, and a narrower, dropped plaster plenum band edged with a wall-lighting slot was used in the corridors feeding perimeter offices and interior classrooms **(7)** in the core zone. On this level, core classrooms and perimeter offices are full height and indirectly illuminated. On the upper levels (6, 7, and 8), the building is widened with a sec-

3→

Lam　**5**　Photos without credits by Scott Simon

E7 University of Lethbridge　225

Courtesy Robbins Mitchell Watson

Scott Simon

6   7

ond narrower band of T's at the perimeter.

The nature of the structure is essentially one-way, with major girders running parallel to the long axis of the building. This limits flexibility and the size of service distribution channels in the other direction. These are concealed above drywall infill panels within the depth of the double-T's which serve as secondary structure. Spaces with maximum service requirements, such as labs, are restricted to the middle band, where services may be run freely in any direction above the suspended ceiling. In the perimeter bands, the visual impact of the lighting system and the exposed structure is sufficiently powerful that the few exposed pipes, ducts, etc., go quite unnoticed.

In the dormitory levels, desire for total flexibility of room arrangement and a minimal budget made complete built-in lighting impossible. Instead, some general lighting was provided from wall brackets, and each student was provided with a portable ''Luxo''-type lamp that could be inserted into bushings built into every bed and desk (12). Concealed lighting was provided for kitchenette (8) and lounge areas, along with some adjustable floodlights to provide flexible accents as desired.

Site lighting design

At Lethbridge, pedestrian and auto traffic are separated, and the need to provide exterior lighting to ensure a sense of security from attack is minimal because of its location in a remote part of Alberta. This remoteness and the need to preserve the unspoiled, empty surrounding landscape from undesirable visual noise presented additional design challenges.

With separated pedestrian circulation, in a locale where none of the surrounding roads are illuminated, roadway lighting could be reduced to a minimum, serving primarily for guidance. From a distance, orientation to the University is provided by the building itself, conspicuous because of its size and well defined by flood-lighting and by spill light from the interior (which also illuminates the immediate surroundings). The site entrance was marked with illuminated graphics, and the roadway was defined by low fixtures (11) mounted at a height that would not disrupt views of the building. Great care was taken to preserve the beautiful, fragile landscape. To this end the large parking areas were hidden behind berms so that they could not be seen from the building, and illuminated from adjustable floodlights mounted within monumental concrete shafts (10) whose shapes will be seen as environmental sculpture rather than visual noise during the day. The floodlighting is oriented away from the buildings so that from within the buildings only the illuminated ground and berms can be seen—no glaring fixtures are visible. The exhaust stack/lighting bridge on the plaza (13) and the integrated air-intake/floodlight housings which flank the building were given similar sculptural roles in the overall design concept.

8

9 Main kitchen (another indirect approach to kitchen lighting which relates the lighting to the equipment rather than the structure is shown in **Fig. 24** on page 28.)

Photos: Lam

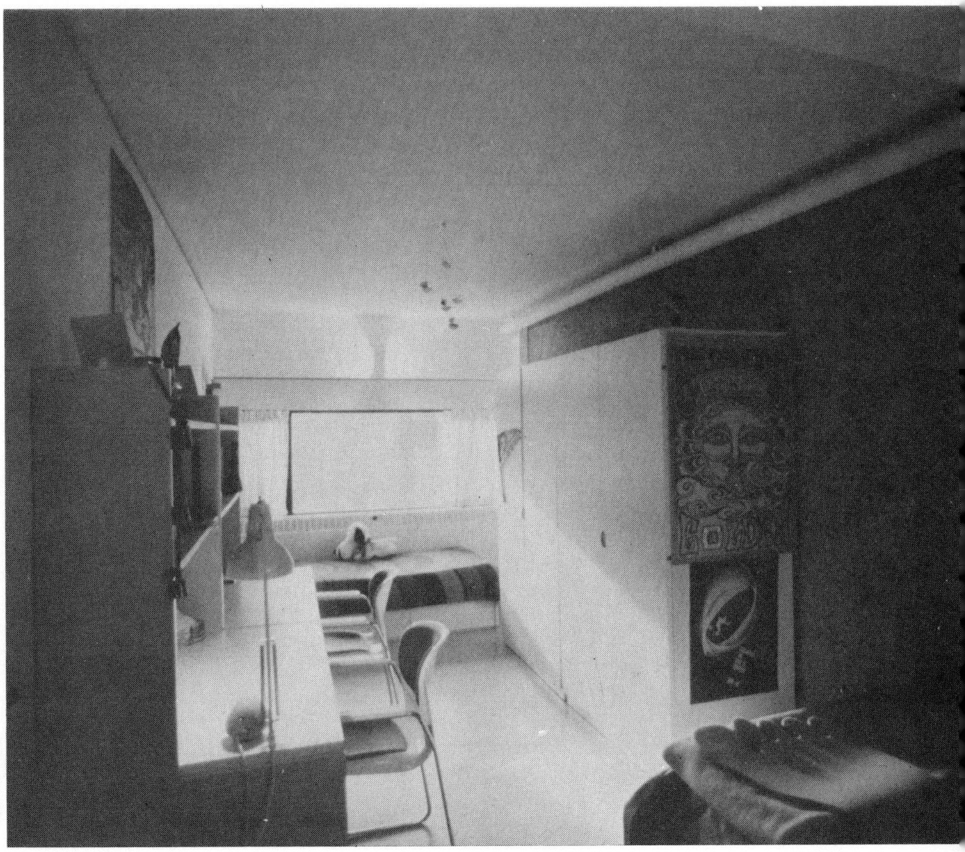

12

10

Courtesy of Robbins Mitchell Watson

11 13

1

MACMILLAN-BLOEDEL BUILDING
Vancouver, British Columbia

E8

Erickson/Massey and Francis Donaldson (architect); Arthur Erickson (partner in charge of design); James Strasman (Erickson/Massey) and Procter LeMaire (Francis Donaldson) (project architects); William Lam Associates, Inc. (lighting consultants); Bolt, Beranek and Newman (acoustical consultants); Lester Beall & Associates (graphics consultants); Reid Crowther & Partners, Ltd. (mechanical and electrical engineers); R. A. Spence, Ltd. (soils engineers); Otto Safir (structural engineers); Laing Construction & Equipment Ltd. (general contractor). Schematic design started 1966. Construction completed 1970.

2

MacMillan-Bloedel presented an opportunity to test the advantages of larger modules. Having created a very classic exterior form—monolithic poured concrete punctured only by crisp square window openings glazed with uninterrupted sheets of glass—architect Erickson was anxious to have exposed concrete structure within.

From the inception of the project, two constraints had forced the design toward a homogenized suspended ceiling solution: cost and a programmatic requirement for a 5-foot partitioning module. These impediments were overcome by an integrated design approach and a more realistic look at the partitioning requirements.

Design

The original mechanical scheme was uneconomical because it was not "pure" enough; for instance, patches of suspended ceiling had been included to take care of mechanical distribution to the interior zones adjacent to the cores. Only slight modifications to the structure were necessary to increase flexibility, to eliminate such ad hoc elements, and to bring the mechanical cost into line.

Flanges of the structural beams were widened to 3 feet, so that the 10-foot-on-center spacing of the beams became effectively 3'−7'−3'−7'−3' for partitioning purposes. This made it possible to

![Typical floor plan]

TYPICAL FLOOR

3 Architectural Record

![Ceiling plan showing mechanical and lighting]

direct lighting: typical floor

partition locations

indirect lighting: plaza level, 25th floor

4 CEILING PLAN SHOWING MECHANICAL AND LIGHTING

create spaces from 7 to 13 or 17 to 23 feet wide with walls running parallel to the beams. Every beam was penetrated at two points, so that air supply and return could be handled from duct bands run through the holes, interconnecting the end service cores **(6)**. This eliminated any need for a second mechanical room on each floor. The edge of the duct band was the logical place to locate indirect cove lighting supplementing light from the perimeter **(5)**.

This combination was more economical than a suspended ceiling with its (necessarily) much larger number of lighting fixtures. Had the integrated solution been found earlier, additional economies could have been realized by reducing the floor-to-floor height by 6 to 12 inches; unfortunately, however, the preparation of new structural drawings would have delayed construction by a season and was therefore impractical.

Lighting distribution was predicted from a model of a single cell and confirmed with full-scale room mock-ups.

It is often difficult to sell a client sight unseen on an unconventional but superior system; full-scale mock-ups were used at MacMillan to demonstrate the superiority of the proposed indirect systems **(11)** over other, more conventional alternatives: suspended ceiling with fully recessed, direct fluorescent fixtures, and

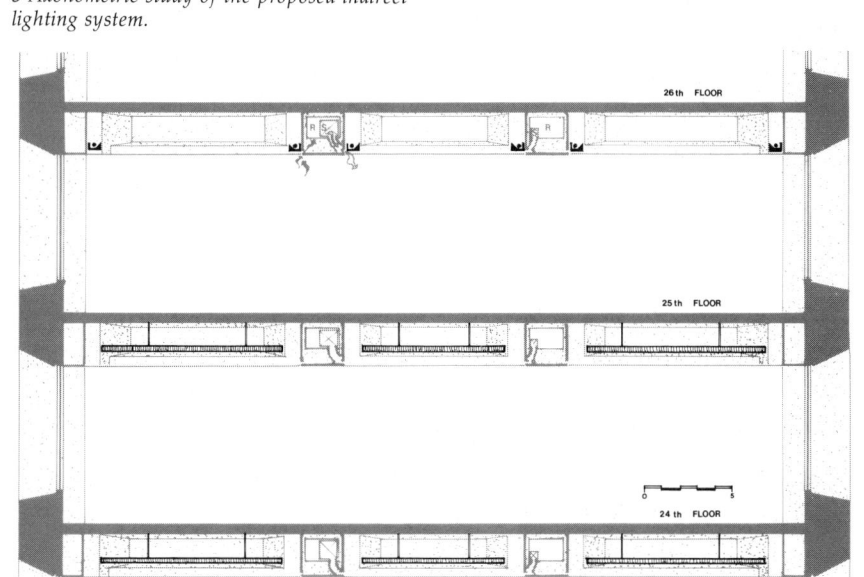

5 *Axonometric study of the proposed indirect lighting system.*

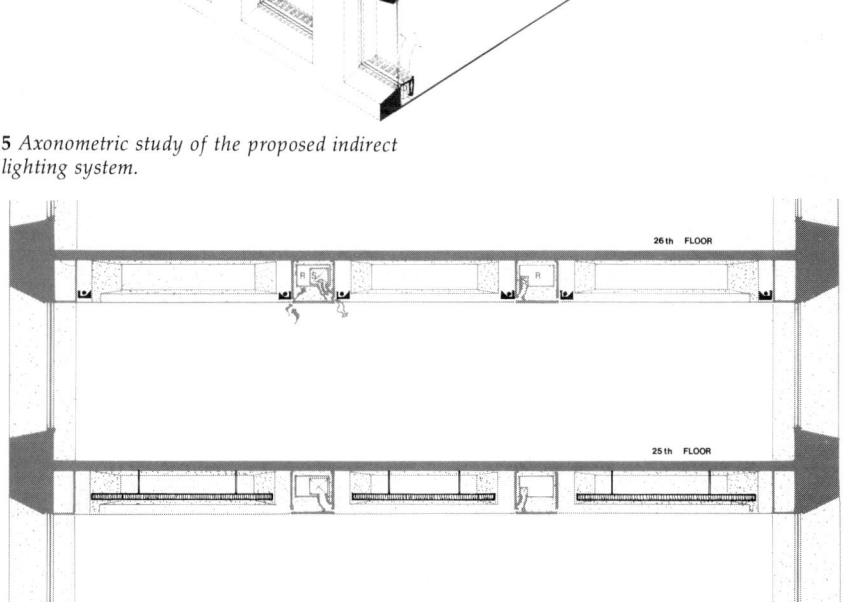

26th FLOOR

25th FLOOR

24th FLOOR

7 Mock-up of typical secretarial pool area.

8 Typical small office as built.

9 Typical small office on the top floor.

Photos by Lam

large surface-mounted fluorescent fixtures which approximated a luminous ceiling. A single indirect fixture with a V profile was also proposed and mocked up as the least–cost acceptable alternative **(10).** The recommended double cove system was unanimously acclaimed as producing the best environment **(15).**

Unfortunately, despite the success of the mock-up, prior leasing commitments based on specified footcandle levels led to the selection of a compromise lighting solution on most floors **(6).** Even then, much better and less expensive lighting was achieved by the integration of structure and mechanical systems to yield biologically satisfying spaces **(13).** Another compromise required on the top floor **(9,12)** because of interference with roof drains makes this building a good "laboratory" in which one may examine a variety of luminous environments under otherwise similar conditions.

In the lobby **(14),** the indirectly illuminated coffers were supplemented by recessed incandescent fixtures to increase the focus on ground-level objects in the high space. Exterior lighting was integrated into the pool edge **(2)** and benches. Floodlighting was supplemented by globes on the plaza to erase any shadows at the lower walls.

Critique

Unfortunately, final detailing of the executive floor ignored several key features of the tested and approved mock-up. Walls and furniture were dark-colored instead of light, reducing their reflectance. Both illumination levels and a sense of spaciousness were further sacrificed by the use of gray patterned glass (instead of clear) for the transoms.

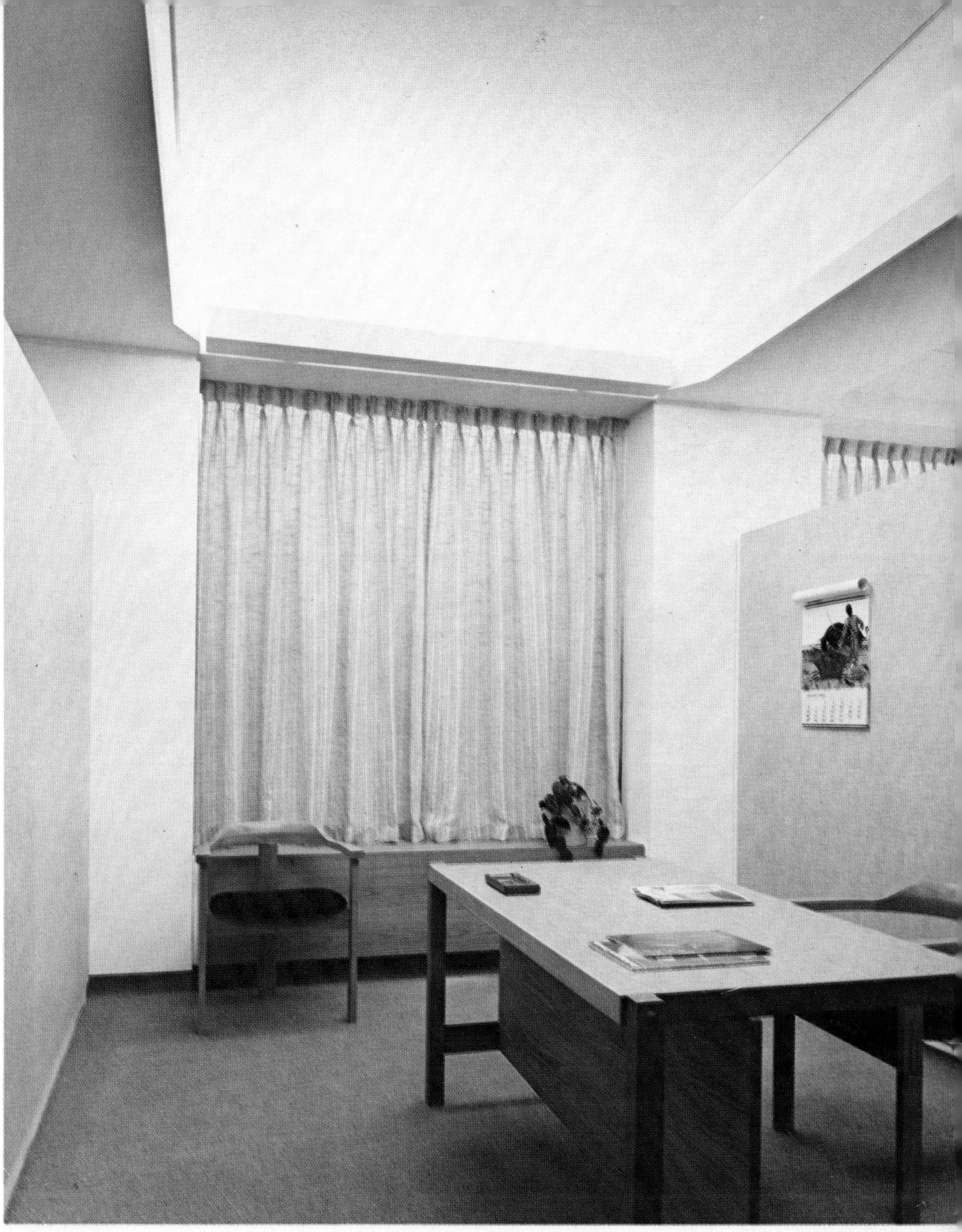

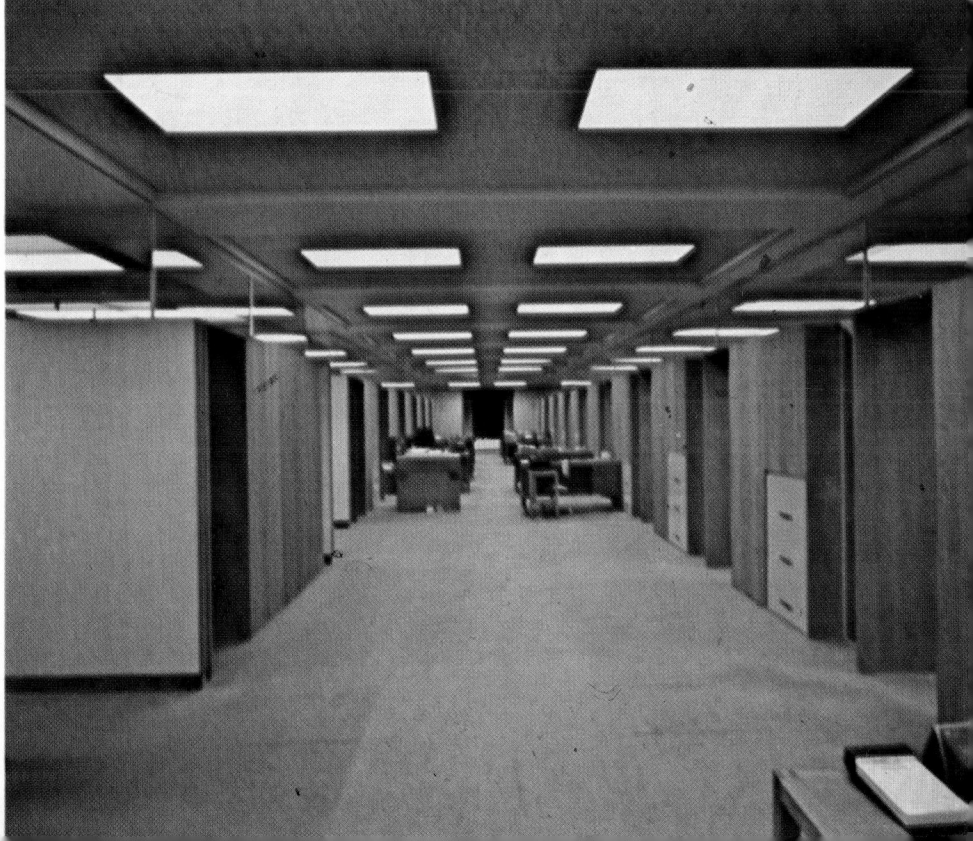

11 *Mock-up of typical indirect coffer.*

Two photos: Bob Roberts

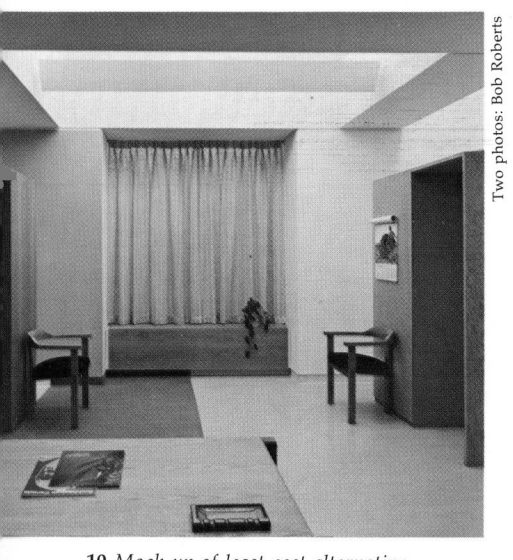

10 *Mock-up of least-cost alternative.*

12 *Secretarial pool area on the top floor.*

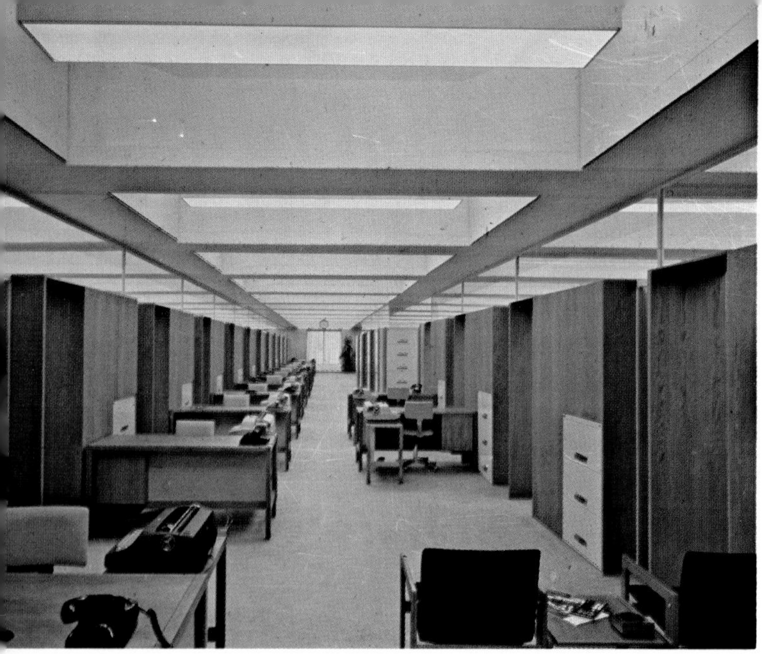

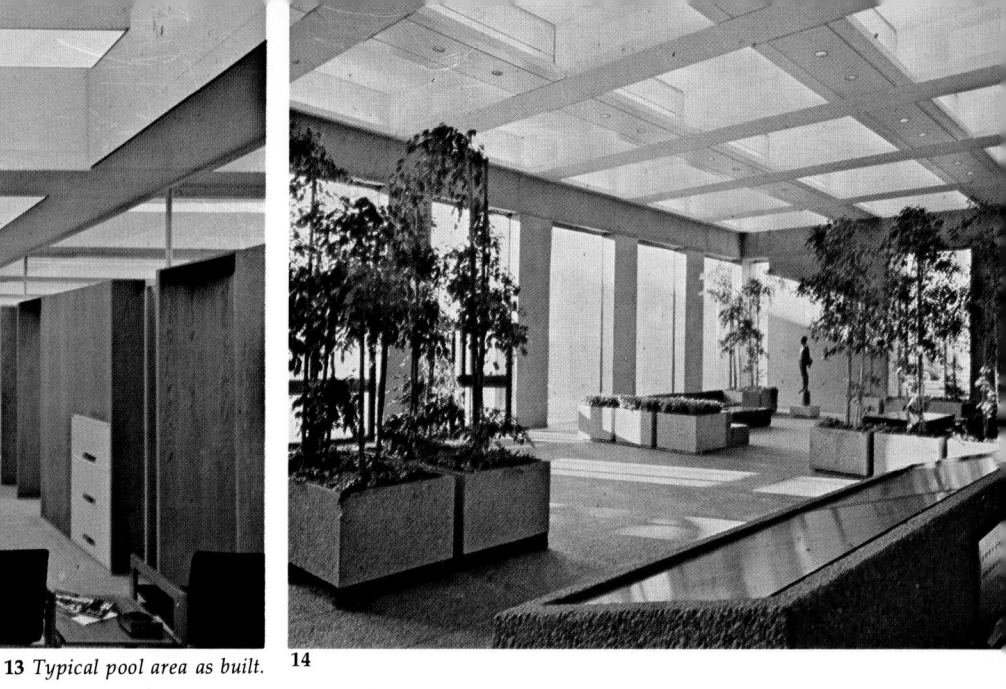

13 *Typical pool area as built.*

14

15 *Executive office.*

Photos: © ESTO

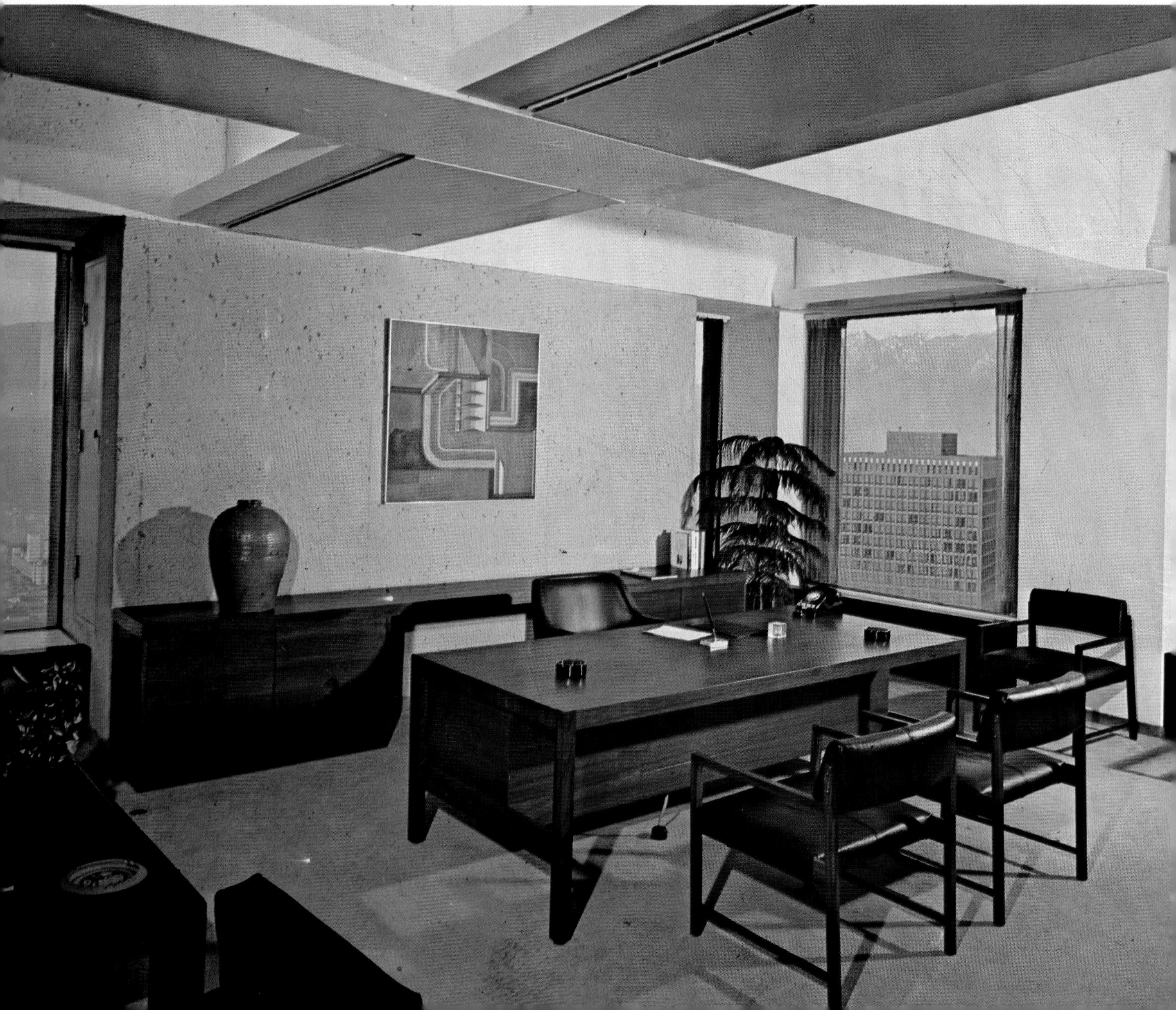

1

PIERREFONDS COMPREHENSIVE HIGH SCHOOL
Pierrefonds, Quebec

E9

Affleck Desbarats Dimakopoulos Lebensold & Sise (architect); D. F. Lebensold (partner in charge); Imre Reichmann (project architect); William Lam Associates, Inc. (lighting consultants); N. J. Pappas (acoustical consultant); ARC—Montreal (graphics consultant); Pierre De Guise et Associés (electrical engineers); Pageaux, Gelinas, Favreau (mechanical engineers); Delorme, Carrier, Bourbonnais et St.-Amant, Vezina et Associés (structural engineers); Janin Construction Co., Ltd. (general contractor). Cost: $6,000,000. Square footage 419,287. Construction completed Fall 1971. Approximate lighting load: 2.2 watts per square foot.

The Pierrefonds Comprehensive High School represented a big step toward the articulated, flexible building. The architects had been commissioned to design two separate high schools (French and English) spread apart on a single large site. Instead, they chose to combine the two in a single structure, designed so that they could be totally separated (per the original program) if the social integration experiment should fail.

Detailed planning came after development of the concept for a system-of-systems (5) which would integrate services, structure, and lighting. The structure was designed to create long bands of indirectly lighted concrete coffers alternating with service channels that could enclose ductwork and unlimited lab plumbing. The structural/mechanical/lighting system was designed around precast concrete channels (3) which contain mechanical services, span up to 70 feet, and double as lighting coves. These rest on channel columns that are paired to create the main service corridors (2) within the building and above the roof. Decking consists of short precast double-T beams spanning between the channel beams. The gaps between the ends of the double-T's provide additional space for ductwork.

The spatial result is large-scale illuminated channels (9 feet wide) that take partitioning on a

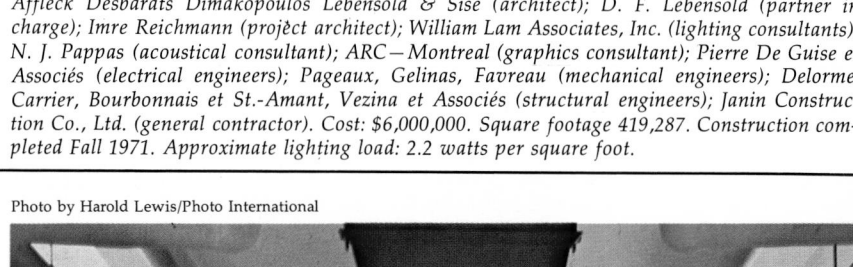

2

3

4

234   *E9 Pierrefonds Comprehensive High School*

9′–4′–9′–4′–9′ rhythm. Partitions parallel with the structure can be located anywhere within the 4-foot bands (the undersides of the service channels). Cross partitions and corridors perpendicular to the channel beams can be placed anywhere without interrupting the lighting system; the fluorescent strip fixtures, which rest freely in the coves, are simply spread apart to accommodate partitions. With this integrated approach, spacious classrooms (10) and other large spaces with high ceilings were possible within a floor-to-floor dimension which with 5 × 5 foot modules and a suspended ceiling would have produced only 8 foot 6 inch flat ceilings.

The indirectly illuminated ceiling coffers cast plenty of light on vertical surfaces such as chalkboards. In addition, walls adjacent to any one of the open channels can be highlighted easily by mounting bare lamps behind the beams.

The channel-beam spacing was increased in the central cafeteria/library area (4,9), and the skylights spanning between the beams were supplemented by incandescent downlights to be used on overcast days and at night.

Site

Driveway and entrance were articulated by a hierarchy of clear globes. Parking lots are illuminated by adjustable floodlights housed in Corten steel shafts that appear like sculptures against the skyline (12).

Critique

Despite full-size drawings and a full-scale mock-up, the cove light fixtures were installed in the wrong position (with the lamps up), making the lamps somewhat visible from a distance and the illumination of the beams slightly spotty (8).

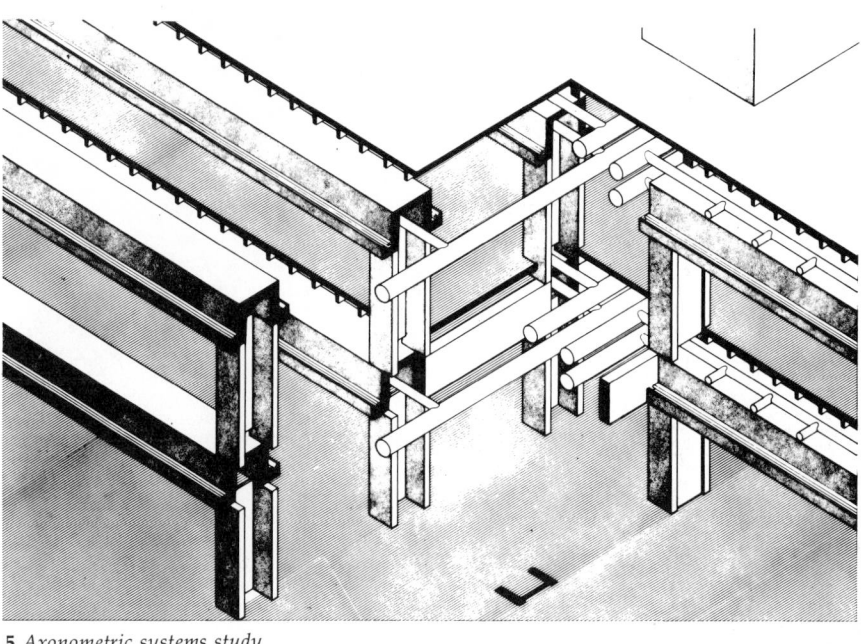

5 *Axonometric systems study.*

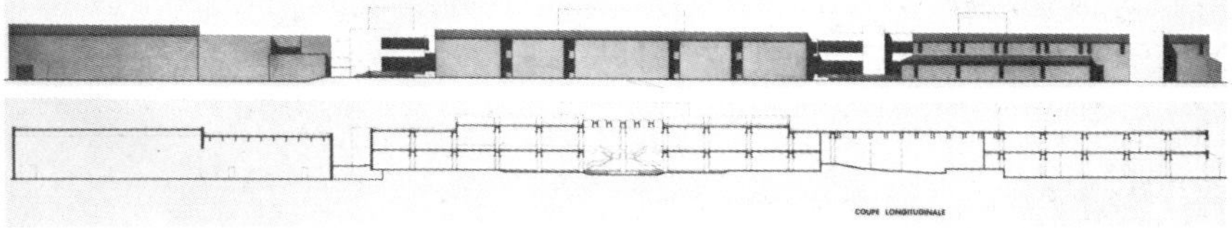

6

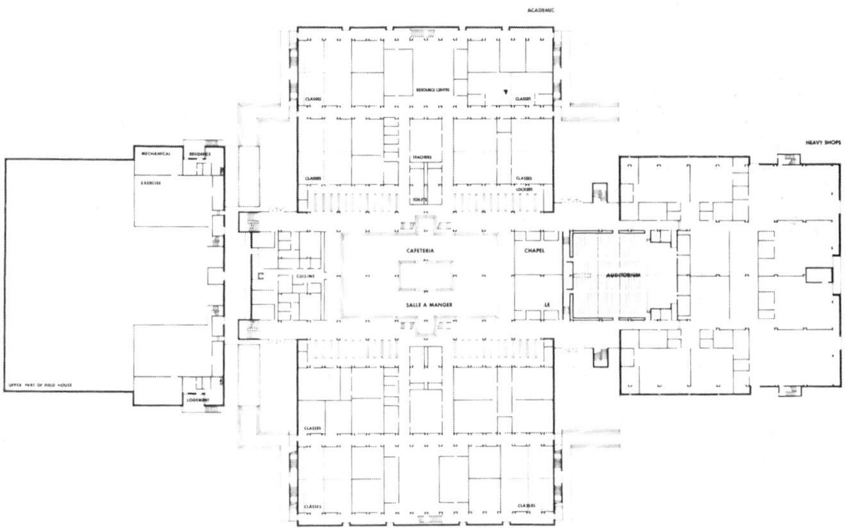

7

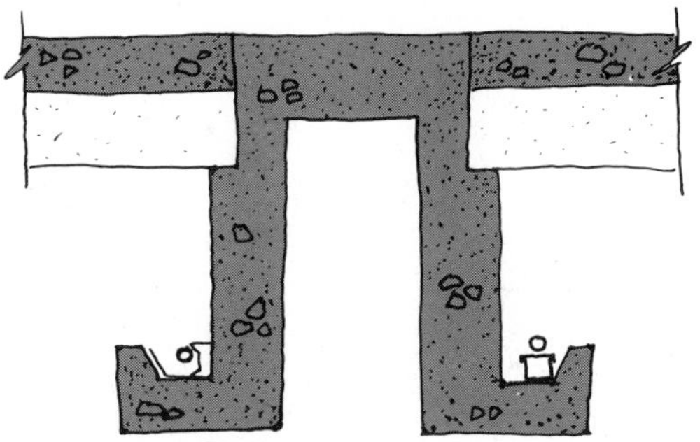

8

AS CONCEIVED   AS BUILT

Ripman

At $14 (Canadian) per square foot, in 1968, this building was as economical as any of the Montreal "systems" school buildings, and if more of this type were built the precast system should be just as fast to erect.

9

10   11

12

CASE STUDIES GROUP F

SEQUENCES OF SPACES WITHOUT FIXED CORRIDORS: FLAT-CEILING SYSTEMS FITTED TO PREDETER-MINED EXTERIOR FORMS

Although articulated building systems such as the ones presented in the previous section offer the greatest potential in providing biologically satisfactory environments suitable to the activities which they house at lowest cost, there are many situations in which a homogenized, neutral solution[1] may be appropriate—or unavoidable. Such circumstances might exist:

1. When scheduling requirements of a tight project timetable can only be met with a steel framing system and maximum utilization of factory-made components.
2. In labor-short locations, or areas without sophisticated concrete technology.
3. When unlimited rather than moderate partitioning and service flexibility is demanded, i.e., in speculative buildings.
4. When a building is designed from the outside in, so that the exterior forms and framing are established prior to design of the ceiling, lighting, mechanical, and partitioning systems. Such a process forecloses the possibilities of developing an integrated system-of-systems.
5. When a preference is expressed for "average" spaces, functionally usable for a wide range of activities but not particularly good for any—a "safe" choice of the developer or designers.

In short, homogenized buildings are usually a compromise, resulting from an inability to arrive at an articulated building system that can accommodate the various projected activity and spatial needs within the budget. When a homogenized building is called for, the primary objective is generally not to create positively expressed spaces, but, on the contrary, to create the most neutral spaces possible. To create spaces which are reasonably satisfactory for all activities, design objectives must be formulated completely and clearly. Achieving these objectives within correctly stated economic

[1] By a "homogenized solution" I mean an approach which conceals all structure and mechanical appurtenances above a suspended ceiling, usually flat and unarticulated, and in which there is little or no evident intent to integrate structural and mechanical systems in such a way as (1) to maximize perceptible room volumes within a given floor-to-floor dimension, (2) to create natural service channels in the structure, and (3) to use the actual surfaces of the structure as sources of illumination for the spaces which they enclose, through the use of indirect lighting (sometimes supplemented by unobtrusive direct lighting).

constraints becomes the problem. Most homogenized buildings are clearly less than optimal, since many desirable design objectives have been compromised for economy—real or imagined.

Design objectives of homogenized solutions—assuming no cost constraints—usually include the following: The ceiling should be capable of distributing air and light in every module. The plan module should allow partitions to be aligned with windows, framing, columns, and other elements; should be nondirectional (so that rooms can run in either direction); and should provide easy access to mechanical, electrical, and plumbing services, without damage to ceiling material during this process or when partitions are moved. (Painting or replacing part of a homogeneous flat ceiling is likely to be conspicuous, while this is not usually the case with ceiling systems articulated in three dimensions because the variation in surface orientation to the light sources is perceived as explaining most changes in color or texture.) Light fixtures should be as inconspicuous as possible, should give off a minimum of direct glare, should cast only moderate shadows, and should allow variation in light output when desired for design or economic purposes. Good acoustic absorption is usually desirable, and good attenuation should occur at partitions. Excessive radiant heat and sound from lighting fixtures and other mechanical components must be avoided.

The most common design errors and compromises of these objectives are:

1. *Use of directional fixtures* (e.g., 1×4 foot) *when the building and/or building module is nondirectional (square)*. Usually dictated by the economy of the 4-foot fluorescent lamp.

2. *The generation of excessive direct glare* as a by-product of a misconceived design goal: the provision of maximum footcandles rather than maximum comfort. Fixtures which produce maximum direct glare can be spaced relatively widely due to their high lateral distribution of light, and the temptation exists to trade an increase in glare for a reduction in the number of fixtures required to achieve a given horizontal distribution of illumination.

3. *Improper alignment of the ceiling and lighting module with structural elements, windows, etc.* Perceptible order in the visual environment facilitates comprehension and relaxes the user. The absence or misalignment of an overall organizing module often leads to visual chaos, which produces an opposite effect. Misalignment of the lighting module is frequently caused by a lack of coordination between standard dimensions of ceiling material and structure. More often, misalignment is the result of deriving the lighting module from the most "efficient" method of providing required footcandle levels, rather than from desirable visual relationships and partitioning studies. Obvious lack of coordination in the visual

environment is distracting and unpleasant, particularly when it involves strong elements of the visual field such as lighting fixtures and structural members.

4. *The generation of excessive heat and/or shadows in work areas* through the unjustified and excessive employment of directional incandescent systems.

5. *Excessive spacing of fixtures,* so that lighting must be rearranged whenever partitions are moved.

A number of opportunities exist for the design team to reduce costs, while simultaneously diminishing the negative effects of compromise solutions. The team should:

1. *Minimize waste of space in the ceiling cavity with an articulated, integrated arrangement of ducts, lights, and structure.*

2. *Write the program for maximum comfort instead of maximum footcandles per dollar.* This allows the use of less efficient but much more pleasant lamps, improves glare control, and permits lamp operation at reduced voltage (which greatly extends lamp life while reducing current consumption) *for incandescent lamps.*

3. *Recognize the presence of daylight as a primary or supplementary light source, and realize that at night, lighting needs are reduced because one expects there to be less light at night than during the day.* Separate switching of exterior modules, where artificial light is usually unnecessary during the day, and other variations of lighting design at the perimeter will permit the realization of considerable economies in operation and create a more relevant luminous environment. A room looks ridiculous when electric lighting is on (and cannot be turned off) in areas already fully illuminated by daylight.

4. *Recognize probable corridor positions when possible.* Less light is required in corridors than in work areas. Around building cores, reduction of lighting levels and the number of fixtures will give extra space for ductwork in the ceiling around the core where it is usually most needed, as well as saving money.

5. *Use the largest possible module for the needs of each particular building to minimize both the number of light fixtures and the sense of spatial fragmentation.*

6. *Avoid excessive window areas, to reduce problems of heat and glare control and associated air-conditioning costs.* Use building forms for louvering and sunshading (for instance, deep reveals with glazing at the inner rather than outer face of the wall).

7. *Minimize fixture size to reduce cost and to minimize visual dominance.*

8. *Consider cost of moving fixtures* (including administrative cost) *during partitioning changes.* This may offset the higher initial cost of smaller modules, which in turn could eliminate the need to move any fixtures during such changes.

There are also opportunities for long-term advances in product design. Striving for the ideal rather than the immediate compromise can create pressure on manufacturers to produce new, desirable products or to modify old ones on a competitive price basis. It was this sort of pressure which finally stimulated manufacturers to offer the multilevel fluorescent ballast as a standard catalog item.

We proposed the use of multilevel fluorescent ballasts for the 1100 Milam Building **(Case Study F3)** in order to save energy and reduce operating costs. Use of these multilevel ballasts would have made it possible to adjust illumination levels to match the spatial distribution of needs, despite a uniform layout of fixtures. While such ballasts were technically feasible at the time, ballast manufacturers were unwilling to undertake the necessary product development until I had proposed multilevel ballasts for a number of major projects and the concept had been incorporated into several important design guideline documents[2], largely at my suggestion.

Recognition of the hard facts of a long-term energy shortage will hopefully lead to an improvement in the boring homogenized environments typical in flat-ceiling office buildings. Increased energy-consciousness should expedite acceptance of nonuniform illumination schemes such as those made possible by the multilevel ballast.

Other energy-efficient tactics which have been applied to programs which might otherwise have been wastefully engineered into homogenized solutions include the following:

1. *Recessed ceiling-mounted fluorescent luminaires can be used for local lighting, usually one per work station.* These must then be relocated as part of the "furniture" with every change in the location of work stations. This scheme will not work unless the ceiling construction and power distribution system can accommodate such movement easily and without damage to the ceiling material. This strategy was used at the Eden Theological Seminary Library **(Case Study B5).** A variant on the approach was used at the AMAX Headquarters Building **(Case Study D7)** where the fixed location of work stations allowed the design of a layout of local (but stationary) recessed fluorescent fixtures coordinated with the layout of work stations. Although this type of local lighting may satisfy "task" needs at the desk, it is important to realize that the satisfaction of biological needs for visual information requires that walls and ceilings be adequately illuminated to meet expectations of the users. It was for this reason that we illuminated the walls at the Eden Library and the ceiling at AMAX in addition to

F1 *Reed College Library, Portland, Oregon* (Harry Weese & Associates/Architects; William Lam Associates/Lighting Consultants).

[2]*For example*, The Economy of Energy Conservation in Educational Facilities, *Educational Facilities Laboratories, New York, July 1973, p. 40* and Energy Conservation Design Guidelines for Office Buidings, *GSA/PBS, Washington, D. C., January 1974, pp. 10–22.*

Morley Baer

providing localized task lighting. (The proposed approach of using recessed fluorescent fixtures placed selectively in a layout coordinated with work stations should not be confused with the prevalent practice of using random, irregular layouts of 2 × 4 lensed fluorescent troffers to achieve numerical footcandle criteria stated as averages. The latter approach merely produces visual chaos and a sense of unpleasant irrelevance in the luminous environment.)

2. *Spaces can be entirely illuminated from portable lamps or from fixtures integrated into furniture units.* One of our earlier projects in which we used this approach is the Reed College Library **(Fig. F1)** in Portland, Oregon, for which we designed the lighting in 1963. At the Reed Library, direct/indirect fluorescent fixtures built into the carrels provide both local task lighting and general room illumination. (The traditional desk lamp which lights both desktop and ceiling above is another familiar example of this lighting strategy.) This approach can be very energy-efficient while satisfying both activity and biological needs for visual information. Building owners and managers have been reluctant to accept such schemes, however, because they are afraid to depart from the conventional high-footcandle, high-energy, high-glare designs (which may be the only thing they have ever experienced). Perhaps clients will be more receptive to new design approaches now that the myth of "high footcandles everywhere" has been exposed for the propaganda which it is and life-cycle costing and energy conservation are beginning to receive more than lip service. It should be noted that furniture-mounted lighting is no panacea because not every room can be broken up effectively and attractively by this type of furniture. This limits the applicability of pure furniture-mounted lighting solutions, and suggests that their real potential can only be realized when they are used in conjunction with other lighting approaches. It is for this reason that we prefer the type of articulated building system represented by the projects in **Case Studies Groups E** and **G,** in which furniture-mounted and portable lighting can be used as appropriate for accent highlighting and for supplementary task lighting where the moderate level of general illumination provided from sources integrated into the building fabric is inadequate to satisfy the needs of users with special and unusually demanding tasks.

1

BLUE CROSS - BLUE SHIELD BUILDING
Chicago, Illinois

F1

C. F. Murphy Associates (architect); William Wuerfel (project manager); Otto Stark (designer); William Lam Associates, Inc. (lighting consultants); Bolt, Beranek and Newman (acoustical consultant); O. Cokliss (electrical engineer); D. Despot (mechanical engineer); L. Moro (structural engineer); Paschen Contractors (general contractor). Cost: $8,250,000. Square footage: 276,000. Construction completed 1968.

The square shape of this building in plan (2) as well as the need for directional freedom in the interior spaces dictated that ideally the fixture in each module should be nondirectional as well as low-brightness.

Design

At the time of design (1965), however, neither the lamps nor the fixture louvering for efficient, economical *square* low-brightness fixtures was available. Consequently, the design team compromised to 1 × 4 foot low-brightness louvers (with a cell one-half inch square) but even then were unable to get approval for the design. The final compromise (1 × 4 foot lensed fixtures) (3) was at least better than randomly placed 2 × 4 foot fixtures (with which equivalent light levels could have been produced at lower cost but with considerably more visual noise). Where the recommended low-glare design was used on the executive floor the superiority of the luminous environment is obvious (4). Fortunately, more appropriate lighting was possible in elevator lobbies (5, 6) and on the main floor.

Architecturally neutral downlight cans in the ceiling coffers illuminate core wells and the lobby floor. The stairway, a major sculptural element during the day, doubles as a chandelier at night (7).

2

3 4

Photos by Harold Lewis/Photo International

5

6

Ripman

7

Balthazar Korab

TIME – LIFE BUILDING
CHICAGO SUBSCRIPTION OFFICE
Chicago, Illinois

F2

Harry Weese & Associates (architect); John F. Hartray Jr. (1st project manager); Robert E. Bell (2d project manager); Tom Devine (3d project manager); William Lam Associates, Inc. (lighting consultants); Delores Miller & Associates (interior design consultants); Cosentini Associates (mechanical and electrical engineers); Office of James Ruderman (structural engineers); Turner Construction Co. (general contractor). Cost: $24,000,000. Square footage: 700,000. Schematic design started January 1964.

1

TYPICAL FLOOR PLAN   0   30'

2

3

Ripman

Architect Weese took good advantage of the fact that most of this building would be used as large open areas. Partitioning would be infrequent. Window height was kept low to decrease air-conditioning loads and sun-control problems (and cost) without sacrifice of the view (6). While low-brightness fixtures would have created a more pleasant environment, much of the discomfort and visual clutter usually associated with lensed fixtures was reduced by using 4 × 4 foot fixtures widely spaced (approximately 9 feet on center). This scheme leaves substantial areas of blank ceiling on which the eyes can rest (5). A range of small room sizes can be created below the gridless ceiling, although the fixture may not always be centered within the room.

On the main floor, a respite from ceiling fixture dominance was achieved by not "homogenizing" the Corten ceiling pan with a uniform pattern of light or luminaires. Rather, fixtures were arranged in the pans in such a way as to define vertical surfaces and edges and to create focus on displays, etc.

Within the core on the main level, the granite used in the walls of the lobby is continued as ceilings. To avoid having to punch holes through the granite ceiling plane for light fixtures, the ceiling was illuminated indirectly from fixtures concealed behind built-in benches in the waiting area (3).

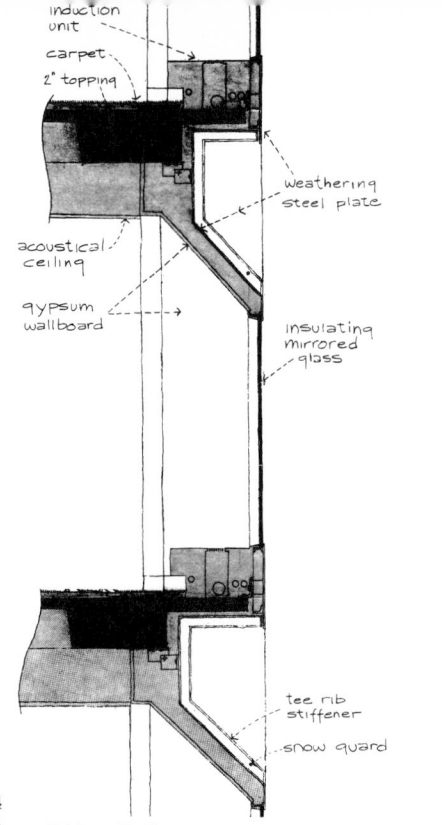

induction unit
carpet
2" topping
weathering steel plate
acoustical ceiling
gypsum wallboard
insulating mirrored glass
tee rib stiffener
snow guard

4

Ripman

5

MARGARET TILTON

6

Balthazar Korab

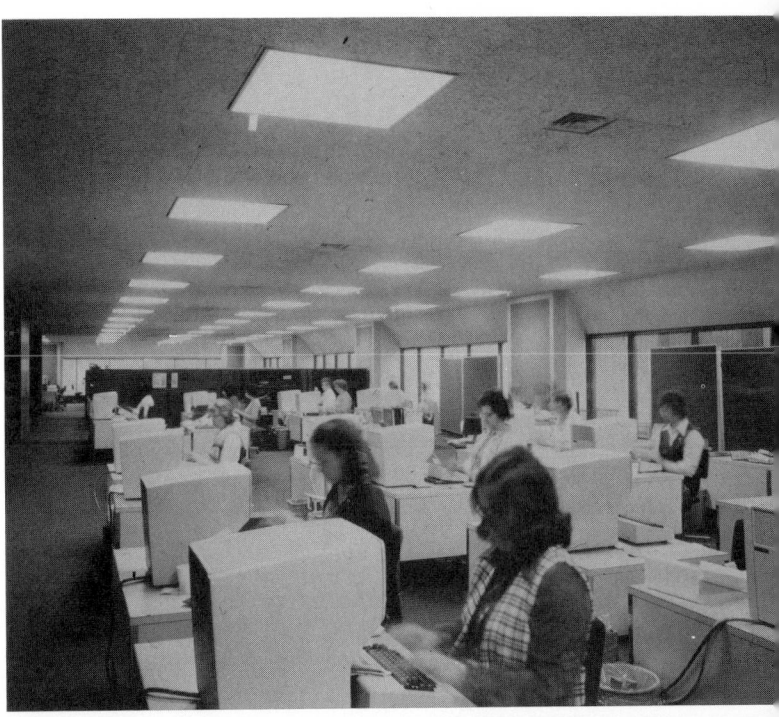

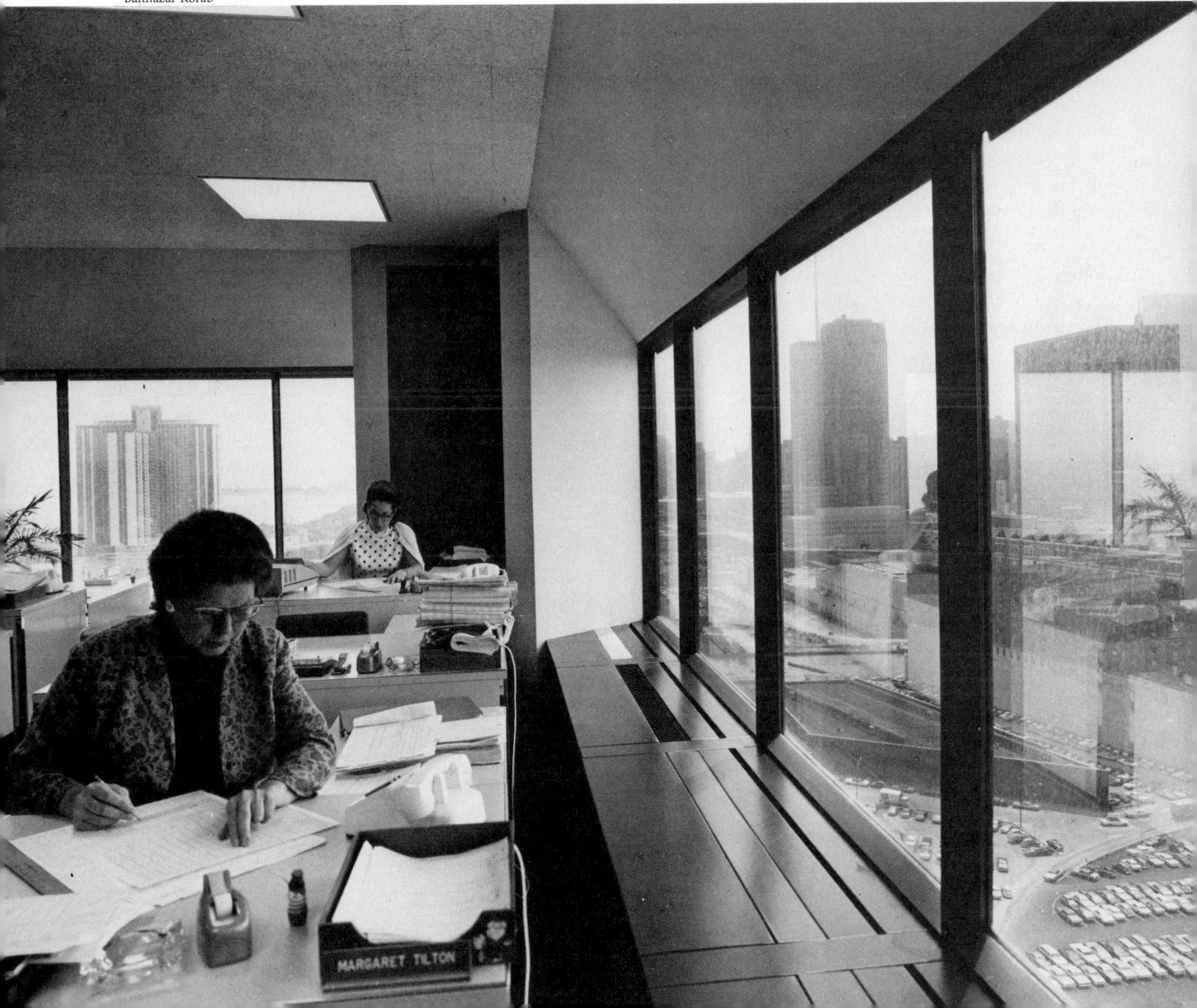

1

1100 MILAM BUILDING
Houston, Texas

JV III: Koetter Tharp & Cowell, Caudill Rowlett Scott, Neuhaus & Taylor (joint venture architects); Charles R. Sikes, Jr. (Neuhaus & Taylor, partner in charge); A. William Modrall, Jr. (Koetter Tharp & Cowell, project manager); Charles E. Lawrence (Caudill Rowlett Scott, director of design); William Lam Associates, Inc. (lighting consultants); Chenault & Brady (mechanical engineers); Walter P. Moore & Associates (structural engineers); W. S. Bellows Construction Corporation (general contractors). Schematic design started December 1970.

The project schedule and program requirements for total partitioning flexibility in this speculative venture dictated a steel-frame suspended-ceiling building based on a 5 × 5 foot module.

Design

By 1970–71, quite efficient and economical 2-foot-square low-brightness fluorescent fixtures were available, but the design team had difficulty in getting approval for a scheme which called for one of these fixtures in the center of each module. At the time, speculative competition was using less expensive 2 × 4 foot fixtures placed randomly to provide an average illumination of 70 foot-candles; furthermore, though the available square low-brightness fixtures were by 1970 as efficient as lensed fixtures—and much more pleasant to look at—the U-shaped lamps required were still more expensive than conventional linear 4-foot fluorescent tubes. Use of a fixture in each module meant increased initial cost over a random scheme. It was recognized, however, that long-range economies could be realized if fixtures could be left untouched each time partitioning was rearranged to suit the needs of new tenants—

approximately every 5 years.

Unfortunately, the tight project schedule made it impossible to offset the increased fixture cost through redesign of the air-handling system, which use of the square fixtures would have made possible. Regular spacing of the 2 × 2 foot fixtures (5 feet on center) would have created a grid of 3-foot-wide channels running in *both* directions at the level of the fixtures above the suspended ceiling. (Using 1 × 4 foot or 2 × 4 foot fixtures arranged end to end allows distribution in only one direction at the level of the fixtures themselves, parallel to the fixtures. Such a system requires greater structural depth for ducts which must run *above* the fixtures in the opposite direction.) If time had permitted redesign of ductwork to fit within the two-way channels created by the pattern of square fixtures, floor-to-floor height could have been reduced by as much as 14 inches per floor. This would have yielded considerable savings in terms of reduced exterior skin, foundation costs, structure, etc., which could have been applied to offset the increased cost of the square low-brightness fixtures.

Another proposed economy was operation of fixtures at reduced output in all but the smallest offices, which would have yielded substantial long-run savings in terms of reduced power cost, extended lamp life, and reduced air-conditioning load. The

3 *Structural, partitioning, and lighting systems.*

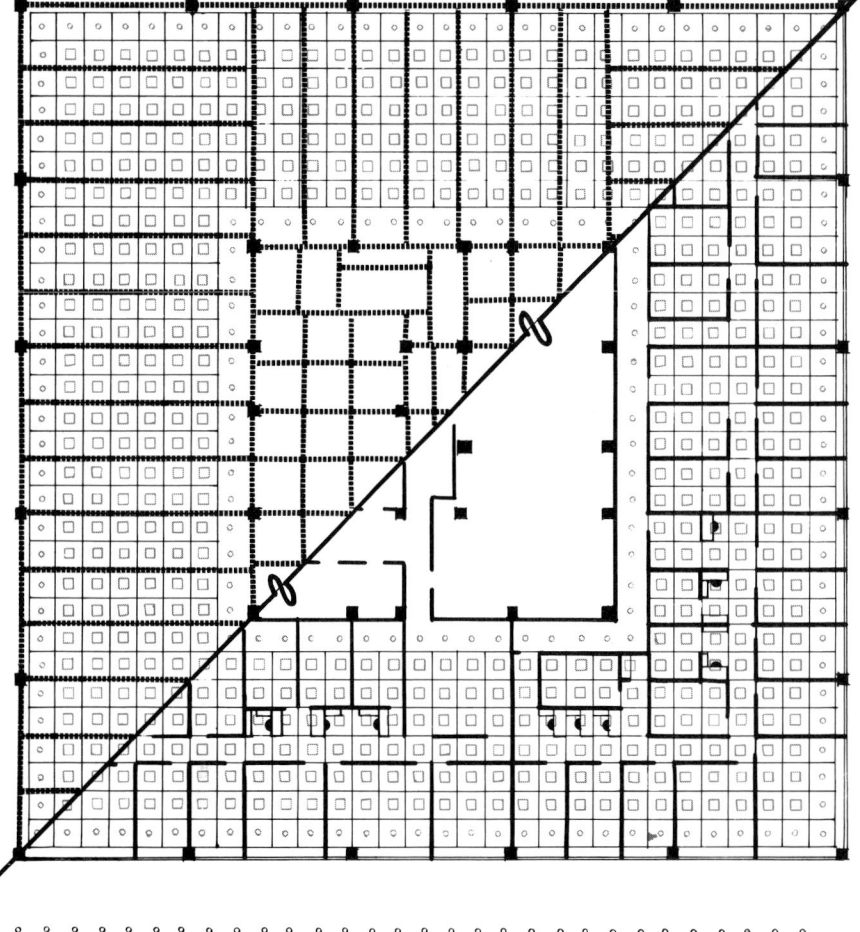

additional initial cost of special "Hi-Lo" ballasts would have been amortized in months.

Elevator lobbies and other circulation spaces were handled consistently with incandescent downlights and wall washers to aid orientation. To expand the spaciousness of the elevator cabs, a mirror ceiling was proposed.

Much of the main-floor concept and detailing was coordinated with the design concepts of other units of the complex. These included the Hyatt Regency Hotel **(Case Study C9)** and a major parking garage, linked to each other and to the office building by second-level bridges which were illuminated in such a way as to emphasize their connecting function.

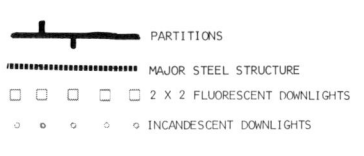

PARTITIONS
MAJOR STEEL STRUCTURE
2 X 2 FLUORESCENT DOWNLIGHTS
INCANDESCENT DOWNLIGHTS

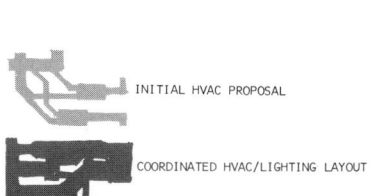

INITIAL HVAC PROPOSAL
COORDINATED HVAC/LIGHTING LAYOUT
2 X 2 FLUORESCENT DOWNLIGHTS
INCANDESCENT DOWNLIGHTS

Critique

The design recommendation to use symmetrical low-brightness fixtures came too late in the design process to allow realization of potential savings in building height, etc., which would have helped to offset the higher initial cost of lighting fixtures. As a result, the scheme was compromised, and minimum cost 1 × 4 foot fixtures were used instead. Had lighting coordination been initiated on this scheme prior to the completion of structural drawings, the final design might have been quite different.

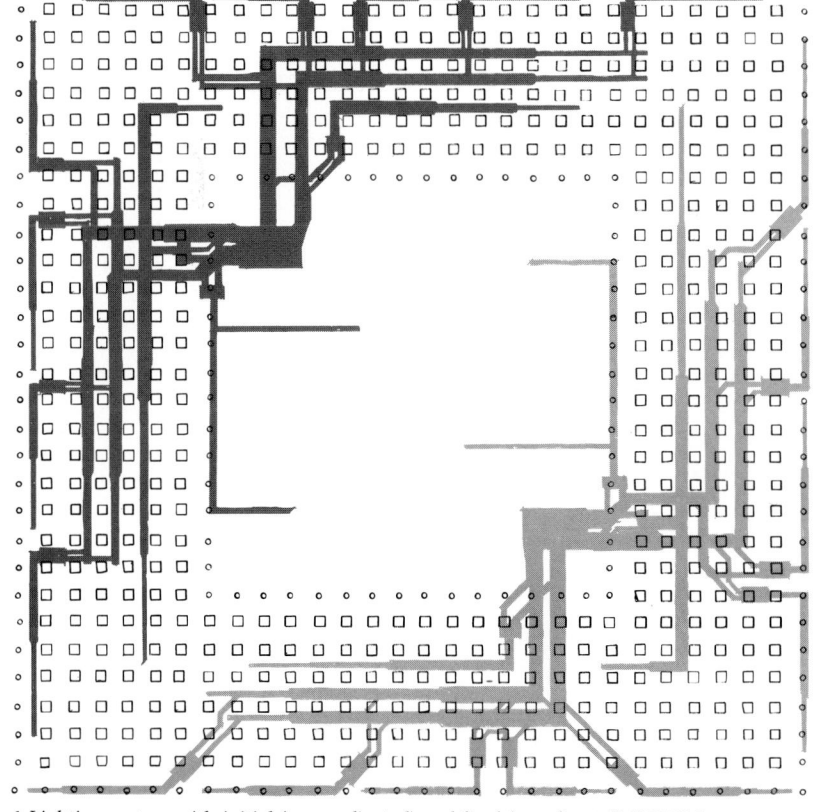

4 *Lighting system with initial (uncoordinated) and final (coordinated) HVAC layouts.*

CASE STUDIES GROUP G

GROWTH SYSTEMS

When integrated systems incorporating structural elements, services, and lighting must be fitted within the constraints of predetermined plans, further expansion of a project is usually possible only in quite large increments. Furthermore, the systems tend to be one-directional, which limits service distribution capabilities, especially service distribution perpendicular to the primary structural orientation. In contrast, modular, articulated integrated systems which incorporate two-way service channels allow much more freedom in planning and growth in any direction, vertical as well as horizontal. Increments of growth can be as small as a single module or as large as an entire university complex. Plans and expressive exterior forms derive naturally from the repetitive, cellular nature of the system itself. Repetition of the same module in large numbers generates substantial cost savings over more ad hoc approaches. If desired, plans can be irregular, and voids can be created at will in the form of courts or multistory open spaces by simply omitting certain modules.

While the nature of a flexible, modular integrated building system dictates the use of columns, the largest possible module should be used which can still accommodate the desired service distribution and partitioning requirements, to minimize visual fragmentation of spaces and to keep the number of columns and light fixtures to a minimum.

The integrated systems presented in this section drew on earlier developments in lighting and air-conditioning detailing from integrated systems worked out within the constraints of predetermined exterior forms, such as those of Place Bonaventure **(Case Study C5),** the Pierrefonds Comprehensive High School **(Case Study E9),** and others.

Even when no growth is expected, the superior service flexibility characteristic of buildings whose form is derived from the systems with which they are constructed—buildings designed from the inside out—makes this type of building particularly suitable when service requirements are heavy and unpredictable.

NASA ELECTRONICS RESEARCH CENTER
Cambridge, Massachusetts

Photos by Ripman

1

The Architects Collaborative (architect); Louis A. McMillen, William Geddis (principals in charge); Joseph Hoskins, Malcolm Ticknor (job captains); Jackson & Moreland (associated firm); William Lam Associates, Inc. (lighting consultants); Jackson & Moreland (structural, mechanical and electrical engineers); Aberthaw Construction Company (general contractor). Cost: $5,300,000. Square footage: 124,000. Schematic design started October 1967. Construction completed Mid-1969. Building lighting load: 3.6 watts per square foot.

Harold Lewis / Photo International

2

In 1966, 70 acres of land near MIT were cleared for a NASA Electronics Research Center designed by Edward Stone. When the very formal initial concept was changed, only the tower and an auditorium unit had been built. The Architects Collaborative was engaged to develop a more informal system of lower structures that could be constructed in a number of stages. Changes in national priorities, however, resulted in cancellation of the Cambridge center when only two TAC-designed units had been built. The center was subsequently taken over by the Department of Transportation.

Design

The design team began with an attempt to achieve the same degree of two-way design freedom as that inherent in the Place Bonaventure "tree" system (see **Case Study C5**). Design freedom was constrained, however, by the predetermined location of the columns (dictated by the layout of caissons already in place for the earlier Stone design). Because it lacked bilateral symmetry and because the implied column spacing was inappropriate (too far in one direction and too close in the other), this foundation layout would have required an awkward and unbalanced tree structure. For this reason the design team abandoned the concept of a tree struc-

ture in favor of cantilevered platforms suspended from split columns (a "table" structure), with major service channels between the platforms and a smaller channel enclosed by paired beams at the center line of each platform. The vertical shafts created between the split columns offered a convenient place for mechanical risers.

Critique

The overly large tree dimensions (in one direction) created overly large spacing of service channels in one direction. That factor, aggravated by poor job supervision, resulted in a few unsightly exposed conduits and other service elements which might otherwise have been concealed. Despite its shortcomings, the system is visually powerful enough to camouflage these irregularities. The table module is unfortunately too large to be perceived as a generating unit **(7)**. After partitioning, there were no spaces large enough to show a complete module, and as a result, its actual form is never apparent **(5,6)**. Furthermore, the "growth" characteristics of the system were not expressed on the exterior, where infill panels were executed in poured concrete. In other projects (such as case studies **G2** (The Bank of Canada) and **G5** (Governors State University) more appropriate, detachable lightweight infill panels were used.

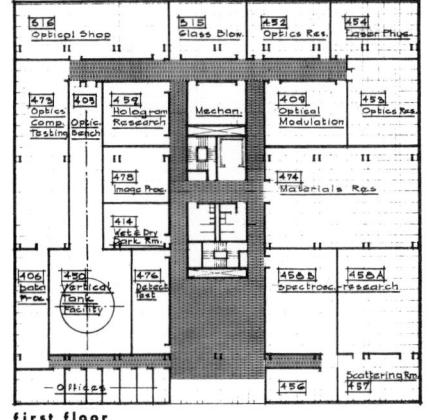

3 **first floor**

ILLUMINATED COFFERS

STRUCTURAL "TABLES"

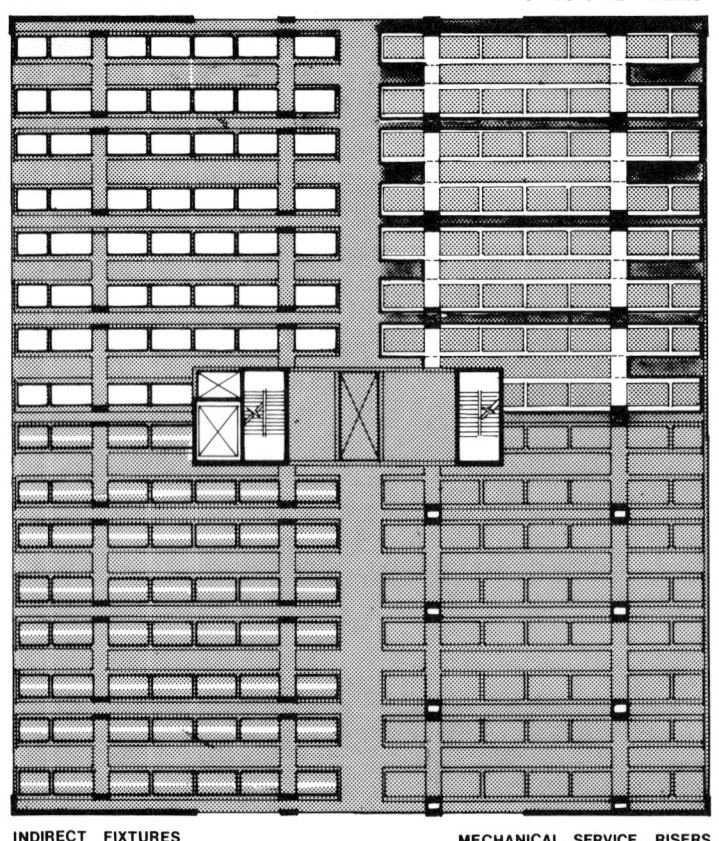

5 6

INDIRECT FIXTURES

MECHANICAL SERVICE RISERS

4 *Reflected ceiling diagram.*

7 *Prior to partitioning.*

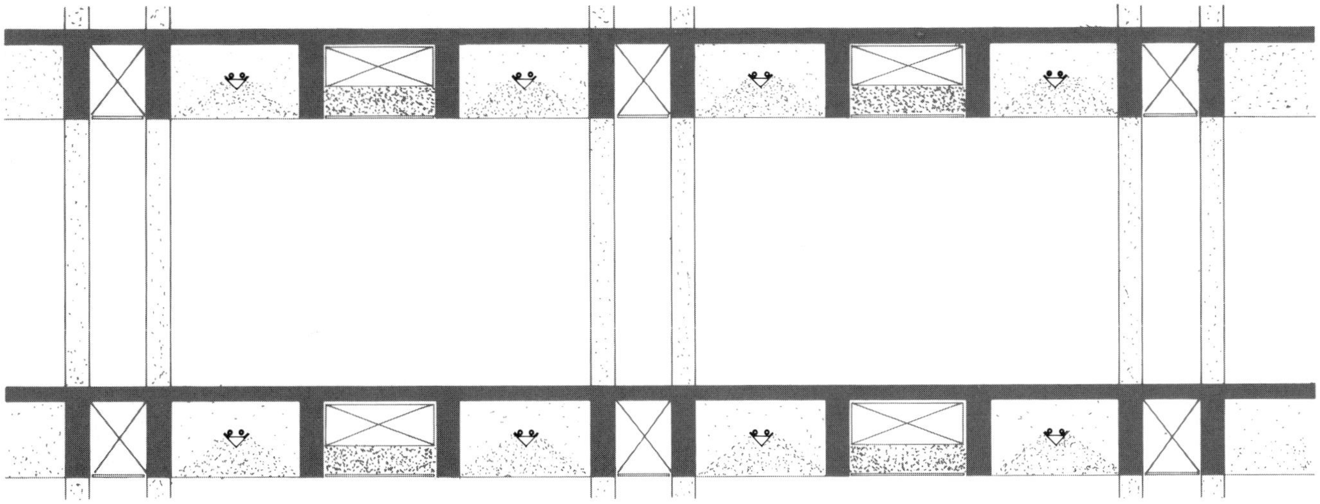

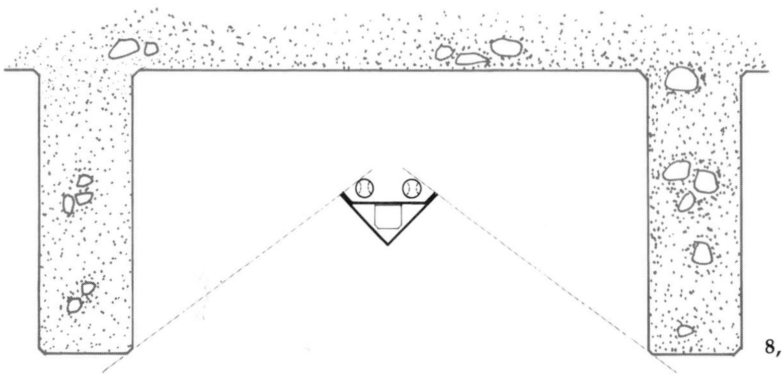

8, 9 *Typical section and indirect fixture detail.*

10

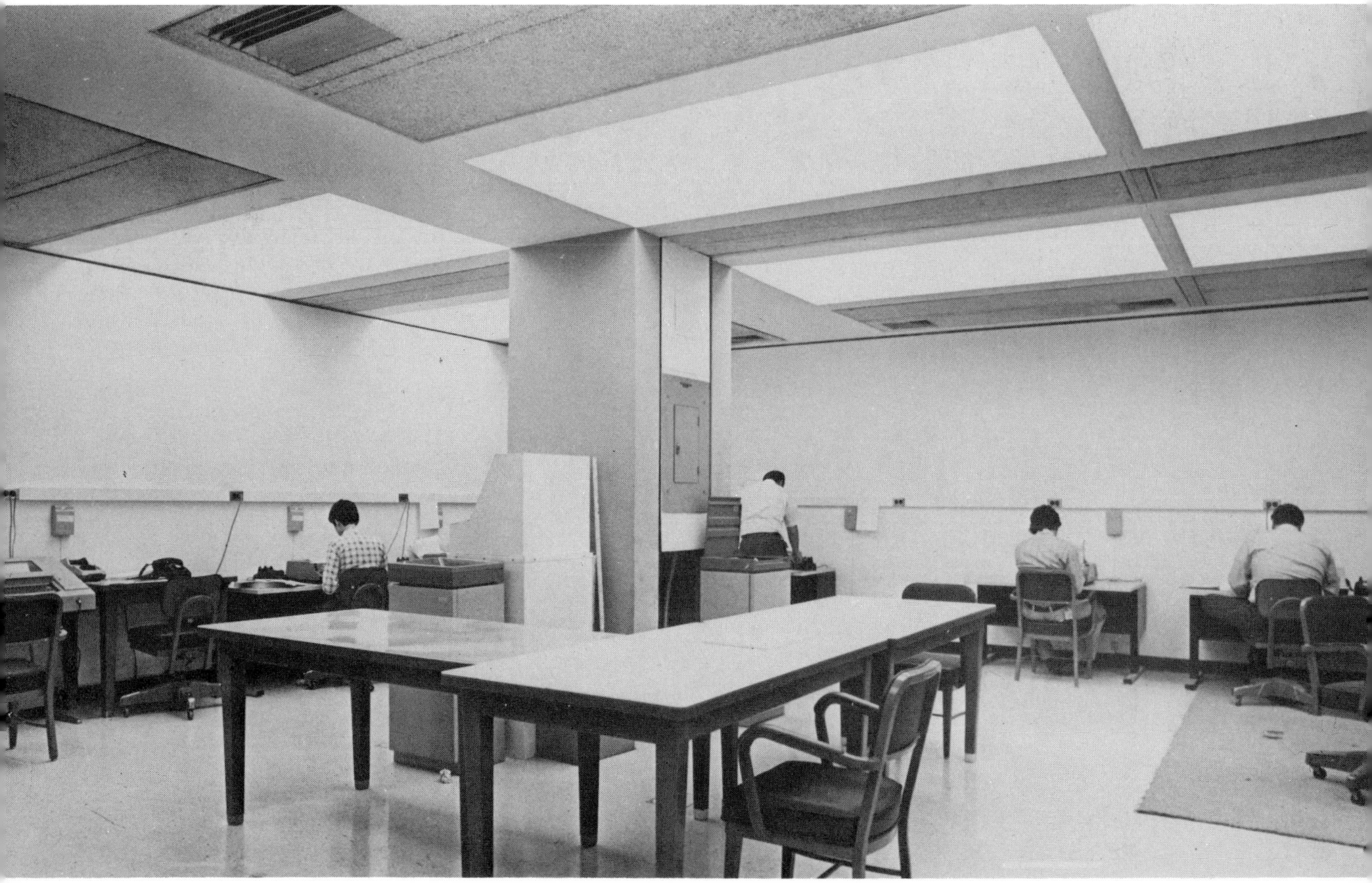

1

BANK OF CANADA
Ottawa, Ontario

G2

Marani, Routhwaite & Dick/Arthur Erickson Architects (joint venture architects); James C. Strasman (project architect); William Lam Associates, Inc. (lighting consultants); John R. Bain Associates Limited (acoustical consultants); Ardec/Brais, Frigon (electrical and mechanical engineers); C. D. Carruthers & Wallace Consultants Limited (structural engineers); Ellis Don Limited (general contractor). Cost: $40,000,000. Square footage: 800,000. Schematic design started 1969. Construction completed 1976.

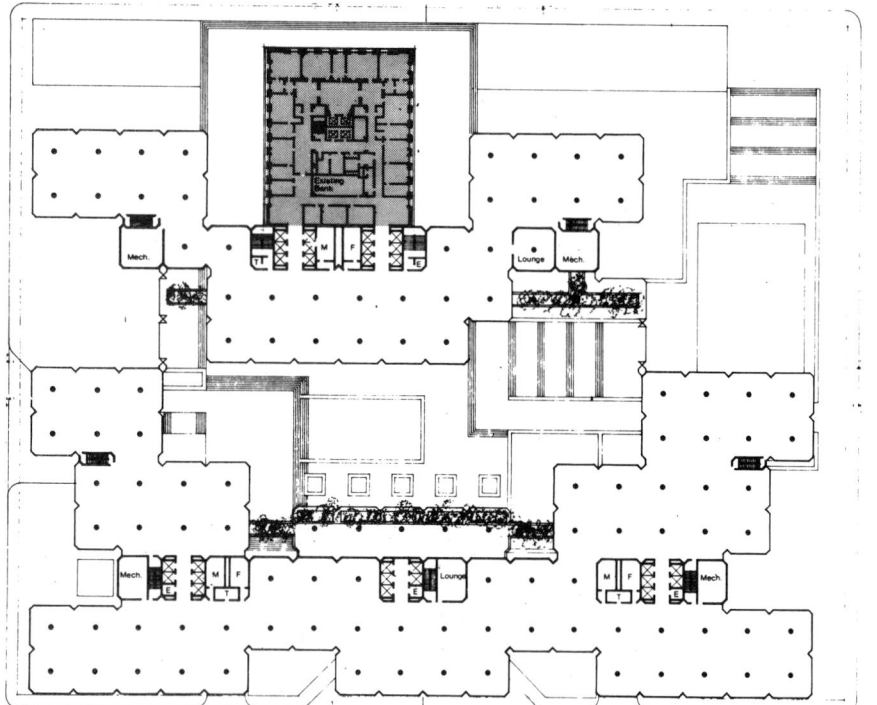

2 *Initial schematic design proposal.*

3 *Final design.*

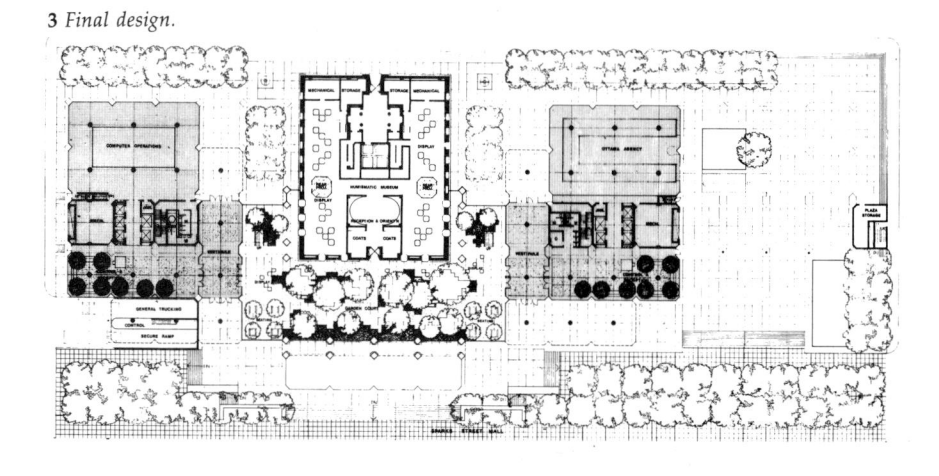

Following the precedent set by Erickson/Massey in their University of Lethbridge project, coordination of architecture and lighting, mechanical, and structural systems began at the stage of diagrammatic planning. The Bank of Canada project (1) was not limited by a predetermined planning diagram or building form, so that it was possible to develop a building system which would achieve all the goals of environment and services. In fact, the organic tree system which was developed allowed such flexibility in planning that it remained unchanged despite several substantial modifications in the plan (2,3). When, for instance, one of the initial clients withdrew from the project, leading to a drastic reduction in planned square footage, only 30 days were required to evolve a new schematic plan for the entire building. No modifications of the tree system and associated architectural details were required.

Design

The organic tree module was a development from the Place Bonaventure and NASA projects. The trees differ from the freestanding structures of Kahn (9) and Wright (7) in that the tree structures were created to frame two-way channels for mechanical services rather than to provide gaps for the introduction of daylight. In each tree, coffers (defined by the arrangement of branching beams

4

that was necessary to create the framing for typical room subdivisions) contain indirect lighting fixtures in integral coves along the lower edges of the structure. A study model **(5,6)** was built to evaluate the concept and to measure the light distribution of the indirect system.

Though most of the spaces were to be used as office landscape, the Bank required that the system should permit the creation of 10- or 15-foot-wide offices. Note the considerable variety of spaces made possible by this tree configuration **(8,11).**

A very important advantage of the tree approach is that mechanical rooms can be located anywhere, unlike post-and-beam systems in which major feeder ducts must usually either penetrate or pass below the beams. The usual problems encountered when large holes must be cut through structural members to accommodate mechanical runs can be avoided if a system permits the elimination of structure along lines of service distribution; tree structures are among the few generic types which permit such elimination. In a tree structure, mechanical rooms can be located wherever they may be required without affecting the layout or detailing of the exposed structure and surrounding spaces.

At the schematic stage of planning a tree structure, the interface between structure and air-

5

6

Courtesy of the Johnson's Wax Company

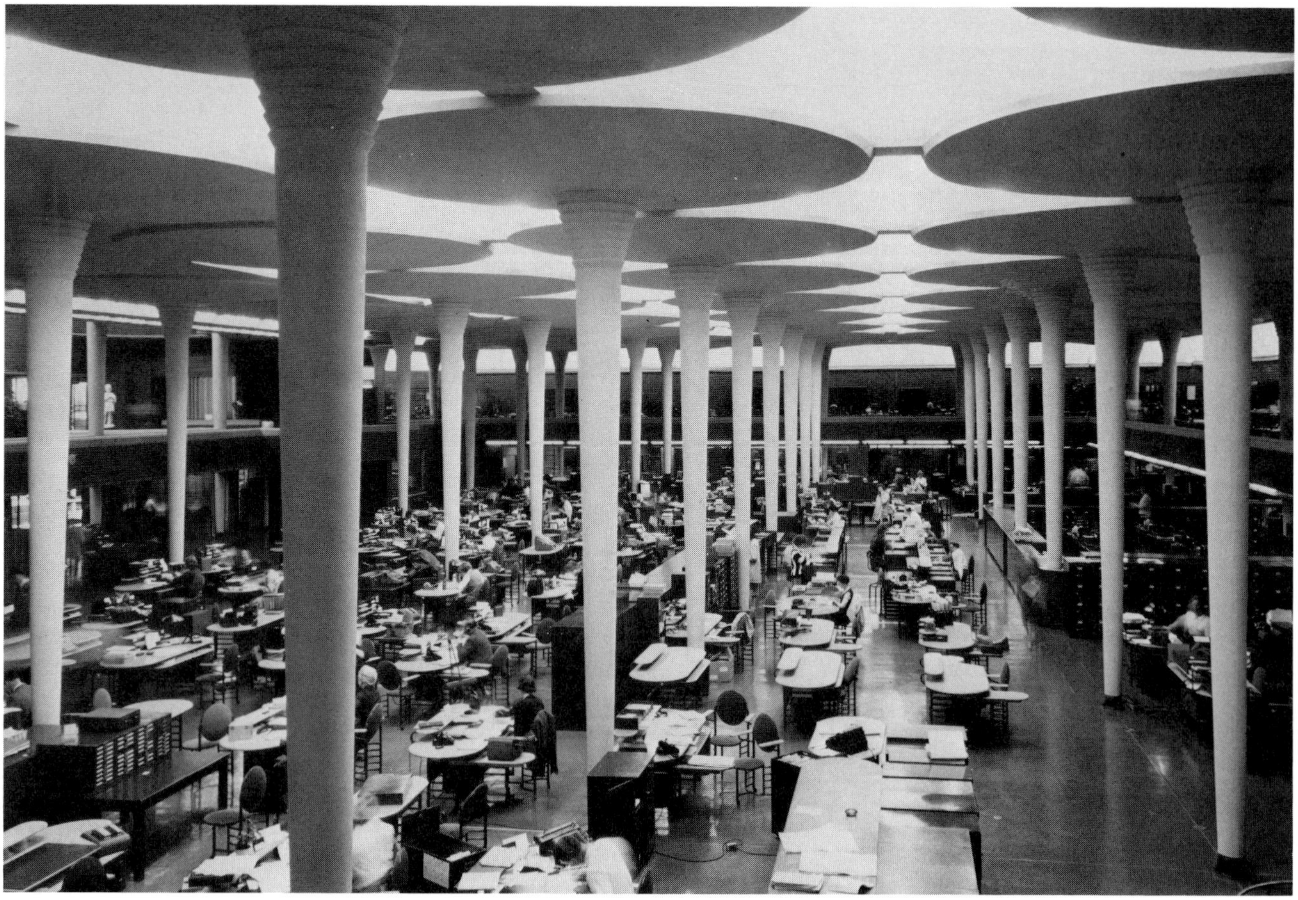

7 *Johnson's Wax Headquarters, Racine, Wisconsin* (Frank Lloyd Wright / Architect).

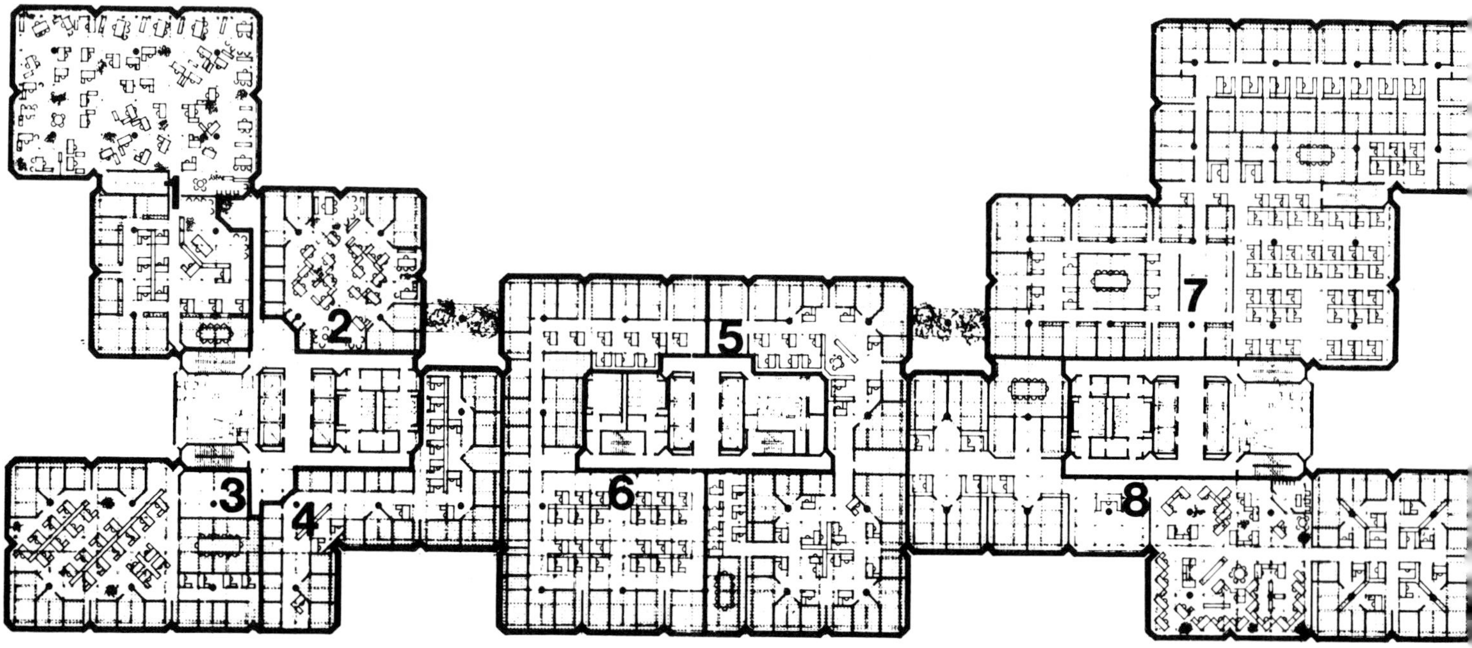

8 *Preliminary partitioning study.*

handling systems is so unconstrained that almost any type of air-conditioning system is feasible—multizone, dual duct, etc. The size of the service channels (12) can be tailored to fit the needs of almost any mechanical system. After tradeoffs in partitioning, flexibility, acoustic separation, cost of forming, etc., have been analyzed, coffers and service channels can be dimensioned to maximize the visible room volume. One system studies alternative is presented in **Fig. 10.** For the Bank of Canada project, a multiduct system was selected. Holes in the perimeter beams of the trees were carefully planned to accommodate all foreseeable future needs, so that almost all trees could be made with identical formwork. A detailed mechanical layout for a similar system is presented in the case study on Governors State University **(Fig. G5–7).**

Evolved from the nature of the system itself, the exterior skin

9 *Olivetti Factory, Harrisburg, Pennsylvania* (Louis Kahn / Architect).

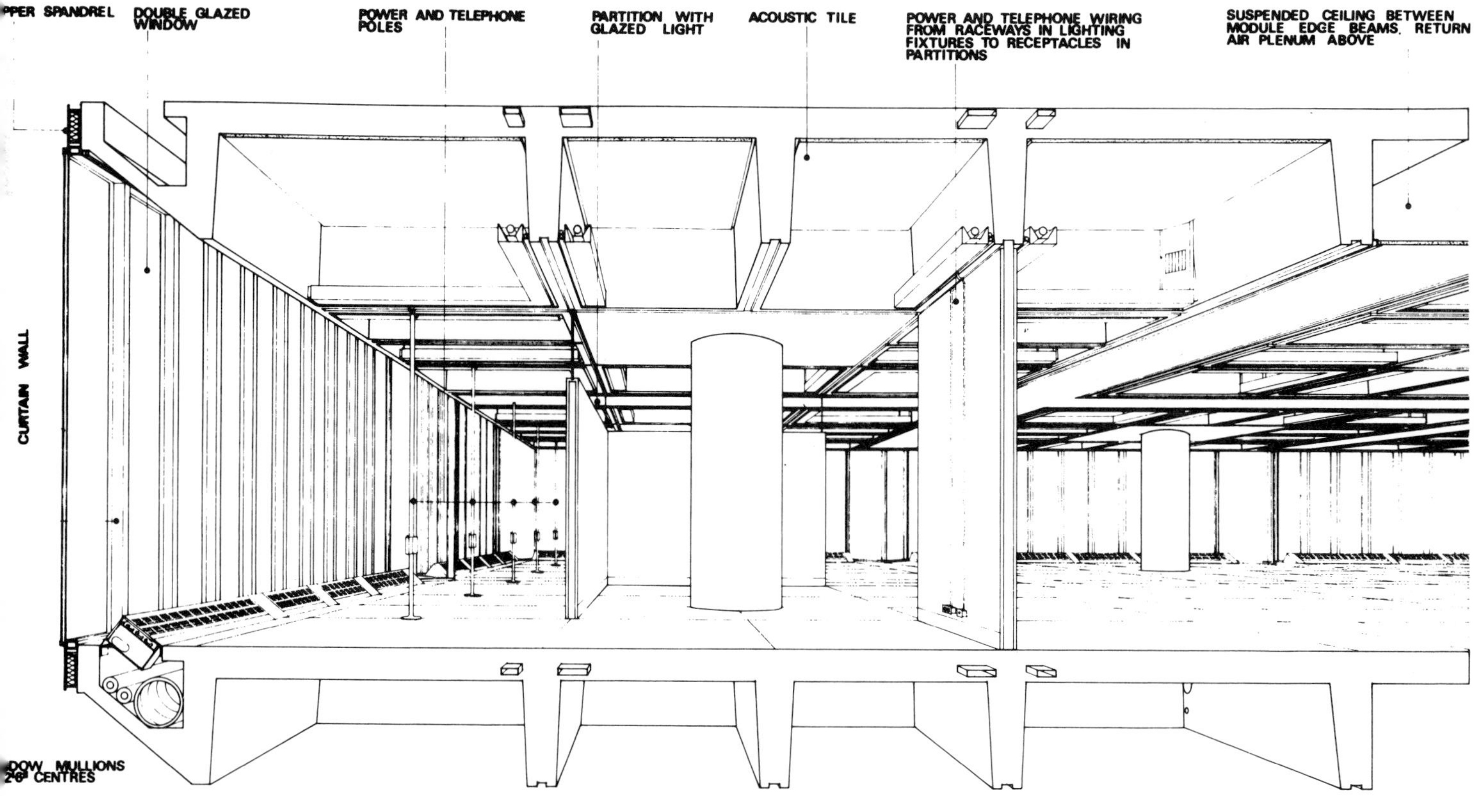

PPER SPANDREL   DOUBLE GLAZED WINDOW   POWER AND TELEPHONE POLES   PARTITION WITH GLAZED LIGHT   ACOUSTIC TILE   POWER AND TELEPHONE WIRING FROM RACEWAYS IN LIGHTING FIXTURES TO RECEPTACLES IN PARTITIONS   SUSPENDED CEILING BETWEEN MODULE EDGE BEAMS, RETURN AIR PLENUM ABOVE

CURTAIN WALL

DOW MULLIONS 26" CENTRES

10 *Design development study for the tree structure.*

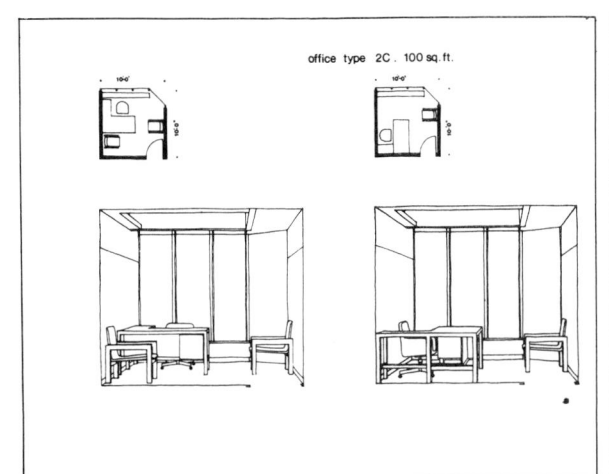

office type 2C . 100 sq. ft.

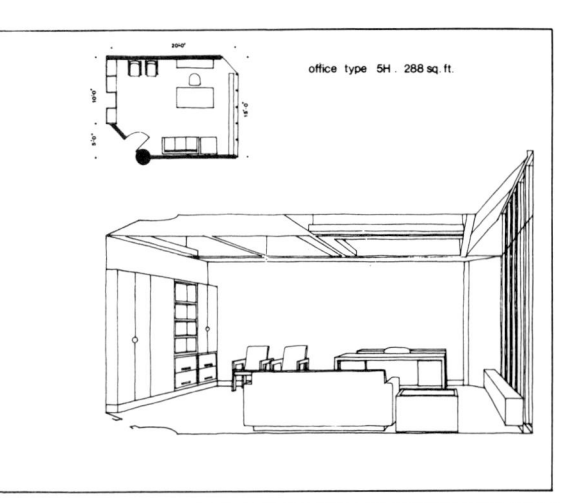

office type 5H . 288 sq. ft.

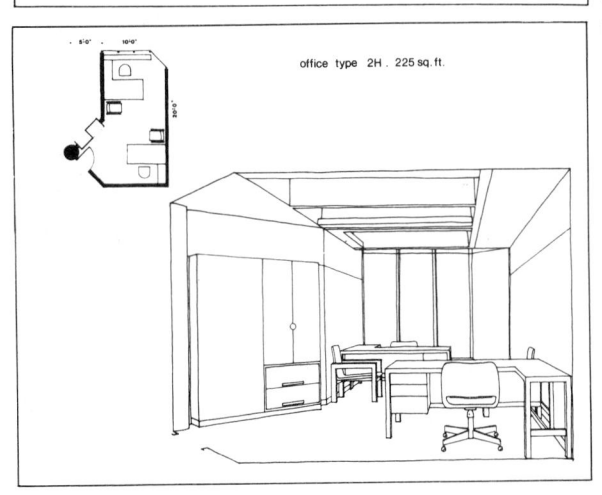

office type 2H . 225 sq. ft.

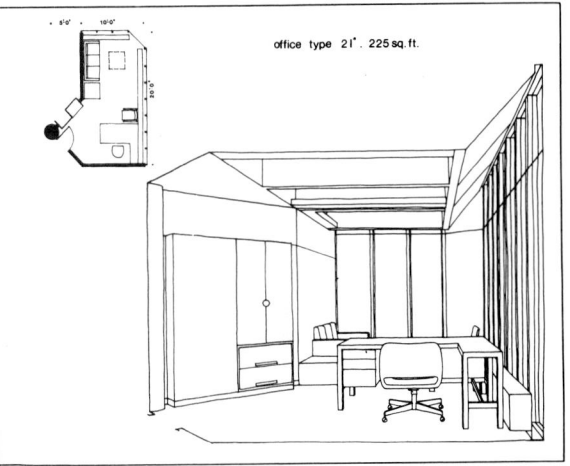

office type 2I⁺ . 225 sq. ft.

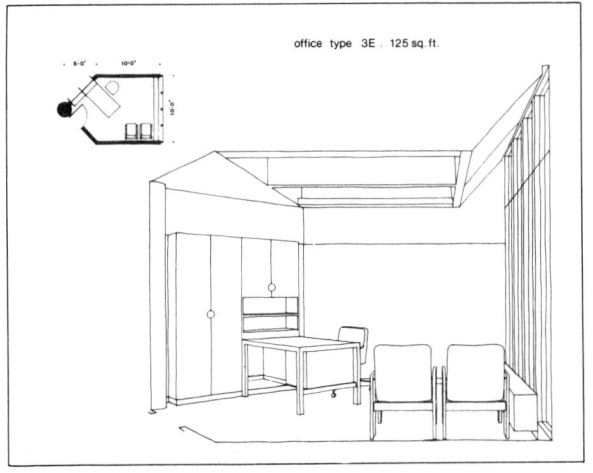

office type 3E . 125 sq. ft.

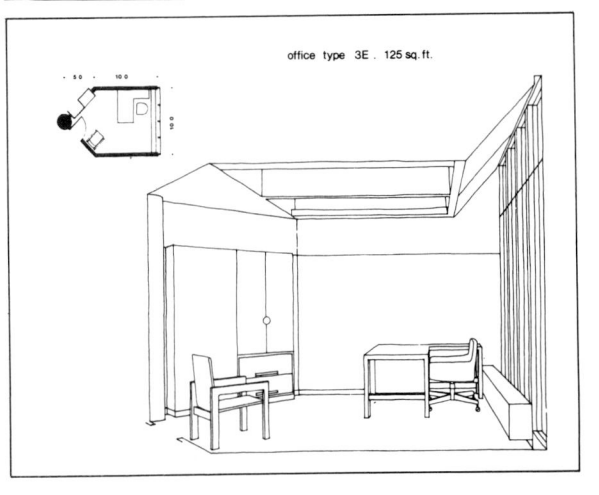

office type 3E . 125 sq. ft.

'Office Landscape' 1547 sq. ft.

11 *Studies of typical office spaces.*

of the building is obviously non-structural and visually reinforces the beholder's awareness of the shape and dimensions of the basic tree module.

Critique

Unfortunately, the proposed indirect lighting scheme was changed to a direct/indirect system **(13),** except on the ground floor and in exterior coffers.

12 *Service channels.*

13 *Typical structural tree.*

Applied Photography Ltd.

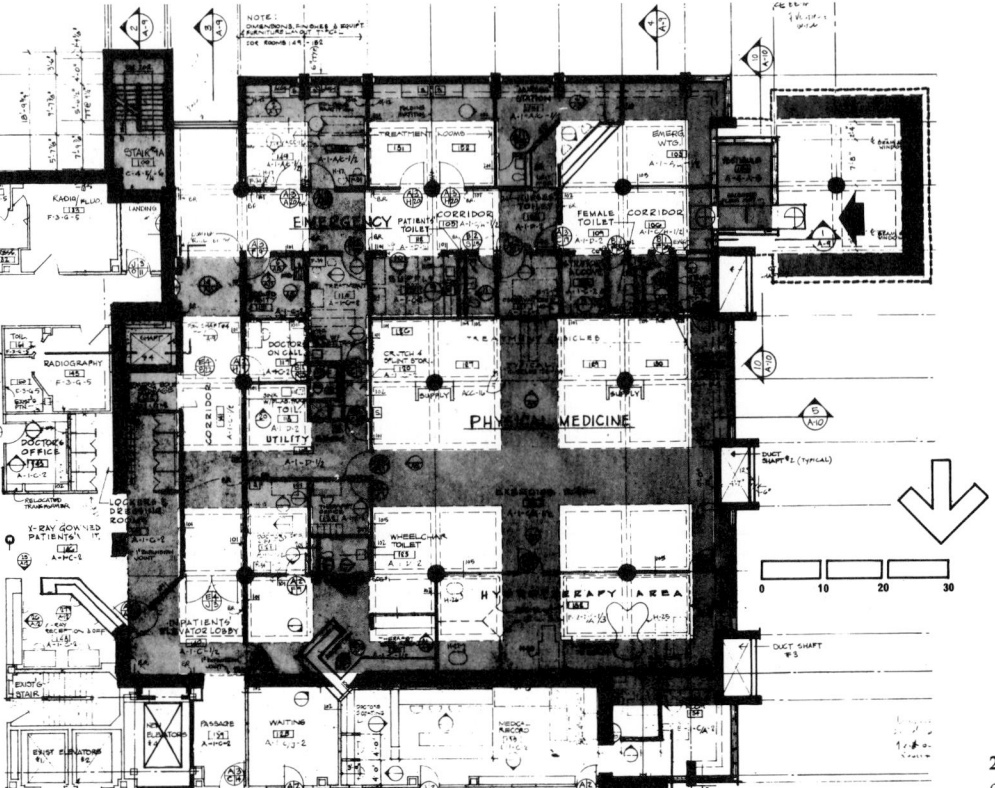

CHARLOTTE HUNGERFORD
HOSPITAL ADDITION
Torrington, Connecticut

G3

Isadore & Zachary Rosenfield (architect); William Lam Associates, Inc. (lighting consultants); Ranger Farrell (acoustical consultant); E. C. Klumb (graphics consultant); Meyers & Locker (mechanical and electrical engineers); Ames & Selnick (structural engineers); Bonvicini Construction Co. (general contractor). Cost: $2,600,000. Square footage: 18,300 (new) plus extensive alterations. Schematic design started November 1970. Construction completed September 1973.

Subsequent to creating an irregular tree structure for the Easton Hospital **(Case Study E6),** the same design team employed the same approach in a second hospital addition, one with fewer constraints in terms of the planning module. Problems of contact with the existing buildings were also simplified; with contact required on only two sides of the new structure, symmetrical trees could be used. A higher proportion of the program is assigned to open space at Charlotte Hunger-

ford **(1)** compared with the Easton Hospital. This makes the building system more easily readable, maximizing orientation and comprehensibility for the users. Omission of the glazing mullions at transoms would have increased this effect.

The 20-foot-square trees bordered by 10-foot-wide service channels provide more than ample service distribution capability and adequate partitioning flexibility **(2).** The arrangement of indirect lighting fixtures within the

tree structures differs from the configuration used at Governors State University, where the coves border the beams which form the branches of the structural tree. At Charlotte Hungerford the fixtures outline the perimeter of the trees **(4),** running along the edge beams which frame the service channels. Since the project was too small to amortize the costs of special formwork, which would have made it possible to cast the coves with the beams, extruded aluminum luminaires were used instead.

2 *Reflected ceiling and mechanical distribution plan.*

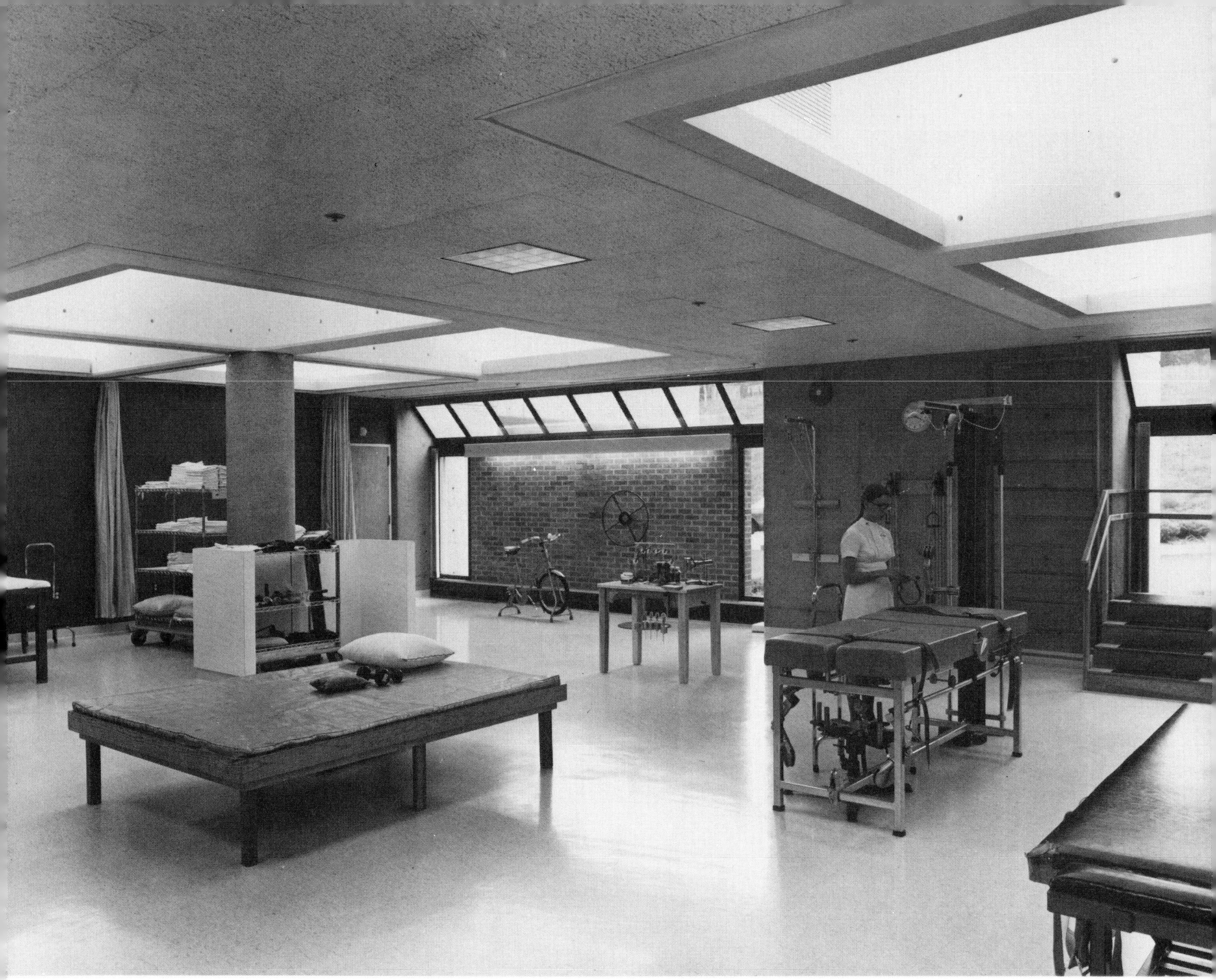

3

4 5

G. Wade Swicord

POLICE ADMINISTRATION BUILDING
Jacksonville, Florida

G4

William Morgan Architects (architect); Thomas A. McCrary (project architect); William Lam Associates, Inc. (lighting consultants); Ed Heist (interior design consultant); Roy Turknett & Associates (mechanical and electrical engineers); Haley W. Keister (structural engineers); Orr Construction Company (general contractor). Cost: $8,500,000. Square footage: 171,000 (enclosed) plus 110,000 (covered parking). Schematic design started 1973. Construction completed 1976. Lighting load: 1.9 watts per square foot (including parking), 2.9 watts per square foot (without parking).

1

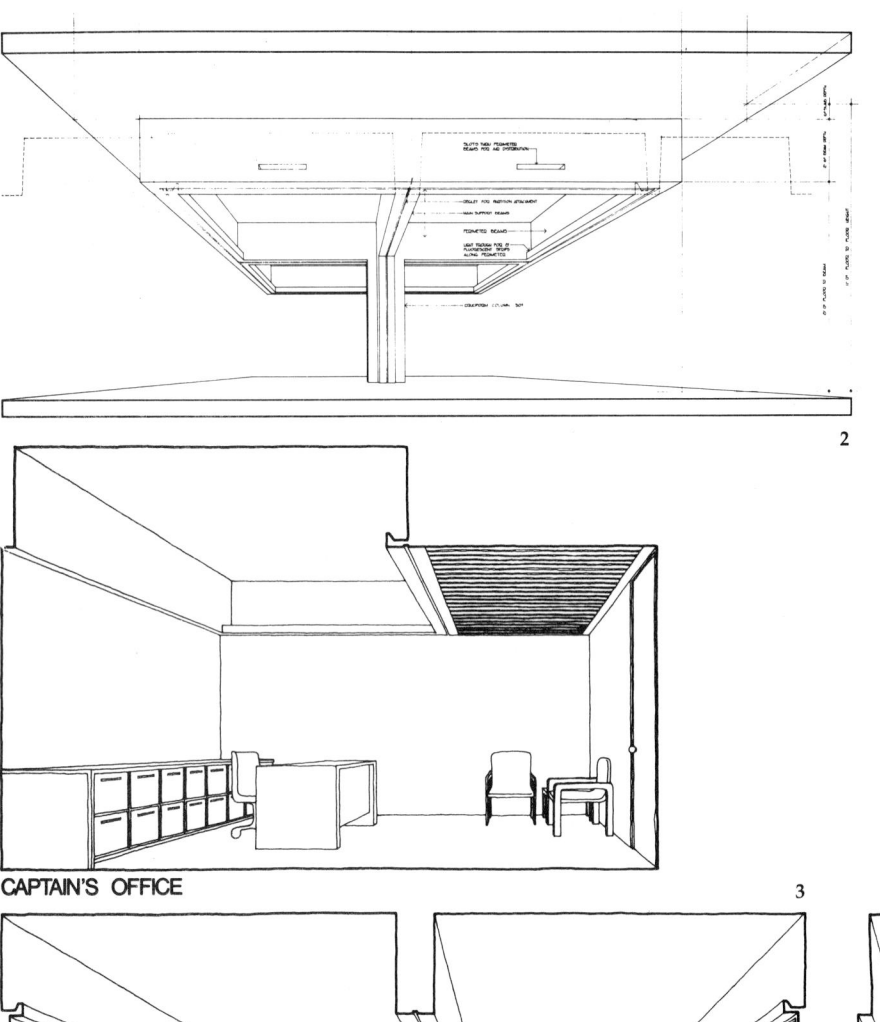

2

CAPTAIN'S OFFICE

3

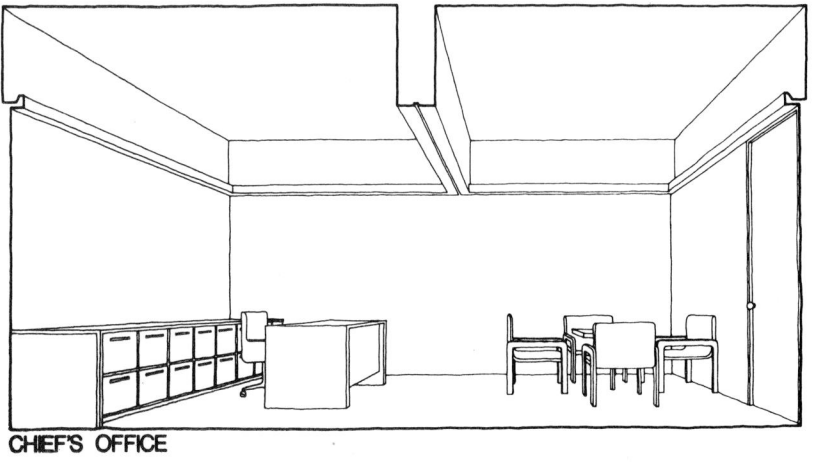

CHIEF'S OFFICE

LIEUTENANT'S OFFICE

The inherent versatility of tree systems was further demonstrated by their application to the complex forms of this project (6). Architect Morgan's competition-winning design had been based on flat-slab construction with plans to apply mechanical and lighting systems in a configuration quite similar to that of a tree system.

Lighting consultation began just before the design development stage. Structural engineer William LeMessurier joined the team for a 2-day squatters session, as a result of which the tree system was adopted as an economically feasible and spatially more desirable approach. Relatively few adjustments of the original plan were necessary to eliminate irregular situations which would have required asymmetric trees. The system was maintained even at the parking level (although the concrete was left unpainted and lower levels of lighting were used), since the service channels were as useful there in terms of providing an inherent visual order as they were in more finished spaces.

Tree spacing was 27 feet on center because of the special parking requirements for quick getaway of police cars—two cars per bay, parked diagonally. To accommodate furniture placement in the corners of the large number of partitioned rooms, X-shaped rather than round columns were considered most efficient (3). The rooms will be very spacious, as at Governors State, with the bottom of the beams 8 feet above the floor and a floor-to-floor height of 11 feet.

Comment

The Jacksonville (four-coffer) tree configuration and dimensions proved adequate to accommodate a wide range of room sizes. These trees were much less expensive to form than 12-cell trees such as those used for the Bank of Canada. For more conventional programs the 27-foot column spacing would prove somewhat tight for parking three cars per bay.

In terms of the detailing of indirect coves integrated with structural beams, it is instructive to compare the sections at Charlotte Hungerford Hospital, the Police Administration Building, and Governors State University (8). Casting the coves monolithically with the structural beams, as at Governors State, gives the simplest and most pleasing appearance. At Jacksonville, precast coves were fabricated separately and field-applied to the cast-in-place beams. The continuity of material gives a better appearance than an applied metal luminaire of the type used at Charlotte Hungerford, but the simplicity of the integral casting has still been lost.

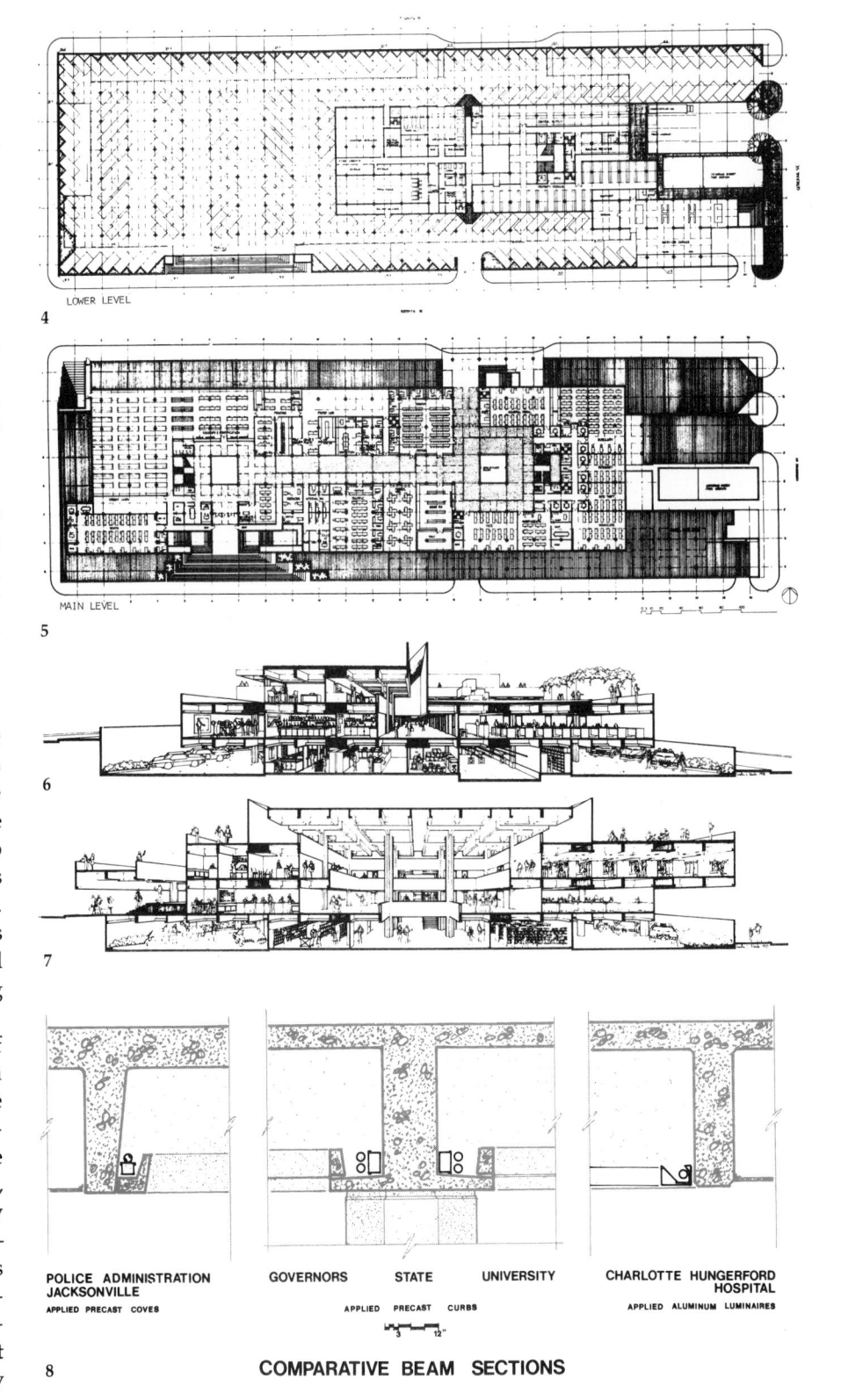

4 LOWER LEVEL

5 MAIN LEVEL

6

7

8

POLICE ADMINISTRATION JACKSONVILLE
APPLIED PRECAST COVES

GOVERNORS STATE UNIVERSITY
APPLIED PRECAST CURBS

CHARLOTTE HUNGERFORD HOSPITAL
APPLIED ALUMINUM LUMINAIRES

COMPARATIVE BEAM SECTIONS

1

GOVERNORS STATE UNIVERSITY
Park Forest, Will County, Illinois

Caudill Rowlett Scott (architects for design development); Evans Associates (architects); Johnson Johnson and Roy (site planning and landscape architects); William Lam Associates, Inc. (lighting consultants); C. P. Boner & Associates (acoustical consultant); McKee-Berger-Mansueto, Inc. (cost consultant); Davis MacConnell Ralston (educational programming consultant); Educational Testing Service (educational programming); Instructional Dynamics, Inc. (educational technology media planning consultant); DeHaan & Reed & Associates (interiors consultant); R. Morse (soils consultant); Brown Davis Mullen & Associates (mechanical engineers); M. Dean Worth (structural engineers). Cost: $19,500,000 (including partitions, lighting, finishes, and built-in equipment). Square footage: 420,000. Schematic design started 1970. Construction completed 1975. Lighting load: 3.3 watts per square foot.

2
3

This university complex was developed around a tree system similar to that of the Bank of Canada. The same tree module **(2)** is used throughout, except where larger, column-free spaces were required (such as the gym and swimming pool). In these spaces, one-way systems are used with a module of beams and voids related to the contiguous tree structures, so that service channels continue uninterrupted. Note the gridwork of service channels and their relationship to the structure and lighting diagrams **(7,8,9)**.

Unlike the Bank of Canada, where small offices would clearly be required, the University could be designed with a 30×30 foot module readily divisible into two or four. In the early design phase it appeared that areas requiring finer divisions would represent only a small portion of the building, and that these could be treated as special cases and given a lowered ceiling if necessary. However, the final programmed landscaping for carrels, etc., made it possible to accommodate all the programmed spaces without resort to such ad hoc variations on the system. Introduction of the integrated system-of-systems approach came after an original design had been developed based on a suspended ceiling system.

Only a single morning "squatters session" was required

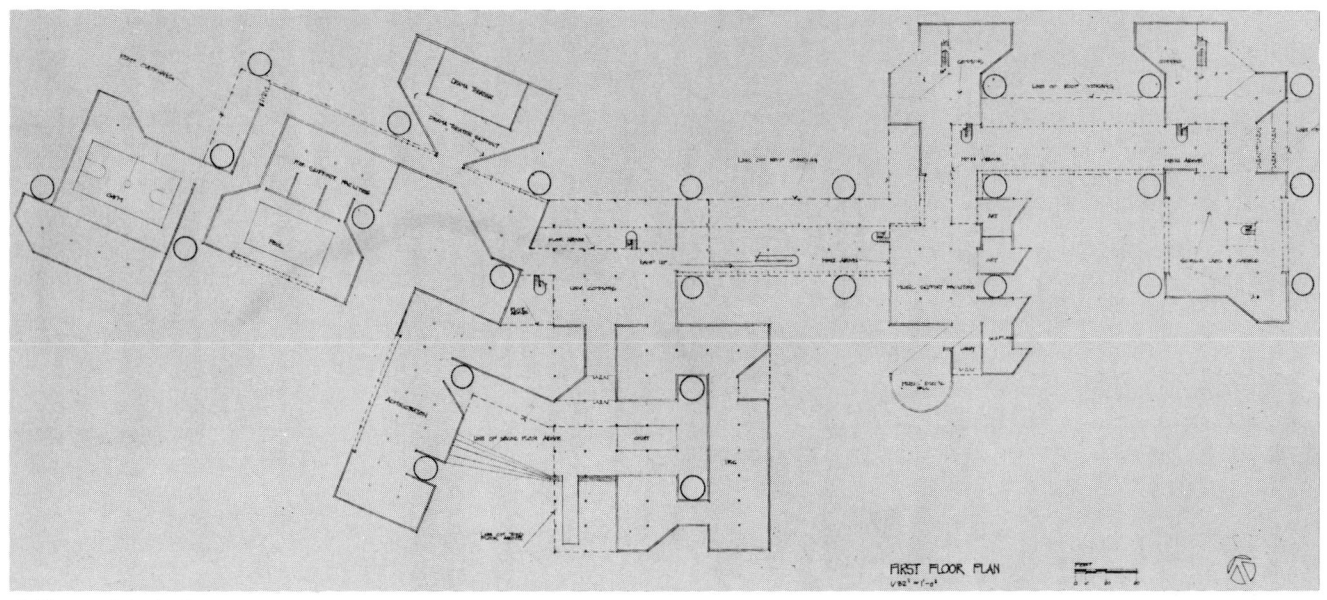

4 *Plan—original scheme.*

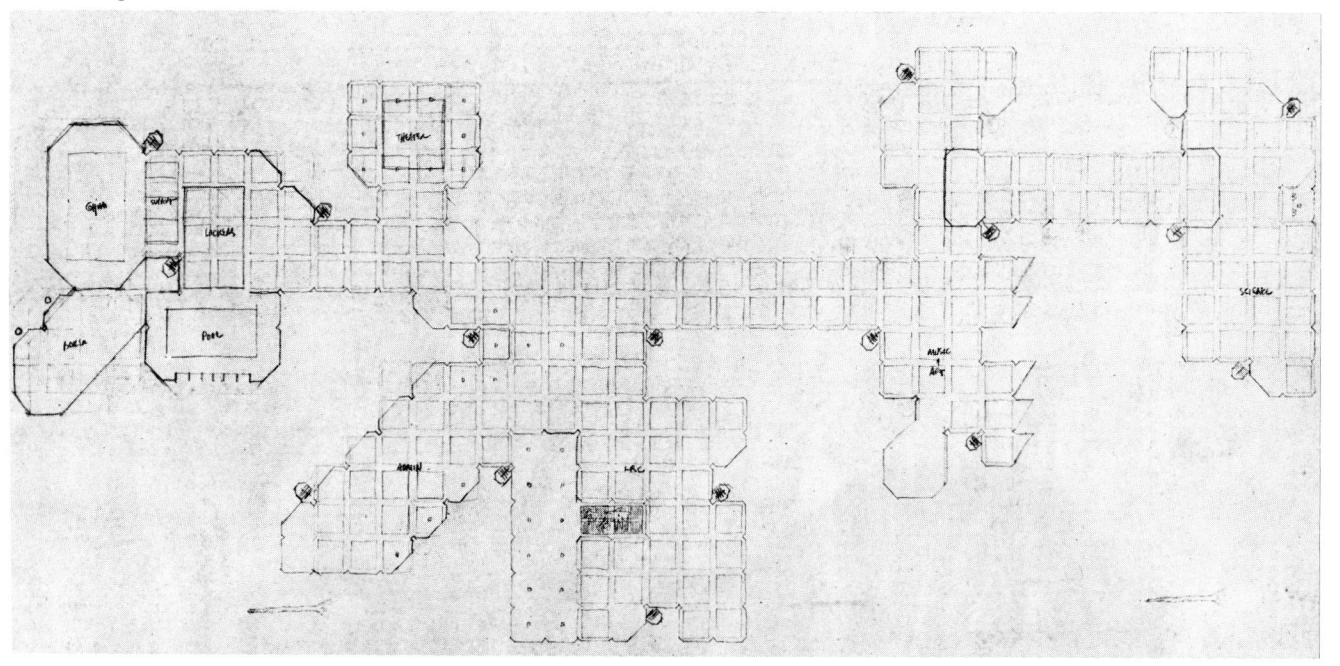

5 *Early systems sketch.*

for the design team to review a number of possibilities and conclude that the tree system looked both workable and economical. Overnight the original plan **(4)** was modified around the tree system **(5,6).** Cost forecasts proved accurate and the building contract was well within the budget. A mock-up **(13)** was built to check light distribution measurements.

The lighting and mechanical systems are designed around the concept of adaptability rather than flexibility. The "trees" are perforated with sufficient holes to accommodate any foreseeable air-conditioning requirement; the natural channels between trees can enclose any foreseeable duct or plumbing requirement. Since ducts and pipes run in clearly defined, unlighted channels, they can be left exposed **(11)** if economy or a need for frequent rearrangement dictate, yet remain inconspicuous because of the strong organization of lighted coffers and unlighted channels.

A number of provisions ensure total lighting adaptability. The fluorescent cove fixtures may at a moment's notice be easily changed to high-output fluorescent lamps, pairs of high-output lamps, or pairs of super-high-output lamps, because the inexpensive cove fixtures are not firmly attached to the structure but merely plug in and rest on the concrete coves. The plan was zoned according to use, and fixtures of appropriate output level were provided in each zone. Provision of an outlet point in the slab in each tree cell allows a single, adjustable fixture or a track system to be attached in lounges and other areas where accent lighting of trees, sculptures, walls, etc., or the creation of another type of environment is desired (i.e., with dimmed rows of decorative lamps). The lowered bands of ceiling between trees do not normally need any additional lighting. However, if they are isolated from the surrounding illuminated coffers (as in a corridor), recessed lights can easily be inserted in the infill ceiling panels. Similarly, important walls in the shadow of the lowered band can also be

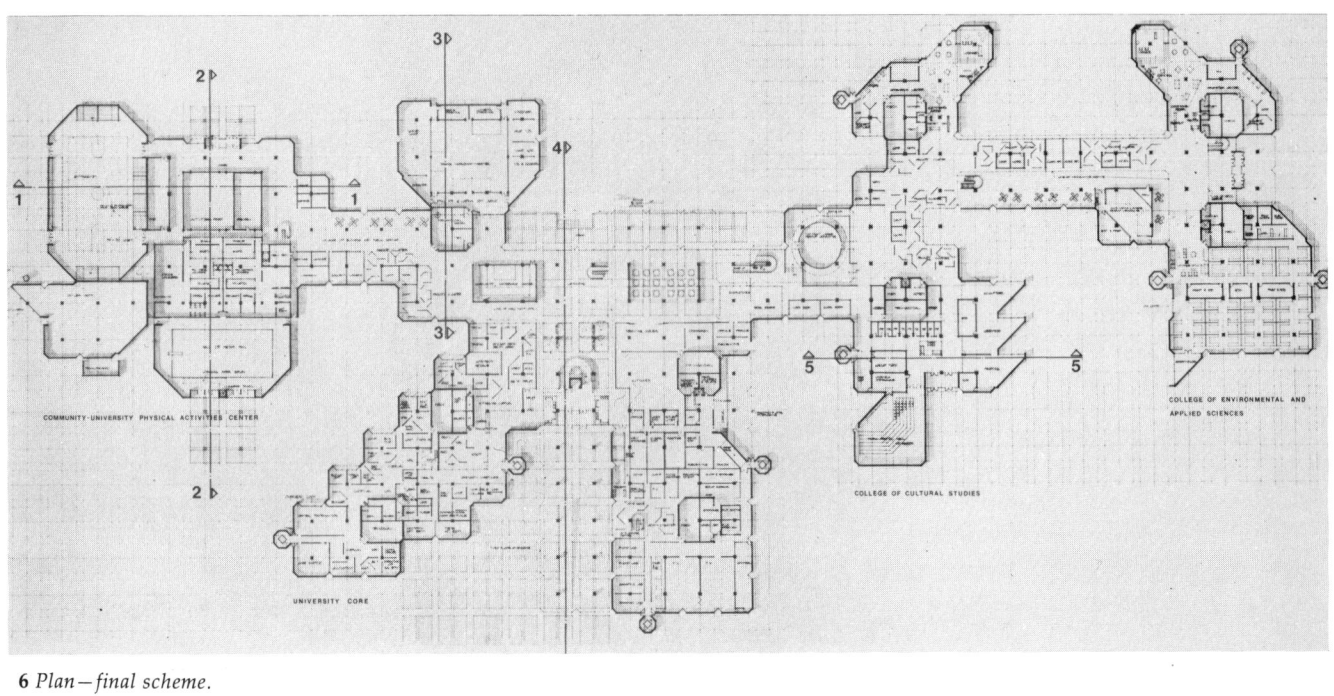

6 *Plan—final scheme.*

7 *Detail of HVAC layout in service channels.*

highlighted with recessed wall washers.

Comment

This building was designed from the inside out. The exterior forms are derived almost entirely from the nature of the interior systems, which are clearly expressed and comprehensible. The underlying unity of the entire complex is immediately apparent.

Monolithic concrete beams and coves with undercut sections obviously cost more to form than simpler concrete shapes to which lighting fixtures are subsequently applied. However, when the scale of the project is large enough the additional investment in formwork can be offset by substantial savings in the electrical contract. Even on smaller jobs, I feel strongly that practical and aesthetic advantages of monolithically formed beams with integral coves are well worth the cost differential, unless the budget is so inflexible that no tradeoffs can be realized (less expensive carpeting, etc). Many who have seen such buildings as Governors State or Quebec Government Center Complex "G" **(Case Study H5)** would agree.

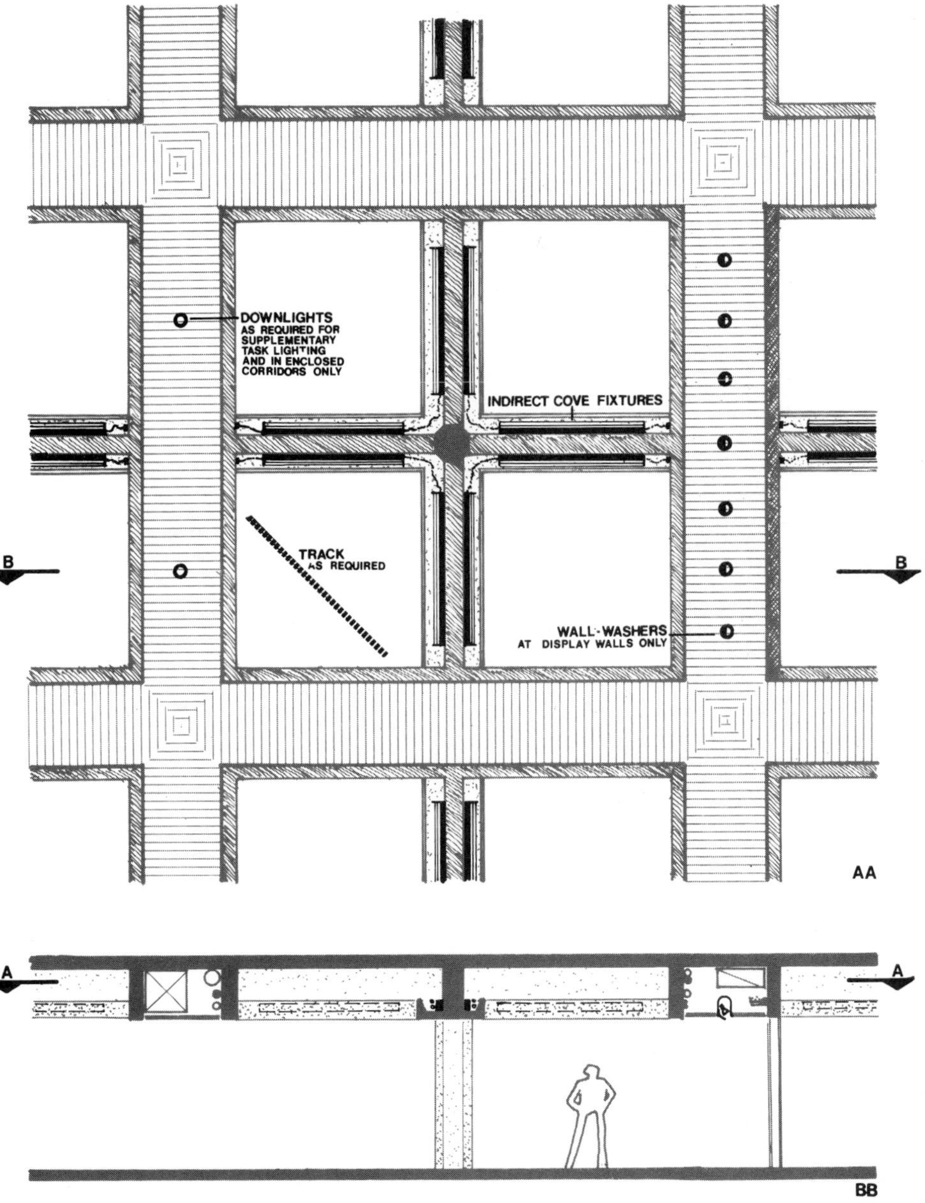

DOWNLIGHTS AS REQUIRED FOR SUPPLEMENTARY TASK LIGHTING AND IN ENCLOSED CORRIDORS ONLY

INDIRECT COVE FIXTURES

TRACK AS REQUIRED

WALL-WASHERS AT DISPLAY WALLS ONLY

AA

BB

8

9

SECTION THRU STREET — MEZZANINE

10

11

13 *Mock-up (used only for measur light levels and distribution).*

14   17

15   18 →

19

16   20

12

CASE STUDIES GROUP H

BUILDING COMPLEXES

1

Photos by Harold Lewis/Photo International

Just as the design options for a single room are reduced when it is part of a sequence of rooms or a flexible building system, so the design (both exterior and interior) of any single building should be influenced by the design of other buildings with which it is grouped, particularly when all are built at the same time to house similar or related activities.

Such principles have long been recognized in the relationship of building exteriors viewed from street and plaza. However, there seems to be less recognition among designers that these principles remain valid *below* plaza levels (within a structure); and that here, in fact, the orientation need is usually even more critical than above ground. Perhaps the failure is more from lack of understanding rather than lack of will. It is true that relationships above ground can be viewed simultaneously while relationships below grade are usually only perceivable in sequence. But designers must understand that the seeing process consists of gathering *and* processing information; of seeing facts rather than only pictures; of being able to see and relate similar elements, though separated by time. Continuity in a sequence (or its absence) is as immediately perceptible as consistency in a grouping which can be seen all at once. The more easily a designer can describe a design concept in words so that a listener can "see" the concept, the more likely it is that casual users of a building will be able to sense its application.

2

CANADIAN CENTER FOR THE PERFORMING ARTS (NATIONAL ARTS CENTER)
Ottawa, Ontario

J. A. Langford, FRAIC, Assistant Deputy Minister (Design) R. F. West, Director of Design, National Capital Region (department of public works); Affleck Desbarats Dimakopoulos Lebensold & Sise (consulting architects); D. F. Lebensold (partner in charge); William Lam Associates, Inc. (lighting consultants); Bolt, Beranek and Newman, N. J. Pappas & Associates (acoustical consultants); Sasaki, Strong & Associates Ltd. (landscaping consultants); Jean Rosenthal (stage lighting consultant); DeLeuw, Cather & Company of Canada (traffic, roads, and parking consultants); Granek, Chisvin, Crossey (mechanical and electrical engineers); Adjelian & Associates (structural engineers); V. K. Mason Construction Co. Ltd. (general contractor). Schematic design started 1964. Construction completed 1969.

The approach to lighting design of the National Arts Center was decorative as well as functional. No preconceptions were imposed on its development. The lighting concept came from:

- Architectural forms and spaces of this project
- Perception principles
- Psychological and physiological needs of the users

- Coordination with structure, mechanical systems, and other details

The validity of this total design approach can be judged in a variety of applications in the Center because of the range of problems which had to be solved, because of the clarity of the architectural concepts, and, most of all, because of the attitude of the architects and engineers which allowed pursuit of the objectives with diligence to details, teamwork, and effective follow-through. The participating design and engineering staffs worked as a truly integrated team.

Design

From a distance, to a person approaching the Center on a sunny day, the overall impression is that of a series of unbroken building masses on connecting platforms

3 *Theater.*

4 *Opera House.*

5

6 *Theater lobby.*

7 *Decorative column ligh*

Macy Dubois/Critic

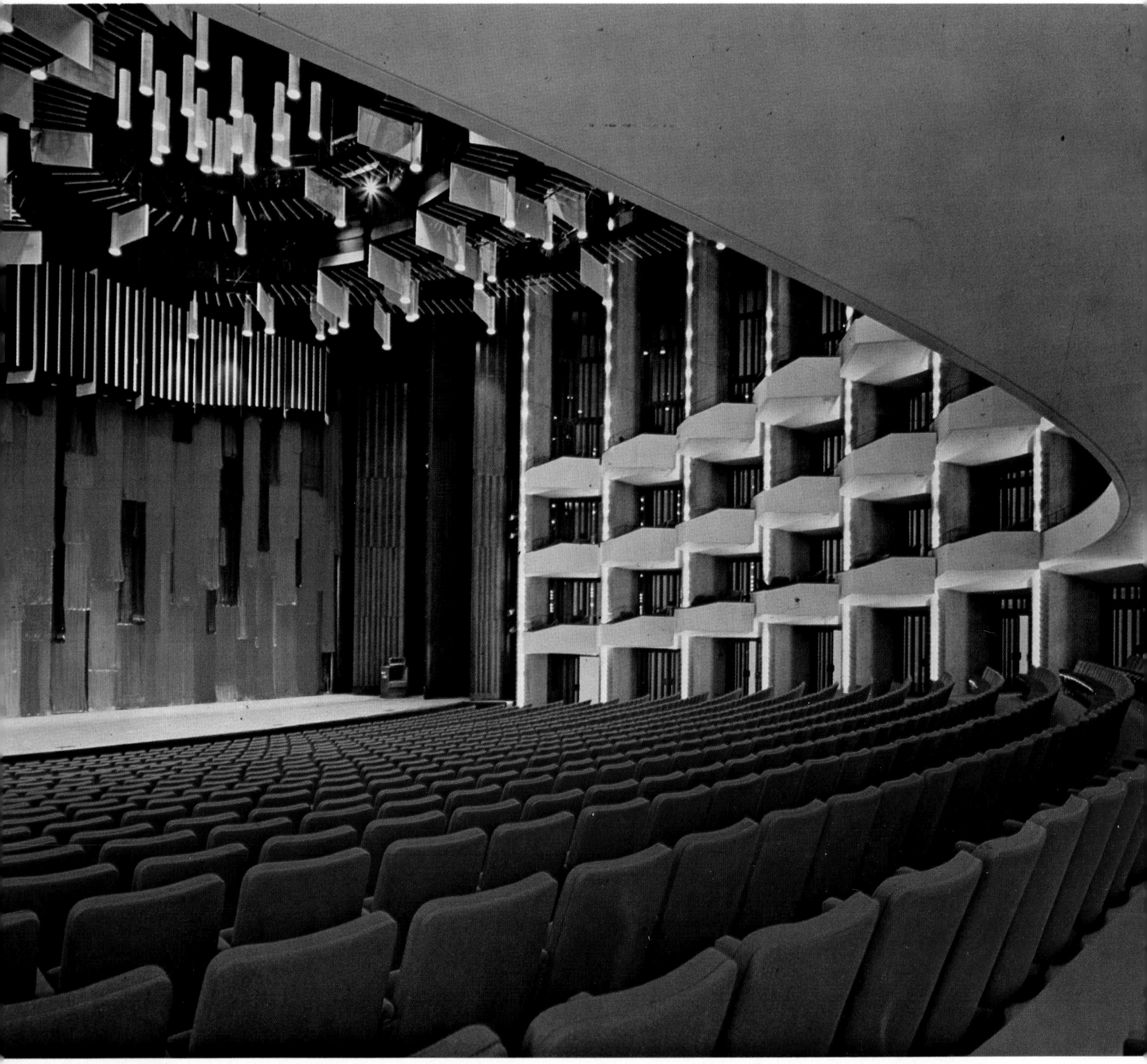

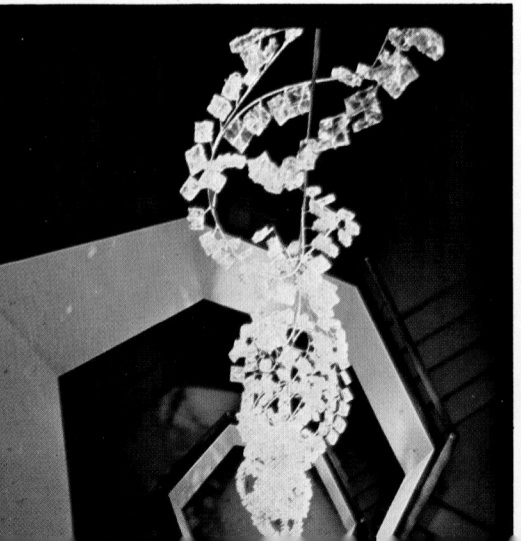

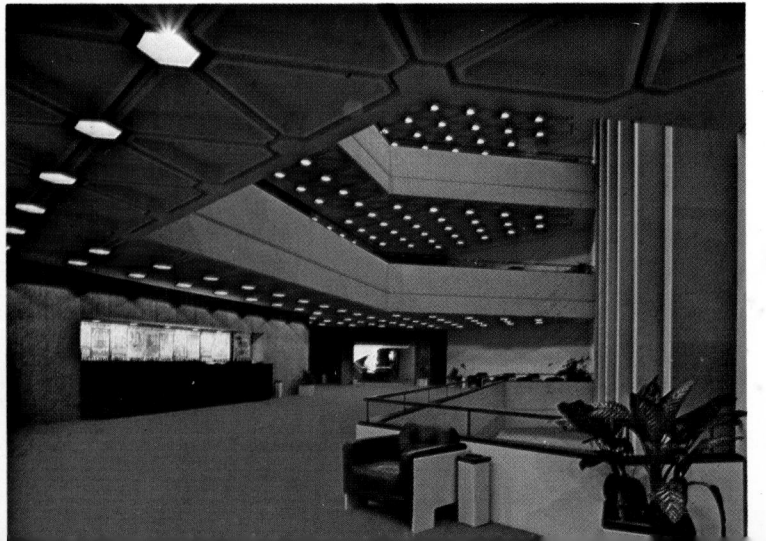

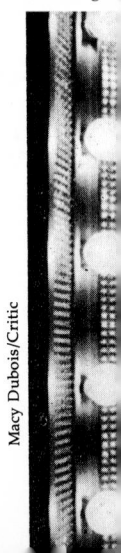

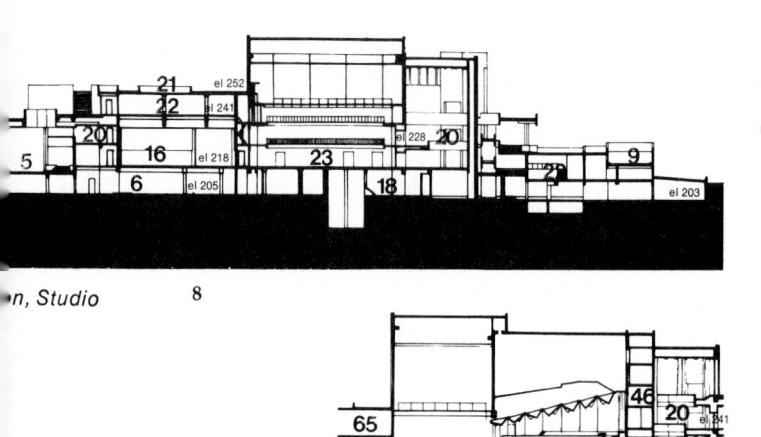

9 *Section, Theatre*

Roger Jowett

10 *Experimental theater.*

and terraces (2). Their hexagonal shapes of various sizes are quite obviously those of several theaters and supporting facilities of stage houses, stair towers, and lobbies.

At close range, when approaching the Center from the surrounding streets, a person's impression of "theater" is reinforced by the presence of billboard/chandeliers (14) which line Elgin Street and mark entrances to the building. Upon mounting the plaza, one gets the impression of public spaces below through the positive expression of skylights penetrating the plaza. Smaller hexagonal forms growing out of the plaza are interesting, but puzzling, and upon inspection turn out to be housings for

11 *Model study.*

12 *Hall lighting during intermission.*

Roger Jowett

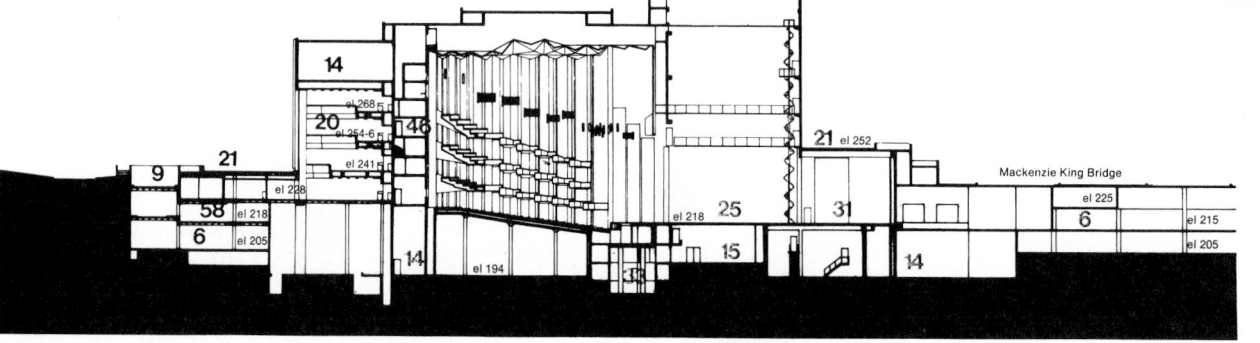

13

Section, Hall

14

15

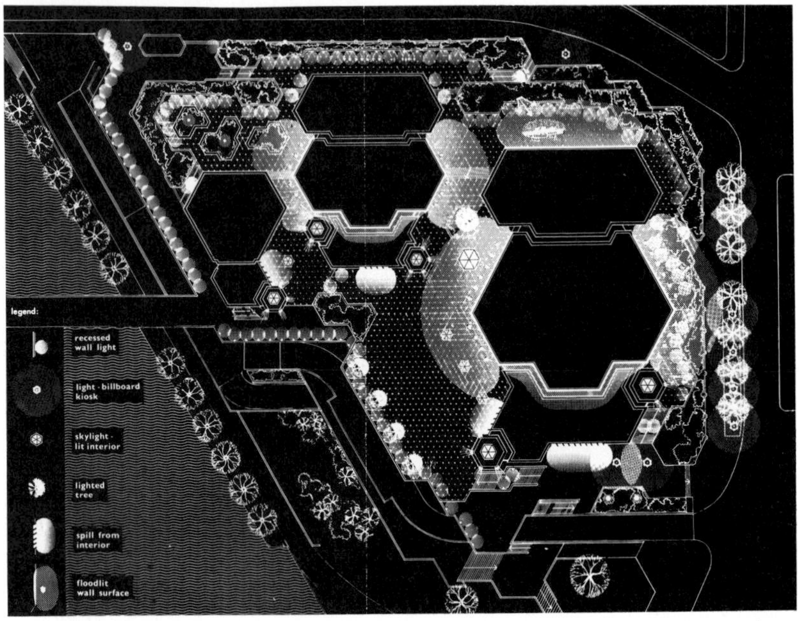

legend:

recessed
wall light

light - billboard
kiosk

skylight -
lit interior

lighted
tree

spill from
interior

floodlit
wall surface

16

floodlights. To a person approaching the Center from a distance on an overcast day, without the crisp definition of form by sun and shadow the buildings tend to become more two-dimensional silhouettes. It was our intention to help maintain depth and liveliness by glowing forms and glitter at skylight openings, stair tower slots, and connecting ceiling planes of lobby areas, as well as with billboard/chandeliers.

From a distance, when one is approaching the Center at night, what is seen can be more totally manipulated, and we chose to compose selectively. Only the forms of the "egg" of the theater and the opera house–concert hall are floodlighted (1). As accessory facilities, the stagehouses were left dark, except for the shadow pattern cast by the floodlit Daudelin sculpture at the rear wall of the opera stagehouse. In the darkness the kiosks sparkle brilliantly, as do the stair towers, with their glass sculptures and patterns of lamps reflected in clear skylights which were faceted and steeply sloping for this purpose. Trees were uplighted, to provide a lighted frame against the background of the city and to add enclosure to the plaza; but the trees were not lit from the street side, where they would be in silhouette against floodlit portions of the Center.

The exterior forms of stair towers and lobby areas were meant to become more mysterious and to remain secondary to the main halls. But the brilliantly lighted sculpture in the stair towers and the illuminated works of art in the lobbies should beckon, seen in silhouette through the architectural exterior screen. The sparking reflections of decorative incandescent lamps in the skylights add further gaiety.

Because of the close coordination of design, it is difficult to say whether the lighting forms were created by the architecture, or whether the architectural forms were created by the lighting design. Both occurred. The clear articulation of the shape of the halls invited their being highlighted selectively. And the housing of the lighting equipment to achieve this purpose became the "raison d'être" for useful, sculptural-scale elements on the plaza (1,18).

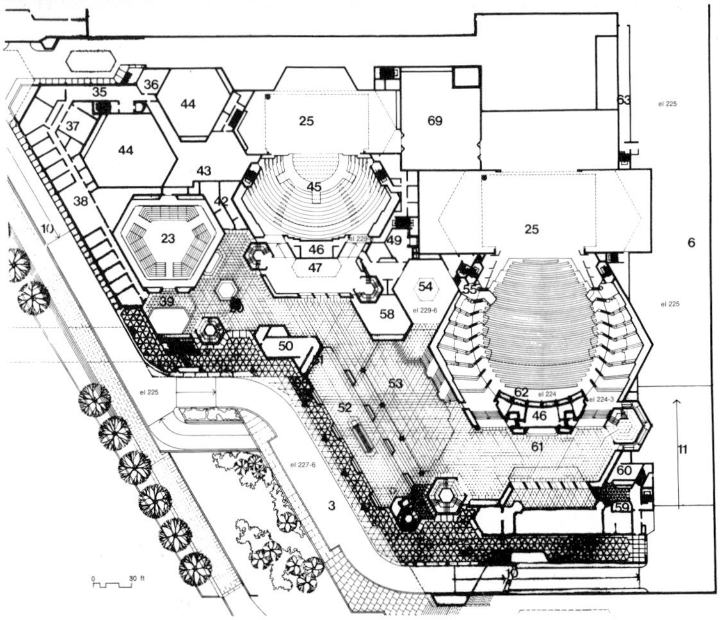

The stair towers derived their shape and slotted corners from the lighting concept that the impression of "theater" and grandeur

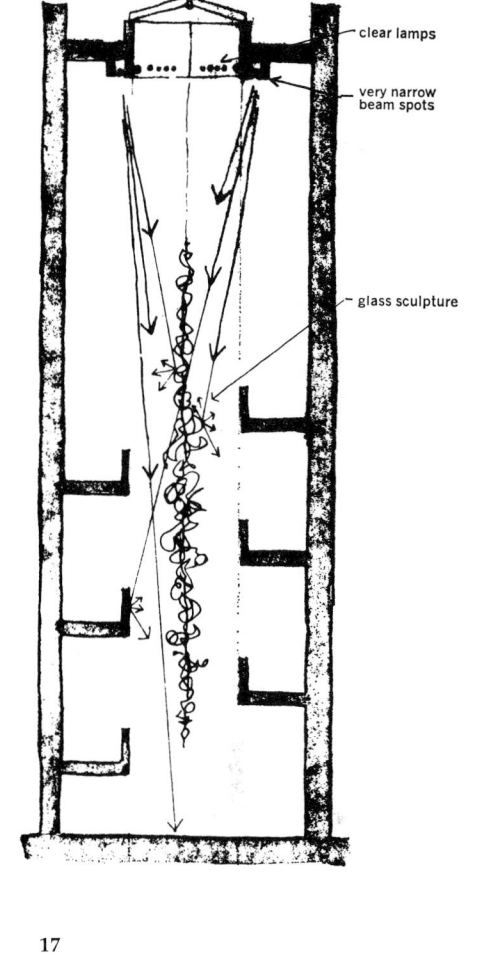

clear lamps

very narrow
beam spots

glass sculpture

17

18

could be heightened by having patrons circulate around a light-reflecting sculpture **(5,18)** illuminated as though by a shaft of sunlight from the top, and by presenting a view to the exterior of a glittery world, unlike that glimpsed in office building stair towers.

Another example, the need for a system of kiosk/sign-chandeliers, arose from the absence of a traditional theater marquee. The design team had to create a new form which would serve as a distinctive nighttime symbol for the theater while displaying advertising posters for current and coming attractions. We chose to develop the design around the hexagonal theater form and the basic interior lighting tool—the exposed, clear, incandescent lamp.

Inside the Center, lighting concepts and details were derived from the thematic architectural forms. The concept of lighting design was to emphasize the most dominant architectural characteristics. The lobby and hall of the opera house are one continuous space, separated only by a screen of unbroken columns, with boxes suspended between them. To emphasize this feature, bare lamp chandeliers are notched into both the hall and lobby sides of each column **(4,7,11,12)**.

The design of the ceiling in the opera hall grew out of the need for an extensive catwalk system for stage lighting and screening for a wide range of randomly placed acoustic reflectors and absorbers. After attempting to leave voids for stage lighting, we decided instead to express the catwalks positively by patterns of light-reflecting white battens, flags, and lighting cylinders, of a scale large enough to distract the eye from the disorderly array of equipment above and arranged to follow the concentric catwalk curves **(4)**. Study models were built to ex-

plore various alternatives **(11)**.

Together the lighted columns and ceiling create a distinct room-size chandelier, unique to the architectural form of the National Arts Center Opera Hall. The effectiveness of this chandelier concept was tested with an illuminated model. By selective dimming and switching of these elements and by highlighting of the curtains, a wide variety of spatial and decorative effects can be achieved. At the beginning of intermission the lighting on the lobby side of the columns is turned on first to expand the space of the hall beyond the columns to the outer walls **(12)**.

The exposed concrete interior walls of the Theater and its hexagonal shape suggested that the walls be highlighted with the same vocabulary of clear lamps used in the Opera House mounted this time behind perimeter beams. The form of the ceiling was again dictated by stage lighting requirements **(3)**. The ceiling structure was created as a series of light-shielding, open-fronted, pyramidal boxes. Their junctions are articulated as part of the house lighting pattern. This room-sized chandelier is also unique to the National Arts Center Theater. A similar edge treatment was used in the experimental theater **(10)**.

In the stair towers, instead of lighting design growing from the shape of the space, an appropriate space was designed to fit around the lighting concept, a spine of brilliantly illuminated, light-reflecting sculpture by William Martin **(5,17)**. A ring of narrow-beam spots around the skylight perimeter is directed only onto the sculpture. The other surfaces of the stairwell receive light only from the sculpture, indirectly. Despite its extreme brilliance, the sculpture causes no glare because it is what one wants to look at (maximum signal-to-noise ratio).

19

20 *Study model.*

Lam

Architecture Canada

21

6 type PS #1 (porcelain sockets)
bulbs: 6 500 RSP
3" dia hole in center of triangular plate
(see above) mounted 1½" below socket
matte black or bronze finish
⅜" solid baffles (by general contractor)
including welded studs for screw-in plate
channel or hollow
steel section
glass
undistorted
lamp reflections
clear lamps @ 5" O. C.
cables woven or wrapped
in gold plated wire beyond
ring as shown
ring
72 stringers gem cut crystal graduated 1½"
dia to 3"

The idea of light-refracting sculpture used in the stairs was used in the salon in a somewhat different form. Here, reflecting elements are simple, graduated strings of glass beads, supported in a "frame" consisting of the edge beam of the skylight well **(19,21)**. This effect was also tested and positively demonstrated by a model **(20)**. Later variations on this theme were important form-givers for such projects as the Hyatt Regency Hotels at O'Hare (Chicago) and Houston **(Case Studies C7 and C9)**. Consistent with the design principle evident throughout, the skylight well was used, not only as the obvious space in which to place a chandelier, but as an integral part of the chandelier itself.

The lighting ceiling system of all lobby areas **(6)** connecting the studio, theater, and opera house was designed as a positive element, recognizing the importance and extensiveness of these surfaces, and as the most continuous and visible element when the spaces are filled with people. Rather than attempting a more neutral ceiling, with inevitable interruptions for access panels, air diffusers, etc., a richly sculptured, removable panel system was devised, using the decorative light fixture as the air supply, with the conical shape of the fixture providing a natural, neatly integrated air-deflecting element for the air diffuser **(6)**. Some of these light fixtures were used to conceal loudspeakers; in these cells, the air diffuser was omitted.

Execution of the lighting concepts was coordinated with the detailing of other building elements, for example, in the lobby ceiling just described. In the opera house column lighting, the column cladding and air ducts, air diffusers, and lighting extrusions are combined. One of the inherent perceptual problems is to generate the appearance of a *band* of light from a series of individual lamps. This was accomplished by lining the gold anodized aluminum reflector with sheets of glass balls. *Each* ball produces point reflections of lamps to any viewing position. (A spherical surface will always have a point of tangency to any viewing position.) In addition, each ball acts as a focusing lens and creates a brilliant spot on the gold backing. The combination creates a rich three-dimensional surface **(7)**. Lamps are not evenly spaced through the vertical length, but spacing increases at the top of the column to produce the effect of "fading out." The decorative light notch is terminated at the bottom by integral ashtrays.

The initial rectangular shape of the column was modified to accept the lighting notch gracefully; thus, the lighting became the "raison d'être" for essentially hexagonal columns, adding further to the architectural continuity of the National Arts Center.

Critique

Floodlighting of the sculpture at the back of the Hall stagehouse was not permanently installed until 1972, although the illuminated sculpture had been a key element in the exterior lighting concept. Temporary lighting was used by the lighting consultant at a "tuning up" session to determine the best arrangement for that particular piece of sculpture.

Also, in 1972, it was decided that the lobby side of the buildings should appear more prominent when viewed from adjacent streets through the intervening park. From this direction the mass of the lobby (initially conceived as fairly transparent) had interfered with the view of the hall itself; uplighting of the screen walls of the lobby restored the integrity of the exterior image.

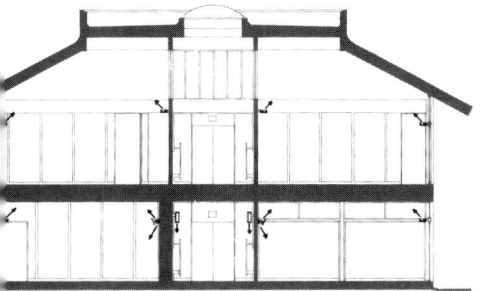

1

C. THURSTON CHASE LEARNING CENTER EAGLEBROOK SCHOOL
Deerfield, Massachusetts

The Architects Collaborative and Campbell, Aldrich & Nulty (architects); Sarah P. Harkness, Herbert K. Gallagher, Sherry Proctor (The Architects Collaborative); Walter Campbell, Carmen di Stefano (Campbell, Aldrich & Nulty) (project team); William Lam Associates, Inc. (lighting consultants); Donald Mitchell, Robert Anderson (educational consultants); Jackson and Moreland (mechanical and electrical engineers); Souza and True (structural engineers). Schematic design started 1964. Construction completed 1966.

At least one of the three small buildings in this project would probably have taken a different form if built separately in a different location. As a cluster, however, it was considered desirable that they be related in interior character as well as exterior forms, insofar as their various uses permitted. Development of a common vocabulary in the detailing and lighting was difficult but possible. The most important common denominator was the strong roof form hovering over its supporting brick walls.

Design

The starting point for the lighting design at the Eaglebrook School was the idea of supplementing the natural lighting by utilizing the white plaster ceilings floating above the perimeter walls to reflect light from fluorescent sources concealed at the top of the walls. Since the walls were interrupted by windows, it was necessary to create a horizontal band across the mullions at that level for continuous lighting and wiring (3). Whereas in some rooms a direct/indirect light distribution would have been best, in others the need to place bookshelves and laboratory cabinets up to that level dic-

Architectural Record.

2

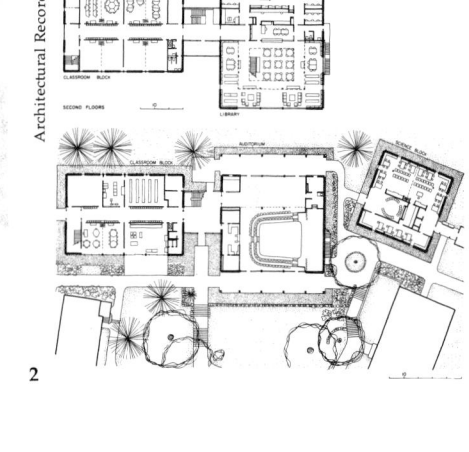

Photos by Louis Reens

3 *Section through classroom building.*

4 *Typical upper level classroom.*

5 *Typical lower level classroom.*

6

7 *Lecture area.*

tated the use of a closed-bottom channel, with light distribution upward only **(4,5)**. This eliminated the potential problems of lamp reflections in the windows below. The channel was "floated" away from the mullions in order to allow a space for upward distribution of air from the brick cavity walls.

This basic light distribution was supplemented from other directions. In the double-loaded corridor building, which has similar height corridor walls and transom above, the indirect lighting was continued from the corridor walls of classrooms, etc. On the lower level, however, no convenient horizontal position was available, so the compromise was low-brightness incandescent downlights recessed in the ceiling **(7)**.

Maintaining the scheme in the library building **(9)** was more difficult because of the presence of a balcony and the greater room size. At the perimeter, physically similar fixtures with two super-high-output lamps were used, with lenses to reduce their brightness when viewed from the balcony. Such reduction of the light spread was in opposition to the objective of illuminating the ceiling as uniformly as possible, but was an unavoidable compromise.

The central portion of the space **(8)** was illuminated from a fluorescent edge slot and by the central skylight (supplemented by incandescent downlights). The edge slot was originally to have been an edge skylight, which unfortunately had to be eliminated to meet budget problems. The central skylight was left totally transparent in order to get undiluted direct sunlight and sky view. The dynamic quality of the space with the introduction of a relatively small area of sunlight (maximum projected area of less than 64 square feet at mid-summer noon) was considered valuable enough in fulfillment of biological needs to offset the possibility that some students might be inconvenienced by the direct sun at times. The chamfered ceiling well provides some transition to the skylight brightness but, more important, brings the perceived size of the modest skylight up to a scale appropriate to the large central well space.

An initial scheme for translucent skylights covering the entire central area was quickly abandoned with the realization that the necessary construction would have appeared "busy"—the translucent glazing would seem glaring on bright days and gloomy on dark days, with no sky view or benefit of direct sunlight penetration. Air conditioning would also have been much more expensive and difficult.

Although some of the inherent drawbacks of large skylights would have been eliminated had low-transmission clear glazing been proposed rather than translucent glazing, the extensive pattern of cast shadows would still have been bothersome. (Such shadows would be more acceptable in a transitional environment such as a public circulation space where orientation needs usually outweigh task needs.)

Since the window band is continued around the corners in which a bathroom is located **(10),** the typical classroom artificial lighting is also continued. Had the window been stopped and the bathroom thereby consciously left "out of the system," a lighting scheme more specifically tailored to the needs of a washroom would have been designed. However, as built, the best trade-off in cost as well as appearance was to continue the system. If this had been a "powder room," the system would have been supplemented by local lighting at the mirror.

8 *Library.*

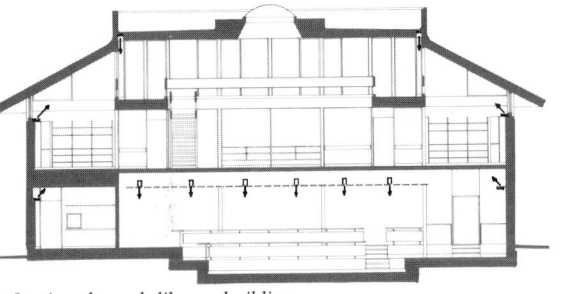

9 *Section through library building.*

11 *Balcony in the library.*

10

12 *Below, right: typical study carrel with integrated local lighting.*

1

FATHERS OF CONFEDERATION
MEMORIAL BUILDINGS
Charlottetown, Prince Edward Island

H3

Affleck Desbarats Dimakopoulos Lebensold & Sise (architect); D. Dimakopoulos (partner in charge); H. K. Stenman (project manager); Vincent Chan (design development); Norbert Schoenauer (town planner); William Lam Associates, Inc. (lighting consultants); Bolt, Beranek and Newman (acoustical consultant); Edward Friedman (concrete consultant); Prof. George Izenour (theatre consultant); Gérard Tremblay (theatre baldacchino consultant); James P. Keith & Associates (mechanical engineers); John Adjelian & Associates (structural engineers). Schematic design started 1963. Construction completed 1965.

When a building complex is unified by exterior forms and materials and by a common roof/ceiling structure, as is the Fathers of Confederation Center, the manner in which the different lighting needs are fulfilled should be consistent with the intent to unify the overall design.

Additional factors made the design problem at the Fathers of Confederation Center much more challenging than that at Eaglebrook. Because of the harsh climate and the shared supporting facilities, the principal circulation is below grade **(7),** which makes the achievement of positive orientation much more difficult. In addition, the Fathers of Confederation complex was intended to serve as a new focal point for the city of Charlottetown. At night, the success of the image would largely depend on the success of the lighting scheme **(2).** The concepts and design were described

2

Roger Jowett

by the author in the following article, reprinted from *Architecture Canada* (12/64):

The architectural concept: Rather than sitting on top of a podium, the masses of library, museum, and theater rise out of the ground from a concourse level which, in the local climate, is the major circulation path much of the year.

The daylight design: By daylight the above ground organization of the masses is clear and powerful. What may not be apparent at first glance is the superb daylight design at concourse level. The narrow skylights surrounding each block allow daylight to define the continuity of those massive walls from concourse floor to skyline . . . a relationship which can best be seen through the open courts (7), but can always be sensed throughout the underground passages, so that the underground and grade level orientation tends to be linked.

Supplementary daytime illumination fills out areas not sufficiently reached by daylight, without nullifying the dominance of the naturally lit areas. The obvious night-time design solution was simply to reverse the daylight effect (2,4).

The 6' × 6' waffle grid is dominant within each of the individual buildings. Even if it were not a visible common denominator on the exterior, consistent handling of the grid had to be the starting point for the lighting design . . . despite the direct conflict between a uniform solution and the varying requirements of theater,

museum, and library. The conflicting demands for unity and difference were resolved by using the same lighting fixture within each coffer, and controlling the appearance of the structure, spaces, and the lighting quality by utilizing variations in lamp sizes, and carefully developing switching and dimming patterns. The universal fixture, a pendent "can" centered in and aligned with the bottom of each cell, was designed to illuminate the cell without bisecting shadows, with separately controlled direct lighting which will appear as the same dark cone even though the lamps vary from 50 to 300 watts.

Most simple of the lighting problems occurred in the library (9) where the requirements are fixed and simply defined. Here diffused lighting is provided by maximum indirect illumination of every coffer, but, since the sand-blasted concrete is not the most efficient reflector, this indirect lighting is supplemented by a direct component from every cell. Fifty watt lamps are used to maintain the pattern in areas (such as at the overhanging soffit) where there is actually no necessity for the light. One may question the relatively low "efficiency" of illuminating the coffers, but the dark color and shadow-casting configuration are precisely the reasons for illuminating the structure, to relieve the daytime gloom of dark ceiling in contrast with bright

window. Spaces not covered by the exposed ceiling grid are illuminated in a neutral manner, indirectly from book stacks or open-cove wall fixtures, by low-brightness recessed fixtures in suspended ceilings, and by local lighting under shelves and cabinets.

The museum (8) demanded a disciplined flexibility . . . flexibility to create the proper focus for a wide variety of possible exhibits, but with a discipline consistent with the monumentality of the Fathers of Confederation complex. Casual arrangements of exposed adjustable lighting fixtures on tracks were thus avoided. Instead, flexibility was gained by:

(1) Highlighting the most likely display planes by arrangements of reflector lamps in the ceiling coffer fixtures, i.e., 300 watt lamps at the

perimeter and over the central well.

(2) Circuiting so that *each* side of *each* concentric square could be switched and dimmed individually.

(3) Adjustable edge lighting concealed from view along the side of the balcony enclosure in one of the galleries allows the upper walls to be lit either uniformly from above or with dramatic effect from below. The actual location and structure of the balcony—originally intended for the outside wall—was changed to make these effects possible.

(4) Special recessed floor fittings to support and electrify posts for self-illuminating mid-floor display panels and cases.

(5) For most exhibits, indirect lighting of the ceiling coffers would probably be dimmed to a very low level for maximum focus on the

3 *Grade plan.*

exhibits. However, the level may be readily increased when a greater component of indirect lighting is helpful or for occasions, such as receptions, when the architectural space is to be emphasized.

The daylighting design (corner window) is a good compromise between providing contact with the outdoor environment and competing visually with exhibits.

In the theater **(5,6)**, many different types of spaces are created with the lighting . . . again primarily by carefully planned switching and dimming patterns with the coffer fixtures. Basic architectural departures from the other buildings were the adjustable shape of the hall and the presence of acoustic clouds which were to be expressed in a positive sculptural manner.

To maximize the expression of the acoustic sculpture as a positive element (rather than a necessary evil) the panels were made translucent, so that when backlighted they become the "chandelier" **(5)**.

Some of the possible spaces to be created in the main hall:

(1) Most dramatic: "chandelier" only, or plus illuminated back wall under balcony.

(2) Neutral: downlights illuminating floor area of *complete* hall, but with walls and "chandelier" remaining unlighted.

(3) Neutral: downlights illuminating floor area of *contracted* hall but with walls and "chandelier" unlighted.

(4) Architectural emphasis: ceiling coffers illuminated plus downlighting of floor ("chandelier" expressed as silhouette). This might be the condition for a lecture-type program, or for daytime concerts when the hall lighting should relate to the daylight conditions outside, or at least provide a pleasant transition during intermissions.

Some change of pace is provided by patterns of bare clear lamps in the lower foyer and refreshment areas.

Some general considerations pertaining to all buildings:

(1) Whenever the coffers are illuminated, *every* coffer in the space is lit. In this way the structure is always perceived as an uninterrupted plane **(4,8,9)**.

(2) Lighting of walls and floor is generally not uniform, but with selected emphasis for purposes of display, expression of structural rhythm, or defining nodes and axes in the circulation pattern **(7,10)**.

(3) All exterior lighting consists of light reflected from and spilling out of the buildings themselves. This was possible because of the limited size of the site **(2)**.

4

5 *Acoustic/lighting sculpture.*

Critique

There has been justifiable criticism of offices and other supporting facilities which are totally cut off from the exterior. In spaces at or above grade which are isolated from outside conditions, dissatisfaction is increased since the daylight is felt to be "so near, yet so far." Awareness of the available alternative is frustrating to the biological need for contact with exterior conditions. Windowless spaces deep in a basement, where daylight is obviously impossible, cause much less irritation to their occupants. However, this tradeoff was consciously decided in favor of maximum monumentality of the principal public elements. Some minimal windows or skylights would have been valuable but could not be accommodated within an already strained budget.

6

Photos by Roger Jowett

Photos by Donald W. Nusbaum

1

FINE ARTS BUILDING
WISCONSIN STATE UNIVERSITY
Stevens Point, Wisconsin

H4

William Wenzler and Associates (architect); Michael P. Johnson (job captain); William Lam Associates, Inc. (lighting consultants); Bolt, Beranek and Newman (acoustical consultant); Edward L. Gingrass (cost consultant); Dolan and Dustin (electrical consultant); Beseke Engineering, Inc. (HVAC consultant); Dega & Stluka (landscape consultant); Lubenow & Gobster (plumbing consultant); Kolbjorn Saether & Associates (structural consultant); A. S. Gillette (theater consultant); C. G. Schmidt, Inc. (general contractor). Schematic design started 1966.

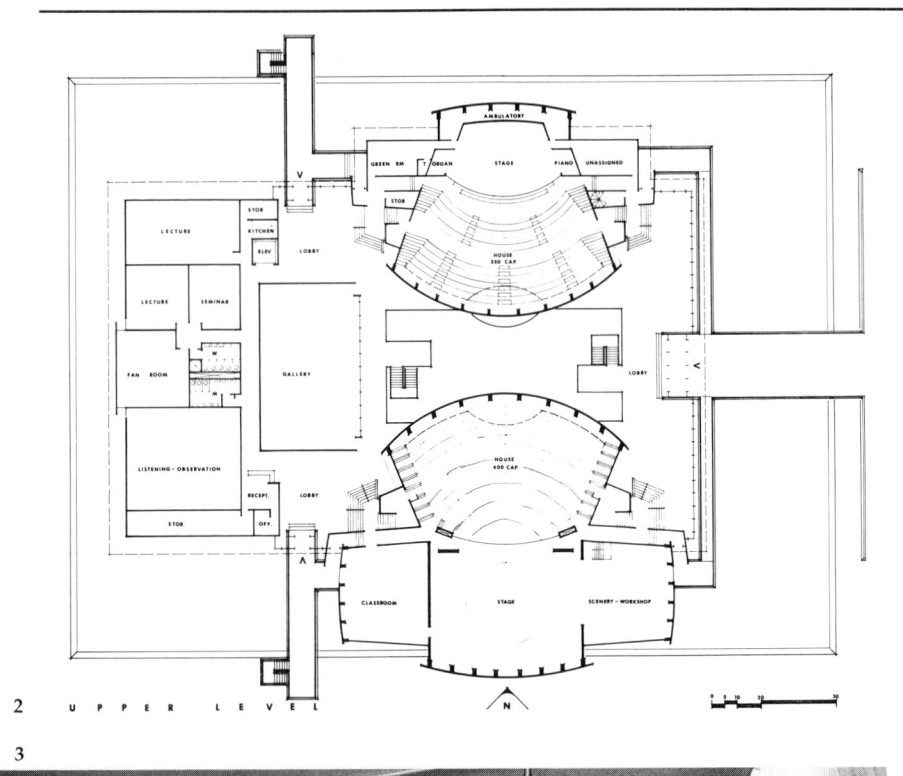

2 U P P E R   L E V E L

3

When main circulation is at grade, defining and distinguishing between the principal units of a complex are desirable but less necessary than when primary circulation is below grade.

Design

At the Fine Arts Building for Wisconsin State University at Stevens Point, edge skylights and coordinated lighting were used to increase the comprehensibility of the forms of theater and hall both from the exterior and within the lobby **(3)** during the day and at night. The ceiling infill was treated as a neutral enclosure for services and as a background for lighting track which allows the focusing of lighting as desired for exhibits and occasions **(4)**.

4 *Exhibition gallery.*

In the hall and theater, the principal elements of the Fine Arts Building, balcony forms were treated as "chandeliers." Used to screen ducts and allow flexibility

in placement of acoustic reflectors and absorption, the wood ceiling took its form and details from the arrangement of lighting. In the concert hall, stage and audience hall function as one room, and therefore the ceiling hovers over both in a continuous sweep; in the theater **(8),** on the other hand, stage and hall are separated and an implied proscenium is created by the interruption of the ceiling plane as it wraps around the lighting bridge (as was the intent at the Beloit Auditorium, **A2).**

The optimum locations for light fixtures suggested the module and joint detailing for the prefabricated wood ceiling sections. The design of the very simple and inexpensive custom-made sheet metal fixtures grew out of the proposed mounting detail. The detailing facilitated installation and makes it possible to relamp and aim these fixtures from the catwalk system above the ceiling **(7).**

Classrooms and studios and corridors occupy the lower level. Rather than treat this level as a basement full of randomly placed ductwork screened by the glare of industrial fluorescent fixtures, the design team attempted to create a restful background of illuminated "bays" supplemented by track-mounted, adjustable incandescent fixtures arranged as required for specific room activities.

Without being any less spartan, mechanical and lighting elements were integrated with the structure. Ducts and pipes were arranged and supported on pipe racks that also support fluorescent strips and wood valances. The pipe supports were meant to extend only as far as necessary (to clear the pipes and ducts) in each instance. Unfortunately, where this concept was not followed and unnecessarily long supports were used, the racks encroach somewhat upon the rooms, particularly the smallest ones.

5 *Concert hall ceiling continues over stage.*

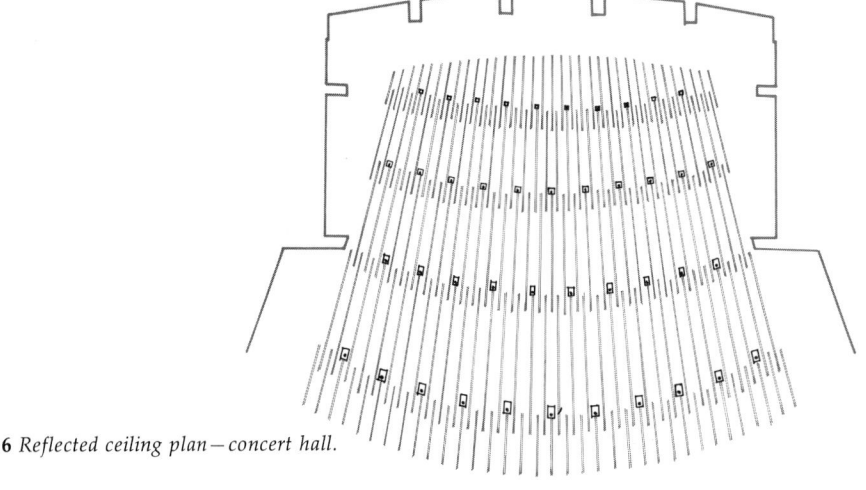

6 *Reflected ceiling plan—concert hall.*

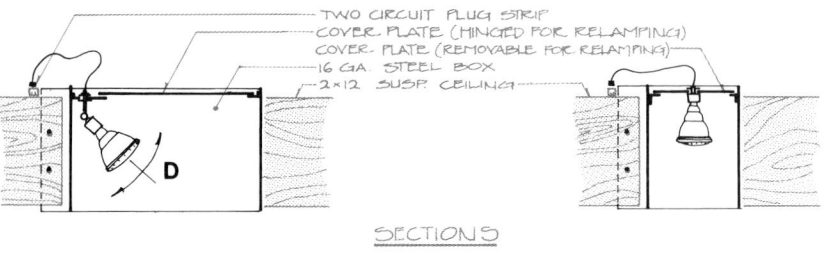

7 *Fixture details—concert hall ceiling.*

8 *Theater ceiling held back to form lighting bridge.*

9 *Sections:* **(A)** *Decorative incandescent globes.* **(B)** *Incandescent work lights.* **(C)** *Stage lighting.* **(D)** *Adjustable spotlights in inexpensive custom sheet-metal boxes.*

Theater.

Concert Hall.

B

10 *Rail lighting details.*

A

6"

Critique

An attempt to modify the structure itself to create integral service channels and lighting coves was handicapped by the lateness of the attempt to coordinate all aspects of design. As a result, on his next similar project (Beloit College, South Campus Complex, [**Case Study C8**]), architect Wenzler began with an integrated design team, so that structural, mechanical, and lighting designs would evolve simultaneously rather than in sequence.

Photos without credits by Ripman

COMPLEX "G," CITÉ PARLEMENTAIRE
Quebec

H5

Fiset & Deschamps-Gauthier, Guite & Jean-Marie Roy (architect); Gilles Guite (partner in charge); Gordon Edwards (consulting architect); William Lam Associates, Inc. (lighting consultants); Leslie Doelle (acoustical consultant); John Schreiber (landscaping consultant) Bernard et Associés (food service consultant) Gilbert, Bourassa, Gagne, Morin (mechanical and electrical engineers) Dufresne, Beaulieu, Trudeau & Associates (structural engineers) Leblanc, Montpetit, Lagace (associated engineers). Cost: $28,000,000. Square footage: 1,030,000 (office space). Construction completed 1972. Lighting loads: 3.5 watts per square foot (tower), 4.2 watts per square foot (low building).

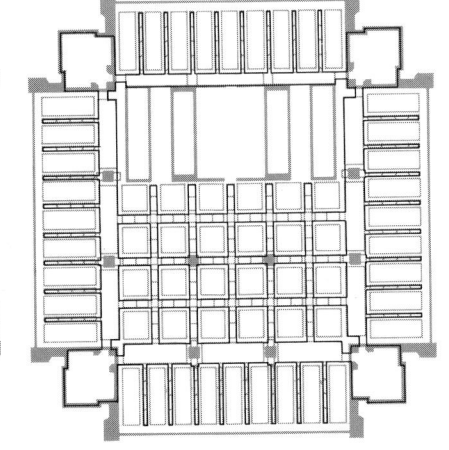

Christian Herdeg

3 *Plan diagrams, tower.*

Early attempts at the integration of structure with mechanical and lighting systems produced buildings such as Weese's IBM-Milwaukee Building **(Case Study E2)** and Skidmore Owings and Merrill's American Republic Building **(Case Study E1).** Though pioneering, these projects suffered from two defects. First, lighted coffers were based on a one-way module too small to be easily integrated into a perception of the created spaces as unified volumes, while the one-way orientation made subdivision of spaces difficult. Second, the integrated systems developed for lighting and air distribution made no provision for flexible distribution of other mechanical services such as plumbing, sprinklers, etc. These problems were subsequently addressed in projects such as the MacMillan-Bloedel Building **(E8)** and the NASA Center in Cambridge **(G1).**

Complex "G" of the Cité Parlementaire, Quebec City **(2),** is among the best and largest projects yet built which incorporates a successful solution to both problems.[1]

Despite the fact that lighting design began late in the Quebec project (the garage level went out to bid simultaneously), it proved possible to redesign a neutral, homogenized suspended-ceiling concept into a well-articulated system integrating architectural, structural, mechanical, and lighting elements. The revised design was built for less than the estimated cost of the original design, without delaying construction.

While a unified design approach suggested the consistent

[1]*Others, which derive an even greater degree of flexibility from the tree-type structural approach, have been completed or are under construction in 1976; for instance, Governors State University **(G5),** the Bank of Canada, Ottawa **(G2),** and Jacksonville Police Administration **(G4).***

STRUCTURE

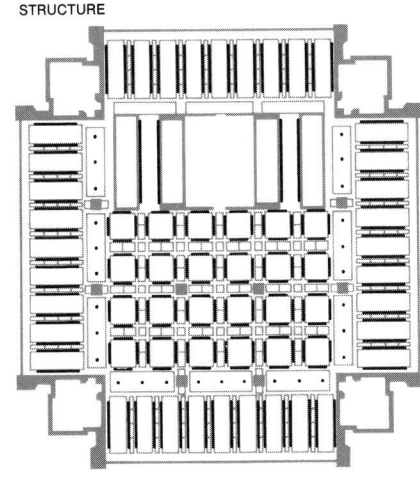

FIXTURE LOCATIONS

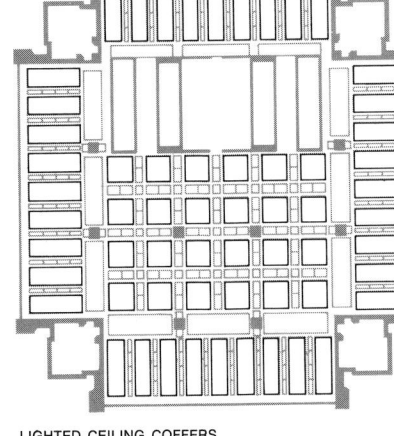

LIGHTED CEILING COFFERS

MECHANICAL DISTRIBUTION CHANNELS

use of a single vocabulary of architectural materials throughout the project, the tower and the low buildings were sufficiently different in volumetric terms that it was by no means obvious that a single structural-mechanical solution could be developed to serve the needs of both. The design team was fortunate, however, in that the perimeter system developed for the tower (3) proved equally suited to the low buildings (8), with their longer spans and cantilevers. Functionally, the extension of one system throughout the project was entirely justified. In both buildings, the predominant activity was to be office work in office landscape arrangements, with enclosed offices the exception rather than the rule. It was assumed that most of these would occur at perimeter locations, to take advantage of the view.

Design

The architectural concept of service cores at the corners of the tower immediately suggested that the usual problems encountered in buildings with exposed structure—running service lines from central core to perimeter—would not be present. It seemed diagrammatically obvious that the most logical distribution of mechanical services would be inward and outward from service bands interconnecting the corner cores.

The problem then became how to enclose and finish the necessary channels. In a relatively simple low building, in which some waste of vertical space would be more tolerable, a network of plaster channels could have been created under the shallowest possible zone of structure. Instead, the design team was able to develop a deep structure which incorporated the necessary service channels while maintaining maximum visible height in between. A key to the solution was the decision to switch to a high-velocity dual-duct air distribution system for the tower (not for the low-rise

4 *Column during construction showing the holes for the service channels.*

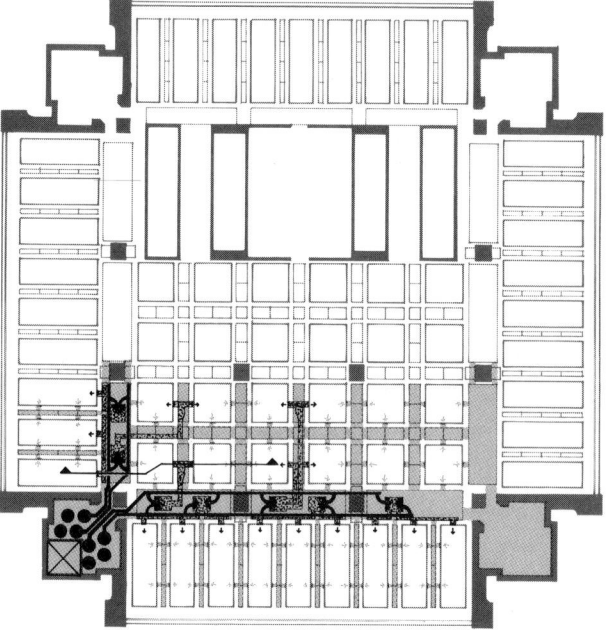

5 *Partial detailed services distribution plan, typical tower level.*

6 *Detailed sections through a typical service channel.*

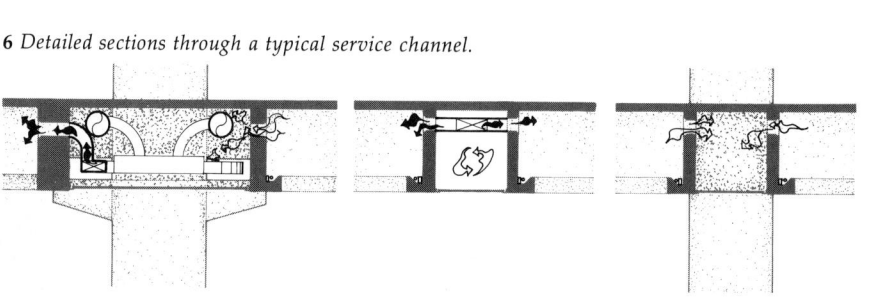

structure), requiring only small holes penetrating the column branches which support the channel beams **(4).** In the service channels, the "shadows" created by the wide columns offered a natural place to locate the mixing boxes. The lowered service channels could thus be placed in the most logical position and still be of only minimum width.

Perimeter spaces are supplied directly from the main channel **(5,7,8).** If these spaces are subdivided, smaller channels spanning to the exterior wall are used for air supply. Economy and flexibility in initial construction and in adaptability of space use were maintained by providing a uniform pattern of holes for air supply and return, etc., throughout the structure. Partitions do not interfere with mechanical outlets since these are located in the sides of the beams **(11),** rather than in the infill surface on the underside (as in the earlier NASA project, **Case Study G1).** Initial skepticism concerning air distribution was dispelled by testing a full-scale mock-up.

Bronze-colored metal infill panels were consciously differentiated from the structure, lest the structure appear too massive.

Where the corridor under the service band is illuminated from adjacent areas, no additional lighting is necessary **(12).** However, when the corridor band is totally enclosed, recessed downlights are added **(10).** The perimeter service system designed for the tower was successfully adapted to the low buildings. Here the deep secondary channel form was even more advantageous structurally for the longer spans and cantilevers. The system was used successfully for areas of office landscape **(12,15),** lounges **(14),** and enclosed offices.

To minimize the size of the integral lighting coves, lighting

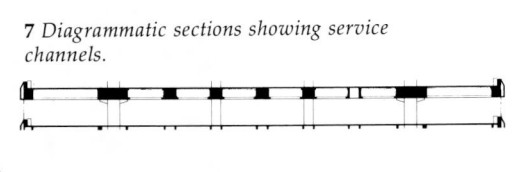

7 *Diagrammatic sections showing service channels.*

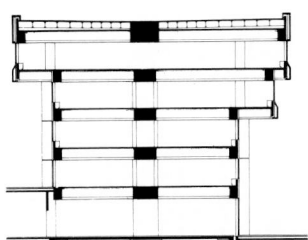

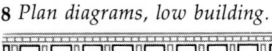

8 *Plan diagrams, low building.*

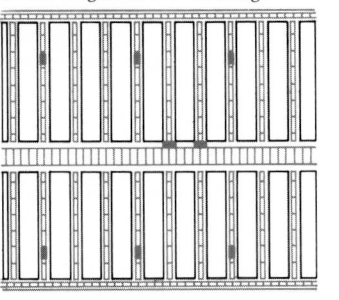

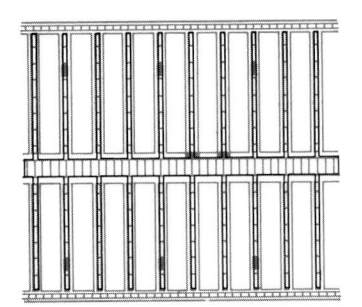

LIGHTED CEILING COFFERS   MECHANICAL DISTRIBUTION CHANNELS

Harold Lewis/Photo International

9

11 *Enclosed conference area (note the unobtrusive recessed air grilles).*

10

H5 Complex "G," Cité Parlementaire   287

12 *Office landscape — low building.*

13   14    15

within the coffers consists of super-high-output lamps in mini-
mum-size strip fixtures in each
cove. The bulky ballasts were
mounted within the adjacent
channel beams and connected to
the fixtures through the regular
pattern of holes provided. Remote
ballasts are acoustically advantageous, particularly in Canada
where quiet super-high-output
ballasts are not available.

To provide orientation to the

major masses above grade in the
levels below the podium, the perimeter corridors which edge
these masses were treated with
metal-slat ceilings and slot lighting
which highlights the walls of the
major masses **(19)**. At the cafeteria level beneath the podium the
infill areas between the major
masses above grade are differentiated with a waffle ceiling **(22)**.
In the cafeteria area itself **(17)**,
where much less light was appro-

priate, standard fluorescent lamps
were used in the indirect coves,
though intended only for use on
overcast, gloomy days. On sunny
days and at night the column-
mounted incandescent fixtures
would be more appropriate for
most occasions.

Edge-slot lighting is used in
washrooms, serving areas for the
cafeteria **(18)**, lower corridors
(19), stairs **(21)**, and snack areas
(20).

16 *Large conference room.*

17 *Cafeteria.*

18 *Cafeteria serving area.*

19 *Slot-lighted corridor.*

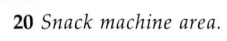

20 *Snack machine area.*

21 *Service stair.*

22 *Corridor edging major building mass*

23 *Commercial area below the podium.*

24 *Auditorium.*   25 *Tower lobby.*

A desire to create terraced forms on the plaza above resulted in an ideal structural form for lighting the auditorium below **(24)**. Edge beams provide natural baffles for wall lighting, which was supplemented by neutral downlights in the coffers overhead and from the lighting/acoustic rig used for stage lighting from the house.

In the high entrance lobby of the tower **(25)**, the usual indirect lighting was supplemented by incandescent downlights used to highlight objects at floor level.

On the exterior plazas, all lighting requirements for safety are satisfied by spill lighting from the building overhangs and interiors **(26)**. Interior lights in perimeter bays are left on at night for circulation within and for protective lighting and image on the exterior **(29)**. Major functions of *exterior* lighting therefore were to illuminate the buildings as focal points in the city, to provide interest, and to define circulation.

Since the daytime image is one of horizontal bands between vertical corner shafts, the corner shafts were highlighted from very-narrow-beam incandescent fixtures mounted in air wells at the corners **(28)**. The horizontals are naturally defined in silhouette against the illuminated ceilings.

Conceptually, emphasis of the terrace horizontals was also desirable, but the means were not so obvious. Recessing lights into the public sidewalk would have created jurisdictional and maintenance problems, while uniform lighting of the great expanses of the other walls would have been extravagant.

Instead, the terracing was defined by selectively illuminating only portions of each wall—those portions which would be relevant to achieving the second objective of guiding circulation. First, lighting was provided from the underside of terraces overhanging truck entrances. In addition, large, cubic precast concrete chandelier/shelters were provided, varying from 8 to 16 feet in width **(27,29)**. These provide shelter where it is needed by pedestrians waiting for a ride. Strings of protected clear lamps within each cube highlight wall and ground surfaces around entrances and provide sparkle **(27)**. The upward light emanated from these shelters provides a subtle wash of light on the otherwise unlit building surfaces and trees. To those persons on the street and plaza or on the floors above, the illuminated cubes identify the points at which the terraces can be penetrated. Seen together or sequentially, they constitute "environmental sculpture." Their presence at the edges of the podium defines its boundaries and frames the view, adding intimacy and a sense of scale frequently lacking in contemporary urban plazas.

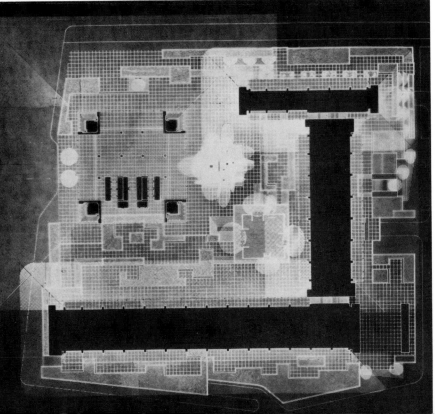

Harold Lewis/Photo International 28

27

Harold Lewis/Photo International

31 *Integrated systems study model.*

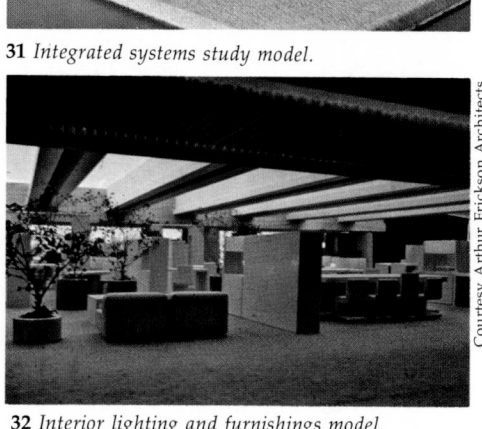

30 *British Columbia Government Center* (Arthur Erickson/Architects; William Lam Associates/Lighting Consultants).

32 *Interior lighting and furnishings model.*

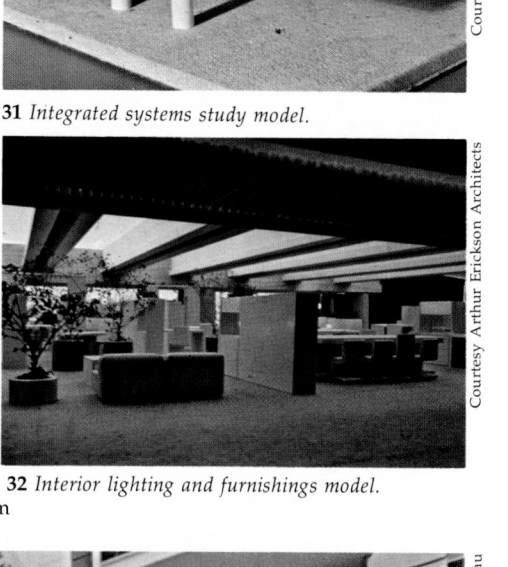

33 *Model Study for Place Guy Favreau.*

Comment

The considerable expanse of first-quality office environment at Complex "G" has proved an invaluable educational experience for both design professionals and building clients. It shows them what is possible—what *can* be achieved as a working environment. Field trips there have led to application of similar systems in the design of a number of major projects. Place Guy Favreau **(33),** a 4-million-square-foot federal government center in Montreal, is being designed with a variation of the Quebec system executed in precast concrete by project architect Gordon Edwards (consultant and principal designer for Complex "G"). Very different in exterior form but similar in its integrated structural/mechanical/lighting system is Arthur Erickson's British Columbia Government Center in Vancouver **(30,31,32),** which spreads out for three blocks, mostly under a park.

Although it may seem extravagant at first thought to demand field trips involving the *entire* design team *and* the clients, experience has proved that the resulting shared experience and common frame of reference for the whole team pays dividends in the final design, while expediting the entire process. A number of design teams have benefited in this way from field trips to Quebec "G," just as the team which designed Quebec "G" drew on experience gained during a field trip to the American Republic Building **(Case Study E1).**

WASHINGTON METROPOLITAN AREA TRANSIT AUTHORITY STATIONS
Washington, D.C.

Harry Weese & Associates (general architectural consultant); Roy Minshew, Stanley Allan (project architects); William Lam Associates (lighting consultant); De Leuw, Cather and Company (general engineering consultant); Bolt, Beranek and Newman (acoustical consultant); Unimark International (graphics consultant); Mueser, Rutledge, Wentworth and Johnston (general soils consultant); Bechtel Associates (general construction consultant). Estimated system cost: $3,000,000,000. Schematic design started 1966. Phase 1 stations completed 1976. Estimated completion of system 1980.

Programming of lighting objectives for the underground stations of the Washington Subway System took place long before the conception of the tubular, vaulted station structures. The basic goal was to give a sense of spaciousness and airiness in order to reduce the natural tendency towards claustrophobia in underground spaces. To achieve this end, wall and ceiling surfaces needed to be well illuminated. The primary design requirement was to provide inconspicuous light sources which would attractively render the enclosing surfaces of the various stations. The integrated structural, mechanical acoustic, lighting, and graphics concept was developed in a morning design session in which representatives of all disciplines participated.

Design of underground stations

The initial architectural program called for related but individual stations, à la Montreal. When the program was revised toward a single design expression for all the underground stations in the system and a tubular design had been developed, the desire to illuminate the vaults from their bottom edges rapidly led to the concept of floating the platforms free from the vaults **(Fig. 100,** p. 89) to use perimeter railings to baffle the light sources (an alternative to using louvered gratings set flush with the floor).

Shielding the lamps by the geometry of platform floor, light sources, and vault instead of relying on hardware such as louvered gratings not only creates a more natural, distractionless space **(1,2)** with more economical lighting equipment and maintenance, but should also reduce vandalism (since the walls are out of reach).

Since the low-positioned light sources mounted in the platform edges could not be used in side-platform stations to illuminate the central portion of the vault overhead without glare to those on the platform, the edge lighting system was supplemented from fixtures concealed between the tracks and, when the tracks are covered by mezzanines, from fixtures concealed in the tops of the ticket kiosks and sign pylons (which are also used to distribute air).

Lighting pylons are also used to light the vaults of center-platform stations. This system proved adaptable to all of the many station configurations. These design concepts were then carried through the other spaces: escalators were "floated" in their tubes **(13,14),** and the pylons which have become symbols of the sys-

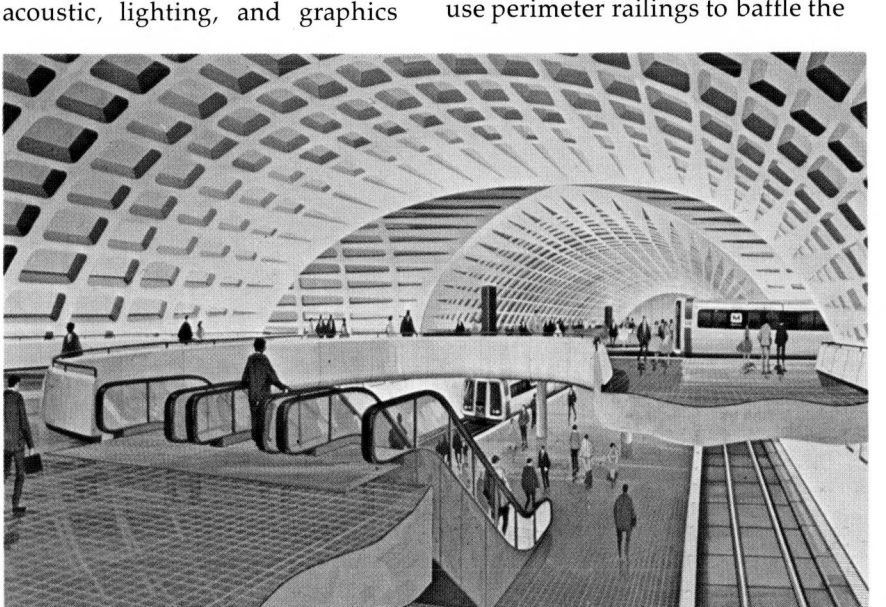

3 *Presentation model.*

4 *Study model.*

5 *Study model.*

6 *Typical map pin study model for site lighting.*

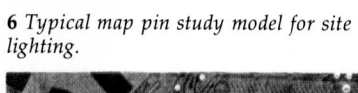

7 *Typical underground station.*

8

9 *Typical entrance to the underground stations.* 10 *Conventional subway signage (in Boston).*

tem were used in the surface stations as spines for distinctive chandeliers. Initially conceived for lighting, the pylons will represent "Metro" at the street level **(9)** — a more classic form than typical subway signage elsewhere **(10)**.

A number of models were built to verify the design and to demonstrate to clients the effect of illuminating the vault rather than aiming the light onto the floor of the stations **(3,4,5)**. The models were dimmable so that a range of luminance levels could be shown and all concerned could be educated in the perception of brightness — that relatively large changes in luminance (approximately doubling or halving) are required to produce a perceptible change in brightness. It was shown that whether their surfaces were illuminated to an average brightness of 2 footlamberts, or 20, the stations would appear quite similar.

The existence of illuminated models probably contributed substantially to the generally high quality of the station renderings, which communicated more realistically than usual both the lighting and a sense of the finished station environment.

A full-scale mock-up in concrete was built to confirm choices of finishes, materials, and lighting **(105,** p. 93**)**. However, the short length of the mock-up (only 6 per-

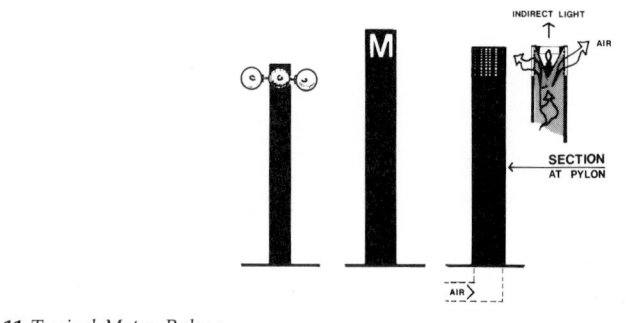

11 *Typical Metro Pylons.*

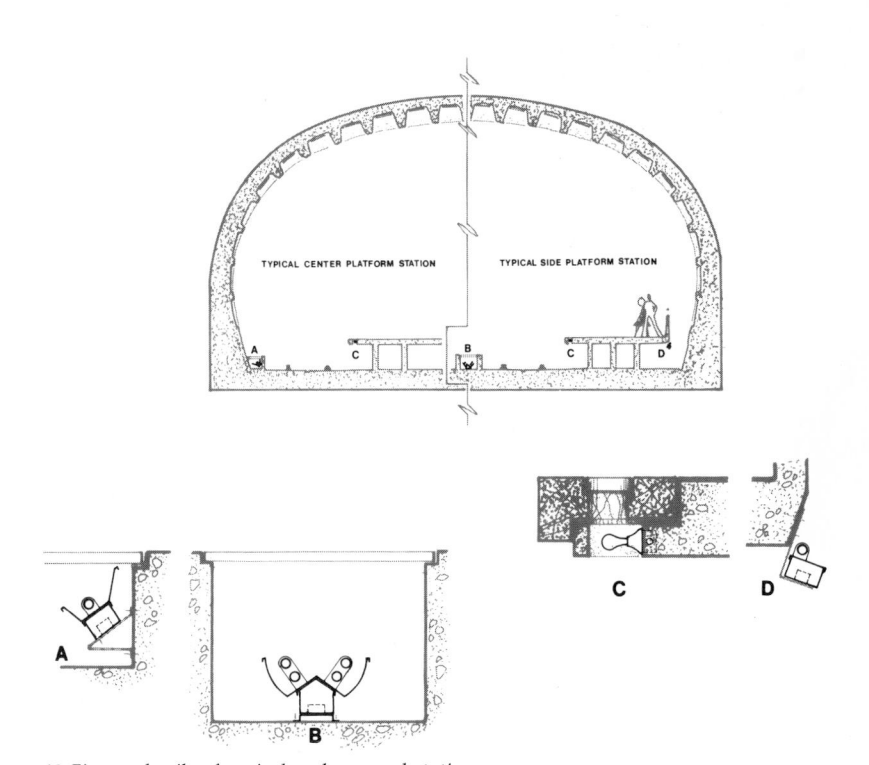

12 *Fixture details of typical underground station.*

13 *Escalator lighting study model (view down into the escalators).*

14 *Escalator as built.*

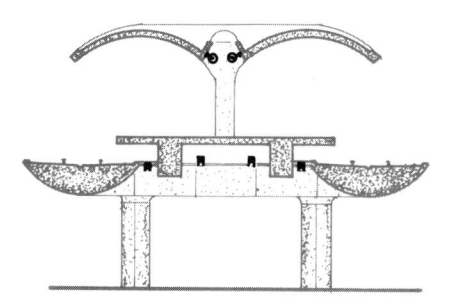

15 *Section of typical elevated platform station.*

Courtesy Harry Weese & Associates

cent of the real length of a station) made any evaluation of the luminous environment somewhat unrealistic. Full-length mirrors on both end walls would have helped, but the cost was not deemed worthwhile since the models had already demonstrated the overall effect.

Exterior lighting

In addition to the conventional objectives of providing adequate illumination for safety, comfort, and visual guidance, two supplementary objectives had to be taken into account during the development of a concept for the exterior spaces of the Washington subway: first, the several exterior spaces of each individual station required unification, and second, the various stations as a group or system needed a clearly interrelated identity. Like the underground stations, the surface rapid transit stations were to follow a single design concept, with variations introduced only as required by special site conditions.

The lighting objectives and constraints were quite different from those of the underground stations, however. Underground, the most difficult objective to achieve is to dispel feelings of gloom which arise from the sensation of being underground and from the transition from exterior to interior brightness levels. In the surface stations, it was easy to accomplish this objective by good daylighting design. Since lighting for physical safety at night[1] requires only minimal illumination levels, which can be provided in many ways, the more challenging design problem was to guide circulation and create an inviting, attractive image for the users of the system and the surrounding communities.

Design of surface stations

To achieve a consistent image for the entire system, the design of surface stations was tied as closely as possible to the already existing design for the underground stations. Platform guide lights and sign pylons were retained. The vaulted canopies,

[1]*It is important here to distinguish between adequate lighting for physical safety and for security. The former implies sufficient light to enable people to move about freely without danger from physical obstructions, while the latter may require considerably higher light levels, especially in high-crime areas, to create a sense of security and safety from attack.*

16 *Typical elevated station.*

17 *Study model of WMATA surface station.*

Courtesy WMATA

Anthony Hathaway/WMATA

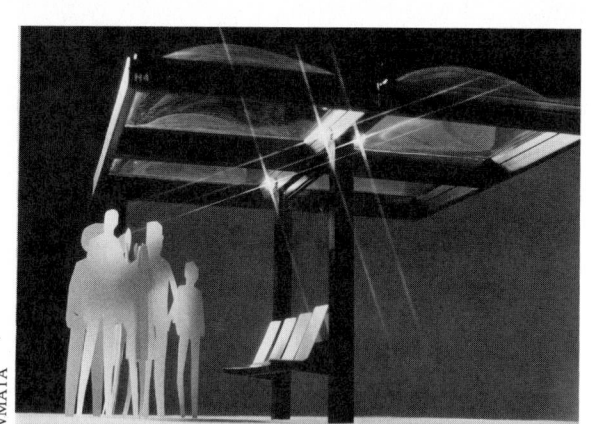

WMATA

18 *Bus shelter study model.*

Gene Streett of Harry Weese & Associates

19

20 *Typical site fixtures and corresponding illumination overlay templates.*

however, are not illuminated in the surface stations during the day since daylight from the open sides and from skylights is well balanced **(19).** At night, the skylights are transformed into a platform-long chandelier of clear lamps **(17).** Beyond the canopy, the theme of exposed clear lamps is continued in the form of the characteristic sign pylon/chandeliers. It is expected that these distinctive clusters of clear lamps on pylon will soon come to mean ''rapid transit station'' to the users of the system, offering an attractive sparkle to the adjacent neighborhoods and highways. The clear-lamp vocabulary was extended to the pedestrian facilities on grade: kiss-and-ride areas, bus shelters **(18),** etc. Major paths were marked with clear lamps, while minor paths were illuminated from more neutral, concealed sources.

Because of the tremendous variation in parking lot sizes and

21
22

EXTERIOR LIGHTING STANDARDS

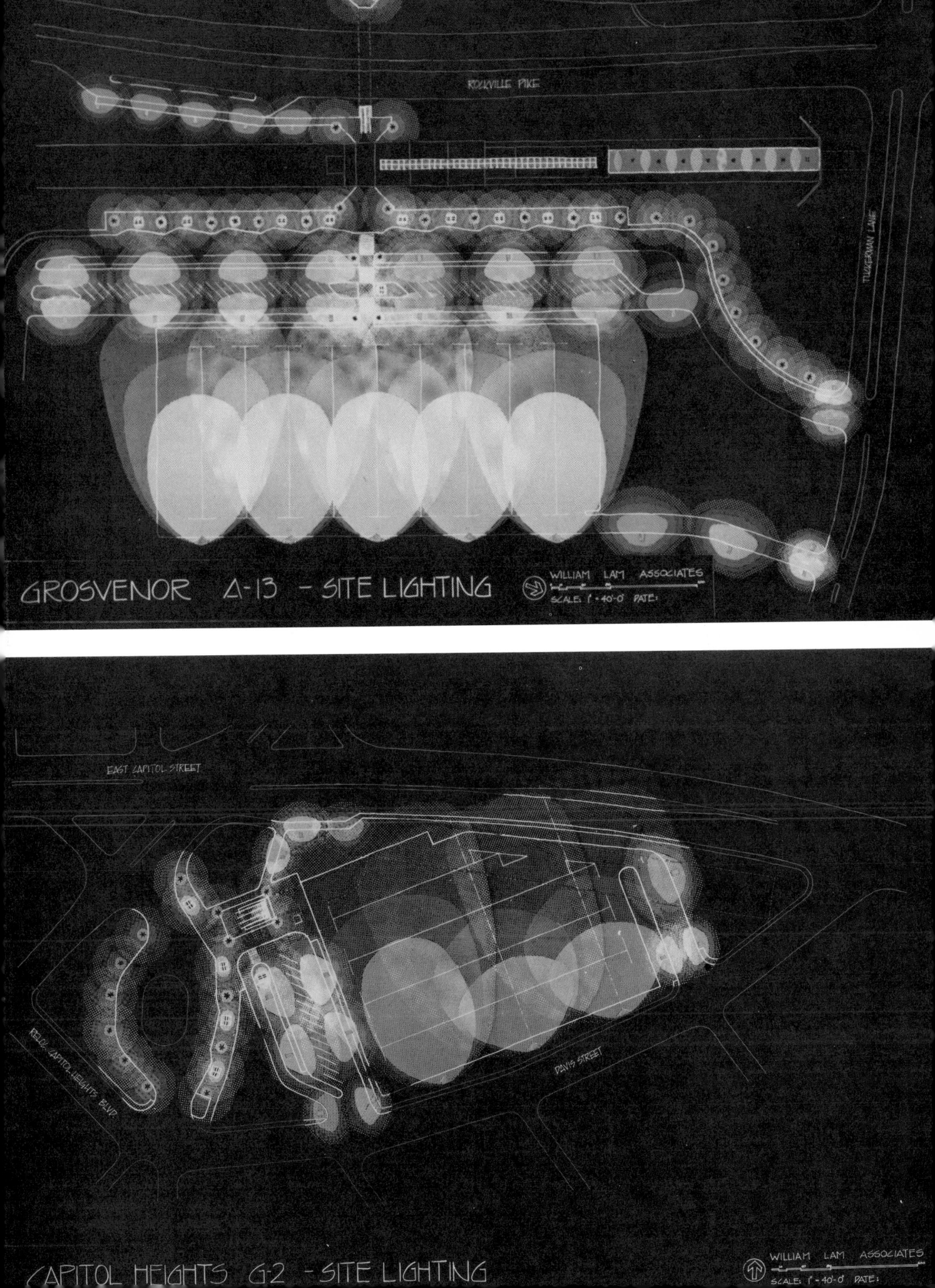

GROSVENOR A-13 – SITE LIGHTING

ROCKVILLE PIKE

TUCKERMAN LANE

WILLIAM LAM ASSOCIATES
SCALE: 1"=40'-0" DATE:

CAPITOL HEIGHTS G-2 – SITE LIGHTING

EAST CAPITOL STREET

EAST CAPITOL HEIGHTS BLVD

DAVIS STREET

WILLIAM LAM ASSOCIATES
SCALE: 1"=40'-0" DATE:

LOCATION _____

PURPOSE OF AREA _____

PART I   SUBJECTIVE EVALUATION

Please read each of the statements very carefully and rate your degree of agreement *in relation to the area you are in now*. In rating each statement, please bear in mind the purpose of the area and the activities that are to take place. If you *strongly agree* with the statement, circle *1*; if you *strongly disagree* with the statement, circle *7*; and if you *neither agree nor disagree* with the statement or you consider it to be irrelevant in the area you are in now, circle *4*.

	STRONGLY AGREE				STRONGLY DISAGREE		
I can see all that is necessary for safe unobstructed movement	1	2	3	4	5	6	7
I don't feel that I am likely to be attacked or molested by someone here	1	2	3	4	5	6	7
I would feel secure and safe from being attacked or molested to walk in this area unaccompanied	1	2	3	4	5	6	7
It is not possible for someone to be moving about in this area totally unobserved	1	2	3	4	5	6	7
The lighting here is adequate for me not to trip or fall over	1	2	3	4	5	6	7
I can recognise someone in this lighting before he is within 10 feet of me	1	2	3	4	5	6	7
I would feel secure and safe from being attacked or molested to walk in this area unaccompanied during the day	1	2	3	4	5	6	7
I feel secure here because it is not possible for an assailant to be hiding nearby	1	2	3	4	5	6	7
I consider this area to be brightly lit	1	2	3	4	5	6	7
I consider the lighting of this area to be highly satisfactory for the activities occuring here	1	2	3	4	5	6	7
I am able to read this evaluation sheet very clearly	1	2	3	4	5	6	7

PLEASE CHECK THAT YOU HAVE RATED EVERY STATEMENT!

23 *Exterior lighting survey questionnaire.*

layouts, it was unusually difficult to design a lighting scheme for the parking lots which could be applied consistently throughout the entire system. Because of the scale of the large lots and their sometimes untidy boundaries, conventional arrangements of poles dispersed evenly throughout the lots would have been potentially confusing to drivers. Instead, a visually simpler and substantially more economical design was developed based on illumination from the outer perimeters of the lots, with light being cast away from the surrounding houses and roadways wherever possible. This system proved feasible for all of the sizes and odd shapes of lots encountered **(20,21,22)**. In each of the lots, the perimeter pattern of floodlighting poles was first designed,[2] and then the number, size, and aiming angles of the light sources were engineered. The designs were checked for consistency using colored map tacks **(6)**. Since the great variety of lot sizes and geometries called for a

[2]*The design process is discussed in more detail on pp. 89–90.*

comparable variety of lamp types, beam spreads and clustering, and aiming angles, all floodlights were housed in uniform shadow boxes, sufficiently large to conceal the largest cluster of fixtures, in order to maintain a neat and uniform daytime appearance.

This approach to the parking lot lighting was made possible by the availability of quartz-lamp fixtures with very narrow vertical and very wide horizontal distribution characteristics, which can deliver "sheets" of light toward distant points. Illumination levels from parking lot fixtures decrease as one nears the station, allowing the distinctive station lighting to become the focus of the user's attention.

Prior to its use in the design of the Washington subway system exterior lighting, this hierarchical approach had been applied and refined during the design of the Forest Park Community College in St. Louis, Missouri and the NASA Electronics Research Complex **(Case Study G1)**. Variations were employed subsequently at Lethbridge University **(Case Study E7)** and Governors State University **(Case Study G5)**.

When the illumination level criteria developed by the consultants for the Washington subway system were questioned by those in favor of much higher industry-promoted light levels, a large field experiment was conducted. Staff members of the Transit Authority, architectural and engineering consultants, and others were conducted on a tour of a number of parking lots, plazas, and a partial mock-up of the proposed design. A questionnaire **(23)** was distributed concerning the qualities of the illumination of the spaces which had been visited, and answers were matched up with the measured illumination levels. The observations clearly verified the validity of the initial criteria.

24 →

Bibliography

I. The Luminous Environment: Criteria, Evaluation, and Design

AIA Research Corporation and Dubin-Mindell-Bloome Associates, Energy Conservation Design Guidelines for Office Buildings, GSA/PBS, Washington, D.C., 1974.

Allphin, W., "Horizontal and Non-Horizontal Visual Tasks in Offices," *Illuminating Engineering*, vol. 60, no. 4.

Appel, John, and James J. MacKenzie, "How Much Light Do We Really Need?" Building Systems Design, February–March 1975, pp. 27–31.

Architectural Research Laboratory, "The Effect of Windowless Classrooms on Elementary School Children," Department of Architecture, University of Michigan, September 1963.

Atkinson, W. H., and R. G. Hopkinson, "A Study of Glare from Very Large Sources," Illuminating Engineering Research Institute Project 59, Paper presented before the Illuminating Engineering Society, Detroit, Mich., September 1963.

Best, Gordon, "Direction Finding in Large Buildings," dissertation, University of Manchester, Institute of Science and Technology, Manchester, England, 1967.

Birren, Faber, *Light, Color and Environment*, Van Nostrand Reinhold, New York, 1969.

—— and Henry L. Logan, "The Agreeable Environment," *Progressive Architecture*, August 1960.

Bitter, C., and J. F. F. A. A. van Ireland, "Appreciation of Sunlight in the Home," reprinted from *Sunlight in Buildings*, Proceedings of the Sunlight Conference of the Commission Internationale de l'Eclairage, Washington, D.C., 1967, pp. 27–37.

Bodmann, H. W., "Illumination Levels and Visual Performance," *International Lighting Review*, 1962.

——, "Quality of Interior Lighting Based on Luminance," *Transactions of the Illuminating Engineering Society*, vol. 32, no. 1, 1967, pp. 22–40.

—— and G. Sollner, "Glare Evaluation by Luminance Control," *Light and Lighting*, June 1965.

Boynton, R. M., "Visibility Losses Caused by Sudden Luminance Changes," Paper presented at the Conference of the Commission Internationale de l'Eclairage, Washington, D.C., June 1967.

Building Research Station, *Integrated Daylight and Artificial Light in Buildings*, Her Majesty's Stationery Office, London, 1966.

Chapman, Dennis, and Geoffrey Thomas, *Lighting of Dwellings*, New Series No. 24, Wartime Social Survey, Atlantic House, Holborn Viaduct, London, 1943.

Chorlton, J. M., "Frequency and Duration of School Visual Tasks," Illuminating Engineering Research Institute, Progress Report No. 3, April 4, 1960.

—— and H. F. Davidson, "The Effect of Specular Reflection on Visibility: Part II—Field Measurements of Loss of Contrast," *Illuminating Engineering*, vol. 54, 1959.

Commission Internationale de l'Eclairage, *Proceedings of Initial Meeting Establishing CIE Study Committee on Psychology in the Visual Environment*, Stockholm, 1968.

Crouch, C. L., "Derivation, Background, and Use of the 'Scissors Curve'," *Illuminating Engineering*, vol. 60, no. 6, June 1965.

Cuttle, C., W. B. Valentine, and W. Burt, "Beyond the Working Plane," No. P67.12, Commission Internationale de l'Eclairage, Washington, D.C., 1967.

Edison Electric Institute, *Street Lighting Manual*, Publication No. 62–34 of the Edison Electric Institute, New York, 1963.

Editors of *The Architects' Journal*, "Special Issue: Artificial Lighting," *The Architects' Journal*, vol. 145, no. 1, January 1967.

Educational Facilities Laboratories, *The Cost of a Schoolhouse*, Educational Facilities Laboratories, Inc., New York, 1960.

Federal Energy Administration, Lighting and Thermal Operations Conservation Paper No. 18, Washington, 1975, II–4.

Flynn, J., and S. Mills, *Architectural Lighting Graphics*, Reinhold Publishing Corp. New York, 1962.

Griffith, James W., *Predicting Daylight as Interior Illumination*, Libby-Owens-Ford Glass Company, 1958.

Hack, Gary, Improving City Streets for Use at Night: The Norfolk Experiment, Norfolk Housing and Redevelopment Authority, June 1974.

Hardy, A. C., "Insolation and Fenestration," *Electricity*, July/August 1967, pp. 268–270.

Hewitt, Harry, "The Study of Pleasantness," *Light and Lighting*, June 1963, pp. 154–164.

——, D. J. Bridgers, and R. H. Simons, "Lighting and the Environment: Some Studies in Appraisal and Design," *Transactions of the Illuminating Engineering Society*, vol. 30, no. 4, 1965, pp. 91–116.

——, J. Kay, J. Longmore, and E. Rowlands, "Designing for Quality in Lighting," Paper presented at Harrogate, England before the Illuminating Engineering Society, May 1966.

Hopkinson, R. G., Architectural Physics: Lighting, Her Majesty's Stationery Office, London, 1963.

——, *A Code of Lighting Quality, A Note on the Use of Indices of Glare Discomfort in Lighting Codes,*

Boldface items are particularly recommended.

Building Research Station, Garston, England, Note No. E 999, April 1960.

————, "Daylight as a Cause of Glare," *Light and Lighting*, vol. 56, no. 11, 1964.

————, "The Lighting of Hospitals," *The Hospital*, vol. 59, September 1963.

————, "A Proposed Luminance Basis for a Lighting Code," *Transactions of the Illuminating Engineering Society*, vol. 30, no. 3, 1965.

————, and W. M. Collins, "An Experimental Study of the Glare from a Luminous Ceiling," Building Research Station, Garston, England, Note No. E 1275.

————, and J. D. Kay, The Lighting of Buildings, Praeger, New York, 1969.

————, P. Petherbridge, and J. Longmore, *Daylighting*, Heinemann, London, 1966.

Illuminating Engineering Society, *IES Lighting Handbook*, IES, New York, Fifth Edition, 1972.

————, *American Standard Guide for School Lighting*, IES, New York, 1962.

Illuminating Engineering Society of London, "Lighting Appraisal and Design," a report of the proceedings of an IES conference at Nottingham University, in *Light and Lighting*, 1965.

International Commission on Illumination, *International Recommendations for the Lighting of Public Thoroughfares*, Commission Internationale de l'Eclairage Publication No. 12 (E-3 3.1), 1965.

Jay, Peter, "Visual Perception and Apparent Brightness," unpublished paper, London, October 1965.

———— and J. Lynes, "Artificial Lighting," *The Architects' Journal*, vol. 145, no. 1, January 1967.

Kohler, W., and W. Luckhardt, *Lighting in Architecture*, Reinhold Publishing Corp., New York, 1959.

Kohn, I. R., "The Influence of Color and Illumination on the Interpretation of Emotions," Thesis submitted to the Psychology Department at the University of Utah, August 1967.

Lam, W. M. C., "Environmental Control—Lighting," *Journal of the American Institute of Architects*, November 1962.

————, "The Lighting of Cities," Architectural Record, vol. 137, June 1965, pp. 210–214, and vol. 138, July 1965, pp. 173–180 (published in two parts).

————, "Lighting for Architecture," in Architectural Engineering, Environmental Control, Fischer, R. E. (ed.), McGraw-Hill, New York, 1964, pp. 118–164; also published in the Architectural Record, vol. 127, no. 7, June 1960, pp. 219–229; vol. 128, no. 1, July 1960, pp. 170–181; vol. 128, no. 4, October 1960, pp. 222–232; and vol. 129, no. 1, January 1961, pp. 149–160.

———— and A. G. H. Dietz, "An Approach to the Design of the Luminous Environment," Report for the State University Construction Fund, Albany, N.Y., 1976.

———— and Jackie Lau, "Performance Criteria: Outdoor Lighting," State University Construction Fund, Albany, N.Y., August 1971.

Lang, R., "An Experiment in Ward Lighting," *Transactions of the Ophthalmological Society*, vol. 71, pp. 563–571.

Larson, Leslie, *Lighting and Its Design*, Whitney Library of Design, New York, 1964.

Lau, Jackie, "Report of a Preliminary Experiment on the Validity of the Use of Models in Subjective Lighting Assignments," University of Strathclyde, Glasgow, Scotland, August 1968.

————, "A Semantic Study of the Concept of Gloom in Lighting," University of Strathclyde, Glasgow, Scotland, April 1967.

Luckiesh, M., and S. K. Guth, "Brightness in Visual Field at Borderline Between Comfort and Discomfort (BCD)," *Illuminating Engineering*, vol. 44, no. 11, November 1949.

Lynes, J. A., W. Burt, and C. Cuttle, "The Flow of Light into Buildings," *Transactions of the Illuminating Engineering Society*, vol. 31, 1966.

Manning, Peter, "Lighting and the Total Environment," Paper presented at CIE conference, Washington, D.C., June 1967.

————, "Lighting in Relation to Other Components of the Total Environment," Paper presented at the Illuminating Engineering Society National Lighting Conference, Churchill College, Cambridge, England, March 25, 1968.

————, ed., *Office Design: A Study of Environment*, Pilkington Research Unit, Department of Building Science, University of Liverpool, England, 1965, chaps. 5 and 6.

————, "Windows, Environment and People," *Interbuild/Arena*, October 1967.

———— and A. Rimmer, "Progress in Daylight Design," *Light and Lighting*, vol. 56, no. 7, July 1963, 188–194.

Markus, T., "The Function of Windows—A Reappraisal," *Building Science*, vol. 2, 1966.

————, ed., "Progress in Daylighting Design," *Light and Lighting*, vol. 106, 1963, pp. 118–326.

———— and A. R. .Hill, "Some Factors Influencing Vision Through Meshes," unpublished paper, University of Strathclyde, Glasgow, Scotland.

Metcalf, Keyes D., *Planning Academic and Research Library Buildings*, McGraw-Hill, New York, 1965, chap. 9.

Ministry of Housing and Local Government, *Planning for Daylight and Sunlight*, Planning Bulletin No. 5, Her Majesty's Stationery Office, London, 1964 (reprinted in 1966).

Moon, Parry, and Domina Eberle Spencer, *Lighting Design*, Addison-Wesley, Cambridge, Mass., 1948.

Ne'eman, E., R. L. Isaacs, and J. B. Collins, "The Lighting of Compact Plan Hospitals," *Transactions of the Illuminating Engineering Society*, vol. 31, no. 2, 1966, pp. 37–58.

Page, J. K., "The Role of Lighting in the Search for Better Interiors — Some Problems," *Transactions of the Illuminating Engineering Society*, vol. 27, no. 4, 1962, pp. 152–169.

Philips, D., *Lighting in Architectural Design*, McGraw-Hill, New York, 1964.

Pratt Institute, "Performance Criteria, Lighting," a preliminary report prepared for the State University Construction Fund, New York, October 1965.

Sampson, Foster K., "Contrast Rendition in School Lighting," Educational Facilities Laboratories, New York, 1970.

Van Ireland, Ir. J., "Two Thousand Dutch Office Workers Evaluate Lighting," Research Institute for Public Health Engineering Report E 39, Delft, the Netherlands, June 1967.

Waldram, J. M., "Design of the Visual Field as a Routine Method," *Transactions of the Illuminating Engineering Society*, vol. 23, no. 2, 1958.

————, "Design of the Visual Field in Streets: The Visual Engineer's Contribution," *Transactions of the Illuminating Engineering Society*, vol. 31, no. 1, 1966.

————, "The Lighting of Gloucester Cathedral by the 'Designed Appearance' Method," *Transactions of the Illuminating Engineering Society*, vol. 24, no. 2, 1959.

Walker, A. E., *A Comparison of a Cut-off Street Lighting Installation with One Approximating to the Semi-Cut-off Type*, Ministry of Transport, Road Research Laboratory Report No. 17, 1966.

Weston, H. C., *Light, Sight, and Work*, Medical Research Council of Great Britain, H. K. Lewis & Co., Ltd., London, 1962.

II.   The Psychology of Perception

Arnheim, Rudolf, *Art and Visual Perception*, University of California Press, Berkeley, Calif., 1964.

Bakan, Paul, ed., Attention, Van Nostrand, Princeton, N.J., 1966.

Bartley, S. Howard, *Principles of Perception*, Harper & Row, New York, 1958.

Bernard, Eugene E., *Biological Prototypes and Synthetic Systems*, vol. 1, Plenum Press, New York, 1962.

Boring, Edwin G., *Sensation and Perception in the History of Experimental Psychology*, Appleton-Century, 1942.

Broadbent, D. E., Perception and Communication, Pergamon, Cambridge, England, 1958.

Campbell, John W., "Color Vision . . . the Land Experiments," in *Astounding Science, Facts and Fiction*, vol. 64, 1960, pp. 83–103.

Gibson, James J., The Perception of the Visual World, Houghton Mifflin, Boston, 1950.

————, The Senses Considered as Perceptual Systems, Houghton Mifflin, Boston, 1966.

Gombrich, E. H., *Art and Illusion, a Study in the Psychology of Pictorial Representation*, A. W. Mellon Lectures in the Fine Arts, Bollingen Foundation, New York, 1956.

Gregory, R. L., Eye and Brain, the Psychology of Seeing, World University Library, McGraw-Hill, New York, 1966.

Helson, Harry, "Illuminating Engineering Research Institute Annual Report," Illuminating Engineering Society, Washington, D.C., 1965, pp. 6–14.

Hering, Ewald, Outlines of a Theory of the Light Sense, Harvard, Cambridge, Mass., 1964.

Hochberg, Julian E., *Perception*, Prentice-Hall, Englewood Cliffs, N.J., 1964.

Hurvich, Leo M., and Dorothea Jameson, The Perception of Brightness and Darkness, Allyn and Bacon, Boston, 1966.

Ittelson, William H., *Visual Space Perception*, Springer, New York, 1960.

James, William, Psychology, Fawcett, New York, 1963 (based on his Principles of Psychology, 1890).

Jay, Peter, "Visual Perception and Apparent Brightness," unpublished paper.

Koffka, K., *Principles of Gestalt Psychology*, Harcourt, Brace & World, New York, 1935.

Land, Edwin H., "Color Vision and the Natural Image," *Proceedings of the National Academy of Sciences*, vol. 45, 1959, pp. 115–129; and vol. 45, 1959, pp. 636–644, (published in two parts).

————, "Experiments in Color Vision," *Scientific American*, May 1959.

————, "The Retinex," *American Scientist*, vol. 52, 1964, pp. 247–264.

Marek, Julius, "Information, Perception, and Social Context, 1 — Simple Level of Perceptual Response," *Human Relations*, vol. 15, 1962, pp. 209–231.

————, "Information, Perception and Social Context, 2 — The Balance and Relevance of Complex Perceptual Responses," *Human Relations*, vol. 19, 1966, pp. 353–380.

Mueller, Rudolph, and the Editors of "Life," Light and Vision, Life Science Library, Time, Inc., New York, 1966.

Neisser, Ulric, Cognitive Psychology, Meredith, New York, 1967.

————, "The Processes of Vision," Scientific American, vol. 219, September 1968.

Sokolov, E. N., *Perception and the Conditioned Reflex*, MacMillan, New York, 1968.

Solomon, P., ed., *Sensory Deprivation*, Harvard University Press, Cambridge, Mass., 1965.

Swedish Colour Foundation, *Attributes of Colour Perception*, Swedish Colour Center Foundation, Stockholm, 1967.

————, *A New Colour Atlas Based on the Natural Colour System by Hering-Johansson*, edited by Anders Hard, Swedish Center Colour Foundation, Stockholm, 1965.

Vernon, M. D., ed., <u>Experiments in Visual Perception</u>, Penguin, London, 1966.

Wapner, S., "An Organismic-Developmental Approach to the Study of Perceptual and Other Cognitive Operations," an article in *Cognition: Theory, Research, Promise*, edited by Constance Scheerer, Harper & Row, New York, 1964.

————, J. H. McFarland, and H. Werner, "Effect of Visual Spatial Context on Perception of One's Own Body," *British Journal of Psychology*, vol. 54, no. 1, 1962, pp. 41–49.

Warr, Peter B., and Christopher Knapper, <u>The Perception of People and Events</u>, John Wiley & Sons, London, 1968.

Yilmaz, Huseyin, and Lewis Clapp, "Perception," reprinted from *International Science and Technology*, Conover-Mast, New York, 1963.

III. Perception and the Environment: Applied Psychology

Black, J. Courtney, "Meaning of Color," Master's Thesis, University of Utah, Logan, Utah.

Bolt, R. H., Stevens, K. N., and W. A. Rosenblith, "A Community's Reaction to Noise: Can It Be Forecast?," *Noise Control*, vol. 1, January 1955, pp. 63–71.

Canter, David V., "On Appraising Building Appraisals," *The Architects' Journal Information Library*, December 1966, pp. 1550–1597.

————, "Office Size, An Example of Psychological Research in Architecture," *The Architects' Journal Information Library*, April 1968.

Cullen, Gordon, *Townscape*, Reinhold Publishing Corp., New York, 1961.

Demos, George D., "Controlled Physical Classroom Environments and their Effects upon Elementary School Children (Windowless Classroom Study)," Research project by the Office of the Riverside County Superintendent of Schools, Riverside, Calif.

Gutman, Robert, "The Questions Architects Ask," *Transactions of the Bartlett Society*, vol. 4, 1965–66.

Halldane, John F., *Architecture and Visual Perception*, Department of Architecture, University of California, Berkeley, Calif., 1968.

————, *Psychophysical Synthesis of Environmental Systems*, California Book Co., Berkeley, Calif., 1968.

Hardy, A. C., "The Colour Coordination of Tile and Other Factory-Coloured Products of the Building Industry in Relation to BS660," The Colour Group, London, 1965.

————, "Colour in Landscape," Paper presented at the International Conference, Keele University, July, 1965.

Healy, Richard J., *Design for Security*, John Wiley & Sons, New York.

Hesselgren, Sven, <u>The Language of Architecture</u>, Student-litteratur, Lund, Sweden, 1967.

Holmberg, L., et al., "The Perception of Volume Content of Rectangular Rooms—Comparison Between Model and Full-scale Experiments," *Psychological Research Bulletin*, vol. 2, 1967, Lund University, Sweden.

————, R. Kuller, and I. Tidblom, "The Perception of Volume Content of Rectangular Rooms as a Function of the Ratio Between Depth and Width," *Psychological Research Bulletin*, vol. 1, 1966, Lund University, Sweden.

————, "Stability of Individual and Group Data in the Perception of Volume Content of Rectangular Rooms as Measured by a Production and an Estimation Method," *Psychological Research Bulletin*, vol. 7, 1966, Lund University, Sweden.

Langdon, F. J., *Modern Offices: A User Survey*, Her Majesty's Stationery Office, London, 1966.

Lynch, Kevin, <u>The Image of the City</u>, Technology Press and Harvard University Press, Cambridge, Mass., 1960.

Manning, Peter, "Appraisals of Building Performance and Their Use in Design," unpublished paper, Pilkington Research Unit, Liverpool, England, September 1967.

———— and Sheila Taylor, "Appraisals of the Total Environment," Pilkington Research Unit, Department of Building Science, University of Liverpool, Liverpool, England, December 1965.

———— and Brian Wells, "An Example of the Semantic Differential," Pilkington Research Unit, Liverpool, England, May 1968.

————, "CIS Reappraisal of an Environment," *Interior Design*, no. 4, 1964.

National Bureau of Standards, <u>Windows and People: A Literature Survey</u>, prepared by B. L. Collins, Washington, D.C. GPO, 1975.

Shafer, Elwood, L., Jr., "The Photo-Choice Method for Recreation Research," U.S. Forest Service Research Paper NE-29, 1964.

Spivak, Mayer, "Archetypal Place," <u>Forum</u>, October 1973, pp. 44–49.

————. "Sensory Distortions in Tunnels and Corridors," *Hospital and Community Psychiatry* (Journal of the American Psychiatric Association), January 1967, pp. 24–30.

Wapner, Seymour, and Heinz Werner, "Changes in Psychological Distance Under Conditions of Danger," *Journal of Personality*, vol. 24, no. 2, December 1955.

Wells, B., "Toward a Definition of Environmental Studies: A Psychologist's Contribution," *The Architects' Journal*, September 1965.

Wolls, R. M., "Some Experiments in Architecture—A Brief Interim Summary of a Research Project into the Effects of the Physical Environment on Behaviour," University of Strathclyde, Glasgow, Scotland, September 1968.

IV. The Physiology of Vision

Appel, J., and J. Mackenzie, "How Much Light Do We Really Need," Building Systems Design, February/March 1975, pp. 27–31.

Blackwell, H. R., "Development and Use of a Quantitative Method for Specification of Interior Illumination Levels on the Basis of Performance Data," Illuminating Engineering, vol. 54, June 1959, pp. 317–353.

———, "The Evaluation of Interior Lighting on the Basis of Visual Criteria," Applied Optics, September 1967.

———, "A General Quantitative Method for Evaluation of the Visual Significance of Reflected Glare, Utilizing Visual Performance Data," Paper No. 50-B, presented at the National Technical Conference of the Illuminating Engineering Society, St. Louis, September 1961.

———, "Lighting Systems for Better Visions," Building Research, Building Research Institute, May–June, 1964.

———, R. N. Schwab, and B. S. Pritchard, "Visibility and Illumination Variables in Roadway Visual Tasks," Illuminating Engineering, vol. 59, no. 5, May 1964.

Boynton, Robert M., and N. Miller, "Visual Performance Under Conditions of Transient Adaptation," Illuminating Engineering, vol. 63, no. 8, August 1968.

Carifa, R. P., and F. W. Hebbard, "Involuntary Eye Movements Occurring During Fixation: Effects of Changes in Target Contrast," American Journal of Optometry and Archives of American Academy of Optometry, vol. 44, no. 2, February 1967.

Chorlton, J. M., "Part II—Field Measurements of Loss of Contrast," Illuminating Engineering, vol. 54, no. 8, August 1959.

Cogan, David, "Damage to Rats' Eyes from Continuous Exposure to Light," Stenographic record of a seminar sponsored by the State University Construction Fund, State University of New York at Saratoga Springs, July 1967.

———, "Popular Misconceptions Pertaining to Ophthalmology," New England Journal of Medicine, vol. 224, 1941, pp. 462–466.

Eastman, Arthur A., "Color Contrast Versus Luminance Contrast," paper presented at the National Technical Conference of the Illuminating Engineering Society, Phoenix, Ariz., September 1968.

Fry, Glenn A., "Assessment of Visual Performance," Illuminating Engineering, vol. 57, no. 6, June 1962.

Griffith, James W., "Analysis of Reflected Glare and Visual Effect from Windows," Illuminating Engineering, March 1962.

———, "Veiling Reflection Studies with Sidewall Lighting," Illuminating Engineering, May 1966.

Hebbard, Frederick W., "Micro Eye Movements: Effects of Target Illumination and Contrast," Final Report of the Illuminating Engineering Research Institute Project, No. 71-B.

Hill, A. R., "A Psychophysical Scale of Visibility," based on a paper delivered to the Research Symposium of Visual Psychophysics and Neurology held at the City University of New York, New York, May 1968.

———, "The Sensory Scaling of Ease of Seeing Through a Mesh," Department of Architecture, University of Strathclyde, Glasgow, Scotland, October 1968.

Hopkinson, R. G., "Daylight as a Cause of Glare," Building Research Station, Garston, England, Current Papers, Design Series 27.

Mackworth, Norman H., "Some Suggested Uses for the Optiscan—A Head-Mounted Eye Camera," Paper 60-WA-304 of the American Society of Mechanical Engineers, New York, October 1960.

———, "A Stand Camera for Line-of-Sight Recordings," Perception and Psychophysics, vol. 2, 1967, pp. 119–127.

——— and Anthony J. Morandi, "The Gaze Selects Specific Features within Pictures," Perception and Psychophysics, January 1967.

Taylor, N. W., "New Light on Visual Threshold Contrast," Illuminating Engineering, vol. 57, no. 3, March 1962.

Thomas, E. Llewellyn, "Movements of the Eye," Scientific American, vol. 219, no. 2, August 1968.

Veiling Reflections Subcommittee of the RQQ Committee, "Present Status of Veiling Reflections Know-How," Illuminating Engineering, August 1968, pp. 433–435.

Wurtman, Richard J., "The Effects of Light on Man and Other Animals," Annual Review of Physiology, vol. 37, 1975, p. 473.

V. Performance, Fatigue, and Stress

Altman, Irwin, "The Effects of Social Isolation and Group Composition on Performance," Human Relations, vol. 20, 1967, 313–340.

Carson, D., and B. L. Driver, "An Environmental Approach to Human Stress and Well Being with Implications for Planning," Mental Health Research Institute Preprint 194, Ann Arbor, Mich., August 1966.

Cook, Desmond L., "The Hawthorne Effect in Educational Research," *Phi Delta Kappan*, December 1962.

Dresler, A., "Fluorescent Lighting and its Effects on the Eye," *Transactions of the Ophthalmological Society of Australia*, vol. 11, 1955, East Melbourne, Australia.

Jacob, E., "Lighting and Productivity," *International Lighting Review*, 1966.

Khek, J., and J. Krivohlavy, "Variation of Incidence of Error with Visual Task Difficulty," Light and Lighting, May 1966.

Myers, Thomas I., "Tolerance for Sensory and Perceptual Deprivation," a chapter in *Sensory Deprivation: Fifteen Years of Research*, edited by J. P. Zubek, Appleton-Century-Crofts, New York, 1967.

National Institute of Occupational Safety and Health, The Occupational Safety and Health Effects Associated with Reduced Levels of Illumination, HEW publication No. (NIOSH) 75–142.

Roethlisberger, F. J., and W. J. Dickson, Management and the Worker, Harvard, Cambridge, Mass., 1966, pp. 14–18.

Stone, P. T., "Ergonomics and the Environment," paper presented at the National Lighting Conference of the Illuminating Engineering Society, Churchill College, Cambridge, England, March 1968.

VI.   Anthropology

Dubos, Rene, *Man, Medicine, and Environment*, Praeger, New York, 1968.

———, **So Human an Animal, Scribner, New York, 1968.**

Hall, E. T., *The Hidden Dimension*, Doubleday, New York, 1966.

———, *The Silent Language*, Fawcett, Greenwich, Conn., 1959.

Jacobs, Jane, *Death and Life of American Cities*, Random House, New York, 1961.

VII.   The Design Process

Banham, Reyner, Architecture of the Well-Tempered Environment, The Architectural Press, London, 1969.

Canter, D. V., "The Need for a Theory of Function in Architecture," University of Strathclyde, Glasgow, Scotland, March 1968.

Horowitz, Harold, "An Introduction to Research Methods for Architecture," *American Institute of Architects' Journal*, January 1964, pp. 62–66.

Illuminating Engineering Society, *IES Lighting Handbook*, Fifth Edition, IES, New York, 1972.

Manning, Peter, "An Experimental Study to Seek More Effective Communication to Architects of the Results of Building Research," Institute of Advanced Architectural Studies, University of York, England.

———, "Multi-Disciplinary Research for Architecture," *The Architects' Journal Information Library*, November 1967.

———, "Systematic Design Methods and the Building Design Process," *The Architects' Journal Information Library*, September 1965.

Markus, Thomas A., "The Role of Building Performance Measurement and Appraisal in Design Method," *The Architects' Journal Information Library*, December 1967.

Studer, Raymond G., "On Environmental Programming," *The Architectural Association Journal*, May 1966, pp. 290–296.

——— and D. Stea, "Architectural Programming and Human Behavior," *Journal of Social Issues*, vol. 22, October 1966.

VIII.   Cost Studies

Loudon, A. G., "Window Design Criteria to Avoid Overheating by Excessive Solar Heat Gains," Building Research Station, Garston, England, Current Papers 4/68, February 1968.

Northern Illinois Gas Company, "Analysis of Lighting Load Effect on Cooling Requirements," paper presented at the American Gas Association Research Utilization and Marketing Conference, Chicago, June 1966.

Tregenza, P. R., "A Study of the Relationship Between the Design Level of Illumination and the Cost of Lighting," *Building Science*, vol. 2. no. 1. March 1967.

IX.   Research Programs, Summaries, Bibliographies, and Indexes

Department of Architecture and Building Science, *Research Bulletin 1*, University of Strathclyde, Glasgow, Scotland, September 1968.

Evans, Benjamin H., *American Institute of Architects' Research Survey*, AIA, Washington, D.C.

Government Social Survey, *List of Published Social Survey Reports*, Atlantic House, London, England, 1968.

Illuminating Engineering Research Institute, *Symposium on Light and Vision Research*, a report of the Illuminating Engineering Research Institute on a symposium held at Soesterberg June 1965.

Illuminating Engineering Society, *Annual Report of the IES Research Institute*, New York, 1961 *et seq.*

Index

A comprehensive index to the case study projects is presented in chart form on the endpaper inside the back cover of this book.

SUMMARY OF BUILDING CHARACTERISTICS

1974																															
(E4)			●						●		●		●		●											●	●		●		
(D7)			●										●		●												●			●	
1973																															
(H5)		●	●						●			●	●		●	●			●					●		●	●	●	●	●	
(H5)			●		●							●	●		●				●							●	●		●	●	
(G4)			●		●							●	●		●			●								●			●	●	
1972																															
(E5)			●						●			●	●			●		●						●					●	●	
(D3)			●						●			●	●			●			●				●			●	●	●	●	●	
1970																															
(G3)			●		●						●	●	●		●			●						●		●	●		●	●	
(G5)			●		●							●	●					●			●		●	●		●	●	●	●	●	
(E6)			●		●						●	●	●		●			●								●	●		●	●	
(F3)				●																				●				●		●	
(C9)		●					●		●		●		●	●	●						●	●		●		●	●	●	●	●	
(C8)							●				●		●			●										●				●	
1969																															
(C6)		●		●			●		●		●													●		●	●	●		●	
(G2)			●		●						●	●	●		●	●		●								●	●		●	●	
(C7)		●	●				●		●					●		●							●	●		●	●	●		●	
(C1)			●			●					●	●	●		●												●			●	
(A1)				●											●	●											●		●	●	
1968																															
(C3)			●			●						●	●			●								●		●	●			●	
(D9)			●									●														●			●		
(E7)			●									●	●						●				●				●		●	●	
(H5)												●	●					●	●				●	●			●	●	●	●	
(F2)		●		●																										●	
1967																															
(C4)					●	●						●												●		●	●			●	
(A6)											●															●			●	●	
(G1)			●		●							●	●						●				●						●		
(E9)			●		●							●	●			●			●				●			●	●		●		
(A8)				●																						●		●		●	

Code	Building	BUILDING ELEMENTS INFLUENCED									DESIGN PROCESS AIDS USED											TIMING OF LIGHTING CONSULTATION				
		OVERALL PLAN	EXTERIOR FORM	STRUCTURAL SYSTEM	ACOUSTICS	MECHANICAL SYSTEM	DAYLIGHTING DESIGN	FURNISHINGS	INTERIOR WALLS	CEILING	FIELD FIXTURE MOCK-UP	FIELD COMPONENT MOCK-UP	FIELD ROOM MOCK-UP	RENDERINGS	FIXTURE MODELS	COMPONENT MODELS	ROOM MODELS	VISUALLY DESCRIPTIVE PROGRAMMING	ACTIVITIES PROGRAMMING	FIELD TRIP	LECTURE	REMODELLING	CONSTRUCTION	CONTRACT DOCUMENTS	DESIGN DEVELOPMENT	PROGRAMMING
	1974																									
(E4)	TOZZER LIBRARY	○		○	◎	○	◎	○	◎	●											●		●	●	●	
(D7)	AMAX CORPORATE HEADQUARTERS	○					◎		○	●			●								●		●			
	1973																									
(H5)	BRITISH COLUMBIA GOVERNMENT CENTER	●	●	●	●	●	●	●		●			●	●			●	●		●	●		●	●	●	●
(H5)	PLACE GUY FAVREAU	●	◎	●	◎	●	○			●			●				●			●	●				●	●
(G4)	JACKSONVILLE POLICE HEADQUARTERS	◎	◎	●		●	●			●											●		●	●	●	
	1972																									
(E5)	SANTA CLARA CIVIC CENTER				○	●				●	●	●	●				●	●			●				●	
(D3)	SUTTON SCHOOL		●	●	○	●	◎	○		●											●			●	●	●
	1970																									
(G3)	CHARLOTTE HUNGERFORD HOSPITAL	●	●	●		●	○	○		●			●								●			●	●	
(G5)	GOVERNORS STATE UNIVERSITY	●	●	●	○	●	●		●	●	●	●	●				●				●				●	
(E6)	EASTON HOSPITAL	◎	●	●	○	●	○	●		●			●												●	
(F3)	1100 MILAM BUILDING																				●				●	●
(C9)	HYATT REGENCY HOUSTON HOTEL	○	○	○		○	○	○	○	◎	●		●	●	●	●					●		●	●	●	
(C8)	BELOIT COLLEGE ARTS CENTER	○	○	○	○	○	○	○	○	◎	●		●		●					●	●		●	●	●	●
	1969																									
(C6)	HYATT REGENCY SAN FRANCISCO HOTEL																								●	
(G2)	BANK OF CANADA	●	●	●	◎	○	○	◎	○	●	●	●	●	●			●	●			●				●	
(C7)	HYATT REGENCY O'HARE HOTEL		◎	◎	◎	◎	○	◎	◎	●								●					●	●		
(C1)	LOYOLA NOTRE DAME LIBRARY				◎			◎		●		●									●			●	●	
(A1)	NEWBURYPORT INSTITUTION FOR SAVINGS							●														●		●	●	●
	1968																									
(C3)	WALTERS ART GALLERY				◎		●			●		●									●		●	●	●	●
(D9)	PLYMOUTH SCHOOLS			●	●	●	◎			●											●			●	●	
(E7)	LETHBRIDGE UNIVERSITY	◎	●	●	○	●				●							●	●		●	●		●	●	●	●
(H5)	QUEBEC GOVERNMENT COMPLEX "G"		●	●	○	○	●			●							●	●		●	●		●	●	●	
(F2)	TIME-LIFE BUILDING									●															●	
	1967																									
(C4)	HUNTINGTON MUSEUM									◎														●	●	
(A6)	CALVARY CHURCH								○																	●
(G1)	NASA RESEARCH CENTER		●	●	○	●	◎			●																●
(E9)	PIERREFONDS HIGH SCHOOL	●	○	●	○	●	●			●	●	●	●													●
(A8)	SAINT THOMAS AQUINAS CHURCH																									●